German Socialism
and Weimar Democracy

Richard Breitman

German Socialism

and Weimar Democracy

The University of North Carolina Press   Chapel Hill

© 1981 The University of North Carolina Press

All rights reserved

Manufactured in the United States of America

Library of Congress Cataloging in Publication Data

Breitman, Richard, 1947–
  German socialism and Weimar democracy.

  Bibliography: p.
  Includes index.
  1. Sozialdemokratische Partei Deutschlands—History.
2. Germany—Politics and government—1918–1933.
3. Socialism in Germany—History. I. Title.
JN3946.S83B73   324.243072   80–21412
ISBN 0-8078-1462-8

To Gloria and Saul

Contents

List of Abbreviations

ABI   August-Bebel-Institut, Historische Kommission zu Berlin

ADGB   Allgemeiner Deutscher Gewerkschaftsbund
            (General Federation of German Trade Unions)

AfA   Allgemeiner freier Angestelltenbund
            (General Free Federation of Salaried Employees)

BA   Bundesarchiv

BVP   Bayerische Volks-Partei
            (Bavarian People's party)

DDP   Deutsche Demokratische Partei
            (German Democratic party)

DGB   Deutscher Gewerkschaftsbund Archiv

DNVP   Deutschnationale Volkspartei
            (German National People's party; Nationalist party)

DVP   Deutsche Volkspartei
            (German People's party)

FES   Friedrich-Ebert-Stiftung

IISH   International Institute of Social History

IWK   Internationale Wissenschaftliche Korrespondenz
            zur Geschichte der deutschen Arbeiterbewegung

KPD   Kommunistische Partei Deutschlands
            (Communist party of Germany; Communist party)

NSDAP   Nationalsozialistische Deutsche Arbeiterpartei
            (National Socialist German Workers' party; Nazi party)

OKH   Oberkommando des Heeres
            (Army Command)

OHL   Oberste Heeresleitung
            (Army High Command or Supreme Army Command)

SA   Sturmabteilung
            (Nazi paramilitary force)

SAPD   Sozialistische Arbeiterpartei Deutschlands
            (Socialist Workers' party of Germany)

SPD   Sozialdemokratische Partei Deutschlands
            (Social Democratic party of Germany; Social Democratic party)

SS   Schutzstaffel
            (Nazi paramilitary force)

Sten. Ber. Stenographische Berichte über die Verhandlungen

USNA   United States National Archives

USPD   Unabhängige Sozialdemokratische Partei Deutschlands
            (Independent Social Democratic party of Germany;
            Independent Socialist party)

Acknowledgments

This book is truly a collective product that evolved over many years, and I am indebted to a great many people. Henry Turner and Hans Gatzke provided me with a sound background in German history and stimulated my interest in the subject. My dissertation advisor, Franklin Ford, supplied good advice, assistance, and criticism of my work. Yet he allowed me the necessary independence to develop my own thinking. I benefited tremendously from contact with Charles Maier, who showed me his own research (which was then unpublished) and introduced me to the intricacies of the interwar period. Stephen Schuker too gave me the benefit of his knowledge and experience. Both Maier and Schuker helped me to find my way into and out of the labyrinth of documents and archives.

Other scholars as well read the manuscript, or portions of it, contributing useful suggestions and thought-provoking criticism. I would like to express my gratitude to Dieter K. Buse, Gerald Feldman, Larry E. Jones, Hans Mommsen, Mary Nolan, Dietrich Orlow, Reinhard Rürup, and Hagen Schulze. Of course, they bear no responsibility for the weaknesses that remain. I am particularly indebted to Susanne Miller, who not only provided advice and encouragement, but also answered specific questions of mine and relayed others to Fritz Heine, to whom I am also grateful. My long interview with the late Ernest Hamburger was one of the most charming and informative experiences I had during my research. He also supplied additional information through correspondence.

My editor, Lewis Bateman, provided judicious counsel and put up with my impatience. A number of my colleagues and friends gave generously of their time and energy. Allan Lichtman, Kathleen Dalton, Ira Klein, Thomas Imhoof, and Richard Streeter contributed non-Germanist perspectives and substantial editing assistance. Major Bernard McDaniel, a very able graduate student, hunted down sources for me. Maureen Miller typed the text, and Eleanor O'Donnell added the bibliography.

The archivists and librarians to whom I am indebted for their assistance in my research are too numerous to be mentioned by name here. I beg the indulgence of those who have been omitted.

My research would not have been possible without financial support from the Council of European Studies, the Center for European Studies at Harvard

University, the Graduate School of Arts and Sciences at Harvard, the Krupp Foundation, and The American University.

Finally, I would like to express my deepest appreciation to my parents, Gloria and Saul Breitman, and to my friends Marc Alexander, Laura Langbein, Christine Marwick, Jeffrey Nelson, Linda and Matthew Ramsey, and Kristi Suelzle. Without their loyal support I would not have had the temerity to carry the long struggle to completion.

German Socialism
and Weimar Democracy

The old slogans have died. The masses no longer believe in them. The full consequences have not yet been drawn from the new democratic form of state. The significance of individual human achievement and individual moral responsibility is not yet perceived. One still believes in the automatic effect of the masses and the substructure; the creative will of the individual, from which everything ultimately derives has not yet been discovered. We are lacking the brains and the capacity to really be able to govern, and the party does everything it can to keep its distance from such qualities. It therefore does not create a bridge to the intellectual (*geistige*) figures of our time, who in large part turn away sharply from Social Democracy. The task . . . is to develop new powers of attraction.

Hugo Sinzheimer to Wilhem Sollman
7 May 1924, Nachlass Sollman 1/19/12.

Introduction

S O C I A L democratic parties in Europe today are neither stalwart defenders nor dedicated opponents of the status quo. Formerly revolutionary movements have cast off their most radical doctrines partly because of the substantial political and economic reforms that have transformed Europe. Most nations in western and central Europe have mixed economies, with varying blends of privately owned and state-owned enterprises. Each state also provides an array of services for its citizens, including health care, employment assistance, unemployment benefits, special assistance to low-income groups, housing, recreational facilities, and free or low-cost education. This welfare state with a mixed economy generally has a parliamentary system of government based on universal suffrage. The strong presidency in France and the continuing political role of the monarchy in Spain deviate slightly from the general pattern, but parliamentary democracy predominates.

European socialist movements have not only accommodated themselves to a postliberal economic order and the political ideals of nineteenth-century liberalism; they helped to establish this combination. Socialist parties and trade unions first came to accept parliamentary democracy and then tried to achieve their economic goals by working through the political system. Even when the outcome was an economy in which privately owned enterprises prevailed, the socialists continued to support the political order.

Social democratic movements had to overcome initial reservations about the limitations of legal political activity. European socialists of the late nineteenth century had regarded legislatures as a forum from which they could explain socialism to workers still uncommitted or politically indifferent. Speeches from the floor of parliament, where socialists were protected by immunity from prosecution, could stimulate class consciousness among workers and promote the growth of socialist organizations. But socialist leaders recognized that they had little opportunity to influence government decisions. Even if late-nineteenth-century socialist parties had captured many seats, they could not have modified existing property relations or redistributed income through legislative action in most nations. Restrictions on the suffrage and limited legislative control of the executive reduced the opportunities for mass parties to make their influence felt. For leading socialists, nineteenth-century "democracy" was worthwhile primarily because it gave workers rights and

3

liberties that could be used in the future battle for socialism. Toward the turn of the century European socialist movements developed greater affinity for representative government. The expansion of suffrage in England reinforced the long parliamentary tradition there. The Dreyfus Affair brought socialists and liberals closer together in France. In Germany, Social Democrats, liberals, and members of the Catholic Center party found common ground in opposing the flamboyant adventurism of Kaiser Wilhelm II.

From World War I until the late 1930s European social democracy developed its characteristic features. Most socialist parties expressed loyalty to their respective nations at the outset of the war, disclosing at least some degree of accommodation with the existing political order. Then as economic crises, international disputes, and fascist movements disrupted postwar Europe, many socialist politicians rallied to the cause of parliamentary democracy. In some cases revolutionary or radical socialists stormed out of their own parties, forming rival working-class organizations. This left-wing competition often restrained social democratic leaders, but it did not ultimately deter them from their moderate course. In Britain, France, Germany, Austria, and the Scandinavian countries social democratic movements sought a parliamentary route to their goals, shoring up existing political systems against radical challengers on the right and left. Rather than promote revolution, social democracy now tried to prevent it.

Indeed, parliamentary government quickly collapsed wherever socialists were unable or unwilling to give it substantial support. The successor regimes varied greatly—Bolshevik Russia, Fascist Italy, and Franco's Spain. Benefiting from firm socialist support, the Weimar Republic in Germany and the French Third Republic lasted much longer. Their eventual collapse did not in the long run divert German and French socialists from their strategy of working through democratic systems. The horrors of the Nazi regime and the disastrous failure of Vichy contrasted with the positive aspects of Weimar and the Third Republic. After World War II, West German and French socialists intensified their commitment to parliamentary democracy. Thus, the transformation of the main branch of western- and central-European socialism into social democracy has molded the contours of European politics in the twentieth century.

Contemporary observers disagreed over the causes of the socialist adaptation to parliamentary democracy early in the century, as many still do today. Lenin argued that an "aristocracy of labor" abandoned the overthrow of capitalism and thereby betrayed the interests of the working class as a whole.[1] From a different leftist perspective, sociologist Robert Michels maintained that as socialist leaders and functionaries gained power and prestige within working-class organizations, they assumed the values of the bourgeoisie. Far from seeing the process of increasing socialist moderation as a conspiracy, Michels described it as an inevitable product of the oligarchical tendencies in modern bureaucratic organizations.[2] Business interests, on the other hand, often suspected that socialist moderation was but a cloak for a continued intent to overthrow capitalism. But particularly in the political chaos of the immediate postwar period, perspicacious businessmen acknowledged that social democratic leaders refrained from revolutionary agitation.[3] Despite its contempt for socialism, big business strongly preferred social democracy to bolshevism.

Historians remain sharply divided in their explanations of what caused the development of social democracy. Many eastern-European historians have accepted the Leninist interpretation that the capitalist system corrupted a working-class elite.[4] Some modern scholars have also retained Michels's view, albeit in a more cautious and qualified form, that the growth of working-class organizations created a bureaucratic elite with a stake in preserving the status quo.[5] In contrast, historian Peter Stearns has argued that working-class organizations in prewar Europe were generally more radical and, above all, more ideological than most workers themselves. Stearns claimed that European socialist movements adapted subsequently to existing political systems in order to deal with the essentially short-term, pragmatic concerns of most rank-and-file workers.[6] These conflicting interpretations rest on fundamentally different pictures of the attitudes and interests of the industrial working class. Better quantitative evidence about socialist membership and voting support as well as in-depth studies of working-class attitudes may eventually clarify the scope of working-class inclinations toward reform or revolution.

A fresh interpretation of social democratic politics in the interwar period must avoid tenuous assumptions and false dichotomies. The view that social democratic leaders consciously chose the status quo over socialist revolution falls into both categories. Although social democratic strategists certainly rejected the risky alternative of socialist revolution, they hardly intended to support the status quo. Party and trade-union officials argued that they could achieve immediate benefits for the working class as well as progress toward socialism within the context of parliamentary democracy.

They were often mistaken in their optimistic expectations. Social democratic organizations not only failed to accomplish major social and economic goals during the interwar period; they sometimes could not preserve the parliamentary-democratic system that was supposed to foster the achievement of their goals. But charges that socialist leaders consciously abandoned or betrayed professed social democratic objectives require specific documentation of intentions that historians have been unable to provide. Political critics, of course, have less rigorous standards.

The German experience provides a graphic illustration of the disparity between the political aims and achievements of European social democracy in the post–World War I era. With a membership of more than one million in 1914, the Social Democratic party of Germany (SPD) was the largest and best-organized socialist party in Europe. The affiliated Free Trade Union Federation, later renamed the General Federation of German Trade Unions (ADGB), then had two and one-half times as many members and similarly possessed a preeminent position among European union federations. The leaders of both the SPD and the ADGB worked to establish parliamentary democracy in Germany and to formulate the early social and economic reforms of the Weimar Republic. Yet despite these efforts, the republic collapsed, preparing the way for Adolf Hitler and the Third Reich.

Given the initial socialist expectations of Weimar, it is no wonder that contemporaries and recent scholars have criticized the quality of the Social Democratic leadership. According to much of the literature,[7] a narrow and entrenched group of leaders dominated these immense mass organizations and presided over their downfall during the Weimar era. Party and union officials developed an excessive concern for the welfare of the organizations, rather than for the cause of socialism, which impeded them from drawing up a suitable political strategy. There have also been discussions of an inappropriate style of socialist leadership. In a recent article one scholar has described the ideal-type of the Social Democratic leader as "the Prussian bureaucrat, whose main characteristics are pedantism [sic], cleanliness, honesty, impartiality, obedience, and readiness for self-sacrifice."[8] In analyzing the SPD's role during the revolution of 1918, Richard N. Hunt has depicted Friedrich Ebert as follows: "He possessed all the virtues of a bureaucrat—administrative skill, level-headedness, and ability to compromise—but also all the defects—a narrow and legalistic vision, a blind trust in experts, and an unreasoning horror of disorder. In a party secretary these faults were no doubt negligible, but history had called Ebert to lead the November Revolution. . . . The failure of the German Revolution was in the first instance a failure of its leadership."[9] The argument seems to be that a different type of leader combined with different policies would have proved more effective.

This line of criticism requires sound inferences about the feasibility of alternative choices and careful scrutiny of relevant evidence if it is to be effective. Both the options available to German Social Democracy and the interpretation of leadership decisions and motivation must arise out of an analysis of the SPD's role in the Weimar Republic. That is the purpose of the present study, which indicates that the strenuous political demands of the Weimar era elicited divergent reactions even within the relatively narrow Social Democratic elite.

Although I concentrate largely on the interaction between the SPD leaders and the parliamentary system, I do not mean to denigrate the importance of the Social Democratic organization as a whole. Most Social Democrats were highly proud that they represented a mass movement. And despite the problems of bureaucratization and ossification described by other scholars, the SPD provided more significant channels for the expression of rank-and-file sentiment than did most other parties at the time.[10] Moreover, there is very little evidence to suggest that the Social Democratic leadership was unrepresentative of its membership or voting constituency in terms of class background.[11]

The vertical links of the SPD leaders to middle and lower levels of the party and to the electorate, however, represent a separate subject that still merits detailed scholarly investigation. More in the way of local studies and quantitative analysis is needed before general conclusions can be drawn with confidence.[12] So my decision to concentrate on the upper echelon of the SPD was in part one of necessity, given the range of unfulfilled research tasks.

There is some logic as well behind the present focus on the SPD leadership. Precisely in the area of governmental and parliamentary policy, party representatives enjoyed a great deal of autonomy, just as many left-wing critics of the party leadership complained. The development of a parliamentary elite at the national and state levels with broad decision-making power[13] was a notable characteristic of the SPD's history even before the Weimar era.[14] The SPD's entrance into coalition governments during the Weimar Republic added to the influence of these "parliamentarians," but at the same time created potential strain between SPD deputies and SPD members of the cabinet. Particularly when there were disagreements within the party elite, perceptions of how the masses would react to certain moves influenced the party's decisions. However, party members could not effectively and directly determine policies, even through the mechanism of the party congress. The SPD elite was in a position to exert its leadership, at least until adverse election results indicated the need for shifts in policy.

What was the general thrust of the SPD's politics during the Weimar Republic? Some western scholars have concluded that the SPD refused to commit itself strongly to a capitalistic republic, thereby weakening a parliamentary system already on shaky ground. The SPD's original socialist objectives allegedly interfered with its more recent democratic affiliation.[15] The present study, building upon recent monographs and primary source research, disputes this interpretation. During the revolutionary period the SPD leaders placed highest priority upon the rapid establishment of parliamentary democracy, neglecting an opportunity to move toward socialism immediately. They also developed the conviction that cooperation between socialists and nonsocialists was essential to make the political system function. Similarly, they believed that joint business-labor efforts could repair the war-torn German economy. The Social Democratic elite's preference for parliamentary democracy based on interparty and interclass cooperation on the whole extended throughout the Weimar period.

However, harsh political realities pressed the SPD elite more and more into a defensive position. After the revolutionary turmoil subsided, the nonsocialist parties of the center, organized business interests, and the military had little need to cooperate with Social Democracy in order to keep the masses in check. Moreover, the repeated foreign-policy crises and negotiations unleashed a nationalistic reaction among many German voters that sometimes threatened the parliamentary republic itself and discouraged the nonsocialist parties from cooperating with the SPD. The SPD leaders were often called upon to sacrifice their economic objectives in order to stabilize the republic. But even when they did so, they could not ensure lasting coalition government at the national level.

The Social Democratic elite thus groped for a strategy that would have preserved parliamentary democracy and at the same time advanced the economic interests of its working-class constituents. The economic, political, and diplomatic constraints of the period doomed this search, which left the SPD leaders with unpleasant and uncomfortable alternatives after mid-1920. The SPD elite rejected the left-wing socialist view that the party should never enter coalitions with nonsocialist parties, but when national economic policy alienated the traditionally socialist segment of the electorate, the SPD parted ways with its coalition partners. Yet a strong SPD presence in the government of the huge state of Prussia served as a stabilizing force even when the party withdrew from coalition government at the national level. This defensive strategy failed during the depression. Although the SPD hoped to prevent an alliance between conservative opponents of the republic and the Nazis, the SPD leaders could not develop a successful approach to interparty cooperation. Previous Social Democratic experience and ideology contributed to that failure.

1. Parliamentarism and Progress

T H E German Reich founded in 1871 was a harsh environment for German socialism. Otto von Bismarck drew up a federal constitution that maximized the influence of the huge state of Prussia, still dominated by the king and the Junker aristocracy. The authoritarian elements of the constitution and the plutocratic character of the Prussian suffrage not only represented major departures from the western liberal model but also served as a barrier to the rise of socialism. Nonetheless, socialist candidates and trade-union organizers gained substantial mass support in the 1870s, which led Chancellor Bismarck to introduce special legislation against German Social Democracy in 1878. For the next twelve years the SPD operated under severe restraints, and many party activists were forced to go underground or into exile.

The antidemocratic features of the Second Reich and government persecution of the early socialist organizations convinced Social Democratic theorists and party officials that there was limited opportunity for gradual progress.[1] Friedrich Engels, one of the founding fathers of modern socialism, wrote skeptically in 1891 about the possibility of a peaceful transition to socialism in Germany: "One can conceive of the old society being able to develop peacefully into the new one in countries where the popular representative monopolizes power, where one has the support of the majority of the people: in democratic republics such as France and America, in monarchies such as England, . . . But in Germany . . . [it is an entirely different matter]."[2] Seven years later Karl Kautsky, the most prominent theorist in the SPD's ranks, essentially agreed with Engels: "Naturally we wish to reach our goal without revolution. The question is whether that is possible. In England yes, but in Germany . . . ? Germany needs a political revolution to reach the point where the English are. . . . Whether we want the revolution or not, whether it brings us victory or defeat, it is our historical task in Germany."[3] Only a revolution could clear the way for socialism in Germany, and the German Social Democrats firmly believed in that revolution. Engels, Kautsky, and the SPD's venerated leader August Bebel had taken Darwinian ideas of progress and evolution, and developed a strongly deterministic brand of Marxism. A socialist revolution need not be "made"; it would simply occur. Social Democratic spokesmen argued that the expansion of working-class organizations and of the SPD's share of the vote in parliamentary elections boded the

9

imminent demise of the capitalist order.[4] Bebel frequently had to revise his forecasts of the date of the collapse, but his faith in continuous development toward socialism remained unbroken.[5]

This belief in the historical inevitability of socialism inhibited Social Democratic leaders from formulating intermediate plans. The SPD not only did little to promote a mass uprising, but some scholars have even argued that it unwittingly stabilized the status quo. According to sociologist Guenther Roth, the extensive branches of the Social Democratic organization directed workers toward short-term limited goals and diverted them from revolution. Moreover, the Social Democratic subculture, a product of social and political segregation, helped workers to gain recognition from their peers, which diminished their sense of isolation and mitigated their resentment of social discrimination. Although the SPD remained opposed to the Second Reich, it mobilized working-class support in such a way that the political system was not immediately endangered. Roth describes Social Democracy as negatively integrated into the Second Reich.[6]

Other factors besides Social Democratic organizations reduced working-class alienation. A substantial increase in real wages from 1880 until the turn of the century provided at least the material basis for the integration of factory workers into German society.[7] The elementary schools, the army, the press, and various kinds of entertainment transmitted bourgeois sentiments to workers. Working-class and nonworking-class attitudes diverged on many issues, but by no means all, even though class antagonisms remained sharp. The dominant culture and the Social Democratic subculture, each in its own way, led the working class away from the path of revolution.

Despite its lack of revolutionary activity, the SPD became a prime target for criticism and harassment up until the First World War.[8] Economic interests and pressure groups worried by the problems of rapid industrialization and urbanization projected their anxieties upon the working class, and Social Democracy served as a convenient scapegoat. Organizations such as the Central League of German Industrialists, the Colonial Association, the Pan-German League, the Agrarian League, and the Reich League against Social Democracy managed to strengthen prejudices against the SPD among nonproletarian elements, particularly those threatened by economic decline.[9] High government officials had reasons of their own to reinforce the SPD's isolation. Antisocialism was the domestic counterpart to imperialism; both policies helped the government to unify an otherwise diverse conglomeration of political and economic interests.

As long as the Social Democratic elite remained confident that socialism was inevitable and imminent, the SPD simply gathered its strength in opposition to the regime and carried on agitation stressing the class struggle. But around the turn of the century the SPD's growth began to slow down, and various groups within the movement openly began to question party strategy.[10] The most fundamental theoretical challenge came from Eduard Bernstein, founder of the revisionist school of Marxism, who questioned prevailing socialist assumptions about economic development, social structure, and the SPD's political goals. Not everyone within the SPD, even among the right-wing forces, was happy about the controversy that Bernstein stirred up, for his ideas threatened party unity. This self-taught writer who had spent years of exile in England raised problems that the SPD wished to avoid. A good many of those problems still lacked solutions during the Weimar Republic.

Bernstein observed that despite the Great Depression of the 1870s and 1880s, capitalism showed little sign of dying. Instead, it was actually creating new occupations and new social strata. The rapid growth in the number of white-collar employees added to the size of the lower-middle class, and contrary to Marx's predictions, small business and small-scale farms had not disappeared. These intermediate social groups might prevent complete social polarization between big business and labor. The new social configuration had obvious political implications.

Bernstein placed great value on parliamentary democracy, arguing that it would almost certainly lead to the abolition of class rule or privilege. If the socialists hoped to gain control of a democratic political system, however, they would need support from other social groups in addition to the proletariat, for the latter might not constitute a majority.[11] The various social strata would have to work out mutually agreeable arrangements to promote the general welfare. Bernstein clearly disagreed with Marx, who had argued that the proletariat's interests were identical with those of the overwhelming majority of society. Marx's claim of proletarian universality made it possible to maintain that socialism benefited virtually everyone. Bernstein's pluralist notion closely resembled that of classical liberalism;[12] various social interests had to be reconciled. Bernstein remained loyal to the goal of socialism, but his advocacy of collective economic principles was considerably less precise than traditional Marxist ideas of socialism. He did not forecast the shape of a socialist economy.

Two clear implications emerged from Bernstein's argument: the SPD should work for parliamentary government, and it should seek some form of cooperation with nonproletarian elements. Although the second position was highly controversial in a society with deep class cleavages, the first had already gained some support among nonrevisionists. Early socialist notions of direct democracy gradually lost favor in the SPD. Karl Kautsky wrote in 1893 that the democratic republic was the concrete form of state within which socialism could be realized.[13]

During the first decade of the twentieth century the SPD Reichstag fraction began the difficult task of pushing the Second Reich toward parliamentary government. SPD deputies insisted that the chancellor had the responsibility of representing government policy before the Reichstag, a stance aimed at forestalling the egregious intrusions of Kaiser Wilhelm II into German foreign policy. By 1908 the SPD delegation pressed for the political responsibility of the chancellor to the Reichstag; a vote of no confidence would then force the chancellor out of office. The only concrete benefit achieved by the Reichstag was a strengthened form of parliamentary interpellation in 1912. After the Zabern Affair in 1913,[14] the Reichstag actually passed a vote of no confidence in the government. Although this action did not force the government to resign, Social Democratic deputies hoped to hold the antigovernment bloc together to move toward parliamentarism.[15] The SPD offered parliamentarism in part as its remedy for the dangerous constitutional defects of the Second Reich.

To exert practical influence in politics, however, meant to accept compromises. Needing to strengthen the SPD's ties with liberal parties in the Reichstag, SPD Cochairman August Bebel played down the party's strident principles, particularly its internationalism and republicanism. By pressing for evolution toward a parliamentary monarchy instead of a socialist republic, the SPD pierced the wall separating socialists from nonsocialists and helped to create a division between leftist and rightist parties instead in the last years before the war.[16] This accomplishment threatened the regime, but it did not satisfy the radical elements within the SPD who doubted the likelihood of peaceful political reform.[17] Moreover, collaboration with nonsocialists called into question the party's doctrine of the class struggle that gave the proletariat a unique and revolutionary mission.

Some right-wing forces within the Social Democratic movement, on the other hand, opposed the use of potentially illegal or risky methods such as a mass strike to pressure the government to accept reforms.[18] At the SPD congress at Jena in 1913, trade-union leader Gustav Bauer rejected the idea of using the mass strike to bring about equal suffrage in Prussia, arguing that the SPD could make progress even with an unequal suffrage. The south German revisionist Ludwig Frank was quite bitter about Bauer's stance, fearing an abandonment of the party's democratic objectives.[19] In the years before the war the SPD suffered a raft of internal disputes over its domestic and foreign policy and over its general political strategy. When Bebel died in 1913, the party lost its most effective unifying force.[20]

The outbreak of the war caused certain changes in the lines of cleavage within the party. The paramount issue within the party fraction at the start was whether the SPD should cease its longstanding hostility toward the government. Although the SPD's decision to vote in favor of the German government's request for war credits shocked many European socialists, even the leftists in the SPD fraction believed that Germany had to defend itself against Russia. The fourteen deputies (out of ninety-two) who voted against war credits in caucus on 3 August, (but did not violate party discipline in the Reichstag on 4 August) objected only to the cessation of political hostilities at home during the war.[21] Other deputies, however, went out of their way to improve relations with the government.

A number of revisionists and a few former orthodox Marxists sought to exploit the convincing display of patriotism by the working class in August 1914 to promote political reform. Ludwig Frank put it most succinctly, writing on 27 August: "For [equal] suffrage in Prussia, we will conduct a war, instead of a general strike."[22] Certainly, quite a number of Social Democrats hoped that the working class would receive favorable consideration at the end of what was expected to be a short and victorious campaign.[23] Revisionist Eduard David had perhaps the clearest vision of how the SPD might expand its pledge of loyalty into a new political strategy.

> In case of a [German] defeat, the Russian government [would be] against democratization; in France a realistic nationalistic government. . . . In case of victory, which is more probable, any thought of revolution and republic in our lifetime would be ended by the return of the Hohenzollern Kaiser at the head of his victorious army. Thus, a *modus vivendi* with the monarchy is necessary. Besides the militaristic, nationalistic wave [there will be] a strong wave of democratic sentiment: the demand of the returning warriors for civic equality. The reform of the Prussian suffrage must be plucked as the fruit; [we would make] concessions on our side to the monarchical form for this price. Parliamentary democratic form of government under a monarchist head.[24]

The moderate course advocated by David expanded upon the SPD's non-revolutionary methods of the prewar period, but David spoke only for a right-wing minority.

Left-wing radicals such as Karl Liebknecht, Rosa Luxemburg, Franz Mehring, and Clara Zetkin, who had criticized the extent of SPD's accommodation to the Second Reich before the war, now found moderation even more repulsive. Faced with antagonistic views, the executive committee and the Reichstag fraction leaders first called for an internal party truce. Party leaders tried to maintain Bebel's policy of preserving party unity. But bitter regional and local conflicts over control of the party press and organization soon broke out. The war also quickly took on a different image. Conservative political groups and economic interests raised public demands for German territorial annexations, which Chancellor Bethmann Hollweg did not repudiate. The war clearly became one of conquest rather than a defensive struggle, which substantially strengthened the antigovernment faction within the SPD.[25]

Finally, the SPD right wing succeeded in bringing about binding votes by the Reichstag fraction on all major decisions. When some of the leftists refused to go along with the majority, they were excluded for violating party discipline.[26] Many of the antiwar deputies of the center-left departed from the fraction as well. The schism culminated with the founding of the Independent Social Democratic party of Germany (USPD) in 1917 as a rival of the SPD.

The removal of the leftists cleared the way for the SPD right wing to pursue political concessions from the government, but this strategy was not very effective. In one area there was some progress. Army officials had forced often unwilling employers to recognize the socialist unions in order to gain the latter's cooperation in the war economy.[27] But all efforts to persuade the government to introduce major political reforms, or to promise such reforms for the future, proved unavailing.[28] Moreover, the SPD objected to many of the government's economic policies. Rising food prices combined with cuts in rations, black-market trafficking, regressive taxes, and restrictions on job mobility antagonized many workers, and the SPD deputies, committed to the support of the war effort, felt frustrated and politically vulnerable.[29] Bound by a sense of national loyalty despite their lack of influence over the government, the SPD deputies refrained from sharp public criticism of government policies for much of the war. The rival USPD thus could more easily exploit growing working-class discontent with the hardships of the war and resentment over the lack of political reform. Although most USPD deputies favored a quick, negotiated settlement to the conflict,[30] left-wing radicals even regarded the prospect of German defeat with equanimity. The International Group, later renamed the Spartacist Federation, held that "the chief enemy is at home."[31]

The government's conduct of war and diplomacy, increasingly dictated by military leaders such as General Ludendorff, became more and more controversial. Many German politicians recognized that the decision to try to break the military stalemate through unrestricted submarine warfare was disastrous. As the political truce lapsed in 1917, the Progressive party and the left wing of the Center party under the leadership of Matthias Erzberger joined the SPD and USPD in criticism of the government. But without the introduction of parliamentary government, the parties were powerless to reverse military or diplomatic policy.[32]

The risks of continuing to support the government became obvious to the SPD leaders in 1917. The Russian Revolution in March demonstrated how wartime dissatisfaction among workers and peasants might swell over the channels provided by working-class organizations. In April serious labor disturbances erupted in Germany when bread rations were cut and further restrictions were imposed on the mobility of labor. Strikers in Berlin and Leipzig called for political changes as well, such as free and equal suffrage and peace without annexations.[33] The SPD leaders dared not oppose the strikes, although they tried to bring about settlements on the economic issues.[34] Spokesman Philipp Scheidemann, who had written earlier that a Russian-style revolution might occur in Germany unless the government changed its ways, went beyond that in May. He warned the Reichstag that if the government prolonged the war in order to secure annexations, there would be revolution.[35] By late June the SPD party council put strong pressure on the fraction to insist on peace without annexations and on parliamentary government.[36] Still, the SPD hesitated to act by itself.

Matthias Erzberger's proposal for a peace resolution by the Reichstag in July 1917 provided the SPD leaders with a new opportunity. They could now move more sharply against the government without danger of being isolated. As a result, the SPD moved quickly to coordinate its objectives with the more modest programs of the Center and Progressive parties, the three parties forming a joint committee (the *Interfraktionelle Ausschuss*) in the Reichstag.[37] The National Liberals also assumed a position on the committee from time to time. Finally convinced of the need to take account of sentiment in parliament, Bethmann Hollweg suggested the reform of the Prussian suffrage to the Kaiser, but it was too late for the chancellor to save his job. The Army High Command demanded the ouster of Bethmann, and the three parties had no desire to prop him up. The chancellor resigned on 13 July, and six days later the Reichstag passed the Erzberger peace resolution, calling for a negotiated settlement on the basis of no annexations.

SPD leaders could now sense that they faced significant changes in strategy. Georg Gradnauer had hinted in late 1916 that the SPD might be willing to work with the bourgeois parties on the basis of parliamentarism and equal suffrage;[38] now that prospect appeared within reach. At the SPD congress in October 1917 Philipp Scheidemann emphasized that the SPD would have an entirely new function in a more democratic political system: "German Social Democracy—I will state it quite openly—has become a party with a direct expectancy (*Anwartschaft*) of state power as a result of the war. In one way or another the parliamentary system will be implemented, and Germany will take a parliamentary-democratic form of state after the war. . . . Today we do not know how the postwar elections will come out, but we may calculate . . . that we will emerge . . . with such great strength that we will not be permitted to enjoy the luxury of opposition."[39] Scheidemann did not promise the delegates socialism, but only parliamentary democracy. Moreover, he implied that the SPD would serve in the government after the war. Otto Landsberg reinforced the commitment of the party to the new political order:

> What reforms do the German people need? We Social Democrats
> know that full democracy can only follow the elimination of class
> antagonisms. In the meantime, a considerable amount can also be
> achieved within the framework of this antagonism. In a state that sees
> its members as citizens and not subjects, that prepares no obstacles to a
> peaceful (but) powerful effort to overcome the principle of economic
> individualism through socialism, the working classes will consider
> themselves part of their state and will do their utmost to maintain it
> and to advance it. In such a state . . . there can only be a parliamen-
> tary form of government.[40]

Landsberg confirmed that party leaders now hoped to achieve socialism gradually through parliamentary democracy rather than suddenly through the collapse of capitalism. The SPD's emphasis on parliamentarism was also expressed by new programs for constitutional reform at the state level.[41]

Evolutionary ideas had seeped into the Social Democratic world-view despite the failure of revisionism to win broad acceptance. Obviously, the wartime experience had a major impact both upon party leaders' view of political opportunities and upon their interpretation of economic development. Political compromise and coalition government with nonsocialist parties now were viewed as legitimate possibilities, and parliamentary democracy would create the foundation for such cooperation. Meanwhile, party leaders saw little chance of a return to prewar economic conditions. Even some former radicals believed that the state-regulated economy of the wartime period would provide guidelines for the evolution of capitalism into socialism.[42] Scheidemann predicted in 1917 that the postwar economy would be influenced by socialist principles, although it would not be fully socialized.[43] A new action program published by the party in May 1918 called for greater representation of all affected strata on state economic agencies, nationalization of private monopolies, and greater state supervision of cartels.[44]

The immediate political problems, however, did not disappear, as Chancellors Hertling and Michaelis resisted parliamentary pressure. As long as the military situation remained favorable on the surface, the SPD refused to ventilate the extent of its dissatisfaction with the government, despite signs that urban workers in some regions were flocking to the USPD.[45] But when General Ludendorff's last offensive failed in the summer of 1918, the interparty committee finally seized the initiative. The SPD representatives insisted on a program based on parliamentary government as well as peace, while the conservative portion of the Center party still had reservations about the former.[46] At this point General Ludendorff also threw his support behind the movement for parliamentary government, hoping that a reformed government could negotiate more favorable peace terms, wanting also to avoid responsibility for whatever settlement was obtained.[47]

When the interparty committee reached agreement on a program that included the responsibility of the government to the Reichstag, the SPD Deputies had to decide whether to join a new cabinet. For a socialist party, the step from opposition to coalition partner was of great consequence. Yet most of the leading Social Democrats had no objection in principle. The debate within the SPD fraction and party council (an advisory body to the executive committee) centered on the practical advantages and disadvantages of government participation at that moment. Numerous speakers contended that the SPD might suffer if it tried to stem the impending bankruptcy of the Second Reich. The supporters of participation had three arguments that overrode immediate party interests: the need to bring the war to a quick end on respectable terms, the danger of a Bolshevik-style revolution in Germany, and the urgency of active SPD support for democratic reforms. The vote in favor of SPD participation in a reformed government was 55 to 10 among the Reichstag deputies and 25 to 11 among members of the party council on 23 September.[48]

The man who exerted greatest influence within the SPD during the critical days of September and October 1918 was Friedrich Ebert, who would also dominate the revolutionary government established in November. Ebert was in many ways the typical second-generation SPD leader. As the son of a tailor, he had no opportunity to advance himself through the educational system. Social Democracy became his career. Born in Heidelberg in 1871, he was trained as a saddler and became an active member of the socialist movement as a youth. After participating in the election campaign of 1890, he was blacklisted by employers as a troublemaker. Ebert then helped to organize a cooperative bakery that soon failed, worked as a newspaper reporter, and ran a restaurant. Finally, he was appointed labor secretary for the trade unions in Bremen, which gave him a respectable position, a dependable salary, and an early political base. The socialist unions helped to bring about his election to the SPD executive committee in 1905, and he served as a liaison between party and union leaders.

Ebert's diligence and attention to detail in office work soon established him as an essential member of the committee, nominally under the leadership of the party's cochairmen, the aged August Bebel and Paul Singer. When Singer died in 1911, Ebert received strong union support for the vacant post of cochairman. But lawyer Hugo Haase, left of center within the party, obtained

Bebel's endorsement, and Ebert refused to accept nomination. When Bebel died two years later, Ebert was elected without difficulty to the other cochairman's post. He also won election to the Reichstag in 1912.

Whereas Bebel had been the undisputed leader of the entire party, Ebert was at first simply the representative of those who directed the practical work of electioneering and organization. He was not a brilliant speaker, and he had little taste for theoretical disputes, whether raised by the revisionists or the left-wing radicals. The pragmatists in the party elite concentrated on the party's immediate tasks; they worried little about long-range objectives. During the war Ebert wished to preserve party unity in support of what he and many others believed to be a war of national defense. When dissidents violated party discipline by voting against the government's successive requests for war credits, Ebert adopted a hard line. His strong sense of patriotism and his insistence on members' obligation to follow party regulations may have contributed to the schism.[49] Since Cochairman Haase soon joined the antiwar camp, Ebert's position made him the leader of the SPD majority, and he continued to gain influence. In early 1916 he was elected cochairman of the Reichstag fraction, serving alongside Philipp Scheidemann and Hermann Molkenbuhr. The aged Molkenbuhr was rarely active, but Scheidemann was a formidable force, joining Ebert as cochairman of the party in 1917.

Scheidemann had more parliamentary experience than Ebert and better oratorical skills as well. The SPD fraction selected Scheidemann (partly at Ebert's urging) to serve in the reformed government headed by Prince Max of Baden in October 1918. Yet Ebert became the dominant figure in the party elite during precisely this period by clinging tenaciously to a consistent line of policy. Ebert wished to ensure the survival of the relations established in 1917 among the SPD, Progressives, and Center, and toward this end he worked to prevent the outbreak of revolution. He is supposed to have told Prince Max that he "hated social revolution like sin."[50] Whether or not this statement was an accurate reflection of his feelings, he certainly would have preferred a parliamentary system of government under a constitutional monarchy to a republic established by revolution. Ebert's wartime experience convinced him that the assistance of liberal political forces, civil servants, and economic experts in the private sector would be essential to any postwar regime concerned with peace and economic reconstruction.

Socialist union leaders showed parallel tendencies, perceiving a need to cooperate with industrialists to prevent economic distress in the postwar period. Carl Legien, chairman of the socialist union federation known as the Free Unions (later as the ADGB), told industrialist Walther Rathenau that a voluntary business-labor agreement would not hinder socialization of the economy, because socialization could only be a gradual process. Industrialists and labor officials concluded most of the terms of a social partnership before the outbreak of revolution. Signed on 13 November, the Stinnes-Legien Agreement gave the unions substantial immediate benefits. Employers granted recognition to the three major union federations and agreed to eliminate the "yellow" or employer-sponsored unions. Both sides accepted the principle of collective bargaining and would have recourse to central mediation organs within each industry. The agreement established worker committees (*Arbeiterausschüsse*) in each plant with more than fifty workers in order to represent labor-union interests, and the eight-hour day became standard.[51]

Legien claimed that this agreement was a step on the way to socialism.[52] More accurately, it was an admission on the part of union officials that capitalism had years and perhaps decades still to live. Paul Umbreit, editor in chief of the Free Union Federation's newspaper, *Korrespondenzblatt*, predicted that it would take thirty or forty years just to complete the educational prerequisites for socialism.[53] In the meanwhile, the new political order and the business-labor agreement were designed to facilitate compromise and cooperation among the diverse political parties and economic interests.

Many prominent Social Democrats accepted the notion that the SPD should form a coalition government with nonsocialists in the postwar period. Trade-union leader Gustav Bauer later confided to German Democratic party official Erich Koch-Weser that in November 1918 all SPD leaders believed a purely socialist government would not be feasible for several years.[54] Eduard Bernstein less discreetly told the SPD congress in 1920: "Yes, even if we had an absolute majority, I would regard the inclusion of bourgeois elements as necessary."[55] The notion of interclass cooperation that stemmed from revisionism took concrete form in the interparty committee of 1917–1918 and the business-labor accord, and survived the revolution of 1918.

The SPD's situation at the end of the Second Reich was in many ways paradoxical. The SPD had a partisan interest in the end of the regime—it was the most likely beneficiary. Yet the Social Democratic elite, unlike its USPD counterpart, sought to work within the framework of the Second Reich despite the growing unpopularity of this approach with working-class constituents. Undoubtedly, SPD leaders such as Ebert and Scheidemann believed it their patriotic duty to secure reasonable armistice and peace terms from the west; revolution, in their eyes, would only complicate this task.[56] More importantly, their evolutionary views of socialism and concern about Germany's postwar economic problems devalued the prospect of socialist revolution. Socialism was impractical or even dangerous at the end of a long ruinous war. Socialists would be blamed for the inevitable problems of economic reconstruction, and monarchist forces might even wage civil war against a revolutionary socialist regime.

Having established links with the government and nonsocialist parties during the war to promote the national interest, the SPD leaders felt that the expected postwar conditions justified closer cooperation on the basis of parliamentary democracy. They did not perceive the arrangements with nonsocialist parties as permanent, nor would such cooperation fundamentally affect the clash of interest between the proletariat and capitalist interests.[57] This position clearly did not take full account of revisionist arguments that interclass cooperation was essential to socialist success. But the revisionist stress on parliamentary democracy took hold, and the pragmatists who dominated the party elite adopted parliamentary democracy as the new solution to an old socialist problem—how to deal with the material needs of workers in the present and push for socialism in the future.

Parliamentary democracy made evolutionary socialism feasible in the eyes of SPD leaders. The parliamentary system would maximize the influence of the SPD, whose deputies had fought their way into the Reichstag despite disadvantageous districting, legal harassment, and a second ballot runoff that usually worked to their disadvantage. Enhanced Social Democratic influence in a parliament with control over the government would make far-reaching social reforms possible; a socialist majority could establish socialism at the appropriate time. The absolutist features of the Second Reich would no longer stand in the way. Parliamentary democracy offered an evolutionary path to socialism, which reduced the tension between the SPD's short-term objectives and its ultimate socialist goals.

But this new Social Democratic strategy brought problems of its own. Nonsocialist parties and business elements sought the SPD's cooperation toward the end of the war partly to help negotiate decent peace terms with the Entente, partly to stave off revolution at home. Once these issues were settled, the future of cooperation was uncertain. Coalition governments and business-labor accords also clashed with the prewar Social Democratic posture of complete opposition to capitalism. The SPD had remained aloof from German society, a position justified by socialist ideology and corresponding to existing class antagonisms.[58] Now the Social Democratic deputies would be forced to compromise with their nonsocialist counterparts, with the rival USPD denouncing every concession to the bourgeoisie. The Independent Social Democrats laid claim to the heritage of German Social Democracy. They argued that they alone continued to carry out the class struggle and to prepare for the collapse of capitalism.[59] This appeal to tradition was potent, and the SPD leaders had to be concerned about a loss of working-class support to their left-wing rivals. If the SPD could demonstrate that interparty cooperation under the framework of parliamentary democracy produced direct benefits for the working class and clear progress toward socialism, then the risk of the new strategy was small. If not, the difficulties of the new political order would rebound upon the fortunes of German Social Democracy.

The SPD leaders had no desire to defend all the political, economic, and military institutions of the Second Reich. But to overthrow them all at the end of the war, they felt, would have been too great a risk for the cause of socialism and too great a danger to German national interest. The framework of parliamentary democracy and the strategy of cooperation with nonsocialist elements reduced the difficulty of stabilizing the economy and negotiating a peace. At the same time, however, this strategy increased the Social Democratic elite's problem of maintaining close ties to the organized working class. The strains and sacrifices of the war, particularly the shortage of food, had intensified working-class resentment of economic privilege and military domination.[60] Even with the end of political discrimination and the prospect of increased SPD influence in government, it was by no means certain that the working class would solidly support the gradualist approach of the SPD leaders.

2. The Limited Revolution

TH E Social Democratic strategy of cooperation with nonsocialist forces on the basis of parliamentary democracy ran into difficulty in late 1918. Despite reforms adopted in October 1918, the institutions of the Second Reich, particularly the position of the Kaiser and the military, blocked a smooth transition to parliamentarism. When the reform government under Prince Max of Baden failed to gain quick command of domestic and international developments, spontaneous uprisings of sailors, workers, and soldiers ended the life of the Second Reich. The insurgents primarily sought an immediate halt to the war, but also a change in government and military institutions.[1] The revolution of November 1918 thus posed a serious problem for the SPD leaders, who had supported and, in the last stage, participated in the wartime government. The antiwar and antigovernment USPD was in a better position to benefit from working-class discontent with the ancien régime. Still, both socialist parties were caught unawares by the suddenness of the revolution.[2]

The Social Democratic leaders had ample opportunity after 9 November to mobilize support for their own conception of the new political order. They succeeded in gaining control of the revolution, not because they read the will of the revolutionary masses on all particulars, but because they possessed superior organization, cohesion, and leadership compared with the USPD. Under Ebert's direction, the SPD treated the revolutionary regime as a kind of caretaker government that would prepare the way for peace and for a Constituent National Assembly elected by universal and equal suffrage. The Social Democratic campaign for the creation of parliamentary democracy succeeded well enough that most of the workers' and soldiers' councils established during the revolution went into political eclipse.

The USPD was sharply divided on the issue of parliamentarism and on the role of the councils. The extreme left regarded parliamentary democracy as "bourgeois" and (thereby) outmoded. The proletariat, which had carried off the revolution, had the right to run the new government through a system of workers' and soldiers' councils that would have both political and economic functions. This leftist viewpoint made the councils seem a threat to parliamentary democracy, stiffening the determination of the SPD leaders to eliminate them. The right wing of USPD, led by party Cochairman Hugo Haase, favored a political order somewhere in between the council system and parliamentarism. The SPD leaders and the USPD left forced the Haase group into an ever more uncomfortable position since it could not agree with either camp. Although the USPD right wing eventually broke with the SPD and departed from the socialist coalition government, the gap between the two wings of the USPD remained. A poorly planned uprising by left-wing radicals in Berlin in early January not only failed to reverse the SPD's domination of the revolution, but also drove the SPD leaders to rely uncritically upon conservative military forces. Not until much later did party leaders recognize that the forces of the old order, including the military, also represented a threat to parliamentary democracy.

The Collapse of the Second Reich

The coalition government established under Prince Max of Baden in October 1918, which included Philipp Scheidemann as the SPD representative, did not fully reflect the will of a parliamentary majority. The new chancellor, a member of the royal family of the south German state of Baden, was not the selection of the coalition parties. Moreover, the government did not measure up to the difficult problems it was called upon to solve.[3] Despite his request for an immediate armistice from the Entente, Prince Max was unable to halt the fighting. Woodrow Wilson remained unconvinced that Germany was now committed to peace and reform, and the Kaiser resisted the one move that might have lent weight to the government's stance—abdication. But the cabinet also had difficulty acting upon domestic reforms, and despite the fact that General Ludendorff had resigned voluntarily, the government lacked full control of the military. Navy officers sought a last-ditch battle with the British fleet while the government was trying to negotiate an armistice. The resulting sailors' mutiny set off a chain of demonstrations and uprisings that culminated in Berlin on 9 November.[4] The vaunted "revolution from above,"[5] the political reforms of October 1918, did not take hold either with the forces of the old order or with the masses.

Up until 7 November Ebert was willing to try to preserve the monarchy if Wilhelm II abdicated.[6] But the contagious uprisings and the formation of workers' and soldiers' councils in many areas forced the SPD's hand. On 7 November Kurt Eisner (USPD) carried out a revolution in Munich and proclaimed a Bavarian republic. On the same day the SPD leaders presented Prince Max with a list of immediate demands: lifting of the ban on public assembly in Berlin; restraint on police and military activity; transfer of control of the Prussian government to the coalition parties; strengthening of the SPD's influence in the Reich government; and abdication of the throne by the Kaiser and the Crown Prince.[7] When the time limit of the SPD's ultimatum ran out on the morning of 9 November with the Kaiser still resisting abdication, the SPD left the government. One SPD deputy in the Reichstag told a National Liberal colleague: "Yes, it was absolutely unavoidable—we cannot control the masses any longer. They have ceased to work and have walked out of the factories. They have now had enough of that swindle. That fellow [the Kaiser] just will not go."[8] In effect, the SPD withdrew from the government in order to maintain its own political base.

Yet the Social Democrats did not quite commit themselves to the revolutionary forces, only to the reconstitution of the government. Ebert still sought to play a kind of mediating role between the officials of the Second Reich and the crowds in the streets. Around noon Ebert, Scheidemann, and Otto Braun met with Prince Max, Vice-Chancellor Payer, and various state secretaries to request that control of the government be turned over to the SPD. Ebert explained that the USPD and the troops in Berlin both supported this move, although the USPD had not yet decided whether or not to participate in the government. Ebert continued: "We also have nothing against the inclusion of representatives of a nonsocialist tendency (*bürgerliche Richtung*); only we must hold the decisive majority in the government." He claimed that this solution alone could restore order and prevent bloodshed.[9]

Ebert's attempt to arrange a legal transfer of power and to hold open the possibility of nonsocialist participation in the new government reflected his respect and consideration for the reform-minded political groups of the Second Reich. The efforts at cooperation during the late stages of the war and the common desire to protect German national interests created a bond between Prince Max and Ebert.[10] As the chancellor turned over control of the government to the SPD leader, he is alleged to have said: "I commend the German Reich to your care." Ebert responded, "I have lost two sons for this Reich."[11] Nonetheless, the legality of the Social Democratic takeover was dubious since the Kaiser failed to authorize it.[12]

Meanwhile, Ebert also sought to work out an arrangement with the USPD. When the two socialist parties began negotiations, however, the future form of the German state was a sticking point. Eduard David was unwilling to concede to the USPD's demand for a republic, promising only the Kaiser's abdication and a regency on behalf of his grandson. Ebert said that the SPD had made no official decision.[13] That afternoon, however, Philipp Scheidemann proclaimed the founding of the republic to an enthusiastic Berlin crowd in order to forestall similar action by Spartacist leader Karl Liebknecht and to canalize the revolution into what he called an "anti-Bolshevist form." According to Scheidemann, Ebert became livid when he heard what Scheidemann had done.[14] Not only had Scheidemann committed the SPD to a decision that Ebert preferred to leave to a Constituent Assembly; the abrupt action also eliminated the possibility of bringing nonsocialist representatives into the new government. The legality of the Social Democratic takeover of the government was exposed as a fiction, and the SPD would have to form a coalition with the USPD alone.[15]

The negotiations between the SPD and USPD continued to go badly throughout the day. The wartime hostility among rival socialist leaders marked the discussions. Georg Ledebour, one of the two USPD cochairmen, flatly opposed the idea of a socialist coalition government. Other party representatives were unwilling to go ahead without the approval of Cochairman Hugo Haase, who was to arrive in Berlin only that evening. Meanwhile, under the influence of Karl Liebknecht, the USPD fraction drew up a list of preconditions for its participation in a government: declaration of a social republic; concentration of all executive, legislative, and judicial authority in the hands of elected representatives of the soldiers and working population; exclusion of all nonsocialists from the government; demotion of all heads of administrative departments to technical advisors of the cabinet; creation of two cochairman posts at the head of a revolutionary cabinet; and the stipulation that the coalition would last only until the armistice. In response, the SPD rejected what it called the suggestion of a class dictatorship, stressing the need to summon a Constituent Assembly to create the new Germany.[16]

During the evening of 9–10 November the negotiating positions of both parties shifted. USPD member Emil Barth, one of the leaders of the radical shop stewards in Berlin known as the *Obleute*, convinced a large assembly of soldiers to summon a meeting of official representatives of the soldiers and factory workers the next day. Barth's success forced the SPD leaders to give renewed attention to the coalition negotiations, and after Haase arrived, the USPD too was willing to moderate its demands.[17] According to the compromise settlement, political power would remain with the workers' and soldiers' councils, and the question of the Constituent Assembly was to be discussed only after the "consolidation of revolutionary conditions."[18]

When several thousand workers' and soldiers' delegates assembled at the Busch Circus on the afternoon of 10 November, Friedrich Ebert announced the formation of a socialist coalition government. The audience applauded wildly, indicating that the fait accompli was popular.[19] The notion of socialist unity, or at least harmony was widespread among the masses; the divisiveness of the wartime socialist schism had not affected the working class to the same degree as the party elites.[20] The two parties each selected three men to form a revolutionary cabinet. Ebert and Haase became the cochairmen, although the former soon gained the upper hand. Indicatively, Ebert moved into the Reich Chancellery, while Haase continued to live in his private residence.[21] Philipp

Scheidemann and Otto Landsberg were the SPD's other representatives, with Wilhelm Dittmann and Emil Barth completing the USPD contingent. Landsberg, a lawyer, suggested the term "People's Deputies" (*Volksbeauftragten*) as a good German alternative to the Bolshehevist "Commissars," so the new cabinet was formally titled the Council of People's Deputies.[22]

The Busch Circus meeting on 10 November also established an Executive Council (*Vollzugsrat*), consisting of seven SPD workers, seven from the USPD and the revolutionary shop stewards of Berlin (the *Obleute*), and fourteen soldiers. Inasmuch as the soldiers tended to be politically moderate, the USPD-*Obleute* group was in the minority. The Busch Circus delegated its supreme revolutionary authority to the Executive Council, which soon led to some confusion. When the Executive Council tried to exercise its authority, it found its path blocked by the Council of Deputies and the existing government bureaucracy.

The Council of Deputies was unquestionably the more active body. On 12 November it declared into law what it termed a purely socialist program. The list of decrees included: suspension of the state of emergency; establishment of the right of assembly and association; abolition of censorship; guarantee of freedom of speech, freedom of the press, and freedom of religion; amnesty for past political offenses; and a number of measures returning workers to their more favorable prewar legal status in contracting employment. The most important economic innovations came about through official ratification of the Stinnes-Legien Agreement,[23] which meant, among other things, the establishment of an eight-hour day in most industries. The most important political reforms were the introduction of equal, direct, and universal suffrage for all citizens over age twenty, and the use of proportional representation in all elections.[24] There was actually nothing here that resembled socialism. The program was an extension of the reforms promised (but not delivered) by the government of Prince Max in October.

Ebert stressed the need for the new regime to work through the existing bureaucracy. On 10 November he asked all high government officials to continue in office, and the Executive Council seconded his request on the following day.[25] The state secretary posts, just beneath the Council of Deputies, were of great significance, especially because the six Deputies did not have time to set policy or to supervise all programs in each ministry. The SPD Deputies wanted to retain the incumbent state secretaries and to appoint other nonsocialists to the vacant positions in order to broaden public support for the government and to spread responsibility for government decisions.[26] USPD Deputy Emil Barth, the most radical of the six, argued that at least the top officials of the Army High Command and the War Ministry should be dismissed. But his USPD colleagues, Haase and Dittmann, wanted the military experts to handle the demobilization, so Barth was outvoted five to one.[27] Only four of the civilian state secretaries resigned voluntarily, and two of these four were replaced by other high-level bureaucrats. Outsiders took over only the Ministry of the Interior and the Food Ministry.[28] The high civil servants of the new regime were predominantly conservative and monarchist.[29]

When government bureaucrats complained that the Executive Council had interfered with matters under their jurisdiction, the Council of Deputies and the Executive Council decided to delineate the functions of each body. On 21 November a joint committee reported that the Council of Deputies would exercise all executive power "except in an urgent, exceptional case."[30] The Executive Council received only the specific right to suppress counterrevolution. Yet City Commandant Otto Wels (SPD) was in charge of security in Berlin, not the Executive Council. In effect, the Council of Deputies removed the Executive Council from the line of authority, facilitating government cooperation with high-level bureaucrats.

One of the earliest and most striking examples of the SPD's willingness to work with the elites of the Second Reich was the Ebert-Groener "pact." In their now famous telephone conversation on the evening of 10 November, Ebert and General Wilhelm Groener discovered a basis for a satisfactory working relationship. The government needed the officer corps to help fulfill the conditions of the armistice and to manage the return of German troops from the western battlefronts and occupied territories in the east. The Army High Command wanted the government to confirm the authority of army officers and to preserve the officer corps. Groener agreed to maintain his post as First Quartermaster, because he, like Ebert, was concerned about the defenseless condition of Germany vis-à-vis the Entente, the danger of separatist movements in a nation less than fifty years old, and what he called the Bolshevist danger within.[31]

Ebert and Groener shared more than a mutual desire to restore order in the midst of a crisis. Both also wished to retain most of the legal and constitutional framework created in October 1918 and to abolish the rule of the workers' and soldiers' councils.[32] Operating under the constraints of uncertain authority and unreliable allies, Ebert and Groener had little opportunity to work out any broad political alliance; in this sense, the Ebert-Groener "pact" is a misnomer. Ebert and the other five Deputies expected that the army leadership would simply carry out the objectives and instructions of the government. Ebert was willing to shore up the authority of the officers, because he felt that this would speed up the demobilization.[33] The contacts among Groener, the Army High Command, and "Chancellor" Ebert[34] created a foundation for more substantial cooperation subsequently, but also intensified the conflict between the SPD and the USPD.

While the right wing of the USPD expected and approved of temporary cooperation among the Deputies, the officer corps, and civil-service personnel, it did not foresee any lasting common aims. The castelike aristocratic officer corps vividly symbolized the militarism and authoritarianism that had pervaded the Second Reich. Given the mutual antipathy between the officer corps and the USPD, Ebert, Scheidemann, and Landsberg were eventually to be forced to choose one or the other. During the tenure of the socialist coalition, high-level civil servants and military officials helped to stymie the USPD on three basic issues: nationalization of industry, determination of the date of elections to the Constituent Assembly, and military reform. But the bureaucrats would not have been successful if they had not been fully backed by the three SPD Deputies. The three USPD Deputies were often at odds with each other, and the left wing of their party was critical of their collaboration with the SPD from the start, which further weakened the USPD's influence within the coalition.

Nationalization

Socialist theorists had traditionally regarded nationalization of industry as the only solution for class exploitation generally, and specifically, for the liberation of the proletariat.[35] It was the essential step toward the goal of a more just, more humane society. Many organized workers, accustomed to hearing this theme, therefore had high expectations when a socialist government took power.[36]

These expectations created a major problem for socialist union leaders, who had just concluded the Stinnes-Legien Agreement with the employers. The head of the construction workers' union, Fritz Paeplow, worried that the accord would not go over well during the revolutionary period when many believed that "nationalization of the enterprises was only a question of days." According to Paeplow, only when the masses regained their senses would they realize the value of the social partnership with the employers. Carl Legien and Robert Schmidt restated the conviction that the achievement of a socialist economy could occur only through a long slow process; attempts to force the pace could only end in chaos. Labor leader Gustav Bauer, later to become chancellor, claimed that if workers in specific factories threw out management officials, "then the good people would stand like oxen [helpless] in front of a mountain."[37] A number of months later Theodor Leipart, another high official in the Free Unions, stated the same position more tactfully:

Will it be possible for us . . . to find such experienced workers' representatives in all firms, that we can with good conscience leave the leadership of the firms to them? Today there can be no talk of that, and I dispute that we will be able to do that in five or ten years. . . . We need the forces that have been active in this area for decades, for centuries, which must place their experience, their knowledge, and their ability at our disposal. We would really be complete fools if we released the large number of capable, experienced, educated managers and wanted to take their place ourselves. No, they should be used (*eingespannt*), they should work in our service and in the service of the entire public.[38]

These pessimistic statements and warnings against hasty action typified the views of experienced party and union officials accustomed to slow progress and to policies that avoided risk.

The revolutionary cabinet did not share the vehemence of these union leaders, but it was nonetheless reluctant to move ahead with nationalization. On 12 November Emil Barth had proposed that the government nationalize mining and other industries, but he was outvoted by a five-to-one margin.[39] Instead, the Council of Deputies established a Socialization Commission on 21 November to investigate the possibilities of nationalization.[40] At Ebert's insistence, a number of nonsocialists were appointed to the commission, which did not convene until 5 December. It lacked adequate financing and staff, and government officials in other departments soon protested against the commission's "encroachments" into their domains. Several of the nonsocialist state secretaries campaigned publicly against nationalization.[41] The Council, meanwhile, gave the Socialization Commission little support.

The issue of nationalization came up at a national congress of workers' and soldiers' council delegates held in Berlin in mid-December. USPD Deputy Wilhelm Dittmann observed that the war-torn economy was less suitable for nationalization than the economy of 1914 had been. He warned that any attempt to nationalize would undoubtedly disturb the already low level of production, and he hinted that economic reconstruction had to precede nationalization.[42] Max Cohen-Reuss (SPD) called economic development an evolutionary process that had been reversed during the war, agreeing with Dittmann that a period of recovery was needed. As proof of the danger of hasty action, he cited the chaotic conditions in Russia, where the Bolsheviks had struck down the old forms of production before the new ones could function.[43] Karl Kautsky stressed that nationalization without support from the majority of the voters might mean civil war, which would further damage the economic well-being of the German people. If socialism was meant to bring general economic prosperity, it could not be reached in this way.[44] A corollary of this argument was that society still consisted of diverse interests whose support was needed for satisfactory economic development. Cohen-Reuss and Kautsky both stressed the importance of the intelligentsia.[45]

The main speaker on nationalization at the congress, USPD economist Rudolf Hilferding, took a centrist position, stressing the importance of nationalization to end class exploitation yet admitting that many branches of the economy were not ripe for state ownership. Ripeness for Hilferding was determined by a high degree of concentration within the industry (oligopoly or monopoly), standardized techniques of production, and secure markets. He argued that the mining of coal, iron, and potash, the refining of iron, and large-scale farming were ripe for nationalization. Despite his advocacy of selective nationalization, Hilferding recommended a compromise resolution to the congress, requesting that the government push ahead with the nationalization of all ripe industries, especially mining.[46] This proposal, which passed without difficulty toward the end of the congress, left the government a free hand. Even when the majority of the Socialization Commission later recommended the nationalization of mining industries,[47] an SPD-led coalition took no action.

Social Democratic party and Free Union leaders tried to justify their caution by pointing out, first, that they lacked the sanction of parliament; later, that they lacked a parliamentary majority. This was indeed true, but in 1918–1919 they had no desire to press ahead with nationalization. The major figures in the Social Democratic movement simply assumed that the opportunity for socialist economics would present itself sometime in the future under more favorable circumstances.

The Date of Elections to the Constituent Assembly

The SPD's campaign for early election of a Constituent Assembly began almost immediately after the ambiguous coalition agreement between the SPD and the USPD was reached on 9–10 November. On 14 November Friedrich Stampfer, editor in chief of the SPD newspaper *Vorwärts*, wrote that a Constituent Assembly would demonstrate that the German republic had an entirely different legal basis from the Bolshevik regime's in Russia.[48] State Secretary for Foreign Affairs Wilhelm Solf also recommended the earliest possible date for elections on the ground of foreign policy.[49] At the meeting of the Council of Deputies on 26 November, State Secretary of the Interior Hugo Preuss announced to a surprised and angry USPD contingent that the elections would take place on 2 February.[50] Three days later the USPD Deputies demanded that the upcoming congress of workers' and soldiers' council delegates have a voice in this decision. Ebert pledged to seek the congress's approval but insisted that election preparations continue. Five of the six Deputies agreed on a compromise date of 16 February, Barth alone abstaining.[51] Meanwhile, Richard Müller, a leading USPD member of the Berlin Executive Council, had announced that the way to the Constituent Assembly lay only over his corpse.[52] The SPD press would later refer disparagingly to Müller as "corpse-Müller."

Social Democratic warnings of the danger of bolshevism in the two months following the revolution were largely a tactical maneuver to win further support for the rapid establishment of parliamentary democracy. The small groups of Spartacists, incorrectly regarded as German Bolsheviks, were without significant influence. But the SPD leaders played upon the fears of the German public, hoping to present their party as the guardian of legitimacy and stability against senseless radicalism. On this slogan the party hoped to attract substantial middle-class support. On the other hand, government officials hoped to exploit the Entente's fears of Bolshevist expansion; German diplomats tried to gain better treatment for Germany by warning of the danger of bolshevism in the heart of Europe.[53] Both of these arguments had their tactical weaknesses. The German government desperately wanted to avoid the entry of foreign troops into Germany,[54] even though this certainly would have prevented the spread of bolshevism. Furthermore, the greater the anxiety about bolshevism in Germany, the more the middle classes might wonder whether a Marxist party could provide sufficient security against the danger.

The debate about the elections was brought before the workers' and soldiers' congress in mid-December, as Ebert had promised. In his opening speech Ebert argued that only the will of the entire German people could provide political legitimacy, and Max Cohen-Reuss then proposed 19 January as the most suitable date for elections.[55] Richard Müller and Ernst Däumig, both left-wing Independent Socialists, wanted the congress to vest political authority in councils composed of manual and "intellectual" laborers; they regarded parliamentarism as outmoded.[56] Finally, Hugo Haase argued that the congress need not choose between a Constituent Assembly and a council system—the two could be combined. Haase also favored delaying the elections until 16 March, stressing the technical difficulties of arranging an election immediately after war and revolution, with soldiers in the process of returning home and voters lacking reliable information. Haase failed to challenge directly the SPD's view that the Constituent Assembly should decide all basic issues, including the existence of the workers' and soldiers' councils themselves. Philipp Scheidemann had indicated to the congress that the councils were a temporary necessity; they could not be made permanent unless they had the support of the majority of the voters.[57]

The SPD leaders won their case regarding the Constituent Assembly with a congress composed primarily of SPD members.[58] Few workers' and soldiers' representatives saw themselves as a legitimate replacement for a democratically elected parliament. But the congress did not necessarily endorse the SPD leaders' plans to refer all basic decisions to the Constituent Assembly. Many workers and soldiers were unwilling to wait patiently for the eventual abolition of the unpopular features of the ancien régime. The congress's handling of military reform revealed a perspective fundamentally different from that of the SPD members of the Council of Deputies.

Military Reform

Ebert's early contacts with General Groener had given both men the impression that cooperation between the SPD and the military was feasible. Although socialist tradition committed the SPD to seek a popular militia, Ebert was nonetheless aware that a powerful army could enhance Germany's international leverage. Moreover, he had no great love for the soldiers' councils, which complained primarily about the authoritarian behavior of military officers.[59] On 3 December Ebert introduced a proposal for compromise: a volunteer military force of 11,000 men initially, organized on a democratic basis, that could supplement the regular army. However, the Army High Command and the officials in the War Ministry had serious reservations and did little to implement the plan.[60] Relying on the Army High Command for its expertise in demobilization, Ebert was unwilling to risk a break, although military officials began to assert themselves more and more openly on political issues.[61] Already on 1 December General Groener urged Ebert to use the army to create "absolute authority" and "real power" in Berlin.[62]

On 8 December Field Marshal Hindenburg sent Ebert a personal letter demanding that the government check the soldiers' councils, restore full authority to the army officers, and summon a Constituent Assembly as quickly as possible. Hindenburg wrote, "In your hands is the destiny of the German people."[63] Ebert's problem was the Army High Command's methods—it wanted to suppress the radical elements in Berlin with a show of force and to impose its demands. Ebert felt that this approach was unwise and unnecessary, at least for the moment.[64] If Ebert sided with the military, he would destroy the coalition government and antagonize many SPD supporters in the process. If he tried to replace the army, the Army High Command might defy the government.[65] Ebert compromised by gaining cabinet and Executive Council approval for the entrance into Berlin of only those troops formerly garrisoned there. Even these soldiers were to receive limited ammunition.

The Army High Command's plan to cleanse the city of radicals and to disarm deserters thus proved politically unfeasible, and General Arnold Lequis lacked enough trustworthy divisions anyway.[66] Without initial government authorization, the Army High Command began to organize volunteer formations of troops known as Free Corps. Placed under the full control of their officers, the Free Corps were not plagued by soldiers' councils or unsympathetic draftees.[67] They would later play a critical role in the suppression of left-wing unrest and strikes.

When the congress of workers' and soldiers' councils met in mid-December, the officer corps and the soldiers' councils were at each other's throats.[68] Soldiers' council representatives from the Berlin garrison interrupted the assembly to present a number of demands for military reform. Walther Lamp'l then presented the case for seven specific changes already adopted in the Hamburg area, including the election of officers. Ebert argued that the "Hamburg Points" should be nonbinding guidelines, but he was outvoted. The congress decided that the reforms should be implemented immediately.[69]

On 19 December Field Marshal Hindenburg sent a telegram to the various army commanders stating that he refused to recognize the Hamburg Points.[70] The leading officials of the Army High Command, War Ministry, Admiralty, and Armistice Commission all indicated to the government that they would resign if the reforms were adopted.[71] The next day General Groener protested against the Hamburg Points in the strongest terms to an expanded cabinet session. Ebert and Scheidemann backed Groener's position, while Barth and Dittmann expressed support for the reforms.[72] The outcome was a decision to apply the reforms only to the troops already home, not to those still on the fronts. The War Ministry would also handle the regulations for implementation. These regulations, eventually issued on 19 January 1919, merely gave soldiers' councils the right to complain about the political content of military orders to the next highest military authority. The law of 6 March 1919 establishing a provisional Reichswehr completed the process of restoring military autarchy.[73] Thus, one of the most powerful institutions of the Second Reich survived with its structure (although not its dimensions) intact. It was to exert a largely negative influence upon the Weimar Republic.

The *Zentralrat*

One major purpose of the December congress of councils was to elect a Central Council, or *Zentralrat*, as the supreme revolutionary authority. The *Zentralrat*'s proposed function, parliamentary supervision, was somewhat ambiguous. USPD delegates Ledebour, Geyer, and Lipinski wanted to specify that the *Zentralrat* have veto power over bills formulated by the Council of Deputies and the Prussian cabinet and have the right of consultation before the Council of Deputies or the Prussian cabinet made any high-level administrative appointments. Ebert countered that the *Zentralrat*, as the supreme organ of government, retained the right to dismiss the Council of Deputies and to appoint a new one, but that was all. The Council of Deputies should possess all executive and legislative power until the Constituent Assembly convened. Surprisingly, USPD Cochairman Haase also supported Ebert's view with slight modification, suggesting that the *Zentralrat* be consulted on legislation. Others on the left wing of the party disagreed strongly. One USPD delegate observed that under Ebert's proposal, the Council of Deputies would be a kind of six-man dictatorship. Either the *Zentralrat* would watch passively, or else it would intervene only to oust the Council of Deputies. In theory, the latter was possible, but it was politically inconceivable. When the congress rejected the USPD delegation's amendment, the USPD refused to participate on the *Zentralrat*, and an all-SPD slate was immediately elected.[74] This outcome further weakened the position of the USPD within the government.

The tendency of the USPD right wing to accept the Constituent Assembly and to limit the role of the council institutions raised the prospect of an alliance with the SPD against the left wing of the USPD. Marxist historian Arthur Rosenberg subsequently described such a party realignment as a sensible resolution of the differences that had existed.[75] But the personal and political antagonism within the Council of Deputies precluded this solution. Haase and Dittmann, both members of the USPD right, distrusted the government's reliance upon nationalistic, antidemocratic administrators, judges, and military officers. Ebert, Scheidemann, and Landsberg, on the other hand, were quite willing to establish themselves as respectable and responsible leaders in the eyes of the nonworking-class strata by cooperating with economic, political, and military elites in the interest of the nation. After a while, the SPD Deputies simply dismissed the warnings from their USPD colleagues about the danger of collaboration with the forces of the ancien régime, and their patience with the USPD grew thin.[76] Then in late December, an unrelated incident brought about a complete break between the two socialist parties.

The Christmas Crisis

On 23 December the People's Naval Division, reacting angrily to the government's refusal to pay their wages as agreed, occupied a government building and abducted City Commandant Otto Wels (SPD) and an associate. The sailors also sealed off the Reich Chancellery itself for a time. The dispute had little to do with politics,[77] but nonsocialists thought the incident showed the lack of order in the city, and Ebert was sensitive to such charges. Seeing a conflict with radical elements in Berlin as inevitable,[78] General Lequis pressed for an immediate attack on the building occupied by the sailors. Both Lequis's chief of staff and General Groener himself threatened to refuse their aid in the future to Ebert if he did not order an attack now.[79] After much of the night passed without Wels's release—the other man had been set free—and after receiving information that Wels's life was in danger, the SPD Deputies approved military action. Early in the morning an assault on the building, accompanied by artillery, killed eleven sailors, while the attackers suffered fifty-six dead. Wels escaped injury and was released unharmed but severely shaken by the whole experience.

The USPD Deputies were furious about not being consulted before the decision to attack, as well as about the loss of lives, which they felt could have been avoided. Dittmann asked insistently who had given General Lequis the authority to use all means available, including artillery, allegedly to rescue the prisoners from the sailors.[80] He did not get an answer. Anton Fischer (SPD), deputy city commandant, subsequently ascribed the attack to the government's bypassing of his authority and to the military's mismanagement of the situation.[81] Finally, Haase made one last stab at defining the proper direction for a socialist revolutionary government: "The cabinet has the duty to reject the old military system before the opening of the Constituent Assembly." When the new *Zentralrat*, composed entirely of SPD members, refused to go along with all the USPD's demands, especially those regarding the military, the three USPD Deputies withdrew from the Council on 29 December.[82]

The collapse of the socialist coalition government not only left the SPD Deputies in command of political power, it also cleared the way for closer SPD cooperation with nonsocialist forces. The USPD leftists saw this SPD strategy as the antithesis of their own purely proletarian course based on the institutions of the workers' and soldiers' councils. The Christmas crisis and the breakup of the coalition increased the likelihood of a violent collision between these antagonistic forces. The right wing of the USPD found little organized support for its efforts to reduce the influence of the elites of the Second Reich before the summoning of a Constituent Assembly. The USPD left refused to pledge its acceptance of parliamentarism, while the SPD Deputies showed little concern about temporary reliance upon civil servants, military officers, and industrial and landowning elites. The intermediate position of the Haase group satisfied neither extreme. Moreover, Haase lacked the weight and firmness to unite his own party behind a clear position.[83]

Despite the withdrawal of the USPD from the government, Spartacist leaders decided to form a new party of their own on 29 December. Joining with radical groups in Hamburg and Bremen, the Spartacists founded the Communist party of Germany (KPD), which combined a number of sophisticated and experienced Marxists with a larger group of utopian revolutionaries. The latter rejected the advice of the majority of the party leaders and refused to participate in the upcoming elections to the Constituent Assembly.[84] Divided from the start, the new party received another blow when the revolutionary shop stewards of Berlin (*Obleute*) refused to join, remaining on the left wing of the USPD.

On 4 January, Prussian Interior Minister Wolfgang Heine (SPD) dismissed Emil Eichhorn (USPD) from his post as chief of police in Berlin. Eichhorn refused to relinquish his office, and on the following day the shop stewards and the KPD leadership arranged a protest demonstration against Eichhorn's dismissal. Much to the surprise of the organizers, tens of thousands joined the protest. Under the impression that a spontaneous revolution had begun, some shop stewards, the central committee of the USPD organization in the district of Berlin, and a few Communist leaders decided to try to overthrow the government by force.[85] But most of the demonstrating workers and soldiers were willing only to speak out against the SPD's policy of collaboration with the men of the old order, not to participate in an armed uprising.[86] By 8 January the poorly organized revolutionaries had clearly failed in their effort to win popular support.

The government appointed SPD Defense Minister Gustav Noske as commander in chief of volunteer troops, which had been moved close to Berlin. Noske told Ebert, "Someone must be the bloodhound; I will not shrink from the responsibility."[87] Various USPD leaders tried desperately to reach a face-saving compromise that would have avoided armed conflict. About 200,000 workers signed petitions at their places of work on 9 January, calling for a peaceful settlement and for the creation of a coalition government in which all the socialist parties were represented. But the SPD leaders were adamant against any concessions, perhaps being influenced by the attitude of high army officials.[88]

Once the battle had begun, Rosa Luxemburg, who had previously opposed the uprising as counterproductive, reluctantly concluded that the KPD could not afford to abandon its supporters.[89] In the indiscriminate violence that accompanied the suppression of the uprising by the Free Corps, Rosa Luxemburg and Karl Liebknecht were captured by Free Corps troops and murdered. By 15 January order was restored.

In one sense, what happened in the streets of Berlin during late December and early January merely confirmed the verdict in the Reich Chancellery; the revolution would not go beyond the formation of a parliamentary republic. In another sense, the "Spartacist uprising" had tremendous significance, if not for the fate of the revolution, at least for the thinking of the SPD leaders. Already committed to a policy of cooperation with liberal political and economic representatives of the bourgeoisie, the SPD leaders now allowed their dislike of left-wing radicals to drive them into uncritical dependence upon military and civilian officials who sought to eradicate "bolshevism" with armed force.[90] Indicatively, the SPD press began to publish recruitment notices for the Free Corps in mid-January.[91] Many left-wing activists never forgave the SPD for its *Noskepolitik*, its sponsorship of military suppression.

Because the radical adherents of the councils were so strident, the SPD leaders easily won their case with most workers and soldiers during the revolutionary period. If the alternatives were parliamentary democracy or proletarian dictatorship, the outcome was not in doubt. German workers were accustomed to regard democracy as an essential component of the socialist program. SPD spokesmen emphasized that as long as the proletariat was not dominant numerically, other social and economic groups had the right to express and defend their interests. Responding to those who saw the workers' and soldiers' councils as the basis for a new democracy, one SPD delegate at the congress of councils in December explained: "If the dictatorial takeover by the proletariat were a true democracy, then the reality must first be that the proletariat is no longer simply a class: there is one collectivity that is the proletariat, and all classes have disappeared. In spite of the revolution, we still have the hard fact that the proletariat is only one economic class. As long as this situation lasts, the takeover of political power by the proletariat [alone] would remain a dictatorship."[92] Not only the Social Democratic position of support for parliamentary democracy but also the strategy of cooperation with nonsocialist elements follow from this implicitly pluralist argument.

This Social Democratic strategy overlooked several factors, however. The revisionists had long since challenged the notion that the proletariat would automatically expand its size and influence. The SPD could not simply wait for the automatic triumph of socialism in the future. Moreover, the SPD leaders underestimated the problems of parliamentary democracy under the prevailing circumstances. Misled perhaps by the particular conditions late in the war which gave the SPD and the Free Unions a pivotal position and which induced many employers to make generous wage settlements with striking workers, most high-ranking SPD officials expected only limited opposition to parliamentary democracy from the right. But there was serious question whether a Constituent Assembly dependent upon the Prussian officer corps and the Reich and Prussian administrative apparatus, representing monarchist as well as republican voters, could erect and maintain a parliamentary republic. Finally, the workers' and soldiers' councils, and even the smaller number of peasants' and agricultural workers' councils[93] were by no means the tools of the radicals. The new institutions reflected a widespread, partially articulated demand for change in the structure of political, economic, and military authority.[94] Working-class discontent with the authoritarian state and with industries characterized by authoritarian management was a powerful force in 1918–1919. If the new parliamentary republic failed to take account of the demand for substantial changes, then it might alienate a significant portion of working-class voters. The SPD leaders could not simply campaign against bolshevism and class privilege. They needed a positive and concrete program that would demonstrate the advantages of parliamentary democracy to the working class.

3. A Shaky Beginning

TH E crushing of the January uprising in Berlin and the elections to the Constituent Assembly did not extinguish the workers' and soldiers' councils. Widespread working-class support for the new institutions still existed, particularly in regions where heavy industry and mining predominated. Some workers supported the idea of giving workers' councils administrative functions in government. Others turned to the councils as an economic institution. Councils within each enterprise (*Betriebsräte*, usually translated as "factory councils") could give workers greater economic authority. But the SPD-led government had serious reservations about these councils and their adherents. The material hardships of the immediate postwar period aggravated conflicts between the government and working-class activists. The fact that the government lacked a reliable armed force and called upon the volunteer Free Corps to control disorder made the situation all the more explosive. Finally, the bitter debate over the Versailles Treaty weakened the government after it had survived its earlier troubles. Although the Constituent Assembly at Weimar succeeded in drafting and passing a democratic constitution, the first fourteen months of the Weimar Republic, concluded by a dramatic military coup, gave little comfort to those Social Democrats supporting the ideal of cooperation between socialists and nonsocialists.

The government's tentative moves on the basic issues of economic policy in 1919–1920 (which will be discussed in detail in chapter four) met strenuous resistance from the nonsocialist parties and from business interests. The SPD leaders recognized the difficulty of reaching agreement with nonsocialists on such issues as nationalization of specific branches of industry and worker participation in factory management, but they felt that the effort had to be made. The SPD elite's highest priority was to maintain the socialist-nonsocialist coalition. Ebert had initiated this strategy before the revolution, and he continued to promote it from his new vantage point as president of the Reich. On the other hand, the SPD could not simply ignore working-class demands for basic social and economic changes. Workers dissatisfied with the SPD could desert to the two Marxist parties farther to the left, both of which decried the limitations of the Weimar Republic.

The SPD elite reacted with alarm and some anger to the various signs that the new republic was on shaky ground. Yet party strategists had no real solution other than to attack the enemies of the republic on the left and right. The first Weimar Coalition governments not only failed to work effectively; the experiment also produced serious strains within the SPD organization, as some party spokesmen began to suggest a policy more closely aligned to the Independent Social Democrats. The result was confusion and uncertainty at all levels of the party.

The Weimar Coalition and
Its Conflict with the Left

The elections to the Constituent Assembly on 19 January 1919 gave the SPD the largest share of the vote—37.9 percent. Under the new proportional representation the party received an almost identical (and record) percentage of the seats in the Assembly, but the results were considerably short of a majority. Meanwhile, the poorly organized and divided USPD obtained only 7.6 percent of the vote, while the KPD refused to participate at all. The German Democratic party (DDP) was the SPD's choice for a coalition partner, but the Democrats, unwilling to be crushed in the SPD's embrace, insisted upon the inclusion of the Catholic Center party. The SPD asked the Democrats and Centrists for unconditional recognition of the republic, adoption of progressive financial policies, support for far-reaching social reforms, and socialization of "presently suitable industries." However, the SPD leaders had already made it clear that they were opposed to hasty nationalization.[1]

The SPD fraction in the Constituent Assembly, now 165 members strong, was divided about whether to invite the USPD to join the government. Some deputies wanted to proceed cautiously and to avoid any commitment; others proposed a full merger of the two socialist parties. Finally, the SPD fraction voted to ask the Independents to join the government if they would recognize the principles of parliamentary democracy and renounce the use of the Putsch.[2] The USPD fraction replied that it could not consider such a move until the existing rule by force had ended and until the SPD leaders made it clear that the achievements of the revolution would be protected.[3] So the SPD opted for a tripartite coalition (Weimar Coalition) headed by Philipp Scheidemann, which was officially established on 10 February.[4] On the following day, according to a prior agreement among the coalition parties, Friedrich Ebert was elected as provisional president of the Reich by the Constitutent Assembly.

Ebert's choice of the presidency surprised many even within his own party who wanted to make this office as weak as possible. The SPD's experience with the Kaiser during the Second Reich made most SPD deputies suspicious of a strong executive.[5] Ebert apparently foresaw that the republic would need a source of political stability and authority, as many of the nonsocialist constitutional experts maintained.[6] But by casting himself as the representative of the whole nation and stressing German foreign policy needs, Ebert created a barrier between himself and his own party.[7] He not only removed himself from internal party affairs, but also adopted a different political perspective than his successors.

Minister President Scheidemann lacked Ebert's skill at negotiating arrangements with the nonsocialist parties, which added to his government's difficulties during the first half of 1919. Yet there were few domestic policy disagreements between the two leading Social Democrats in the government. When Scheidemann presented his program to the Constituent Assembly, he omitted any mention of the remaining revolutionary institutions, stressing that the unity of the Reich would be protected by a strong central government and by the establishment of a sovereign Constituent Assembly.[8] In an interview with an American journalist on 4 February, he was more explicit about the workers' and soldiers' councils: "The council system is the schematic reflection of an institution that perhaps may be suited for Russia, which possesses no organized working class. . . . For decades we have had in the Social Democratic organization and in the unions the proper (*berufene*) representation of the workers. . . . In a revolutionary period of transition the workers' and soldiers' councils may well have done many useful things. After this period of transition, which must be regarded as ended with the convening of the Constituent Assembly, the workers' and soldiers' councils would be . . . costly obstacles to every orderly administration."[9] Scheidemann's policy toward the councils was simply a more forthright statement of the position already taken by the revolutionary Council of Deputies.

In some areas—Bremen and nearby port cities, Braunschweig, and Düsseldorf—KPD and USPD adherents of the councils clashed with troops sent in by the national government to restore order.[10] Yet most workers' councils accepted their own demise without serious resistance. In contrast, factory councils and pit councils in the mining industries enjoyed widespread and vigorous support, especially in the Ruhr district. In part, this was the result of dissatisfaction with the meager economic benefits that the unions had obtained from employers since the revolution.[11] The newly organized councils were not only able to articulate specific local grievances better, but they were more willing to use the strike to back up their demands. The mining unions were constrained by the Stinnes-Legien Agreement and by subsequent negotiations with employers' federations as well as by the government's attempts to discourage strikes. The factory council also offered the worker the chance to gain a new position of authority within the firm and to escape complete dependency upon the "master in his house," the all-powerful employer and his representatives.[12]

After the *Zentralrat* voted its approval of the socialization of "ripe" industries in mid-December, the factory-council movement in the Ruhr gained in strength and in scope. By 11 January 1919 the total number of workers on strike in the Ruhr had risen to 80,000.[13] Many local SPD organizations joined the USPD and KPD in support of miners' demands for the immediate socialization of the coal industry and the establishment of councils within each firm.[14] Workers' and soldiers' council delegates from throughout the district met in Essen on 13 January with representatives of all the mining unions and voted to begin the socialization of all mining industries. A man named Ernst Ruben, a jurist and an SPD member, was elected as "people's commissar," and nine additional commissioners were also chosen—three from each socialist party. Convinced that change was indeed taking place, most of the striking miners returned to work.[15]

Theoretically, the new government too was committed to the socialization of mining industries. The government sent its own socialization experts to observe and discuss the situation in the Ruhr, but it had no intention of abandoning the parity principle established by the Stinnes-Legien Agreement. As early as 28 January Defense Minister Noske was asked whether he was prepared to take military action in the Ruhr. Noske replied that he did not yet have sufficient manpower. Ebert was already convinced that the decisions made by the Essen assembly had been taken under the threat of violence on the part of the radicals.[16]

Meanwhile, the Ruhr socialization commission developed its plan for a hierarchy of mining councils: the lower levels to supervise management of the individual firm and the implementation of union contracts, the highest level to direct the socialization of mining industries in conjunction with the government.[17] The commissioners believed that there was a clear connection between the council system and socialization.[18] Whether the average worker perceived the same relationship is open to some question. One observer in Essen reported in mid-February: "The workers, namely the mining workers, have obtained their material goals. The question of socialization may still cause a certain unrest among the proletariat, the workers meaning syndicalization rather than nationalization. This is an idea that the numerically very weak Communist circles know how to spread, while the Majority Socialists reject it—but more quietly."[19]

Government support of a strong system of factory councils might have received a favorable response from most miners, even if the ownership of the firms was left in private hands.[20] However, this was exactly the kind of action that the SPD leaders were unwilling to take without first ascertaining the positions of business and labor organizations, then proceeding carefully through the parliamentary process. Moreover, the initial indications were unfavorable, as even the socialist union heads felt that the factory councils would antagonize employers, endanger the gains already achieved, and interfere with industrywide collective bargaining by the unions.[21]

During negotiations with representatives of the Ruhr movement in mid-February, Labor Minister Gustav Bauer (SPD) and Economics Minister Rudolf Wissell (SPD), both of whom had made their mark previously as Free Union functionaries, refused to allow the councils the right of control over mines and factories. When the council representatives threatened to call a general strike, Wissell responded that the Constituent Assembly alone could grant demands such as the miners wanted.[22] Wissell suggested instead that the factory council should receive information from management only on labor relations matters, and that it should participate only in decisions on dismissals of workers and employees.[23]

When the issue of the factory council became entangled with that of the soldiers' council, any chance for a peaceful settlement quickly vanished.[24] Numerous soldiers' councils in the area had been feuding with Defense Minister Noske for some time, refusing to recognize the government's ordinance of 19 January, which had effectively restored the authority of army officers. On 11 February Noske authorized General Oskar von Watter, commander of the Seventh Army Corps, to arrest the members of the soldiers' council in Münster. Workers'- and soldiers'-council delegates in Essen responded on 14 February with a threat to call a general strike in three days unless the government rescinded Noske's action and disarmed the Free Corps in the area. Instead, Noske sent more troops into the Ruhr on the next day. A local USPD-KPD meeting in Mülheim on 16 February declared an immediate general strike throughout the Ruhr, preempting the decision of a larger assembly scheduled to meet in Essen on 18 February. According to one SPD participant at the Essen conference, some 500 delegates out of a total of 650 favored a "reasonable" socialization.[25] The SPD delegates immediately presented a motion condemning the Mülheim strike decision and the occupation of the mines by armed bands. When this move failed, the SPD representatives walked out, publicly denouncing the strike, which was called off three days later.[26]

In the central-German industrial area, where there was another sizable movement to bring about socialization through a system of factory councils, the entrance of the Free Corps set off a general strike on 22 February. A regional assembly of miners formulated demands for the creation of miners' councils and factory councils with the right of participation in management decisions, and the socialization of those industries ready for public control. All three socialist parties in the area took part in this assembly, with the USPD being the best represented. The strike proved to be quite effective. When the railroads stopped service, the government in Weimar was briefly cut off.[27] Again, the presence of the Free Corps eliminated the possibility of compromise. The government relied upon its volunteer troops to defend the parliamentary system against a perceived Communist assault.[28]

Under the impact of the central-German strike movement as well as political unrest in both Bavaria and Braunschweig, the cabinet began to give ground. An official statement denounced the "tyranny" exerted by radical elements and warned against the consequences of economic disorder and acts of violence. Still, the government pledged support for the goal of economic democracy to be built upon the foundation of factory councils.[29] The SPD fraction immediately introduced a bill into the Constituent Assembly that declared the resources of the soil to be the property of the nation, and urged public operation of mining and energy-production industries in part through factory councils.[30] Nonetheless, the Berlin workers' council delegates voted to declare a general strike on 3 March.[31]

On 4 March local SPD officials in Berlin met with the cabinet and got a firm commitment that factory councils would be "anchored" in the constitution and allowed to participate in socialization measures.[32] The same day the government officially proposed broad but vague legislation that made state takeover of mining industries possible;[33] until this point the draft of the constitution had not contained any provision for the expropriation of private property. These concessions brought most SPD members back into the fold in Berlin and in central Germany, but the KPD and the USPD continued to endorse the general strike in Berlin.[34] Incidents of plundering and occasional attacks on police then precipitated a major armed battle.[35]

Defense Minister Noske, who had been given virtually dictatorial power by the Prussian government, declared a military state of siege in and around Berlin. General Walther von Lüttwitz occupied Berlin with his 31,000 volunteer troops, and began to put down the insurgents, who, according to military estimates, numbered some 15,000.[36] When wild rumors about incidents of Spartacist terrorism began to circulate, Noske issued the following order: "The brutality and bestial behavior of the Spartacists fighting against us obliges me to . . . [order that] any person who bears arms against the government troops will be shot on the spot."[37] The granting of life-and-death authority to the ill-disciplined volunteers led to numerous excesses, including the shooting of twenty-nine disarmed prisoners from the People's Naval Division. The strike was called off as early as 8 March, but fighting with the use of bomber planes, artillery, and machine guns continued through 12 March.[38]

Although Communist leaders had carefully instructed their local affiliates to avoid armed action,[39] SPD officials generally regarded the far left responsible for the fighting because of their past experience with "bolshevism" and their concern for the security of the new democratic system.[40] The SPD leaders viewed the military action as necessary to prevent Germany "from becoming another Mexico" plagued by endless Putsches. In late March Otto Wels claimed that the government would have been overthrown without the Free Corps.[41] But the bloodshed in which some twelve hundred people lost their lives seriously tarnished the image of the government.

The radical miners in the Ruhr, who mounted a new strike campaign with substantial effect at the end of March, persisted with their call for factory councils and socialization. In addition, they pressed for material goals that the unions had been unwilling to support—a six-hour day for miners, a 25 percent pay raise to compensate for inflation, two-thirds retroactive pay for strikers, adjustment of pension payments—as well as certain limited political demands: implementation of the army reforms passed by the *Zentralrat*, dissolution of the Free Corps, and resumption of relations with Russia.[42] They resented the excesses of the Free Corps and the state of siege that denied them their civil liberties.[43]

One radical worker explained why the Ruhr movement had challenged the government: "If we revolutionary workers are now of the conviction that an improvement [in our condition] must take place, and we find that the present form of government does not allow us this, and we believe that a council government works better, then we have the right to demand that also. . . . Therefore, we reject being called Spartacists. No one is more concerned about the German fatherland than the proletariat. We form the foundation of the Reich, we are the base."[44] This statement certainly reflects the reservations of factory-council activists about the new parliamentary system. But by treating this viewpoint as outright hostility to democracy, the SPD leaders and the government added to their difficulties. Moreover, the SPD leaders overreacted to the outward appearances of radicalism. When Carl Severing became government commissar for the Ruhr in early April, he told the delegates of one conference of "revolutionary mining workers" that this title alone indicated that they wanted to overthrow the government.[45]

The government was forced to concede a seven-hour day for miners in April 1919.[46] Overworked and underpaid during the war, miners were too impatient to be swayed merely by promises of future improvements. But with the full backing of the government and the party leadership, Severing refused to negotiate on the "political demands" of the Ruhr strikers. He issued an ordinance obliging all male inhabitants between the ages of seventeen and fifty to obey the orders of local officials to maintain the economy, under penalty of a five-hundred mark fine or one year in prison. He sent troops to the mines to "protect" miners willing to work.[47] Under this pressure, and with some additional concessions on economic issues by the government, the strike movement collapsed in late April.

The SPD leaders overcame the working-class threat to their strategy of interclass cooperation by a combination of coercion, compromise, and the promise of future reform through the parliamentary system. But the result of such methods, particularly the use of the Free Corps, was substantial working-class alienation. And it proved to be exceedingly difficult to balance the interests of the various existing economic, social, and political groups in the heated political climate of 1919.

The one big success for the new regime in 1919 was the passage of a constitution that reflected a careful blend of socialist and nonsocialist aspirations. The constitution was designed to be a compromise right from the start. Immediately after the revolution Friedrich Ebert chose Hugo Preuss, a well-known liberal republican, but in no way a socialist, to fill the key state secretary of the interior post and to write the government's draft of the constitution. Furthermore, Ebert helped to provide Preuss with as much independence as possible during the crucial month after the revolution.[48] Social Democratic deputies eventually raised some objections to Preuss's first draft, but the praise far outweighed the criticism.[49] The main opposition to Preuss's approach came initially from the state governments, including some Social Democratic ministers therein. Whereas Preuss wished to strengthen the national and provincial levels of government at the expense of the states, the state ministers (particularly the Prussian ministers) sought to preserve as much of their authority as possible.

Under the Second Reich the huge Prussian state had been the bastion of reaction, but the Social Democrats who sat in the Prussian cabinet in January 1919 saw no justification for dismembering a state that contained some three-fifths of Germany's population. Prussian Minister President Paul Hirsch (SPD) argued that a democratic Prussia could guarantee a democratic Germany.[50] Preuss was soon forced to adopt Max Weber's plan of leaving Prussia intact but limiting its influence in the upper house of the national parliament.[51] This body, named the *Reichsrat*, was to be composed of delegates selected by the state governments, but Prussia received far fewer seats than its proportion of the population would normally indicate. Half of the Prussian delegates were to be selected by provincial assemblies, instead of by the state government, and the provincial delegates were not bound to obey the instructions of the Prussian cabinet.

Social Democratic ministers and deputies had direct influence upon a number of provisions in the constitution. Ebert insisted upon a section listing the fundamental rights of German citizens, and Carl Legien asked for the inclusion of the right of unionization. Against Preuss's objection, the SPD also required that the voting age be lowered to twenty.[52] The SPD deputies in the Constituent Assembly wanted a pure parliamentary system; if a presidency existed at all, it should be as weak as possible.[53] Liberals such as Hugo Preuss, Max Weber, and Erich Koch-Weser, felt that the president had to be strong enough to provide a check on parliament.[54] This position coincided with Ebert's, so the SPD fraction could not carry its view. The SPD fraction also wanted a weak upper house of parliament, but it preferred a lower house with strong powers vis-à-vis the states.[55] The party had to settle for stronger state powers (Articles 12 and 14) than it would have liked.

Were the Social Democratic representatives consciously aiming for a pluralistic democracy based on the parliamentary system in 1919? The results are plain enough, but statements of political philosophy by the most influential SPD figures at the time are few and far between. Friedrich Ebert wrote in 1920 that he had tried to overcome social divisiveness through his political activity.[56] Gustav Radbruch, the only real constitutional theorist in the SPD fraction, explained four years later that the general will was not really arrived at through the free decision of equal individuals. The parliamentary balance of power was actually determined by the relative strength of the various social strata. Radbruch further argued that the dominant line of cleavage, that between capital and labor, could only be bridged by a coalition government in which both were represented. Democracy reflected the current state of the class struggle and made it possible to carry on the class struggle with nonrevolutionary means.[57]

The effort by Social Democratic leaders to find an agreeable basis for political and economic compromise with liberal and Catholic political forces, while leaving the way open for the expected evolution of capitalism to socialism, was most clearly expressed where the constitution listed the fundamental rights and duties of the German people. The right of unionization (Article 159) was guaranteed for all vocations, but so was the right to own property (Article 153), free choice of trade (Article 151), and the right of inheritance (Article 154). Specific provisions for well-defined interests were also written in. Article 129 protected the acquired rights of government officials and soldiers, Article 137 protected the existing religious societies, Article 147 allowed for private confessional schools, which were of great importance to the Catholic population. Article 157 guaranteed the right to work, and Article 164 granted state protection to the independent middle class (*Mittelstand*) in agriculture, business, and commerce. The SPD had resisted this last provision because of its political tone—but also because the Social Democrats tended to view the *Mittelstand* as an outmoded stratum.[58]

The measures meant to open the way for the development of a more equitable economic order were Article 151, which required the economy to provide each citizen with a worthy human existence; Article 155, which declared the distribution and use of the land and its mineral resources under state supervision; and Article 156, which allowed the government to nationalize property with proper compensation, and to regulate production in the interest of the community. The Social Democratic fraction wanted to leave the question of compensation open, but it did not insist, and the socialist parties were outvoted.[59] A later addition, Article 165, establishing a system of factory councils, will be discussed in the next chapter.

Perhaps the most serious constitutional weakness from the SPD's point of view, the creation of a presidency with significant powers independent of parliament, was aggravated at the last minute by an amendment passed over the opposition of the socialist parties. Under Articles 48 and 49 defining the president's "emergency powers," the amendment eliminated the requirement that the Reichstag give ex post facto approval to presidential ordinances during an emergency. Instead, the president had only to notify the president of the Reichstag of his decrees, although the Reichstag could still lift any such ordinance by a majority vote.[60] Another potential check on parliament was the provision for popular initiative and referendum, which corresponded to old SPD demands. However, the SPD fraction no longer placed any emphasis on direct public decision-making.[61]

By and large, the SPD deputies and leaders of the party organization were quite satisfied with the final result, which was passed by the Assembly on 31 July, becoming law on 11 August. To be sure, party spokesmen stressed that a "bourgeois phalanx" had triumphed over the socialists on many points, but they claimed that the Weimar Constitution fulfilled the SPD's prewar demands and offered opportunity for the evolution of economic democracy as well. On 31 July Eduard David boasted in the Constituent Assembly that Germany now had the most democratic constitution in the world.[62] Otto Wels made the same claim in a private meeting of high party officials, indicating that this was not a slogan intended merely for public consumption.[63]

Most prominent Social Democrats saw no contradiction between their democratic political philosophy and the principle of the class struggle, properly defined as an ultimate opposition of interests between labor and capital.[64] Political and economic cooperation with other classes and parties could in no way conceal essentially divergent interests, but most SPD leaders believed that time was working in their favor.[65] Consequently, the slogan of the class struggle need not be raised at each juncture.

The SPD leaders relied upon the parliamentary process to solve the immediate problems of a pluralistic society until the development of capitalism produced a more homogeneous social structure better suited to socialism. But Weimar democracy rested on the assumption that the diverse interests all recognized certain fundamental common interests. As Ernst Fraenkel wrote later with an eye toward Weimar's impending collapse: "The danger for parliamentarism does not lie in compromise, but rather in the eventuality that compromise will no longer be possible, since opposing interests are too strong to be held together by a common bond."[66] The Constituent Assembly at Weimar, like the Frankfurt Parliament of 1848, did fine design work. The problems came in implementation.

Counterrevolution

The Entente's ultimatum forcing Germany to sign the Treaty of Versailles set off a wave of popular discontent that soon began to threaten the republic. Precisely because Germany had installed a western-style democracy, everyone from General Ludendorff to President Ebert (and a large number of voters) had expected a generous Wilsonian peace. The harsh terms dictated at Versailles disillusioned the new converts to republicanism, weakening the republican parties in the process. Right-wing denunciations of the government and the republic itself set off angry reactions among prorepublican groups. The highly charged political atmosphere in the latter half of 1919 put a strain on all the parties of the Weimar Coalition, but particularly on the SPD.

The Treaty of Versailles ruptured the tripartite coalition government. After a period of indecision, the Democrats refused to participate in a government willing to sign such a treaty. Some Social Democrats also wanted to reject the peace terms, but the possibility that rejection would set off renewed warfare sobered most of the delegation. The closest vote, not the final vote, in the SPD fraction was 75 to 39 in favor of acceptance.[67] Scheidemann, however, resigned in outrage, stating publicly: "What hand would not wither which placed this chain upon itself and upon us."[68] Thereafter, Scheidemann's stock fell rapidly within the SPD elite. One SPD deputy commented pithily in her memoirs: "A minister president of the Reich with a withered hand was too big a target."[69]

Ebert settled upon his close friend Gustav Bauer as Scheidemann's successor. Party Cochairman Hermann Müller (-Franken), the favorite of the SPD fraction, at first planned to remain outside the government, but he later resigned his party post and became Bauer's foreign minister.[70] The first head of a Weimar cabinet to be given the title chancellor, Bauer was much more patient than the mercurial Scheidemann, with whom he did not get along. However, even sympathetic observers would note that Bauer's appointment indicated Weimar's lack of established political leaders of international rank.[71] On 23 June Bauer announced that the government had no choice but to sign the treaty.

The treaty affected the military directly, reducing in stages the size of the army to one hundred thousand men, and emasculating the navy. Although Generals Groener and Seeckt agreed upon the futility of armed resistance and managed to prevent a last-ditch stand, other high-ranking officers would have preferred to go down fighting rather than accept such peace terms. Motivated by self-interest and by a belief in the indispensability of a strong military force, the bulk of the officer corps quickly turned against the government. Some officers spoke openly of creating a government with dictatorial powers in an effort to stave off foreign pressures to dismember the army.[72] Lieutenant Commander Hermann Ehrhardt, head of a naval brigade, was one of the most outspoken officers.

Social Democratic ministers received warnings about the danger of reactionary military activity throughout the latter half of 1919. Private citizens, local SPD organizations, and the SPD press all criticized Defense Minister Noske's confidence in antirepublican military men. But Noske saw himself as a broker between the officers and the politicians, not as the bearer of supreme civilian authority. He also saw little need for the commotion.[73] Finally, some top SPD officials turned against the government. Scheidemann, who had moved into the vacant post of party cochairman, gave a well-publicized speech in October entitled "The Enemy is on the Right."[74] He also initiated a memorandum sent by the executive committee to the SPD ministers in the Reich, warning of the danger of a reactionary uprising, and demanding changes in government policy, particularly with regard to the Reichswehr.[75] Scheidemann argued that the ideal government would be a purely socialist one—certainly a new position for him. Party Cochairman Otto Wels raised the idea of an ultimatum to the government; if the SPD's demands were not met, it could pull out of the coalition. Even Prussian Agriculture Minister Otto Braun, who foresaw serious economic consequences if the SPD left the government, acknowledged that the party was not making sufficient use of its leverage within the Weimar Coalition.[76]

The SPD critics of the Bauer government suffered a blow when on 13 January 1920 police and military guards fired upon unruly left-wing demonstrators organized by the Independent Socialists and the Communists to protest pending factory council legislation.[77] Forty-two demonstrators were killed and some one hundred were wounded. The government pointed to the incident as still another proof of the violent and antidemocratic inclinations of its rivals on the left. Chancellor Bauer's warning that the SPD's withdrawal from the government would lead to a Bolshevist coup and a subsequent uprising by reactionaries now served to quiet his critics within high party ranks. On 27 January the members of the party council and the Reichstag fraction gave the government a vote of confidence.[78]

For the officer corps, quick action to prevent the imminent reduction of the Reichswehr and the navy was urgent, and General Walther von Lüttwitz took it upon himself to develop a plan of action. Generally regarded as the most powerful man in the army, Lüttwitz intended to give the government one last chance to move in the right direction. If the government tried to carry out the terms of the Versailles Treaty, he was prepared to overthrow it and to appoint Wolfgang Kapp as his new chancellor. Kapp was a middle-level civil servant (*Generallandschaftsdirektor*) in eastern Germany who had a close political relationship with General Ludendorff. Lüttwitz merely wanted to install a new cabinet in which Noske and "reliable" Social Democrats might be included, but Kapp and his associates sought a full-scale dictatorship.[79] Ehrhardt's naval brigade, camped near Berlin, was eager to act before it was forced to dissolve.

Lüttwitz requested and got a face-to-face meeting with President Ebert on 10 March, presenting a list of demands that included: appointment of a new foreign minister, more forceful presentation of the army's needs to the Versailles powers and to the Economics Ministry, dissolution of the Constituent Assembly and the holding of new elections, ouster of the Army High Command chief, General Walther Reinhardt, and creation of a new post of Supreme Military Commander. Ebert replied that he still hoped for some concessions from the Versailles powers regarding the Reichswehr; otherwise he rejected Lüttwitz's demands.[80] Noske then intervened and turned the tense session into a stormy one, denouncing an impending military revolt and informing Lüttwitz that he was placed on indefinite leave.[81]

Secure about the loyalty of the Reichswehr as a whole, Noske believed that his warnings would dissuade Lüttwitz and Ehrhardt. His mistake nearly proved fatal to the government. When Noske learned on the evening of 12 March that Ehrhardt's troops were moving toward Berlin, he hastily summoned his top officers. Noske and General Reinhardt both wanted to meet force with force, but the other generals demurred. Most generals regarded the risk of a leftist uprising as too great for the military to begin a fight with its own troops. Noske's final remark was a sad, rhetorical question: "Am I then entirely abandoned?"[82]

Those ministers in the Reich and Prussian governments who could be reached were called to a 4 a.m. meeting to discuss the options: whether or not to order military resistance to the coup, and whether or not the government should remain in Berlin. No one spoke in favor of surrender. The ministers finally decided that they dared not overrule the leading generals, so armed resistance was eliminated. After a long debate in which Noske and two Democratic ministers favored flight and David, Bauer, and Ebert opposed it, the former group won out. Only Vice-Chancellor Schiffer (DDP) remained in Berlin to represent the Reich government. Ebert, Bauer, Noske, and Müller caught a 6:15 a.m. train to Dresden, where they hoped to reestablish the legitimate government.[83]

With Ehrhardt's troops virtually at their heels, the departing SPD ministers and Ebert made the crucial decision to call for a general strike as a means of resistance to the coup. Understandably, the public generally regarded the strike proclamation as a government decision, although technically, only the SPD ministers present and Ebert were involved.[84] However, the government paid the cost of printing and distributing the proclamation.[85] The SPD ministers who had authorized the general strike soon learned that the Reichswehr's generals were more worried about the strike than about the Putsch. Consequently, the SPD ministers backed off from the strike after 13 March; Noske actually denied it had been officially authorized and condemned it.[86] But other groups had already adopted the strike on their own.

Carl Legien, chairman of the executive committee of the ADGB, refused to leave Berlin on 13 March in spite of his advanced age and ill health. After receiving a report from the SPD executive committee on the events of the previous night, the union leaders called for their members to go on strike.[87] To win as much support as possible, the ADGB leaders invited representatives from the SPD, the USPD, and two smaller socialist union organizations to a joint meeting to plan the strike. At first, the USPD refused to cooperate in any way with the SPD. By the afternoon, the Independents were willing to participate in a general strike, but not for the restoration of the Bauer government— only for a workers' government.[88] Otto Wels agreed to USPD Cochairman Artur Crispien's call to arm the workers and to force Noske's resignation, but Wels reminded Crispien that this was not a battle of socialists against non-socialists, but of republicans against antirepublicans. The help of Noske's troops (if available) could not be spurned. Crispien became angry by about 8 p.m., shouting that the USPD could not sit at the same table with the SPD.[89] The old antagonisms prevented joint socialist action even during the crisis.

That evening the ADGB and AfA federations issued a unified strike proclamation, the SPD stood by its earlier, semiofficial announcement, and the USPD released its own. Only the Communist leadership held back, arguing that there was no difference between Kapp and Noske.[90] The KPD reversed its decision the following day when its Berlin leadership received word that local KPD organizations in the Ruhr and central Germany were joining the increasingly powerful strike movement.[91]

The strike was so effective that the Kapp government was soon isolated and helpless. Water, gas, and electricity in Berlin were shut off on 14 March. The railroads stopped service on the following day.[92] Another crucial factor that paralyzed the new regime was the refusal of most officials in the Chancellery, the Finance Ministry, and the Reichsbank to follow its orders. One of Kapp's associates received the runaround from the bureaucrats in the Finance Ministry, and the new government had no funds.[93] Most of the undersecretaries in the Reich Ministry of the Interior collectively decided not to serve the Kappists.[94]

Meanwhile, the departed members of the old government were not faring so well. In Dresden, General Georg Maercker showed an ambiguous attitude toward them, so the ministers decided to proceed to the more hospitable city of Stuttgart. Their Odyssey stumbled onward, first by car, which ran out of gas, then by train, which was boarded and searched at several stops by armed men whose allegiance was not apparent. One of the men walked up to Ebert and asked for identification. Ebert handed him identification, which he read aloud: "Friedrich Ebert, *Reichspräsident.*" The armed man returned the document without blinking. Ultimately, the train reached Stuttgart safely.[95]

The Putsch revealed the multiple fissures that had developed during the past year within the country. Most prominent industrialists appear to have been surprised and upset by the coup. Although industrial interests shared some of General Lüttwitz's goals, such as new elections and a stronger, more conservative government, his poorly planned conspiracy seemed to destroy the hope of achieving these objectives by legal political means. The National Association of German Industry, unwilling to oppose the coup, put out a cryptic statement that it remained true to the principles of the business-labor agreement, "however the political situation of Germany might be structured." Industry was clearly opposed to the general strike, a weapon explicitly renounced in the Stinnes-Legien Agreement.[96] The business-oriented People's party actively condemned the strike, while adopting a wait-and-see position on the Putsch.[97] The largely monarchist National People's party (DNVP) regretted only the amateurism of the coup.

The ministers in Stuttgart refused to negotiate with the Kapp government. However, Justice Minister Schiffer, who had remained in Berlin, feared that a bloody conflict and a left-wing uprising would erupt before the issue was resolved. He therefore disobeyed instructions and began negotiations with Kapp's representatives. Even a few SPD figures became marginally involved. Prussian Minister President Paul Hirsch, Prussian Finance Minister Albert Südekum, and Berlin Chief of Police Eugen Ernst sat in a room next to the negotiations in the Ministry of Justice from 15 to 17 March. When consulted about amnesty for those involved in the Putsch, Südekum and Hirsch pledged that, although the SPD could not vote for such a bill in parliament, the party would allow it to be passed somehow.[98]

On 17 March the ministers in Stuttgart first learned that the Berlin negotiators had agreed to certain conditions to obtain Kapp's resignation: spring parliamentary elections, direct popular election of the president,[99] a reconstitution of the government, and an amnesty for those implicated in the Putsch. More than one cabinet member was driven to despair about how the unions, Independent Socialists, and Communists would exploit this "deal."[100]

On 17 March ADGB Chairman Carl Legien told USPD members Rudolf Hilferding and Wilhelm Koenen that he wanted to form a workers' government which would repudiate the coalition with the bourgeois parties, defend and increase the political and social rights of workers, purge counterrevolutionaries from the administration and the army, and arm the proletariat.[101] Legien had a strong weapon to employ. The unions refused to end their general strike unless the government met nine demands, including decisive union influence over the formation of new governments in the Reich and in Prussia; a purge of counterrevolutionary elements from positions of influence in public administration and in the economy; immediate action to socialize "ripe" branches of the economy and to convene a new Socialization Commission; and replacement of disloyal military formations by new ones drawn from the republican segment of the population. The most specific demand was for the resignations of Defense Minister Gustav Noske, Prussian Interior Minister Wolfgang Heine, and Prussian Railway Minister Rudolf Oeser.[102]

The union leaders justified their demands by citing the procrastinations and failures of the Constituent Assembly:

> There may be doctrinaire democrats who feel that such an arrangement is incompatible with the constitutional rights of representative government. We can only say one thing to them: a parliamentarism that rigidifies in its outward forms without concerning itself with the living, effective forces of the people, is a danger to the commonweal. The monarchist Putsch has demonstrated how easily democratic governments and popular assemblies can be driven out. What cannot be driven out, overturned, or dissolved, however, is the working population, the only lasting factor, the source of all state-sustaining forces. . . .
>
> The unions . . . [want] a new order that corresponds to the wishes of the people and guarantees a secure future. The unions have sought this responsible task just as little as they have sought to organize the political general strike. But history, which was stronger than the

government and the public's representation, has put them in this position and given them this mission.[103]

When representatives of the DDP and the Center complained of the unions' usurpation of power, Legien warned that if no agreement were reached, there would be civil war in Germany.[104] After Chancellor Bauer and some of the other ministers had arrived from Stuttgart and joined the negotiations, the government agreed to a slightly tempered version of the union demands. The union leaders were also told that Noske and Heine had already tendered their resignations.[105] But the agreement broke down almost as soon as it was concluded.

In a dramatic meeting with the president on 22 March, Wels and Legien both insisted on Defense Minister Noske's ouster. Ebert countered with his own threat to resign. Wels overtrumped Ebert, raising the idea of an extraordinary party congress at which he and the entire executive committee would resign. Ebert was forced to give way.[106] He approved of Noske's orientation against the left, but he knew that an SPD congress would never sustain Noske. Ebert told a Democratic politician the next day, however, that Noske would be back in office in less than three months.[107]

Renewed union pressure forced the parties and cabinet members to resume negotiations on the same day. First Legien asked the two socialist parties to form a government consisting solely of workers. He also demanded the purging of reactionaries from the army and the security police, as well as the withdrawal of troops from Berlin. USPD Cochairman Crispien showed only mild interest in participating in a coalition with the Social Democrats, confidently predicting that "conditions are developing by themselves toward our view." Foreign Minister Hermann Müller argued that a workers' government was untenable on grounds of foreign policy. Bauer finally accepted all but the first union demand, committing himself only to discuss that matter with the nonsocialist parties and the SPD fraction.[108]

The cabinet adamantly opposed the idea of a workers' government, regarding it as unconstitutional, since it would lack a majority. Democrat Erich Koch-Weser, using rhetorical overkill, called it a "council republic" (*Räterepublik*) that the DDP would not support for one day. Eduard David replied that the SPD would never participate in such a venture, and President Ebert also believed that a SPD-USPD coalition was impossible. He suggested that if the cabinet resigned now, he would allow it to remain as a caretaker government, and he could simply reappoint it in two weeks when the commotion had died down. Chancellor Bauer concluded by assuring the others: "No differences of opinion over government policy. I am holding fast to the [Weimar] coalition."[109]

The Democrats were plainly worried that the SPD would abandon the Ebert-Bauer-David line. Wels and Scheidemann, the party cochairmen, had supported at least the most immediate demands of the unions, and both thought cooperation with the USPD would be desirable. But from 19 March on, the organizational leaders showed some willingness to temper the union demands in order to mollify the nonsocialist coalition parties.[110] Wels believed, mistakenly as it turned out, that the USPD now recognized the necessity of a coalition with nonsocialists; by joining the Weimar Coalition, the USPD could strengthen working-class influence within it.[111] The Democrats perceived the situation more accurately; they had to form a united front with the Social Democrats, preventing the latter from working with the Independent Socialists. Delay was their best weapon.[112]

Later that day the SPD fraction approved the idea of a workers' government, provided that the DDP and the Center agreed—an unlikely event. The SPD executive committee also publicly pledged a decisive move to the left. Some SPD officials clearly wanted to add the USPD to the Weimar Coalition; Wels, Scheidemann, Müller, Paul Löbe, and Franz Krüger, the last the head of the party organization in the district of Berlin, fell into this category. But no one in the upper levels of the party hierarchy was willing to sever ties with the nonsocialist parties to form a fragile coalition with the USPD alone. Bauer reassured the anxious nonsocialist ministers that the USPD, even if invited, would never serve in a cabinet with the bourgeois parties, which turned out to be correct.[113]

Legien continued to brandish the threat of a general strike and the possibility of civil war. But the nonsocialists soon realized that the crisis was ebbing, and they refused to consent to the union demands. When Ebert finally authorized Legien to try to form a government himself, he lacked the backing of either socialist party and gave up the attempt. The SPD deputies settled upon their conciliator, Hermann Müller, as the new chancellor, and Ebert and the nonsocialist coalition parties ratified this choice.[114] The well-respected Otto Braun, a consistent advocate of coalition government with the nonsocialists, replaced Paul Hirsch as head of the new Prussian government, and Carl Severing took over the key Prussian Ministry of the Interior.

When the SPD fraction nominated Otto Wels to become Noske's successor,[115] Wels declined, perhaps influenced by Schiffer's warning that there would be a mass exodus from the Reichswehr if Wels took it over.[116] The new Defense Minister was Otto Gessler (DDP), whose tenure lasted throughout much of the Weimar period. When Otto Braun pressed the Defense Ministry to oust reactionary officers from the Reichswehr, Gessler refused to permit such civilian interference.[117] The appointment of Gessler and the Kapp Putsch itself ironically removed the Reichswehr still further from republican influence.

When the Democrats and the Centrists joined the conservative parties in calling for spring elections, Chancellor Müller agreed, thereby limiting his maneuverability.[118] The continuation and radicalization of the general strike in the Rhineland-Westphalia area, the creation of a radical "Red Army," the renewed specter of bolshevism, and the repeated intervention of the Free Corps against the radicals with the same disastrous consequences as in 1919 absorbed the government's attention and eliminated any remaining chance for reforms.[119] ADGB Chairman Legien was too concerned about the violence and the unreliability of the USPD to consider a resumption of his strike. Repeated protests against the government's continued use of the Free Corps did not disguise the unions' retreat from their ultimatum.[120]

Legien and other socialist union leaders tried to revise the political-system and the terms of interclass cooperation in March and April 1920, which indicates that they had second thoughts about the SPD's policies during the revolutionary period. The November Revolution and the Constituent Assembly had secured neither the parliamentary republic nor the expected range of social and economic reforms. Legien's criticism of the government resembled grass-roots complaints of late 1918 and early 1919. The retention of anti-republican personnel in the civil service and the army, the lack of structural economic reform, and the SPD's seeming subservience to its coalition partners all aroused working-class resentment. The government's use of the Free Corps and the state of siege magnified rank-and-file discontent. The socialist unions responded to these sentiments even though union leaders were by and large men with a stake in the political and economic order. Their criticism could not be dismissed as the impatience of inexperienced young workers or the excesses of revolutionary hotheads.

But the nonsocialist parties charged that the union attempt to tip the political balance to the left violated the established political processes. Many prominent Social Democrats not only agreed with bourgeois objections to the union position; they also perceived that the union demands would force the SPD to cooperate with its left-wing rivals. Limited on the one side by its commitment to coalition government with nonsocialists, and on the other side by its concern about the antidemocratic intentions of the Independent Socialists and Communists, the SPD resisted the pressure from its union allies.

By early 1920 the SPD had foresaken the possibility of a bold, independent course. The opportunity to curtail the political and economic influence of established political and economic interests hostile to parliamentary democracy had passed. The Weimar Republic was no tabula rasa, and the SPD was constricted by the positions taken by its nonsocialist coalition partners. The only hope for significant new reforms lay in developing new programs and policies to which nonsocialist parties and nonproletarian interest groups could agree. But socialist ideology itself represented an obstacle to innovation in the area of economic policy, as events from 1919 to 1921 demonstrated.

4. The Failure of Structural Economic Reform

T H E First World War had brought the state a much greater role in the German economy. At the end of the war many businessmen hoped to remove their enterprises from the yoke of state controls,[1] particularly since the Social Democrats, their traditional antagonists, would obviously exert great influence within the new system of government. Labor's attitude toward state intervention in the economy was ambiguous. Many Social Democrats regarded the free market system as outmoded, but few had any precise notions about state economic regulation beyond the traditional socialist solution of nationalization of industry and agriculture. Frantic about the shortage of food in 1918–1919, Social Democratic ministers had no intention of trying to expropriate large landholdings, which might have further depressed agricultural production. And nationalization of industry would have complicated the working relationship between the SPD and its coalition partners.[2]

In this uncertain climate the first Weimar Coalition government showed interest in a number of schemes designed to modernize the relationship among business, labor, and government, rather than displace private enterprises with state agencies. Technocracy and planning were generally popular ideas in postwar Europe and the United States.[3] The German case was unique only in that a socialist politician with strong ties to the socialist unions became one of the leading advocates of a planned economy, regarding it both as a source of greater economic efficiency and as a means of progress toward socialism. But nonsocialist parties disputed the first contention, and many socialists quarreled with the corporatist features of the new proposals. The result was a complete stalemate in the area of economic policy, which allowed organized business interests to increase their economic leverage.

Rudolf Wissell was at the center of the early disputes. A metalworker by trade, Wissell was an experienced ADGB bureaucrat and self-educated writer with more than a streak of independence and stubbornness.[4] Wissell had joined the revolutionary cabinet in December 1918, taking responsibility for social and economic affairs. There he came into contact with Wichard von Moellendorff, undersecretary in the Economics Ministry and a former aide to prominent industrialist Walther Rathenau. During the war both Rathenau, who directed the War Ministry's Raw Materials' Section, and Moellendorff had written of the need for a postwar planned and controlled economy to be

59

built upon the foundation of wartime regulations.[5] But instead of direct bureaucratic controls imposed by the state, Rathenau and Moellendorff wanted
administrative boards in each branch of industry composed of representatives
from business and labor. A corporatist structure at the national and regional
levels would not only satisfy business's desire for self-regulation (*Selbstver-
waltung*), but would also make it possible for the state to pursue the goals of
national economic solidarity and German autonomy. Administrative determination of pricing, production, and the level of foreign trade would replace
the decisions of the free market.

Aware of all the obstacles to nationalization of industry, but impatient for
some sort of government action, Wissell adopted the essence of the Rathenau-
Moellendorff approach to economic policy. For the time being, the government could help to regulate industry properly and fairly; eventually, public
controls could lead to nationalization.[6] After becoming economics minister in
the Scheidemann government, Wissell set a number of specific regulatory
bills before the cabinet and the Constituent Assembly.[7] Taken together, they
embodied the concept that Wissell and Moellendorff called the "common
economy" (*Gemeinwirtschaft*). Under the pressure of strikes and local uprisings, the Reichstag took the first step toward the common economy on 13
March 1919 by establishing a National Coal Council to regulate the coal
industry and set prices.[8]

Wissell was not the only SPD minister concerned with developing an
appropriate response to the economic demands of working-class demonstrators. Minister of Labor Gustav Bauer, soon to become chancellor, was drawing up provisions for the creation of workers' councils within each factory,
bilateral (worker-employer) regional councils in each industry, and a National
Economic Council. The factory councils were to have supervisory functions
over management, while the joint business-labor economic councils were to
help increase production and to protect the public interest.[9] There were certain
similarities between this plan and Wissell's common economy. Both schemes
allowed for representative bodies to participate in administering whatever
industries might be nationalized, and in supervising privately owned busi-
nesses. Bauer also made it clear that the National Economic Council (*Reichswirtschaftsrat*) would include representatives of industry, commerce, handiwork, and agriculture; it was not to be a mere tool for labor to extend its
influence.[10]

By early April Wissell realized that it might be possible to alter this council
structure to suit the needs of his common economy. When Bauer presented a
revised draft of his proposal to the cabinet on 7 April, by providential accident
or as a result of Wissell's influence, the Labor Ministry had adopted much of
what Wissell wanted. Bauer even mentioned that the economic councils for

each industry would fulfill collective economic functions (*gemeinwirtschaftliche Aufgaben*). When a question was raised about the term *gemeinwirtschaftlich*, Wissell quickly explained the extensive regulatory functions that he foresaw. Unfortunately for him, Bauer wanted to use the term only in a general sense—collective economic functions as opposed to functions within an individual enterprise—and the cabinet voted to substitute a less ideological word (*gesamtwirtschaftlich*).[11] Nevertheless, the incident showed how Wissell was trying to harness the council system to power his new economic model.[12]

When it became clear that some sort of factory-council legislation was inevitable, anxious socialist union leaders decided to make the best of a bad situation by participating in the drafting of detailed proposals. Within a short time the government and unions reached a compromise that reassured the latter. The main function of the factory council was defined as supervision of the fulfillment of contracts, which would still be negotiated between unions and management. Although the factory council was given the right to participate in decisions directly connected with labor relations, e.g., dismissals and overtime, it was effectively transformed into a representative organ for the unions at the factory level.[13]

The union federations gained direct influence over the upper levels of the projected hierarchy of councils. Workers' councils and the Chambers of Commerce in each district were each to select representatives to the bilateral economic councils, but local unions were to elect a portion of the workers' delegation. In addition, the unions and employers' associations were to select the membership of the technical boards (*Fachgruppen*) for each branch of industry. Both the regional councils and the national boards would send delegates to the National Economic Council, which would also include some public and consumer representatives.[14] The socialist unions were generally pleased with this overall structure, but employers who were consulted during May and June could not countenance the factory council's role in management of the firm, so the issue remained unsettled.[15] The government was still operating on the basis of an attempt to reach a consensus, not only among the coalition parties but also among the major interest groups.

Wissell thought that this dual structure of regional economic councils and national industrial boards, with the National Economic Council at the top, would be an ideal setup to manage production.[16] However, he had yet to secure cabinet approval for the principle of a planned economy or for any specific economic policies. In May the Economics Ministry finally spelled out its comprehensive program, which was formulated by Moellendorff and cleared previously with Labor Minister Bauer.[17] The ministry proposed to create the hierarchy of councils through special legislation, instead of through the slower procedure of an amendment to the constitution. Other industries besides coal then could be placed under public management more quickly. To strengthen the government's economic leverage, the program called for a capital levy, with payment in the form of stock to be rewarded by a lower rate of taxation. The result of this tax would be to give the state a share in the ownership of many large industrial enterprises without complete expropriation or costly compensation payments. Administration of the state's holdings would be placed in the hands of a nonpolitical National Assets Bank. Moellendorff also suggested state orders and purchases of specific commodities, which might then be exported to improve the balance of payments and raise the level of employment. The program included government subsidies to wages and salaries in order to mitigate the effect of rising food and clothing prices, and a variety of limitations on the right to strike, including a requirement that 90 percent of the workers affected must approve any strike by secret ballot.

Both Wissell and Moellendorff understood that the Democrats, by and large believers in a free-market economy, would not go along with such a program. Accordingly, Moellendorff also composed an assessment of the Weimar Coalition government's failures for the consideration of the SPD ministers.[18] He cited the government's inaction, especially in the realm of economic policy, as the cause of much of the discontent and radicalism infecting the workers. Moellendorff and Wissell called for the creation of a coalition government with the USPD, which they perceived as willing to support the construction of a new economic order.

The Democratic ministers got wind of the Economics Ministry's intentions and preempted Wissell by suggesting that the cabinet set up an economic subcommittee, consisting of the ministers of economics, treasury, and food. The subcommittee would have to clear all projects affecting the economy. The cabinet approved this idea on 6 May, despite the fact that it was obviously intended to block the adoption of Wissell's common economy.[19] The SPD ministers were upset by the blunt criticism of the Weimar Coalition contained in the Wissell-Moellendorff political statement,[20] and they were unwilling to consider bringing the USPD into the government, which would have disrupted the Weimar Coalition.

The Allied powers then communicated the terms of peace to Germany. According to the treaty, Germany had to refrain from adopting any measures that interfered with the trade of the Entente nations for a period of five years. This provision placed another substantial obstacle in the way of economic planning and Wissell's hopes for economic autarky.[21] Wissell's plan next drew a crossfire of hostile reactions from the other ministries. Food Minister Robert Schmidt (SPD) wrote up a critique that described the common economy as incompatible with the SPD's Erfurt Program of 1891 and insufficient to satisfy the adherents of factory councils.[22] Treasury Minister Georg Gothein (DDP) argued that the best way to rebuild the economy was to remove stifling government controls, not to add more of the same.[23] The unions opposed the co-optation of economic interest groups by the state, because it would have endangered their negotiating position and infringed upon their strike prerogative.[24]

Wissell's first reaction was to offer his resignation and that of Moellendorff,[25] but these were apparently not accepted. Details of the Wissell-Moellendorff plan were then leaked to Georg Bernhard,[26] editor in chief of the *Vossische Zeitung* and a well-known supporter of the planned-economy concept. Bernhard's articles about the proposal made public debate inevitable, much to the cabinet's displeasure.[27] Wissell next took his case to the SPD national congress in mid-June, giving a lengthy speech that stressed two themes: the need for structural economic change and the incapacity of the existing coalition to achieve it. Wissell claimed that he would support socialization of specific industries insofar as it was then possible, but that the rest of the economy had to be planned and controlled. Wissell received an enthusiastic response from the congress, because he offered evidence to support the convictions of those SPD members who suspected that the government had no clear economic policy other than to return to the prewar capitalist order.[28]

Other cabinet members present at the congress were extremely defensive about the government's failure to achieve structural economic reform. Eduard David argued that if large numbers of workers were discontented with the government, the government itself had good reason to be upset with the economic selfishness of the people. Robert Schmidt claimed that the cabinet did have a clear policy—socialization of specific industries—while Wissell was accused of wanting only diluted socialization.[29] Hermann Müller claimed that the USPD would not support the common economy anyway, and he urged the party congress not to take action on Wissell's proposal. In a rare show of independence, the congress disregarded this advice and approved the resolution that Wissell had advocated.[30] Nonetheless, the outlook for the common economy remained doubtful. The hostility of the upper circles of the SPD, and DDP, the trade unions, and the employers' associations were formidable obstacles.

On 7 July Wissell called for a clear government economic program, and the other ministers responded with a chorus of criticism of the *Gemeinwirtschaft*. Bauer cited Rudolf Hilferding's concern that it might preserve capitalism, Müller warned that the capital levy would have disastrous effects, and several speakers said that they saw no possible alignment of parties that would accept this kind of planned economy. When Bauer asked if anyone present supported

Wissell's plan, no one answered. Bauer concluded that the government would pursue a policy of socialization.[31]

Wissell then told the SPD fraction that he intended to resign. The fraction requested that he wait for a hearing, and on 10 July Bauer, David, and Wissell all came to the fraction meeting to present their respective views. Perhaps recognizing that there was no immediate prospect of nationalization, most of the deputies who spoke found a kernel of truth in Wissell's complaints and urged a compromise. Fraction cochairman Paul Löbe had learned from Wissell privately that the latter was interested in becoming minister of labor, but Wissell insisted on prior approval of his plan. Under the circumstances the fraction concluded that there was no alternative to Wissell's resignation, but it did not repudiate Wissell or his plan. When the SPD executive committee later criticized Wissell publicly, the fraction came to his defense.[32] The government's essentially passive approach to economic policy remained an irritant to many SPD deputies, and Wissell continued to act as one of their spokesmen.[33]

The Wissell-Moellendorff scheme did have serious weaknesses.[34] Organizational complexity made it costly and unwieldy, and there was little assurance that the business-labor boards would have been able to perform the tasks for which they were designed. Even so, it was the only attempt by a prominent Social Democrat to impose state influence over private economic decisions. The common economy met that need by making business and labor representatives responsible for collective economic goals, which would have limited labor's bargaining position, but enhanced its influence over the formulation of economic policy.

The common economy rested upon the assumption of consensus, but it was precisely the lack of consensus within the Weimar Coalition on economic policy that made its passage impossible. If the Social Democrats had to impose any economic policy upon unwilling coalition partners, they preferred the traditional socialist goal of nationalization. They were willing to postpone that until more favorable circumstances arose in the future. By doing so, they renounced the possibility of influencing the pace and direction of economic evolution.

Economic Minister Schmidt grudgingly sanctioned a gradual dismantling of the existing state controls in late 1919. However, the return to a free market was not rapid enough for Prussian Agriculture Minister Otto Braun (SPD), who urged Schmidt to drop controls on farm products to encourage farmers to raise production. Schmidt countered that if the consumers' interests were not protected by holding down the prices of bread, milk, potatoes, and meat, then the Communists and Independent Socialists would successfully exploit widespread consumer discontent.[35] Nevertheless, Schmidt did remove price controls on some nonessential goods, and he reduced the number of enterprises regulated by the government. With the SPD ministers in disagreement, it is not surprising that confusion reigned within party ranks. Worried about the election campaign in 1920, one SPD member complained, "When the opposition asks us: 'Does the SPD stand on the principle of the controlled economy or the free economy?' we can't give a clear answer."[36]

The rejection of government controls and of economic planning did not completely undermine the factory-council legislation, which was still designed to implement the principle of codetermination by workers and salaried employees at the level of the firm. Hugo Sinzheimer spoke out in behalf of the factory councils at the SPD congress in June 1919, and the congress approved two resolutions calling for a constitutional amendment to this effect.[37] But Chancellor Bauer chose to move cautiously, first consulting with employers' and employees' representatives, later working to obtain the consent not only of the Center party, but also of the Democratic party, which had left the coalition government for a time after the signing of the Versailles Treaty. The SPD should have had enough leverage to get a strong bill approved by the cabinet, but the SPD ministers tried to meet even the shrillest objections halfway; the Prussian minister of commerce, a Democrat, once complained that the government draft was nothing less than "organized bolshevism."[38]

The draft legislation accompanying Article 165 of the Weimar Constitution, which pledged codetermination through a system of councils, was sent to the Constituent Assembly on 21 August. In contrast to Bauer's previous proposal,[39] factory councils were accorded equal rights to decide labor-relations issues only in conjunction with the unions. The councils' right to arbitrate in threatened strikes was removed; now they could only appeal for outside arbitration. The introduction to the bill read: "Unlike contract and labor-relations matters, leadership of production itself naturally cannot be the subject of negotiations between two equal sides, with arbitration by an outside body in case of disagreement. In reality, that would involve management in a chain of negotiations and conflicts that a fully nonresponsible group would settle. [Whatever the form of ownership of industry] . . . leadership is always unified and incorporated in one body, and no other solution is conceivable."[40] Despite the rather drastic change in the spirit of the original proposal, the National Association of German Industry still found the measure unacceptable.[41]

When the Democrats expressed a desire to rejoin the Reich government in September, the SPD fraction agreed, under the condition that there would be no further weakening of the factory-council legislation. Just two weeks later, the SPD fraction learned that both the Center party and the Democrats had opposed the basic principles of the bill in committee, allegedly giving way only after Bauer had threatened to resign. But their next move was to raise procedural obstacles. In November both parties still objected to the idea that workers would not only have their own councils in each firm and region, they would also have direct representation on the National Economic Council and the district economic councils alongside of business.[42] Another bitter pill for the nonsocialists was a provision allowing the council delegates in each firm with more than one hundred salaried employees or more than five hundred workers to sit on the board of trustees and to examine the firm's books. One Democratic leader objected that this procedure would wreck industry's traditional understating of profits: "German industry has become great not on the profits it has displayed but on those it has hidden."[43]

The Center party ultimately reached agreement with the SPD, even expressing agreement with the SPD's move to reduce the minimum size of the firm to be covered by the bill to one hundred persons.[44] But the Center insisted that the Democrats consent to the legislation also, and the DDP insisted on its right to make changes in the details.[45] Finally, the parties agreed on a compromise giving the factory council the right to examine the firm's yearly balance summaries and to receive quarterly reports, but denying it access to the books used to prepare the summaries.[46] Furthermore, the factory council's right to appeal for outside arbitration was not binding upon the employers.[47] Delaying tactics by the Democrats stalled the legislation until after the new year, much to the SPD's discontent.[48] Final passage occurred on 18 January.

The legislation was one of those compromises that satisfied almost no one. At its meeting in December, the SPD party council criticized Bauer for his handling of the bill, even though he claimed that the Democrats and the Center had given in on most disputed points.[49] Industrialist Ernst Borsig was so enraged by the result that he suggested a mass lockout to other employers. But most industrialists recognized that some sort of bill was necessary to prevent mass unrest and the possible defection of the SPD from the coalition. The conscious aim of the Democrats was not to prevent passage of the bill— only to weaken it as much as possible.[50]

The modest hopes of the SPD backers of the compromise were thoroughly dashed by subsequent developments. A provisional National Economic Council was appointed in August 1919, but the Reichstag kept adding additional representatives of various economic interests to the new body. When the National Economic Council first met in May 1920, it had altogether 326 members.[51] At best, it served as an unwieldy forum for the discussion of important economic issues. Much of the work was delegated to committees and subcommittees. The provisional council, however, often tied up proposals that otherwise might have gone directly to the Reichstag. There was a limit to what could be gained by airing all points of view on a given issue.

The district economic councils and the district workers' councils needed to provide essential support for the National Economic Council never materialized. Most disillusioning, perhaps, was the ineffectiveness of the provision allowing the factory council the right to have representatives on the firm's board of trustees. Despite union efforts to instruct workers in how to use their authority on these boards, industrialists nullified the impact by sharply curtailing the functions of the trustees, and by transferring power to administrative councils on which workers were not represented.[52] The growing trend toward the vertically integrated concern also hindered the work of the factory council. The legislators had mistakenly assumed that all relevant economic decisions were made on the level of the individual factory. Finally, the law rested on the premise that workers in a particular factory were supported by a strong union. Where there were many different craft unions within a given firm, employers found it convenient, even desirable, to conduct contract negotiations with factory councils.[53]

Article 165 of the Weimar Constitution and the factory council legislation succeeded to a degree in mitigating the worker's sense of dependency. However, they neither transformed the worker's actual authority within the firm nor gave him or her greater influence upon the direction of macroeconomic policy.[54] Social Democratic leaders simply had not pursued these wider goals with any consistency. Rather, they hoped that a social partnership in some form could promote economic recovery and economic progress. As Philipp Scheidemann told the delegates at one party conference: "We want to bind intellectual and manual laborers into an organizational unity and to interest all productive powers as thinking human beings in the result of production, which in the final reckoning is designed for the general welfare."[55] The establishment of increased production as a superordinate goal and the SPD's willingness to allow the Democratic party to influence the factory-council legislation brought about a weak institutional reform. The factory-council amendment, like the abortive common economy, could not serve as convincing evidence of progress toward socialism.

Nationalization Efforts After the Kapp Putsch

When Scheidemann's government had introduced its socialization law and coal law into the legislature in March 1919, it had also printed up and distributed more than one million copies of a proclamation headlined, "Socialization is here!"[56] But the bills only provided general authorization for the government to nationalize industries in the future, as well as specific regulation of the coal industry. The failure to nationalize at least the coal industry stirred up considerable frustration and resentment within the SPD ranks. One delegate to a party conference later complained: "What is left of the big fuss that we also made over socialization in the days after the revolution? Nothing but the placards on the street corners saying, 'Socialization is here!' "[57] It was precisely this attitude that union leaders took into account in setting forth their demands in the days immediately following the Kapp Putsch.

The agreement that the unions extracted from the governing parties by means of the general strike in March 1920 abruptly revived the debate over nationalization. The ADGB leaders expected that the provision giving the unions decisive influence over the composition of the national and Prussian governments would clear the way for action.[58] To be sure, this prospect dimmed when the Weimar Coalition was reestablished under Hermann Müller's leadership, but nationalization of the coal industry remained a prime union goal during the next year.

Not only did union spokesmen denounce the influence of the coal companies over the whole economy and the spiraling coal prices; the political consequences of continued private ownership of coal now seemed dangerous to the union leaders. The leaders of the huge coal trusts are enemies of the democratic state, warned mining-union leader and SPD deputy Otto Hue.[59] Rudolf Hilferding, the cautious USPD advocate of nationalization, also noted in late 1920 that the refusal to nationalize explained the working class's inability to secure political power.[60] But the major SPD spokesmen did not share the unions' view that nationalization was necessary to protect the democratic system. Otto Wels cited only the argument of increased worker productivity and the need to protect German concerns against takeovers by foreign capitalists as justifications for the proposed nationalization of the mining industries.[61] The speaker for the SPD fraction at the 1920 party congress continued to warn against hasty experiments that might discredit socialism.[62] All Social Democratic initiatives were soon reduced to what the liberal nonsocialists found acceptable, and the SPD was willing to cooperate with the USPD only insofar as the latter respected these ground rules. Under these circumstances business interests who opposed any nationalization had far more leverage than unions supporting it.

After some delay, Hermann Müller's government authorized the establishment of a new Socialization Commission for the purpose of making detailed socialization proposals.[63] In the Reichstag, SPD financial specialist Wilhelm Keil called for socialization of both the coal and potash industries, but he warned that these moves would not create much revenue for the Reich. Rather, their purpose was to strengthen the mining workers' confidence in socialism and to raise production generally. A DVP spokesman replied that the nonsocialist parties had no interest in strengthening the workers' trust in socialism, and he denied that a public takeover would increase productivity.[64]

First convening in late April, the new Socialization Commission immediately divided into pro- and antinationalization factions. Caught in the middle was Undersecretary Julius Hirsch of the Economics Ministry, who had proposed a reform of the existing regulatory bodies in the coal industry. The legislation of March 1919 had established a National Coal Council and a National Coal Association.[65] The former body contained business, labor, and government representatives, while the latter was a compulsory syndicate composed solely of representatives of management. When the Coal Association forcefully pressed its views on prices, production levels, and wages, the Coal Council lacked the data and the political cohesiveness to make a convincing challenge on behalf of public interest.[66] As a remedy, Hirsch proposed to abolish the Coal Association and to give its functions to the Coal Council. All of the concerns' price-setting, profit targets, and depreciation practices would be subject to the Coal Council's inspection and regulation. This plan was designed to protect public interest better than had been done under the previous arrangement. But industrialist Walther Rathenau gave it a negative appraisal, which ended the chances of the Hirsch proposal.[67] Like many proposed compromises in 1920, the plan went too far for the industrialists and not far enough for the advocates of nationalization.

The Socialization Commission subcommittee on the coal industry continued to debate the issues. Advocates of nationalization, such as USPD economist Rudolf Hilferding, argued that the owner-entrepreneur was already a thing of the past; he had essentially turned over leadership of the firm to salaried managers. From this change Hilferding drew the conclusion that the owner no longer held an important role in production, which meant that state ownership was indeed feasible. The state could hire professional managers just as well as the present owners. Backed up by Christian union leader Friedrich Baltrusch, statistician Dr. Robert Kucynski, and Georg Werner, head of the federation of technical employees and officials, Hilferding claimed that nationalization of the industry would not disturb production. The owners or stockholders could be paid off with state bonds, while workers, employees, technical experts, and consumers would gain direct influence over management through their representatives on the National Coal Council. This plan resembled the majority report of the first Socialization Commission, which had been written by economist Emil Lederer. On the other side, Walther Rathenau and Theodor Vogelstein argued that the entrepreneur would remain an indispensable part of the industry for some time, suggesting that his replacement might be possible in thirty years.[68]

When the discussion of coal reached the full Socialization Commission, the political situation was no longer favorable to reform. The elections of June 1920 left the SPD as the strongest party, but just barely so, and the Weimar Coalition no longer possessed a majority. Since the USPD refused to join a coalition with nonsocialists, the SPD withdrew from the government. A minority coalition of the DDP, DVP, and Center was formed by Konstantin Fehrenbach (Center). The new chancellor pledged to continue the policy of socialization, but the inclusion of the business-oriented People's party made action seem less likely than ever. In fact, Economics Minister Ernst Scholz (DVP) worked closely with coal magnate Hugo Stinnes on this issue.[69]

Even though they were now outside the government, SPD leaders continued to express concern about the danger of economic experiments. Friedrich Stampfer defined socialization as the transformation of the capitalist economy into socialism without damage to the economy, asking the government to reach a reasonable settlement with the advocates of coal socialization.[70] Stampfer was in effect requesting some sort of compromise that could be described as socialization to the SPD's following; the vagueness of the term made it possible to use socialization even for a proposal that left the entrepreneur in his position.

There was some movement toward compromise in the Socialization Commission. After an 11 to 11 deadlock between the Lederer-Hilferding proposal and Rathenau's suggestion of gradual expropriation over thirty years, five supporters of the first plan agreed to accept the second one if their own was rejected by the government. ADGB officials Otto Hue and Paul Umbreit were among this group.[71] But industrialists Hugo Stinnes and Carl Siemens had voted for the Rathenau proposal only because it had been the lesser of two evils. After the threat of immediate nationalization was eliminated, a number of businessmen began to work out new proposals and new delaying tactics.[72]

While the Socialization Commission made strenuous efforts to foresee the *economic* implications of reform of the coal industry, the political parties and government ministers worried about the political consequences of action or inaction. At each stage of the political debate economic interests strained to exert maximum leverage upon the political parties with which they had influence. The government's conduct, covered only by a thin veil of bureaucratic rationalization, was essentially an attempt to avoid being torn apart. In the last resort the Center party and the Democratic party held the decisive middle ground.

The cabinet rejected the Hilferding proposal for complete nationalization of the coal industry, but a cabinet economic subcommittee pronounced the Rathenau plan viable.[73] Meanwhile, Stinnes was expounding his own plan, which provided for management of the coal industry by coal producers' and coal consumers' representatives. At first glance this looked attractive, but Stinnes was actually suggesting a trust for heavy industry that was patterned after his own corporate empire. The biggest coal consumers by far were the iron and steel industries! This proposal was sent to a new reconciliation committee, which was supposed to work out differences of opinion on the issue.[74]

Within the Democratic party fraction and a special DDP committee on socialization, there was a consensus that the Rathenau scheme went too far and that a limited profit-sharing plan might be a useful gesture to win increased worker loyalty. The committee concluded that the DDP should work closely with DVP industrialists Stinnes and Albert Vögler. Although the liberal Hirsch-Duncker unions were affiliated with the DDP, their representatives were not aggressive or knowledgeable enough to rebut the arguments of those Democrats who championed industrial interests. Former state mining official Georg Gothein was not challenged when he claimed that coal-industry profits were actually too low.[75]

Christian union leader Imbusch, after supporting nationalization throughout most of 1920, finally wearied of the whole struggle, voting for the Stinnes plan in the reconciliation committee. Industrialists Stinnes, Vögler, and Paul Silverberg also won over two other members of the seven-man committee, but the joint subcommittee of the National Economic Council and the National Coal Council was dissatisfied and sent the draft back to an expanded reconciliation committee.[76] When President Ebert pressed the cabinet to take a clear position in early December, the ministers decided to wait for the committee's report, postponing a decision until January.[77] January came and went without the report being issued. Despite Labor Minister Heinrich Brauns's protest, the cabinet continued to wait.[78] The final stage in this ludicrous process came when Economics Minister Ernst Scholz insisted on a study of whether nationalized coal mines might be liable to seizure by the Entente as part of German reparations. An opinion written by the Foreign Ministry foresaw this possibility, although a committee of experts later determined that such a move would be illegal.[79] By that time the Fehrenbach government had resigned, and there was little further prospect of nationalization.

What might the Social Democrats have done to force an end to the delays? They apparently never considered the extreme weapon, a motion of no confidence, despite the minority government's dependence upon SPD toleration.[80] One SPD deputy called for a plebiscite on socialization,[81] but nothing came of that suggestion. At a private meeting of the party council in December 1920 fraction spokesman Karl Hildenbrand said that the SPD itself was partly to blame for the lack of action: "We ourselves don't even know how much and what should be socialized." He argued that the SPD had to reject the far-reaching demands of the Independents and the Communists, wait for the government to introduce a bill, try to reach agreement with the liberal parties, and pass it with the help of the working class.[82] In late January the USPD, which had hitherto insisted on expropriation without compensation, voted unanimously to drop this demand in the hope of creating a united socialist front on the basis of the ADGB's more moderate program.[83] The SPD congress in 1921 also voted its approval of the ADGB position on socialization,[84] but the fraction showed no sign that it wanted to break with the liberal parties.

The SPD's new Görlitz Program of 1921 reflected not only the party's commitment to the notion of interparty cooperation, but also its uncertainty about the type of economic policy suitable for the period of cooperation. Heinrich Cunow, editor of the socialist journal *Neue Zeit*, drafted a statement for the program commission calling for a transfer of private monopolies into a socialist "common economy" (*Gemeinwirtschaft*). Eduard David wanted to redistribute wealth through a common form of production, but he defined socialization as the end of exploitation and improvement of productive output through better organization and technology. Further distancing himself from any expropriation, David argued that socialization involved a rejection of the means and methods of bolshevism. Hermann Müller wrote that a socialist economy developed gradually out of an economic order dominated by large concerns.[85] In short, the economic terminology was both abstract and ambiguous.

The program commission's final draft contained one reference to common ownership: "The large, concentrated economic concerns, insofar as they have already become private monopolies or have obtained a dominating position in the economic life of the nation, are to be converted into the socialist common economy through common ownership (*Vergesellschaftung*) of the capitalist means of production, while at the same time all available social forces (*Kräfte im Volk*) will be trained in the planned expansion and erection of production to the highest level of technical development and job satisfaction (*Arbeitsfreudigkeit*)."[86] Friedrich Stampfer, editor in chief of the SPD newspaper *Vorwärts*, rewrote this draft just prior to its presentation to the party congress, replacing *Vergesellschaftung* with the word *Sozialisierung*,[87] which was open to various interpretations. During the discussion at the congress Heinrich Ströbel argued that the SPD should explain to the masses exactly what socialization was and how it could be accomplished. The party could then win the members of the Christian unions away from the Center party and the Hirsch-Duncker unionists away from the DDP, if the nonsocialist parties still refused to cooperate with the SPD on this issue.[88] Stampfer's rebuttal offers a revealing glimpse into the thinking of the SPD leaders. "We are proceeding on the way from capitalism to socialism; that we know. How long this road is, we don't know; none of us knows that. No one is in a position to sketch out every step of the way in detail ahead of time and to claim how it must be done. But that is the great danger of these socialization prophecies, which are also in large part thoroughly un-Marxist, for the essence of Marxism is the clear belief in the inevitable and necessary process of evolutionary development. . . . What happens if one tries to socialize suddenly, that Russia has shown us. That road we don't want to take.''[89] The First World War and the disruption of the Russian economy by revolution and civil war had heightened the SPD leaders' concern for restoring production and for making full use of the nation's economic resources, including the skills of owners and entrepreneurs.

Hermann Müller stated quite explicitly at the congress that the SPD had to enter coalitions with the nonsocialist parties in upcoming years in order to reach socialism by way of democracy. The SPD would be forced to deviate from its socialist philosophy and to make compromises as a result.[90] But party leaders had little sense of what sort of economic compromises to pursue. Socialization and socialist common economy were slogans expressing hopes for progress. They did not represent practical plans to convert capitalism into socialism.

Abandonment of traditional socialist economic policy left a gap in the party's stance that was never really covered by specific proposals for social reform and progressive taxation. Rather, the party's priorities shifted into the purely political sphere, or remained limited to the defense of economic gains originally regarded only as a first step, such as the eight-hour day. The German economy was rebuilt, but the Social Democrats had little chance to determine how the pieces of the expanding economic pie were distributed. Instead, the chaotic social consequences of an uncontrolled inflationary reconstruction brought the Weimar Republic itself into danger. The SPD was called upon to preserve a poorly functioning political system within which they could exert only limited influence. The chance to reduce the economic and political power of large industrial interests through nationalization did not return again.

5. Defense of the Republic, 1920–1922

D E S P I T E the shock of the Kapp-Lüttwitz Putsch and the complications of the general strike, the Weimar Coalition parties remained in agreement on some basic principles. They recognized that the regime needed additional protection and a period of stability. None of the three parties cared to risk another brush with civil war. But their differences in perspective, produced in part by considerations of self-interest, made it difficult for them to decide how to protect the republic. The SPD reversed its previous stance and focused on the danger of counterrevolution by right-wing extremists, whereas the Democrats and the Center were more concerned with the threat of a Communist uprising. There was a greater consensus in the realm of foreign policy. The SPD, DDP, and Center generally agreed that revision of the Versailles Treaty and reduction of German reparations obligations would be possible only after Germany at least made some effort to show the Entente nations its good intentions.[1] However, the temptation to maneuver for a reduction or delay of reparations payments was everpresent. The reparations bill, announced by an Allied commission in 1921, required large sacrifices from German taxpayers, and only a reduction of the burden could have cooled the domestic political debate over how to raise the tax revenue.

From 1920 to 1922 the SPD leaders were usually willing to commit the party to coalition governments that would defend the republic and pursue a conciliatory foreign policy toward the west. The alternative to SPD participation was too often a right-wing government that included the National People's party (DNVP), which was openly committed to a restoration of the monarchy. Fearful of both the domestic and foreign repercussions of such a government, the Social Democrats again shouldered political responsibility under difficult circumstances.

Yet the government's inability to draw up an effective economic program raised serious doubts among SPD officials, who were worried about the reaction of the SPD's working-class constituents. Not only the party itself but the republic as well might be in danger if inflation ran out of control and reparations remained unsettled. Even SPD participation in coalition government might not provide the republic with needed political stability.

A Tactical Retreat

Hermann Müller, who became chancellor in April 1920, carried out the SPD's coalition strategy in a capable but uninspiring fashion. Despite his obvious intelligence and conciliatory manner, the former commercial employee and journalist lacked the capacity to inspire his ministers and to develop among them a sense of collegial loyalty.[2] Party representatives they remained. The unassertive chancellor had agreed in advance to new elections in June, which gave his government something of a lame-duck status. Müller declined to seek additional support on the left, believing that the "reasonable" group within the USPD (Hilferding, Breitscheid) was losing ground to the advocates of a proletarian dictatorship.[3]

Most members of the SPD party council agreed that there was little prospect even for a temporary truce with the USPD during the election campaign. Although aware that working-class sentiment, particularly in Rhineland-Westphalia, had shifted to the left, numerous members insisted that the SPD's coalition with the DDP and the Center was unavoidable.[4] At another conference of high party officials in May, Wilhelm Sollmann, editor of the *Rheinische Zeitung*, played down the goal of a socialist majority in the June elections. Even if this unlikely event occurred, Sollmann said, the SPD would still have to work with the existing administrative apparatus and within the limitations of the current economic situation.[5] Sollmann's implication was clear; the SPD could not dispense with its bourgeois allies, whatever the election results.

Some of the dissenters within the party elite agreed with the party leadership on this point at least. Scheidemann, the main speaker at the May 1920 conference, blamed Noske for much of the SPD's political misfortune. At the same time, however, he lashed out at the USPD, claiming that its leaders had divided the working class and weakened the republic. He summed up his attack on all the enemies of democracy with the slogan: "Without Ledebour, [there would have been] no Lüttwitz." Although noting that the SPD's withdrawal from the Weimar Coalition might be popular with the party following, Scheidemann rejected this course, calling it a surrender of the republic to its enemies.[6]

The election results provided little comfort for any of the coalition parties. The SPD saw its share of the vote plummet to 21.6 percent from 37.9 percent a year and a half earlier. The party's participation in government decisions to make use of the Free Corps and the renewed military action against left-wing activists in April 1920 cost it dearly with working-class voters. Of course, the lack of achievements in the realm of economic policy was also a factor in the decline. At the same time, the SPD probably lost some of its nonworking-class voters from 1919. The Democrats suffered an even more disastrous defeat, falling from 18.6 percent to a mere 8.3 percent, with its middle-class voters deserting in droves to the People's party (DVP). The DVP's improvement from 4.4 percent in 1919 to 13.9 percent in 1920 was in part the result of better organization. Unlike in 1919, the party mounted a full slate of candidates, and foreign-policy expert Gustav Stresemann provided effective campaign leadership.[7] But the DVP's attacks against the SPD and the Weimar Coalition obviously made an impression upon middle-class voters. The Center party fell from 19.7 percent to 13.6 percent. The new Bavarian People's party (BVP), which had split off from the Center, accounted for much of that loss by collecting 4.4 percent. Even if this more conservative Bavarian Catholic organization were considered part of the Weimar Coalition, the coalition parties no longer commanded a majority.

The extremist parties at both ends of the political spectrum benefited from the government's unpopularity. The National People's party, openly monarchist, rose from 10.3 percent to 14.9 percent. The USPD made strong gains, moving from 7.6 percent to 17.9 percent, and the Communists, competing for the first time, garnered 2.1 percent.

The elections of June 1920 marked a major turning point for the Weimar Republic. In his memoirs, Arnold Brecht, a high civil servant and loyal republican, lamented that after 1920 there was never a democratic majority in parliament to sustain the democratic features of the constitution.[8] At the time, however, the significance of this election was not perceived. Despite the setback, SPD officials expected to regain their losses with more skillful tactics. The impending schism within the USPD, already looming on the horizon, also offered grounds for hope. As soon as inflation, unemployment, and political violence finally subsided, the voters would be less responsive to demagogy, so the SPD strategists reasoned. But how could the interests of the party and the republic be protected in the meantime?

President Ebert called upon the SPD, still the largest party in the Reichstag, to try to form a new government. This time Hermann Müller turned first toward the USPD. On 11 June he wrote to the USPD fraction: "The participation of the USPD in the government of our young German republic appears to me to be especially necessary, since only a coalition government strengthened from the left can defend our republican institutions against all attacks from the right, prevent reactionary incursions against the eight-hour day and the postwar achievements in the area of social reform, which corresponds to the republican and pacifist ideas of an overwhelming majority of the German people."[9] Artur Crispien's response on behalf of the USPD, delivered only four hours after the invitation was received,[10] blamed the growing reactionary danger upon the SPD's policy of compromise with the existing bureaucracy, the military, and the capitalist parties. Crispien pledged the USPD's allegiance to an all-out class struggle and to the capture of political power by the proletariat alone, leading to the realization of socialism. If events created the need for a socialist government, Crispien said, the USPD would consider a coalition with the SPD only if the former held a majority within the government and dominant influence over its program.[11] There was not a word about the defense of the republic.

On 13 June 1920 at a joint meeting of the SPD fraction and party council Hermann Müller summarized the pros and cons of government participation. The economic situation was expected to worsen in the next few months, and there was no hope of Allied concessions at the upcoming Spa conference. The new government thus would bear serious burdens. The biggest disadvantage of leaving the government, Müller said, was that the army would fall under the control of unreliable people, particularly if a right-center coalition was formed. Eduard Bernstein added that the bureaucracy too would be controlled by the right, noting that in view of the widespread misery, he was not at all discouraged by the election results. Coal-mining official Otto Hue and right-wing Social Democrat Eduard David favored participation in the new government even if it included representatives of the DVP. Several speakers suggested a minority Weimar Coalition government, which might conceivably escape a vote of no confidence. But the fraction majority sided with Otto Wels, Franz Krüger, and Adolf Braun, who argued that it was tactically wise to go into opposition.[12]

The SPD leaders, particularly those whose primary responsibility was to run the party organization, wanted to stem losses to the USPD; what better means was there than a respite from governmental responsibility? They hoped that the DVP's inclusion in government might force it to assume responsibility for unpopular but necessary foreign-policy decisions.[13] Friedrich Stampfer later described the rationale for the SPD's withdrawal, demonstrating at the same time that its fundamental strategy of support for the republic remained unaltered: "The Social Democratic fraction was content to be freed of direct responsibility for government, and ready to support a nonsocialist government against dangerous attacks (*Stösse*) from the right or the left."[14]

Coalition policy was a sensitive issue at the SPD congress in October 1920. Cochairman Otto Wels complained that some of the same comrades who had demanded a withdrawal from the government in June were already impatient; they asserted that the SPD should either join the government or else overthrow the minority government that Konstantin Fehrenbach (Center) had established.[15] As a result, the executive committee and the Reichstag fraction explicitly gave the congress a chance to approve or reject the June coalition decisions. The leadership's resolution stated further that the SPD would only consider reentry into the government if it served the interests of the proletariat: specifically, if it advanced the "democratization" of the Reichswehr, the socialization of ripe branches of industry, and a pacific foreign policy.

This formulation left the executive committee and the fraction with plenty of room for tactical maneuvers. However, a Saxon delegate named Ernst Eckstein proposed an amendment stipulating that the SPD should not cooperate with any party that did not support the republic in principle and in fact. This wording was designed to rule out coalition with the DVP, which was still not a committed republican party.[16] Although the SPD executive committee normally took a stance on each proposal before the congress, Wels said nothing about the Eckstein amendment. Wels's silence was an indication that he did not support the amendment but could not afford to oppose it. The congress passed the amended resolution unanimously. Wels salvaged what he could by persuading the party council that the restriction should not apply to the state governments.[17]

The minority coalition (Center, DDP, and DVP) headed by Fehrenbach survived until May 1921. Angered by Germany's failure to disarm its civilian population and by its delinquency in reparations payments, the Allied powers then issued their "final" payment plan in the form of an ultimatum (which became known as the London Ultimatum). They set total reparations payments at 132 billion gold marks (about 33 billion dollars) and threatened immediate occupation of the Ruhr district if Germany refused to comply. Furthermore, the yearly reparations installments of two billion marks plus 26 percent of the value of German exports had to be paid in gold or foreign exchange. As a gesture of indignation, the Fehrenbach government resigned on 4 May. The DVP may have provided the main impetus for such a move,[18] but it was doubtful in any case whether the coalition parties would have been able to agree on any other response.

Forced to act quickly, the SPD executive committee, party council, and fraction met in joint session on the morning of 10 May. Reversing its stand of June 1920, the SPD elite was now willing to share responsibility for an unpopular foreign-policy decision, fearing that rejection of the ultimatum would mean war and the destruction of Germany. The vote in favor of joining the government was 56 to 20 in the fraction and 28 to 10 in the party council.[19] More controversial was the question whether the remaining USPD deputies—the left wing of the party had since joined the Communists—[20] should be asked to join the new parliamentary combination. *Vorwärts* Editor Friedrich Stampfer felt that such a coalition could not work. Nonetheless, an SPD delegation asked the USPD fraction if it would join the SPD and the Center in a government that would accept the Allied terms. After the Independents began to debate the issue, the SPD went ahead alone. Learning of the SPD's move, the USPD then voted not to enter, pointing out that it was still willing to form an all-socialist government. The SPD did not pursue this possibility.[21]

Ebert insisted on appointing Centrist Joseph Wirth, formerly finance minister in Fehrenbach's government, as chancellor-designate. The votes of the USPD, almost half of the Democrats, and some DVP deputies enabled Wirth to survive a vote of confidence and to pledge acceptance of the Allied ultimatum on the evening of 10 May,[22] even though his cabinet was not yet complete. Finally, Ebert exerted strong pressure on the Democrats to join Wirth's government.[23] Otto Gessler continued as defense minister, and Eugen Schiffer became minister of justice. The third Democrat from the Fehrenbach cabinet, Interior Minister Erich Koch-Weser, was now dropped in favor of the SPD's Georg Gradnauer, formerly minister president in Saxony, who may have been Ebert's personal choice.[24] USPD representatives, generally in harmony with the SPD on questions of foreign policy, told Wirth that he could also expect their parliamentary support if his policies were satisfactory.[25] But disagreements over taxation policy soon divided the two socialist parties from the nonsocialists.

The Economy and the Great Coalition

The economic impact of the war, combined with Germany's postwar armistice and reparations obligations, substantially aggravated social and economic tension. The nation as a whole had become considerably poorer, but each social group wished to minimize its losses. Big business and in particular heavy industry found itself in a relatively advantageous position. During the war large industrial enterprises had profited greatly from war contracts at the expense of small business and the consumer.[26] At the same time, real wages for skilled workers declined substantially from their 1913 levels, in some cases by as much as 46 percent.[27] The postwar surge in wages and fringe benefits partly compensated workers for this wartime loss. Leading businessmen tolerated the rise in wages, the intervention of the state into labor disputes, increased social welfare legislation, and government subsidies for essential consumer goods only as a temporary necessity required to prevent the masses from going "Bolshevist."[28] They hoped that these concessions could be revoked as soon as possible in order to restore their necessary profit margins and to facilitate expansion of investment.

The postwar inflation resulted from a variety of factors, including the method of financing the war, high government spending and low tax revenue, combined with a liberal credit policy by the Reichsbank. Industry and agriculture managed to erase their debts and keep prices rising ahead of wages, securing additional profit for investment.[29] Meanwhile, business interests (which were far from unified on the desirability of inflation) attacked the excessive cost of "inefficient" state-run enterprises, such as the railroads. They also denounced government efforts to hold down the prices of potatoes, grain, coal, and clothing beneath the market price through economic controls. Production allegedly could only be increased by removing the fetters of the controlled economy.[30] This attitude clashed head-on with consumer complaints about the rising cost of living and with labor's reliance upon state intervention for a better deal.[31] Buffeted by conflicting pressures, the government lacked the legal authority and the political cohesion to combat inflation effectively.

The tax program originally established by Finance Minister Erzberger in late 1919 relied primarily upon direct taxes that hit the upper-income levels (and corporations) the hardest. Erzberger wanted not only to compensate for past dependence upon excise taxes, but also to bring about a redistribution of income in favor of wage and salary earners in order to strengthen their loyalty to the new republic. New government spending programs and social legislation were aimed at the same goal. But increasing pressure from interest groups upon the nonsocialist parties worked to frustrate what was intended to be a progressive tax system. By fiscal year 1922 some 75 percent of government revenue from income taxes was obtained from payroll deductions from the earnings of workers and employees, while wealthy individuals benefited from delayed payment with a rapidly depreciating currency.[32]

Acting as his own finance minister, Chancellor Wirth had appointed Robert Schmidt (SPD) as economics minister. On 17 May Schmidt presented the outlines of a new Economics Ministry plan for the taxation of "real values" (*Erfassung der Sachwerte*).[33] He argued that wage and salary earners, pensioners, and those with savings accounts had suffered badly from inflation, but owners of property in agriculture, industry, and real estate had not been significantly affected, because the value of their holdings rose proportionally to the fall in the value of the mark. Given the desperate need for tax revenue to meet the initial reparations payments and to balance the budget, the government should first look toward this unearned (relative) increase in the value of property. Schmidt then suggested that the government seize approximately 20 percent ownership of farms, commercial enterprises, and housing. Farmers and householders would then pay off a compulsory mortgage, whereas corporations would surrender roughly 20 percent of their stock and pay dividends on it. This action was supposed to yield some twenty billion (paper) marks annually, which was almost half of the estimated yearly reparation bill.

Wirth did not take to the Economics Ministry's proposal. Following the advice of his state secretary in the Finance Ministry, Heinrich Zapf, the chancellor believed that existing taxes, such as the corporation tax and the tax on wealth, could be increased with less difficulty. Reconstruction Minister Walther Rathenau[34] criticized partial state ownership as a dangerous limitation upon economic freedom, suggesting in its place a tax on capital gains achieved after 1 January 1919. Vice-Chancellor Gustav Bauer and Interior Minister Gradnauer were unwilling to force the cabinet to choose between the Economics Ministry and Finance Ministry plans, because such a decision would endanger the coalition. So Rathenau's idea, plus a scaled-down version of Schmidt's tax, this time applicable only to industry, were left on the table for further consideration.[35]

Wirth leaned more toward Rathenau's view as time passed. The imaginative Rathenau was not only an economic expert in his own right, he was also involved in continuing reparations negotiations—specifically, to allow for part of the German debt to France to be paid through the delivery of industrial goods.[36] Rathenau and Wirth shared a more ambitious goal that became apparent during the summer of 1921. They both sought to convince the Allied powers to lighten Germany's total reparations burden.[37] Wirth and Rathenau found it inopportune for the Social Democrats to raise their demand for massive new taxation, especially through such a controversial method. The easier course chosen by Wirth was to delay consideration of new taxes until reparations negotiations were completed. If the SPD had refused to go along, it could have been cast into the role of an unpatriotic spendthrift, eager to give more German money away than was actually necessary. But as negotiations dragged on and tax revenues lagged, inflation escalated, weakening public confidence in the government.

On 26 August 1921 Matthias Erzberger, left-wing member of the Center party, former finance minister, but most famous as the man who had headed the German armistice delegation, was assassinated by two young nationalists. Carelessness in his personal finances had left Erzberger politically vulnerable. The conservative press and DNVP spokesman Karl Helfferich had carried on a vendetta against him for years. His critics resented his efforts to design a progressive system of taxation and his continued support for a conciliatory foreign policy.[38] Coming only a couple of months after the murder of an Independent Socialist politician in Bavaria, as well as after a year of nationalist resistance to legislation disarming Germany's civilian population, the Erzberger assassination represented the capstone in what seemed to be a coordinated campaign of terrorism against the republic.[39] Secret paramilitary organizations, openly tolerated by the Bavarian government, were a threat to any prominent republican politician; the attack on Erzberger was regarded as an attack against the republic itself.

Wirth and President Ebert agreed that the murder was incited by the agitation of the right-wing nationalists. Wirth also wanted firm action against the antirepublican threat to prevent working-class strikes and violence, which had followed the Kapp-Lüttwitz Putsch.[40] On 29 August Ebert used his emergency powers under Article 48 to issue an ordinance giving the Reich minister of the interior the authority to ban periodicals that called for acts of violence or that made contemptuous references to the constitution or state institutions. It also permitted him to prohibit meetings or demonstrations having the same goals.[41] The implementing regulations issued on the following day gave state and local authorities similar powers.

The effectiveness of the emergency measure varied according to the political composition of each state government. The socialist coalition in Saxony made more vigorous use of its powers than Reich Interior Minister Gradnauer did, while the conservative Kahr government in Bavaria refused to permit Gradnauer to intervene at all in Bavarian affairs. Because of this Bavarian resistance, the ordinance was ineffective where the problem was most severe. Within a few months the Reich government decided to allow the ordinance to lapse.[42]

More significant than the legal changes were the political repercussions. The SPD, USPD, and the socialist unions agreed to pressure the government to act against the radical right. The USPD also approached the SPD executive to discuss the possibility of a joint SPD-USPD-KPD policy regarding inflation and taxes. The SPD executive committee categorically refused to conduct discussions with the Communists, since they had been depicting the SPD as responsible for inflation. The USPD representatives then agreed to leave out the KPD, and Otto Wels triumphantly notified local SPD officials that the USPD had made an about-face on the issue of coalition with nonsocialists; it was said to favor SPD participation in the Prussian government.[43] Such USPD support would have reduced the political liability of the SPD's coalition policy, something which the SPD officials would have welcomed.

DNVP leader Oskar Hergt, claiming that the entire proletariat had declared war against the right, reacted by inviting the DVP to merge with the DNVP. Fearing that complete political polarization between supporters and opponents of the republic could lead to civil war, Wirth angrily attacked Hergt's speech. The chancellor announced publicly that if, despite his efforts, civil war resulted, he would take the side of the workers.[44] When Otto Wels quoted Wirth's statement a few weeks later at the SPD congress at Görlitz, there was frenzied applause.[45] There were few bourgeois politicians whom the SPD leaders felt that they could rely on; Erzberger had been one, and Wirth, the son of a master mechanic from Baden, was another.

Like Chancellor Wirth, the SPD leaders sincerely wanted to avoid extreme political confrontation, for they feared that the working class would be essentially isolated, as it had always been during the Second Reich. Franz Krüger told the SPD congress that the working class alone, if necessary, could defend the republic, but at the cost of terrible suffering and economic damage. Stressing the point, Hermann Müller warned that the party must avoid another two-front war against counterrevolutionaries and left radicals like that of March 1920.[46] Wirth and the SPD leaders agreed that the best way to protect the republic was to continue the SPD's policy of cooperation with nonsocialist parties and to keep the monarchist DNVP at a distance. But the more moderate People's party under the leadership of foreign-policy specialist Gustav Stresemann looked increasingly responsible to the SPD leaders.

Shortly after the Erzberger murder, some leading figures in the SPD, among them Otto Wels, Hermann Müller, and Franz Krüger, began to prepare the party for the creation of Great Coalition governments (SPD, DDP, DVP, and Center) in the Reich and in Prussia.[47] Even such a well-placed member of the Prussian fraction as Albert Grzesinski did not understand why Wels, Müller, and Krüger had suddenly decided to trust the DVP.[48] The answer lay partly in Wirth's strategy on reparations and partly in the DVP's growth and influence.

Wirth had begun to make progress in secret negotiations with leaders of industry toward raising the foreign exchange Germany needed to pay its reparations. In return for certain concessions, a number of industrialists had offered to raise up to 1.5 billion marks in gold, foreign exchange, or credits held by industry abroad. Wirth offered them a guarantee against both socialization and Schmidt's plan for taxation of real values (*Erfassung der Sachwerte*). He also hinted at other tax alleviation, and he told the other government parties that the entry of the DVP into the cabinet would be the natural consequence of such an agreement. Although the executive committee of the National Association of German Industry voted on 13 September to offer its help to the government, it held back from a specific commitment, something that Wirth had wanted before the opening of the SPD congress.[49] Informed of the prospect of a short-term reparations solution, the SPD leaders wished to prepare the party for a political arrangement that might temporarily dispose of the festering reparations issue.

Yet it would be a mistake to interpret the developments at the Görlitz congress purely as the result of an impending deal between the government and German industry. The SPD leaders had always believed it necessary to cooperate with the nonsocialist parties during the early years of the Weimar Republic.[50] The recent election results made it clear that the Democratic party had failed to develop into the large, middle-class republican party that the Social Democrats had hoped for. Meanwhile, the DVP had shown significant strength and had gradually moved away from its monarchist orientation, although it remained divided.[51] As Eduard Bernstein stated with his characteristic candor: "The People's party has great social power; it is actually the party of the German bourgeoisie. Behind it stand finance, industry, and the intelligentsia in Germany. We must try to hitch this party to the wagon of the republic."[52] The notion that the Weimar Republic required the political and economic support of those with economic experience and ability[53] led the SPD to its decision to try to work with the DVP.

At the Görlitz congress Otto Wels, Hermann Müller, Carl Severing, and Otto Braun spoke strongly in favor of a resolution repealing the 1920 Eckstein amendment barring a coalition with the DVP. The leadership presented a new resolution defending the policy of coalition, which was to serve the following goals: defense of the republic; protection of the popular right of self-determination at all levels of government; democratization of the administration and republicanization of the army and police; protection and expansion of social legislation; and a foreign policy of reconciliation, including fulfillment of reparations obligations through taxation of property.[54] The opponents of the resolution argued that the coalition in the past had achieved little, that the DVP was hostile to workers and their interests, and that the new policy would hinder reunification with the USPD.[55] Actually, the SPD leaders hoped that the Independents would be "reasonable." In confidential discussions preceding the congress Hilferding had told Wels that the USPD would observe benevolent neutrality toward a Great Coalition government under Wirth. However, Hilferding overestimated the moderating trend within his party; the USPD fraction backed off from any such commitment.[56] The SPD congress approved the Great Coalition resolution by a 290 to 67 vote in spite of the obvious dissatisfaction of the Independent Socialists. USPD deputy Kurt Rosenfeld complained a few months later: "The SPD prefers the Great Coalition to the unification of the proletariat."[57]

The new Görlitz Program, part of which has already been analyzed, reflected a tentative SPD effort to broaden its appeal. No longer could the two socialist parties simply trade votes back and forth, Otto Wels exclaimed. But when he argued that the SPD had to expand its base of support beyond existing limits, he mentioned only the need to win over those workers then supporting the Center and the DNVP.[58] Over some opposition, the congress agreed to tone down socialist rhetoric about the class struggle, but party leaders did not venture so far as to present a positive program addressed to the needs of civil servants, white-collar workers, and farmers.[59] Ideology and caution combined to restrict political innovation. Many Social Democrats still held the illusion that the natural development of capitalism would drive the independent middle class, salaried employees, and wage earners in both city and country together. Hence they saw little need for special appeals to nonworking-class strata. Even the SPD's willingness to work with the DVP was not a sign of any fundamentally new openness. The defense of the republic required the SPD's participation in government, and given the weakness of the DDP, the SPD was forced to take the DVP in the bargain. *Vorwärts* accurately caught the spirit of the new SPD policy regarding coalition by describing it as a tactical turn.[60]

Immediately after the close of the SPD congress, Wirth's attempt to establish the Great Coalition ran into trouble. First of all, the chancellor still lacked a clear statement from industry on how much foreign exchange it could raise. When representatives of the four parties met in secret to discuss a possible government program, the DVP agreed to recognize the constitution and defend it with all legal means. The three nonsocialist parties then reached a consensus on the outlines of a tax program, which included a loan in foreign exchange from industry, accelerated collection of an existing wealth tax (*Reichsnotopfer*), and new consumer taxes. But the representatives of the SPD claimed that their fraction would regard this program as insufficient. They wanted more than a hypothetical approval of the principle of *Erfassung der Sachwerte*. The other parties argued that to undo the damage from any such tax, there would have to be a change in the labor relationship (*Arbeitsverhältnis*), a euphemism for saying that the eight-hour maximum workday would have to be abolished.[61]

Extremely skeptical about the prospect for a satisfactory tax agreement with the DVP, the SPD fraction then asked the USPD under what conditions it would be willing to join the existing Wirth government.[62] This was a sensitive question for the USPD, which was genuinely sympathetic to the objectives of the Wirth government. In their response the Independents admitted that a foreign policy of reconciliation and fulfillment and a democratic domestic policy corresponded to the interests of the proletariat. However, they presented a list of minimum demands to which any government they joined had to agree: balancing the budget through taxation of property, wide-ranging judicial reform (election of jurors), removal of monarchist civil servants and military personnel, and socialization of mining industries. The USPD also wished to find out how the nonsocialist coalition parties regarded such a program.[63] The SPD leaders were no doubt discouraged by the mention of socialization. Hermann Müller noted the progress of the USPD, which no longer rejected coalition with nonsocialists in principle, but he did not push very strongly for its entry.[64] The Democrats disposed of the matter by demanding that the USPD renounce any attempt to attain the "council republic" by force.[65] There were still enough radicals left in the USPD to block such a pledge.

Thus, the SPD stood alone against the other coalition parties on the tax issue. Wirth now clearly rejected the idea of *Erfassung der Sachwerte*, but the SPD negotiators were suspicious (and justifiably so) of a mere voluntary effort by the industry to raise foreign exchange. As a minimum condition, Wels and Wilhelm Keil insisted that the legal authorization for *Erfassung* be approved by the Reichstag. If industry then failed to raise anything like the one billion gold marks needed, the government could quickly take its share of property as a substitute. Keil also warned the others that the SPD would not consent to new consumer taxes unless the government came up with a comprehensive plan to halt inflation.[66]

In the midst of the unsettled tax and coalition negotiations, the League of Nations committee entrusted with the partitioning of Upper Silesia between Germany and Poland announced a settlement depriving Germany of the bulk of the industrial area as well as a number of cities that were predominantly German. Although all parties, with the possible exception of the USPD,[67] were angry, there was a bitter dispute over the appropriate government reaction. Rathenau and other Democrats urged the resignation of the entire cabinet in protest, while Georg Gradnauer pointed out that this gesture would not change the League of Nations' decision in the slightest.[68]

Under these circumstances Wirth was on shaky political ground. He tried to get the National Association of German Industry to clarify the details of its credit offer, but within the Association opposition to a loan to the government was growing. Some industrialists now took the view that the London Ultimatum payment schedule had to be renounced as unfulfillable.[69] The Social Democrats, who continued to insist upon an agreement on a common program before the establishment of a Great Coalition government, did not feel responsible for the tax deadlock, since actual implementation of *Erfassung der Sachwerte* would only be required if industry failed to raise sufficient foreign credits.[70]

The result of all this bargaining was a stalemate that did little to promote effective government. The Center party fraction actually joined the DDP and the DVP in calling for Wirth's resignation; Deputy Spahn said that the Center would have no objection if President Ebert again chose its man Wirth to form a new government, a stipulation that the Social Democrats insisted on. Claiming that the government had abjectly submitted to the loss of much of Upper Silesia, DDP chairman Petersen and DVP leader Stresemann kept their parties out of the new government. Industrial interests within the DVP wanted nothing to do with a Great Coalition under Wirth, and somewhat dubious itself about the chancellor, the DDP did not want to be seen as a laggard in defending Germany's honor.[71]

The Mining Group of the National Association of German Industry, following the lead of Stinnes and Alfred Hugenberg, decided that it could offer the government credits only if all economic restrictions were removed and publicly owned firms, especially the railroads, were returned to the private sector.[72] The chancellor then asked industry merely to lend the government enough to meet the reparations installments due in January and February, but industry representatives denied this request also.[73] All parties were now back to where they began, but in the meantime speculation against the mark had increased, inflation had accelerated, and the minority government had become weaker.

Having overridden considerable intraparty opposition to create a basis for the Great Coalition, the SPD leaders were upset.[74] Their reaction was tempered by their respect for Wirth, who admitted he was disillusioned. The SPD policy makers lacked a feasible solution of their own for the economic and financial mess. Although *Vorwärts* editorialized on behalf of the socialization of mining industries, Scheidemann conceded privately that this was impossible.[75] When the socialist unions, backed reluctantly by the SPD, again raised the demand for *Erfassung der Sachwerte*, Wirth ruled it out on political and diplomatic grounds: "The goal of our entire policy must be the reduction (*Abbau*) of the London Ultimatum. It would therefore be false if the London Ultimatum were declared at the moment perhaps eighty percent feasible by means of the taxation of real values."[76]

When the nonsocialist majority in the tax committee of the Reichstag began to cut the government's rather limited tax request, the two socialist delegations on the committee began to work together.[77] But the distance that remained between the two parties was revealed on 17 January when Wirth hinted that his government might collapse if there were no tax compromise.[78] This prospect soon forced the SPD negotiators to accept a new bill for a compulsory loan in place of the plan for taxation of real values. The new measure required the wealthy to lend the government the equivalent of one billion gold marks at low interest. The SPD leaders then called upon Wirth to exert his influence upon the other parties, including the DVP, whose support might be needed to pass the bill.[79] Wirth did, and a compromise was reached on 25 January, but despite Wirth's plea, the USPD refused to support it.[80] Eduard Bernstein, who had already left the USPD to rejoin the SPD, complained: "The Independents are prepared to die for the republic in case of emergency, but they are not ready to grant it the means to life."[81]

Within the SPD fraction there was quite a struggle over the bill. Paul Löbe suggested joining the USPD in opposition, but Hermann Müller persuaded the deputies to support the government. Eduard David, a consistent supporter of coalition government, admitted that the bill did not provide for reasonable taxation.[82] The SPD came to the support of Wirth's coalition despite the inadequacy of the financial package. The oft-repeated statement that the

SPD's highest priority was the maintenance of the republic and of a stable, democratic government was verified,[83] but opposition within the party elite to this strategy was growing.

Stepping forth as the spokesman for the SPD's dissidents, Philipp Scheidemann expressed irritation privately at the price the SPD was forced to pay to maintain Wirth: "The lack of goals and style in party policy hurts me like a blow in the face. The tarantella (*Gedudel*) in the Reichstag and the acceptance of all taxes that are demanded and sanctioned by Stinnes and his Stresemann-men . . . where are our goals, our reins, driver, and whip anyway?"[84] In the face of internal opposition, those SPD leaders who had been inclined toward a Great Coalition were forced to reverse course. Hermann Müller told Wirth that the presence of the DVP in the government would be a great political burden for the SPD, and Otto Wels made it clear that the SPD's willingness to sacrifice its economic and social policies to keep Wirth's government afloat had limits.[85]

The reluctance of the liberal parties to resist interest-group pressure, to establish an effective financial program to meet domestic needs and reparations payments, and to erect the Great Coalition has been cited by one historian as a turning point in the fortune of Weimar parliamentary democracy.[86] The liberal politicians who were eager to establish a government and program designed to stabilize republican institutions were outvoted by representatives of economic interests and by political leaders disinclined to take risks. This failure on the part of the liberals made it more difficult for the SPD leaders to defend political cooperation to their constituents. Whatever luster they had managed to give to the idea of a Great Coalition was now badly tarnished.

The Enemy Stands on the Right

On 4 June two would-be assassins tried to dowse Philipp Scheidemann with prussic acid. Only slightly injured, Scheidemann denounced the continuing campaign of murder and terrorism conducted by reactionaries. The attack against him, Scheidemann told a crowd of some 40,000 in Kassel on 8 June, was really another attack against the republic.[87] That struggle claimed another victim on 24 June when Walther Rathenau was shot dead on his way to the Foreign Ministry.[88] The Jewish industrialist had become the target of vicious anti-Semitic propaganda, especially after becoming foreign minister, and even respectable conservatives, such as Karl Helfferich, used him as the target of their wrath against fulfillment policy. On 23 June Helfferich had claimed that Rathenau had betrayed the French-occupied Saar district.[89] When news of the murder reached the Reichstag, there was tumult. Seventy-two-year-old Eduard

Bernstein approached DNVP deputy Helfferich and shouted, "Murderer." Some of the Communist deputies tried to attack Helfferich physically, but they were blocked by Wirth, Reichstag President Paul Löbe, and other Reichstag officials.[90] Löbe claimed that a secret conspiratorial organization was behind the murder, and that those politicians who vilified government leaders were partially responsible. Otto Wels interrupted to lead three cheers for the republic. Wirth, who had been a close personal friend of Rathenau, concluded a passionate speech in the Reichstag on 25 June by elaborating on a slogan already used by Scheidemann: "There stands the enemy that drips its poison into the wounds of the people. There stands the enemy—and there is no doubt about it—this enemy stands on the right."[91]

Although the Nationalist party had no direct complicity in the murder, Wirth accepted the claim of the leftist parties that the murderers were inspired by monarchist agitation. To act against the terrorist danger, the government believed it necessary to place limits upon various constitutional rights and liberties. On the afternoon of 24 June the government requested and got an emergency decree from President Ebert that resembled the one used after the Erzberger murder. Assemblies, demonstrations, and organizations endangering law and order, advocating acts of violence, or expressing contempt for republican institutions could be banned. Mindful of the previous conflict with Bavaria, Reich Minister of Justice Gustav Radbruch gave initial jurisdiction to the state governments. The ordinance provided that in case of disagreement between the Reich and state governments, the former could appeal to a new Court for the Protection of the Republic. Three of the court's seven members were to be named by the head of the Supreme Court, and four would be appointed by the Reich president. This court was also to have jurisdiction in censorship cases arising from the other provisions of the decree.[92] But there was a serious loophole in the emergency decree. Officials of rightist associations could deny responsibility for acts committed by individual members, and thus the question of the associations' culpability had to be thrashed out in court.[93]

Convinced that this decree represented a step in the right direction, both socialist parties wanted stronger action, calling for permanent legislation and for the elimination of antirepublican elements from government administration, police, and the army. The socialists demanded a national police force that would intervene when states failed to act against right-wing radicals.[94] Yet at the same time, the two parties were concerned that states such as Bavaria might use the new legal weapons, not against the intended targets, but against Communists and socialists, as had been done in the past.

In the wake of the Rathenau assassination and the perceived need for strong action against the extreme right, the SPD and USPD submerged longstanding disagreements. The change of mood in the USPD fraction was particularly striking. Former Communist Paul Levi suggested that socialist and union representatives, including members of the Center party, form a government to combat the threat from reactionaries. Wilhelm Dittmann also favored USPD entrance into the government under certain conditions.[95] On 26 June Rudolf Breitscheid countered the arguments of Georg Ledebour in favor of continued opposition. Breitscheid maintained that the republic, the most favorable foundation for the struggle for socialism, was in danger, and the USPD had to show the public that it was willing to defend the republic with all means. Robert Dissmann's rebuttal was that the USPD had to go beyond the mere defense of the republic to solve the nation's social problems, which was presently impossible because the bourgeoisie still held the real power.[96] Nonetheless, Breitscheid's view of party priorities was beginning to gain ground within the USPD fraction. Responding to rumors about a change of policy in the USPD, *Vorwärts* welcomed closer relations with the Independents but made it clear that the SPD would adhere to the necessary coalition with the nonsocialist parties.[97]

The socialist parties and unions organized a joint demonstration on 25 June, a general strike on 27 June, and another on 4 July, all of which were immensely successful. For a time the Communists too were involved, but the SPD soon accused the KPD of trying to exploit the proletarian demonstrations and to foment violence, so contact with the Communists was broken off.[98] The SPD leaders then formally invited the USPD to join the government,[99] which caused some problems for the other coalition parties.

The Democrats and Centrists had gone along with the emergency decree and the government's antimonarchist proposals only reluctantly, while expressing misgivings about the strikes and demonstrations. The Center party fraction decided to accept the USPD only if there was no other way to save the "fatherland."[100] Democratic party official Anton Erkelenz elaborated on his party's difficulties:

> I personally am also of the opinion that the entry of the Independents poses a fateful question for us. Viewed from the higher political perspective, such an entry is desirable and necessary. However, one cannot judge the matter only from this viewpoint. . . . One must also look at the practical effects, and there is no doubt in my judgment that the simple entry of the Independents into the government would be a severe blow for us from which we could never again recover. But it would be a different matter if one also popped the question to the People's party, and if it rejected joint participation with the Independents. Besides the fact that the People's party itself would suffer a

serious crisis then, we would have the possibility of competing against it in an entirely different way than if the invitation had not been issued.[101]

Primarily worried about the attitudes of its voters and about the position of its main competitor, the DVP, the DDP fraction could not accept all the SPD's suggestions.

When the SPD leaders pressed for an invitation to the USPD to join the government, the two nonsocialist coalition parties requested the simultaneous entrance of the DVP.[102] Now the SPD found itself in an uncomfortable position. The USPD's new-found willingness to cooperate with nonsocialists did not extend so far as to include the DVP. At a time when the nonsocialist parties were voting down the proletarian program for the defense of the republic in the Reichstag,[103] it would have been most awkward for the SPD to consent to the DVP's entrance into the government. Hermann Müller assured the USPD that the SPD would not consider a widening of the government to the right. But Müller and Adolf Braun advised labor leader Theodor Leipart not to try to force acceptance of the proletarian program by means of a general strike.[104] Müller also told the SPD fraction that refusal to compromise would force dissolution of the Reichstag and new elections. He feared that this would result in internal disunity ("Mexican conditions") and in the formation of a new government too weak to be able to negotiate abroad.[105] Concerned about a substantial loss in electoral strength, the USPD fraction also wished to avoid new elections. On 14 July the two socialist parties simply announced the formation of a joint parliamentary group (*Arbeitsgemeinschaft*) to facilitate closer cooperation,[106] which did not disrupt the equilibrium of the fragile coalition government.

The government had proposed a Law for the Protection of the Republic, a weaker bill than the proletarian program. Because the government bill entailed modifications of the rights of free speech and free assembly guaranteed in the constitution, a two-thirds majority in the Reichstag was required for passage. The government thus needed the support not only of the USPD but also of the Bavarian People's party and, to be safe, at least part of the DVP. Genuinely shocked by the Rathenau assassination and willing to go a bit further in his commitment to the republic,[107] DVP leader Stresemann mustered a majority of his delegation after the Reichstag weakened the bill. On 18 July the USPD fraction voted its approval of the Law for the Protection of the Republic by a 40 to 17 margin, and it agreed to postpone consideration of its entrance into the government until the fall. The government could now avoid issuing an invitation to the DVP, and the immediate crisis was over. The Law for the Protection of the Republic passed the Reichstag by more than the needed two-thirds margin on 18 July, and a modified version of a bill regulating the conduct of civil servants was approved somewhat later.[108]

The new law gave the Reich and state governments substantial authority to act against subversive organizations. But the SPD originally wanted an effective weapon against monarchist or antirepublican influences in state and society; what it got instead was a law to preserve order.[109] Both the way in which the law was constructed and the way in which it was interpreted prevented broad application against all enemies of the republic. One was not permitted to advocate or attempt the overthrow of the parliamentary-republican form of government by force, to use insulting language to describe it or members of the government. Yet one could legally advocate a change in the system of government through constitutional means. The republic had to put up with an openly monarchist party such as the DNVP.

The Reich government still could not enforce its laws over Bavarian resistance, so it was compelled to compromise again.[110] Despite their unhappiness with the situation, SPD officials recognized that the use of force against Bavaria was infeasible, as Bavarian nationalist military associations were too strong.[111] Moreover, the Reich coalition was too fragile to risk a test of strength with Bavaria. Under these circumstances, President Ebert found it advisable to press for a peaceful solution with Bavaria, even though it meant that the Law for the Protection of the Republic would not be fully enforced there.[112] But the settlement of this dispute in no way eliminated Bavarian complaints about the Reich government and its authority, as the events of 1923 would demonstrate.

The SPD leaders consistently showed their willingness to cooperate with the nonsocialist parties during 1920–22 in the interest of stabilizing the republic and promoting a foreign policy of fulfillment. Neither of these major goals of the Social Democratic movement, Karl Kautsky emphasized, could be reached by the proletariat alone.[113] The question was whether the other coalition parties were willing to make hard and often unpopular economic decisions and to strengthen the political system against violent attack. The specter of proletarian unity, the danger of massive strikes and demonstrations, and the fear of how their middle-class constituents would react made the DDP, Center, and DVP leery of close contact with the SPD. The mere existence of a Great Coalition, reassuring as it would have been, could not have strengthened Weimar's foundation unless the various parties also could have agreed on a program that would counteract the economic and social forces pushing their constituents in different directions.

6. The Crises of 1923

THE Weimar Republic came perilously close to extinction in 1923. Reparation disputes with France intensified the nationalistic climate that had prevailed since the Treaty of Versailles, weakening further the position of the republican parties. Moreover, catastrophic inflation alienated millions of suffering German voters of all classes from the political system. With the parties unable to agree upon economic remedies, the government had to resort to the presidential emergency powers and to special enabling laws to meet the economic crisis. Even so, the hyperinflation continued to accelerate until a new currency was introduced in November. One of the results was a serious erosion of parliamentary authority.

The French and Belgian occupation of the Ruhr, a reaction to the breakdown of the reparations system, provoked a vigorous but ill-conceived German response. In addition to wrecking the budget, the German government's campaign of passive resistance in the Ruhr brought the army and right-wing paramilitary organizations into closer contact, as both prepared for the possibility of war. Some antirepublican activists sought to exploit the charged atmosphere in order to establish a dictatorship, with or without the support of the military. Hitler's Beer Hall Putsch was only one of a number of schemes devised during this period to overthrow the parliamentary republic. Although it refrained from right-wing adventures, the German army was able to expand its own authority during the state of emergency, which again posed a threat to the parliamentary system.

The SPD elite was torn between its concern for the survival of the republic and its fears about the health of the Social Democratic movement. The loss of parliamentary authority made the Reichstag fraction leery of participating in coalition government, except when there seemed to be no other way to preserve the republic. The hardships of inflation, the weakening of social reforms, the rise of left-wing sentiment within party institutions, and the growth of mass support for the Communist movement all induced SPD leaders to take a more reserved attitude toward cooperation with nonsocialist parties during 1923.

The SPD's swing to the left began in the fall of 1922. The reunification of the SPD with the remnants of the USPD forced party leaders to take greater account of left-wing sentiments against coalition government. The two organizations each ratified the merger separately, but at the same time, 122 delegates at the final USPD congress (out of a total of 192) signed a resolution sponsored by Robert Dissmann, one of the leaders of the metalworkers' union, which blamed the SPD's policy of coalition with nonsocialists for the lack of socialist achievements.[1] USPD Cochairman Artur Crispien denounced as an illusion the view that political cooperation between socialists and non-socialists could harmonize relations between opposed classes.[2] The organizational terms of the merger strongly favored the SPD,[3] but the political effect was to strengthen the left-wing opposition to the SPD leaders. According to one tabulation, more than two-thirds of the seventy USPD deputies soon aligned themselves with the left wing of the united party.[4] For the first time there was a substantial possibility that the left might gain a majority in the SPD fraction.[5]

Although the SPD congress ratified a resolution stressing the importance of holding onto positions of power in government in order to defend the republic,[6] Hermann Müller warned the other parties that the SPD was not unconditionally in favor of coalition government. Yet he said little about what constructive political role the SPD might play in opposition. Müller viewed withdrawal from the government simply as a way to limit the alienation of the rank and file and to rebuild the party's strength.[7] Reversion to the long Social Democratic tradition of opposition still had a powerful appeal, partly because of the lack of positive results from coalition government, partly because political separation seemed to correspond to the sharp class divisions still pervasive in German society.

Müller optimistically forecast a major increase in working-class political influence as a result of the merger, but there was at least some concern as well that the nonsocialist parties might form a counteralliance.[8] Prominent Independent Socialists such as Rudolf Hilferding, Rudolf Breitscheid, and Wilhelm Dittmann added distinction and political talent to the higher ranks of the SPD, which had limited quantities of both. On the other hand, the most persuasive spokesmen for the left-wing opposition—Robert Dissmann, Siegfried Aufhäuser, Toni Sender, Heinrich Ströbel, and Kurt Rosenfeld—all came to the reunified party (known for a brief period as the VSPD) by way of the USPD. Among the leaders of the newly emergent left, only the Saxon journalist Max Seydewitz had been with the SPD throughout.[9] The merger thus gave the adherents of traditional socialist principles—primacy of the class struggle, the political strategy of fundamental opposition—the opportunity to recruit support for their views within the SPD organization. When Toni Sender argued that participation in past coalition governments had not hindered the development of fascism, when she urged the SPD to abjure responsibility for political developments, she struck at the essence of the political strategy that the SPD leaders had promoted since November 1918.[10]

In view of the new balance of forces within the reunified party, the SPD leaders were forced to put greater pressure upon Chancellor Wirth to come up with an effective economic program, although they stressed that they had no desire to overthrow Wirth's government.[11] Knowingly or unknowingly operating under a false premise, Wirth replied that no antiinflationary policy could be successful until Germany had reversed her negative balance of trade, improved the mark's rate of exchange, and lowered the cost of its imports (and reparations payments). Wirth perceived the key to the solution in aid from abroad, not in new German efforts. The chancellor hoped for a massive foreign loan to help support the mark and for a longer-term moratorium upon reparations payments in cash, and perhaps also upon payments in commodities. Wirth ignored contrary advice from a committee of international economic experts (including John Maynard Keynes) that the German government itself had summoned.[12]

Wirth's major initiative was not economic but rather political. In order to demonstrate to potential foreign creditors the stability of his government (and perhaps also to make a show of solidarity against further reparations payments), Wirth proposed to expand the coalition to include representatives of all political and economic forces whose cooperation was regarded as necessary for economic reconstruction.[13] This was an obvious attempt to bring more representatives of industry into the cabinet, whether or not the DVP formally joined the coalition. Hermann Müller made it clear, however, that the SPD's attitude toward such a step would depend on the government's program: "The attempt to save the situation through our own strength must be made."[14] *Vorwärts* warned the chancellor that a government which rejected the SPD's antiinflation program and which tampered with the legal restriction on the length of the workday would force the SPD into opposition.[15] The other ministers showed little interest in the tough measures suggested by the SPD: compulsory collection of foreign exchange from business, ban of currency speculation, acceleration of tax collection. By early November Hilferding, Breitscheid, Wels, and Müller were discussing with nonsocialist politicians alterations in the government to make it more effective. DVP leaders seemed intent on forcing the chancellor himself to resign.[16]

A number of leading industrialists urged the government to abandon the demobilization ordinance, which had established the eight-hour workday, in order to allow industry to expand production. Hugo Stinnes expressed this view most forcefully in a speech to a subcommittee of the National Economic Council on 9 November, calling for the implementation of a ten-hour day without payment for overtime, and a ban on strikes in essential industries.[17] The SPD and the socialist unions were willing to negotiate specific exceptions to the eight-hour day, but they insisted it be maintained in principle.[18] The Stinnes proposal, coming soon after a similar one made by August Thyssen, was a power play by heavy industry against the government and against its gestures at fulfillment of reparations obligations.[19] On 10 November the DDP published its economic program, which included the determination of the length of the workday by free agreement, rather than by law, and the elimination of government economic controls. The DDP wanted Economics Minister Schmidt to resign, suggesting Hans von Raumer (DVP), an industrial executive, as his replacement. Finally, the DDP called upon Wirth to appoint Gustav Stresemann, leader of the DVP, to the cabinet.[20]

The chancellor had originally intended to add to his cabinet men with a background in business and finance. He had not committed himself to the inclusion of the DVP in the coalition. But the DVP informed Wirth that it regarded the mere appointment of business "personalities" as insufficient, and leaders of both the DDP and the Center urged Wirth to accept the Great Coalition.[21] Pressed into a corner, Wirth sent one of his state secretaries to the SPD fraction on 13 November with the message that the three parties had demanded the inclusion of the DVP. If the SPD rejected this course, Wirth said, then the government would resign.

Fraction cochairman Hermann Müller, relaying this ultimatum to the SPD deputies, repeated Wirth's view that influential circles abroad wanted all important economic interests represented in the government. Müller himself appeared to be deeply disillusioned with the DVP and recommended that the fraction reject the ultimatum. Breitscheid objected to Gustav Hoch's suggestion that the party force new elections, because this step might have provoked a fascist coup. On the following day the SPD fraction voted not to join the Great Coalition by a 150–20 margin.[22] Wirth was then forced to resign.

Friedrich Stampfer later claimed that the desire not to endanger the fragile union of the two socialist parties was a major consideration in this SPD decision.[23] Two scholars have discovered recently that President Ebert also had a role in ousting the Wirth government.[24] Ebert did not wish to push the SPD out of the government, but he was convinced that a different chancellor could handle currency and reparations issues better than Wirth, with whom Ebert had quarreled over foreign policy. Knowing how the SPD might react to a Great Coalition, Ebert pressed for it anyway, recognizing that Wirth might become a casualty. The SPD could always enter a new government later, or so the SPD leaders believed.[25]

When the Center party shunned further initiative, Ebert authorized Wilhelm Cuno, an executive of the Hamburg-America shipping line, to form a government. The SPD leaders had no personal objections to Cuno, a Catholic who was without political affiliation. But Hermann Müller told the chancellor-designate that the Great Coalition remained out of the question.[26] Unwilling to bring in the DNVP, unable to get the support of the SPD, Cuno turned to a new device, a cabinet above parties, i.e., one in which the parties were not expressly represented. The need for this so-called nonpartisan solution drama-tized the fact that the German parties hesitated to take political responsibility in order to avoid problems with their constituents. Party representatives could tell their supporters that they were not responsible for the actions of the government, even though one or two members of the party might hold cabinet posts.

Instead of granting Cuno a vote of confidence, the Reichstag merely took notice of the government's program—this much both the SPD and the DNVP were willing to do. The impending crisis with France over reparations made it necessary to establish a government capable of negotiating. For this reason the SPD exercised restraint. Another important factor for the SPD was its concern that the Great Coalition government in Prussia might collapse if the SPD disavowed Cuno.[27] Without SPD control of the key Prussian Ministry of the Interior, the republic would have been even more vulnerable to an attack by counterrevolutionary forces. But the weakness of the new Reich govern-ment led to further speculation against the mark and to anticipatory price increases by industry. Even before the Ruhr crisis, Germany's hyperinflation had begun.

Ruhr Invasion and Hyperinflation

The Franco-Belgian decision to take sanctions against Germany for its failure to meet reparations obligations soon led to a full-scale military occupation of the Ruhr. Foreign troops severed Germany's most important industrial district from the rest of the country. The storm of outrage in Germany against this punishment induced the Cuno government to refuse all cooperation with the occupiers, who retaliated by taking what they wanted. Meanwhile, the Ger-man government assumed the costs of passive resistance—subsidies to in-dustry, unions, newspapers, political parties, state and local governments— while there was little effort to raise new taxes.[28]

The government found it easier to adopt the policies of passive resistance and unlimited use of the printing press than to abandon them, despite their consequences. The shutdown of the Ruhr led not only to acts of sabotage directed against the French but to economic, social, and political turmoil within Germany. An index of the cost of food prices (July 1922 equals 100) rose from 804 in November to 5,120 in April; 6,758 in May; and 13,673 in June.[29] Millions of Germans helplessly watched the virtual destruction of savings, debts, and fixed incomes. Delayed tax payments on the wealth, income, and corporation taxes became worthless to the government, while payroll taxes from wages and salaries assumed almost all the burden of what tax revenue there was. Of course, the inflation itself was a form of governmental taxation.[30] Despite the ability of the unions to renegotiate wages frequently, and ultimately, to win contracts basing wages on the dollar rate, taxes deducted from paychecks and the lag in time between payday and shopping day cut badly into the worker's income.[31]

Social Democratic leaders thought that it was out of the question for a working-class party to call for an early end to passive resistance, thereby violating the united front of national solidarity against the French and exposing the SPD to renewed accusations of lack of patriotism. Instead, the SPD was forced to seek constant adjustments in the tow of a runaway economy without a driver at the controls. But, suffering from inflation, unemployment, and political uncertainty, many rank-and-file Social Democrats grew impatient with the party leadership's passivity. In the face of economic and foreign-policy disaster, the SPD was widely perceived as the "fifth wheel" on the government's cart, Rudolf Breitscheid complained.[32]

The problem was that alternatives to toleration of the Cuno government merely increased the dissidence within the SPD. A group on the right that included Prussian Interior Minister Carl Severing, Frankfurt University professor Hugo Sinzheimer, and *Rheinische Zeitung* Editor Wilhelm Sollmann believed that only the Great Coalition could solve the economic-diplomatic crisis.[33] Sinzheimer wrote to Sollmann: "The overthrow of the government is without purpose if . . . a new government with a strong program is not formed. . . . Naturally, only the Great Coalition is worthy of consideration . . . [even though] a stormy path lies ahead of us." Sinzheimer recommended that Hilferding, Adolf Köster, and Gustav Radbruch from the SPD, and Siegfried von Kardorff and Stresemann from the DVP join a durable government that would call upon the public to make real sacrifices, ending the reparations and Ruhr crises.[34]

At the end of July some thirty left-wing deputies held a special conference in Weimar, concluding that the SPD must try to overthrow Cuno but then remain in opposition and seek closer relations with the KPD. The two parties would push the course of extraparliamentary action. When a three-man delegation tried to present the conference's resolution to the SPD executive committee, the latter refused to give them a hearing, hinting that such factionalism could cause another party schism.[35] The left wing then published its demands and carried its arguments into the SPD fraction. In early August Toni Sender presented a resolution expressing lack of confidence in the Cuno government and calling for a sharp turn to the left: "The government as well as the nonsocialist parties have demonstrated that they were neither capable nor willing to take prompt action and to demand a sacrifice from the propertied, which could have prevented the complete collapse of our economy and finances. Therefore, the fraction rejects the Great Coalition. [It is] the highest duty of the hour for the United Social Democratic party to summon together all proletarian forces in a decisive struggle against the bourgeoisie in order to increase the power of the proletariat, and to use this social power to achieve its own demands."[36] However, the fraction majority lined up behind a long resolution drafted by Paul Hertz, another former Independent Socialist, which denounced the inflation, the sabotage campaign against the French in the Ruhr, the ties between the Reichswehr and nationalist organizations, and the government's lack of activity on all fronts.[37] The Hertz resolution called for heavier taxation of property and warned that the SPD's attitude toward Cuno's government would be determined by his response.

When the Communists introduced a motion of no confidence against the Cuno government, the SPD was forced to come to an immediate decision. On 11 August the SPD fraction issued an appeal for a new government on the broadest possible basis, which was followed two days later by an 83–39 vote in the fraction in favor of a Great Coalition. Although the SPD did not get everything it had asked for, the fraction grudgingly agreed to join the government headed by DVP leader Gustav Stresemann.[38] On 13 August some forty-odd leftist deputies issued a statement proclaiming their continued opposition to the Great Coalition but pledging to avoid a party schism. At the vote of confidence for the new government the next day, forty-five SPD deputies were absent, a gesture of strong disagreement, even if it was not a violation of fraction discipline.[39]

Otto Wels emphasized to Chancellor Stresemann and representatives of the other parties that the SPD supported the political system but insisted upon effective leadership: "His [Wels's] party only supports the Stresemann cabinet, because it is the last cabinet possible on a constitutional basis. Social Democracy is also prepared to defend the republic by means of armed force against Bolshevist-worker unrest under some circumstances. It must demand, however, that everything be done to maintain the interests of the state against the leaders of the economy."[40] Lasting SPD participation in a broad-based government hinged on the government's success in halting inflation, calming popular unrest, and meeting the threat of counterrevolution. If the coalition government did not pursue these objectives forcefully, the SPD opposition could only gain further support for its negative attitude toward the principle of interparty and interclass cooperation.

Within seven weeks, the DVP fraction demanded the lengthening of the workday. Stresemann, Labor Minister Heinrich Brauns (Center), and Food Minister Hans Luther (unaffiliated) all agreed that such a move was economically desirable.[41] Stresemann proclaimed his intention of requesting an Enabling Law from the Reichstag that would give the government the power to issue economic ordinances.[42] The SPD fraction reacted with consternation at what appeared to be a rude challenge from heavy industry and the DVP.[43] At cabinet meetings in early October, Interior Minister Wilhelm Sollmann complained that the workers were being asked to make the main sacrifices, and Reconstruction Minister Schmidt argued that the eight-hour day was the only material benefit that the workers had left from the revolution.[44]

The SPD ministers convinced their fraction to support the proposed Enabling Law as long as it could not be used to alter the length of the workday. In addition, Schmidt suggested that the government introduce a separate bill that would maintain the eight-hour day in principle but allow for exemptions under specified conditions. He warned that this was the limit of the SPD's concessions.[45]

Declining at first to defy his own party for a compromise with very uncertain prospects, Stresemann instead tendered his resignation to President Ebert. When he was quickly reappointed, he tried unsuccessfully to persuade the DNVP to support (without actually participating in) a government without the SPD. The SPD leaders then refused point-blank to support a minority government of the three middle parties.[46] Stresemann was forced to accept a solution along the lines of Schmidt's suggestion, telling a colleague that this really represented greater concessions by the SPD than he had expected.[47] Finance Minister Hilferding bowed to the wishes of Stresemann and the DVP and submitted his resignation, following the example of Economics Minister Raumer.[48]

Hermann Müller had persuaded the majority of the SPD fraction that the alternatives to the Great Coalition were even worse. A dissolution of the Reichstag at that moment bore the risk of disintegration of the Reich itself. Müller also argued that the workers would suffer more at the hands of a government in which the SPD was not included. The Enabling Law did represent a short period of "dictatorship," i.e., government without parliamentary participation. Unless the government acted quickly, however, he said, there was a danger of a real dictatorship. The SPD's participation in the government offered some assurance that civil war could be prevented; the Great Coalition became the antidote for further outbreaks of violence.[49] But twelve left-wing SPD deputies walked out of the Reichstag before the vote on the Enabling Law, and another thirty-one issued a statement explaining that they had submitted to the fraction's decision under protest. They called for the next party congress to make a conclusive decision.[50]

The Enabling Law squeaked by, despite an apparently lopsided 316–24 margin in favor. If all deputies had been present, 306 votes would have been required for passage. But since enough absences would have defeated the bill, most of those who were opposed simply did not show up for the vote. Two days before the vote Rudolf Breitscheid had presented Social Democracy's rationale for supporting the measure, and he echoed Hermann Müller's line of argument succinctly: "If we have to choose between the dictatorship of the sword and that of a parliamentary cabinet, we certainly prefer the latter."[51] This remark was an indication of the SPD's concern not only about the nationalist paramilitary associations, but also about the stance of the Reichswehr itself.

Danger of a Coup—Preventive Measures

At the time of the Kapp Putsch in 1920 the Reichswehr had vacillated in its loyalty, and nothing that occurred during the next two years made the military seem more reliable. In 1922 Otto Braun and Carl Severing had complained to President Ebert about the Reichswehr's symptomatic practice of using decorations with monarchist insignia.[52] Unable to bring about a change in the attitude and composition of the officer corps, Social Democrats in the Reich and Prussian governments tried at least to restrict the activities of the rightist paramilitary organizations, whose size and equipment were formidable.

The Prussian government kept an eye upon Adolf Hitler even during the early Bavarian phase of the Nazi party's existence. A secret intelligence report sent to Prussian Interior Minister Severing in October 1922 described Hitler as the new-found savior of nationalist circles. A Prussian police agent presented a detailed description of Hitler's appearance, mannerisms, and personality, concluding laconically: "He is very temperamental."[53] Clearly Hitler had not yet established a national reputation. The Nazi movement was only one of the many nationalist and anti-Semitic organizations hostile to the Weimar Republic. By the next month, however, the Prussian government found Nazi disregard for state authority to be serious enough to justify preventive measures. Prussian Interior Minister Severing invoked the Law for the Protection of the Republic to ban the party throughout the state.[54] But the Bavarian government was so closely linked to the many "patriotic" paramilitary organizations that it was generally unwilling to act even against the Nazi extremists.[55] And Prussia could not act outside its own borders.

From mid-1922 on, trade-union officials and local SPD organizations in Bavaria issued alarming reports about the danger of a rightist coup there. With the Reichswehr expected to abstain from action against the right, the superior strength of the nationalist associations and the sympathy that they enjoyed among the Bavarian police seemed to guarantee the outcome. One union official made a gloomy forecast: "If the Reichswehr fails, the working class is done for." Local party and union bodies drew up some sketchy plans for responding to a coup, forming security detachments that could be activated in time of danger.[56] Yet the Bavarian Social Democrats felt that any sustained preparations by working-class organizations to fight a coup would be insufficient at best; at worst, SPD paramilitary activity would provoke the Bavarian police to intervene against the left.[57]

Nor was Bavaria the only area in which developments appeared ominous. ADGB leader Theodor Leipart told Prussian Minister President Braun in October 1922 that some 80,000 nationalists were arming in the state of Thuringia with the assistance of the Reichswehr, intending to overthrow the republic. Braun responded pessimistically: "Conditions in the Reichswehr appear very suspicious to me also, but as things now stand in the Reich, I don't believe that a change will take place soon."[58] Another instance of the Reichswehr's collaboration with right-wing extremists came to light when police in Altona raided the office of a Reichswehr liaison man, threatening him with arrest. They uncovered documents indicating that the nationalist volunteers were being prepared to suppress internal unrest, and that the Reichswehr was spying on local SPD and union officials. The Reichswehr commander in the area, a Major Helfritz, seems to have acted on his own initiative rather than on orders from above, but the information was disquieting nonetheless.[59]

The man who tried to reconcile the military's demand for stepped-up preparations against foreign enemies with the SPD's demand for isolation of right-wing antirepublican forces was Carl Severing. His background in union and government negotiations undoubtedly gave him a certain amount of experience for this new task, but he was not really suited for a situation in which his opponents failed to recognize the validity of his goals. Nor did he enjoy sharp personal conflict; he looked for an easier route. Instead of challenging the army directly, Severing attempted to reach a compromise with Defense Minister Gessler and then to hold him to its provisions.

Severing and Gessler signed an agreement on 30 January 1923 pledging cooperation between military and civilian administrative officials on matters of national defense. To avoid undesirable publicity (about German treaty violations), specific arrangements between regional army commands and provincial governors were to be made verbally. Meanwhile, the Reichswehr was supposed to reduce its support for private paramilitary forces, with a view toward termination by the end of March.[60] According to Severing's state secretary, Wilhelm Abegg, Severing himself wrote out the text of this agreement, which in Abegg's view gave the military too much leeway.[61] But that was not the only problem. Defense Minister Gessler's assent carried little weight with General Hans von Seeckt, who thought that the nationalist associations might prove useful in case war with France or Poland broke out. Moreover, local Reichswehr officials did not take injunctions against cooperation with extremists too seriously.[62]

Severing continued to complain to Gessler about contacts between the Reichswehr and the far right as well as about illegal supplies of arms.[63] But even a more specific set of guidelines on Prussian-Reichswehr cooperation issued at the end of June failed to resolve Severing's grievances. Disputes over these issues flared up sporadically throughout the 1920s.[64] Ultimately, Minister President Braun felt compelled to terminate Prussia's cooperation with the military regarding border defense because of his dissatisfaction with military compliance.[65]

Severing's attempts to work out mutually agreeable terms with the military in 1923 demonstrated that some Social Democrats shared some of the nationalist indignation at the French and Belgian occupation of the Ruhr. But other Social Democrats regarded Severing's methods as compromising Prussia and benefiting the reactionary forces, which was also the retrospective judgment of Wilhelm Abegg.[66] Yet a diametrically opposite policy conducted by the SPD-led government of Saxony was even less successful.

Unusual political conditions in Saxony made the regional SPD organization receptive to the idea of a proletarian defense force to meet the threat from the far right. A long governmental stalemate had been broken when a leftist-dominated SPD congress voted to formulate a joint action program with the Saxon Communists, including a provision for the establishment of proletarian "hundreds." This agreement created the prospect of a coalition government between the SPD and the KPD in Saxony. When established SPD politicians refused to work with the KPD, the SPD Landtag fraction elected a relatively unknown candidate, Erich Zeigner, to head the Saxon government in early 1923. Zeigner's cabinet was composed entirely of Social Democrats, but the minority government was dependent upon Communist support in parliament. Rising unemployment, hyperinflation, and sharp disputes between the Zeigner government and the military made the situation in the state all the more delicate.[67]

Outside of Saxony (and Thuringia where similar political conditions prevailed), high SPD officials and SPD ministers in state governments had no desire to cooperate with the Communists. During 1921 and 1922 the KPD had tried to strip the SPD of its working-class following, pursuing the so-called "united front from below." During 1923 the KPD central committee had shown signs of diminishing its attacks against the SPD and focusing on the danger of fascism, although the left Communist faction put up strong resistance to each step toward moderation.[68] Nonetheless, a proletarian defense force under Communist influence would not have strengthened the Weimar Republic, as leading Social Democrats recognized.

In one well-publicized speech in March, Severing derided the KPD leaders, calling them political children.[69] Severing and other SPD officials were concerned that stepped-up Communist agitation, particularly in the Ruhr where the Reich and Prussia could not exert direct authority, would incite the working-class population already angered by the inflation and the French occupation.[70] Severing requested Chancellor Cuno to ban the proletarian hundreds throughout the Reich, but Cuno hesitated because of demands to act similarly against the Bavarian paramilitary groups, action which he found politically impossible.[71] Severing then did what he could alone, banning the hundreds throughout Prussia in 12 May.[72] Of course, this move had no effect upon Saxony, where incidents of mass violence and Minister President Zeigner's repeated denunciations of the Reichswehr were bringing matters to a head. But a crisis in Bavaria momentarily eclipsed the difficulties in Saxony.

Article 48

On 26 September Chancellor Stresemann bowed to the inevitable and called off passive resistance to the French occupation of the Ruhr. Chaotic economic conditions and the danger of separatist movements left him little choice but to go to the bargaining table. The outraged Bavarian government suddenly declared a state of emergency. It then appointed as its commissar with full executive powers Gustav von Kahr, a leading nationalist politician who had close ties with the nationalist paramilitary organizations. His antipathy toward the SPD was notorious.[73]

Stresemann's response was a blend of firmness and conciliation. He requested and received from President Ebert a declaration of emergency (under Article 48) throughout the Reich, thereby superseding the Bavarian emergency ordinance. Stresemann hoped to restrain Kahr and to prevent the right-wing paramilitary associations from expanding their influence outside Bavaria.[74] Social Democrats in Munich quickly sent a three-man delegation to Berlin to warn party and government leaders about the danger of fascism in Bavaria. According to an account written years later by one of the delegates, Finance Minister Hilferding agreed with their assessment, favoring Reich intervention to arrest Adolf Hitler. Interior Minister Sollmann declined to support such a move, because he was more worried about conditions in the Berlin area—a possible coup by nationalist forces.[75]

The Bavarian commissar became a constant irritant to the Reich government. Kahr criticized the Stresemann cabinet as being under Marxist influence. In his own realm he clamped down on the Bavarian branch of the SPD and sent police to occupy the headquarters of the SPD newspaper in Munich.[76] Kahr officially canceled the Law for the Protection of the Republic, and he refused to obey Defense Minister Gessler's order to ban the Nazi newspaper, the *Völkische Beobachter*, for its unseemly attacks against Stresemann and General Seeckt. (Both men were said to have Jewish wives.) The Bavarian commissar went so far as to force the Bavarian division of the Reichswehr to take an oath of obedience to the Bavarian government. Despite all these provocations, Stresemann wanted to avoid forceful action against Bavaria that might threaten his government and further strain the loyalty of the army.[77] He was supported in this stance by Labor Minister Heinrich Brauns (Center), Agriculture Minister Gerhard von Kanitz (unaffiliated), Economics Minister Joseph Koeth, and even President Ebert.[78] Defense Minister Gessler, who had initially ruled out the use of force against Bavaria, increasingly came to agree with the SPD ministers that Bavarian defiance required some sort of punitive action.[79]

Gessler shifted his concern to Saxony, however, after Minister President Zeigner publicly denounced the ties between the Reichswehr and right-wing nationalist organizations.[80] Gessler was extremely sensitive about the so-called "Black Reichswehr," the illegal forces with ties to the army. He feared that the Allied Military Control Commission would respond to Zeigner's exposés by imposing further sanctions against Germany. Moreover, Zeigner's criticism of Gessler gave the clash a personal tinge as well,[81] and Gessler threatened to resign if Zeigner were not restrained.

On 10 October Minister President Zeigner consented to the entry of two Communists into his cabinet and also appointed KPD leader Heinrich Brandler to a high-level position in the chancellery. In accordance with a secret decision in Moscow, the German Communist leaders now tried to insert their people into positions of influence so that they could issue arms to the proletarian hundreds. The outbreak of revolution seemed near.[82] On 13 October General Alfred Müller, the Reichswehr commander in Saxony, banned the proletarian hundreds in the area. Comparing the Dresden police force to robber barons and Chinese bandits, Müller also issued an ordinance placing all state and local police under his authority. On 18 October he demanded that the Saxon government repudiate a speech made by KPD Finance Minister

Paul Böttcher in which the latter had called for an armed uprising by the proletariat.[83] Zeigner responded with more revelations about the Black Reichswehr in Saxony.[84]

By this time Chancellor Stresemann was fed up with Zeigner. Gessler insisted that the Reich intervene immediately against Saxony, and Labor Minister Brauns argued that Saxony was a greater threat than Bavaria. The SPD ministers, who had earlier taken a somewhat naive view of Communist intentions,[85] opposed displacement of the Saxon government as unconstitutional and politically unwise; the Reich could not act against Saxony while tolerating Bavaria's behavior. The Social Democrats also insisted that decision-making authority, transferred under the state of emergency to Gessler, remain with the full cabinet. Robert Schmidt suggested that the cabinet induce Zeigner to resign voluntarily. Otto Meissner, aide to President Ebert, reported that Ebert had already requested Zeigner to resign and authorized the cabinet to increase the pressure.[86]

Ebert's feelings in this matter were apparently mixed. Never sympathetic toward the Communists, he had been acquainted with the KPD leader Brandler before the war when both were involved in the trade unions, and he detested the man. But Ebert was more concerned about Bavaria, and he at first resisted the idea of displacing the Saxon government.[87] An article in *Vorwärts* on 28 October stated that the Reich government had the right to intervene but only to halt Communist activities.[88] Stresemann was not contradicted when he later claimed that the SPD had suggested the arrest of the KPD ministers in Saxony.[89]

After a long discussion in the cabinet on 27 October, Stresemann presented the terms of an ultimatum that he was sending Zeigner: in effect, either Zeigner dissolve his government and form a new one without the KPD, or else a Reich commissar would be given full power in Saxony until a constitutional government could be formed. The SPD ministers did not object to this stance.[90] That evening the SPD leadership sent a formidable delegation to Dresden in order to put pressure on Zeigner, who may already have been contemplating resignation.[91] Hilferding, Sollmann, Dittmann, and Georg Gradnauer apparently succeeded in their objective until news of Stresemann's ultimatum leaked to the press. Under pressure from the SPD Landtag fraction to resist the ultimatum, Zeigner told the SPD delegates that he would have to delay his resignation.[92]

The time limit of Stresemann's ultimatum expired on the evening of 28 October, but Stresemann led the Social Democratic ministers to believe that he would not act before the cabinet could meet the next day. Under the same impression, President Ebert signed the decree authorizing the removal of the Saxon government on the morning of 29 October. That same morning, however, Stresemann appointed his party colleague Dr. Rudolf Heinze as Reich commissar for Saxony. Heinze began to carry out the deposition of the Saxon government almost immediately—even before receiving specific instructions from Stresemann.[93] Army troops cleared the Saxon ministers from their offices while a military band performed outside. The Landtag building was shut down, and Heinze released to the press a list of new cabinet members that he had drawn up.[94]

Social Democratic leaders immediately complained to Stresemann that Saxon workers would regard Heinze as a reactionary. Stresemann allegedly replied in tones of disbelief: "Our good old Heinze?"[95] After a strained conversation with the chancellor, Otto Wels and Wilhelm Dittmann won his approval for their plan to go to Dresden and bring about the formation of a parliamentary government that did not include the KPD. Heinze was instructed to cooperate. After learning that the Saxon Democrats were willing to tolerate a minority SPD government, Wels and Dittmann fought hard to impose this solution upon the SPD Landtag fraction and the SPD state committee. The assertive Wels ultimately got his way. The Landtag fraction approved a new government headed by a more cautious SPD leftist named Fellisch. Wels and Dittmann climbed aboard a 2 a.m. train and headed back to Berlin, expressing their contempt for the Saxon leftists. Dittmann later wrote: "What we had gone through in those last twenty-four hours seemed like a fairy tale to us."[96]

Stresemann had acted quickly, and in certain respects he had calculated neatly with regard to the simultaneous crises in Saxony and Bavaria. By intervening in Saxony first, he had cut the ground out from under his Bavarian critics, who had been trying to portray him as soft on Marxism. The quick return to parliamentary government in Saxony, accomplished through the mediation of the SPD cochairmen, eliminated the possibility of a stormy constitutional confrontation over the use of Article 48. Moreover, Communist plans for an uprising then were canceled, except in Hamburg, where local officials received mistaken information from Saxony. This isolated KPD revolt was easily suppressed by police.[97] The fiasco exposed the miscalculations and backbiting among Communist leaders in Dresden, Berlin, and Moscow.

The balance sheet was not entirely positive, however. Stresemann had only limited control over the actions of Defense Minister Gessler and the military during this crisis, and his problem in this regard soon became even more serious. The Reich's use of Article 48 against a recalcitrant state government put the Reichswehr in a position to dominate events. Precisely this fact made Stresemann's handling of the dispute objectionable to the SPD Reichstag fraction, where a major reconsideration of the party's coalition policy now took place.

At the fraction meeting on 31 October Hermann Müller first analyzed the immediate situation.[98] Müller believed that the Saxon intervention had been unnecessary. The same result could have been achieved through mere pressure on Zeigner. Meanwhile, the nonsocialist ministers in the Reich would not support intervention against Bavaria, which he felt to be an urgent need. The Democrats and the left wing of the Center party were willing to support some lesser form of action against Bavaria, such as blocking payment to the Bavarian division of the Reichswehr as long as it remained disobedient—so much for the immediate prospects of continued coalition government.

If the SPD abandoned the government, Müller continued, then DNVP leaders Hergt and Helfferich were prepared to take positions in it, which might well have serious repercussions on the SPD's ability to maintain its presence in various state coalition governments. On the other hand, Müller did not expect that a rightist government in the Reich could maintain a parliamentary majority for any substantial length of time. If such a government were formed and then collapsed, rightists might try to rule through Article 48 or even to impose changes in the constitution. Alternatively, a minority SPD government might increase separatist agitation, bringing about the breakup of the Reich.

Müller recommended that the SPD remain in the government if certain stipulations were met. In particular, the military state of emergency had to be lifted, the government had to take steps to enforce the constitution against Bavaria, and right-wing radicals had to be removed from the Reichswehr. Müller's position was consistent with the view expressed in *Vorwärts* that the state of emergency had robbed the coalition government of all meaning, since the chancellor and the defense minister were not even required to inform the cabinet of their decisions.[99] If participation in government failed to give the SPD leverage over the government's most important policies, it served no purpose and actually damaged the party politically.

Paul Löbe stated outspokenly that the SPD could no longer fight for the republic because the masses no longer saw it as worthy of defense. Capitalists, the military, and "usurers" were allegedly just as strong as they had been under the monarchy. Löbe then offered the traditional socialist prescription: "Back to the pure class struggle." His judgment was that the parliamentary system could no longer provide the basis for compromise among the present parties.

Carl Severing, Rudolf Wissell, and Eduard David from the right, and Wilhelm Dittmann and Rudolf Breitscheid from the center attacked Löbe's views. Severing disputed the comparison of Weimar and the Second Reich, David noted the prospects for reparations negotiations involving the United States as a participant, and Wissell argued that the SPD had to try to preserve the republic, which meant staying in the government. Dittmann believed that the party should maintain the positions it had won until the end.

The centrist group headed by Müller essentially got its way—a large majority approved the stipulations for continued SPD participation. That same evening the text was communicated to the Chancellery by telephone.[100] In his statement to the cabinet on 1 November, Robert Schmidt placed primary emphasis on the need to lift the state of emergency, which, in the SPD's view, was responsible for the crisis in the first place. Stresemann responded, however, that the government could not accept an ultimatum from any party. Defense Minister Gessler laid down the gauntlet with the remark that if the SPD left the government, the Bavarian crisis could be solved easily by way of peaceful agreement.[101] Gessler may have been influenced by General Seeckt, who had expressed this view on the same day, and who was under pressure from rightist elements to become head of a new government.[102]

Over Stresemann's resistance, the other ministers concluded that further efforts to reach a compromise with the SPD would only be counterproductive. This intransigence created a problem for Stresemann, who now rejected the idea of a coalition that included the DNVP. At the final conference with the SPD ministers, Schmidt again indicated that a compromise might still be reached, but there were no takers.[103] The normally reserved Schmidt wept as he spoke of the years he was imprisoned (during the Second Reich) for pursuing his party's political goals.[104] Now all the progress seemed endangered. With nineteen deputies dissenting, the SPD fraction voted to withdraw from the Great Coalition on 2 November.[105]

Since there was no clear combination that would command a majority in parliament, the rump cabinet continued in existence for a few weeks. Ebert discouraged General Seeckt from trying to form a government and held to Stresemann while other candidates were being considered.[106] Ironically, the most pressing problems were disposed of during precisely that period. There was further progress toward a reparations settlement and French evacuation of the Ruhr, and the new currency, the Rentenmark, was introduced on 15 November. The KPD withdrew from the coalition government in the state of Thuringia, eliminating the tension there. Most fortuitous, however, was the turn of events in Bavaria. Hitler's "Beer Hall Putsch" was poorly planned, but the government in Berlin held limited resources. If the Bavarian government had joined the Nazis, the Reich would have faced civil war.

On the night of 8–9 November 1923 Prussian Interior Minister Severing (SPD) was summoned to the Reich Chancellery around midnight. There a number of cabinet members were discussing with General Seeckt the possibility that Hitler, if he triumphed in Munich, might lead a march on Berlin.

Severing asked the general how the Reichswehr would react in such an eventuality. Seeckt answered that the Reichswehr would not fire upon the Bavarian division of the Reichswehr, whose commander had cast his support to Commissar Kahr. (The initial reports received in Berlin were that Hitler and Kahr had joined forces. Only later did it become clear that Kahr had repudiated the Putsch after he had gotten out from under gunpoint.) Angered by Seeckt's reply, Severing then turned to President Ebert and snapped, "Under these circumstances I have nothing more to look for here." He walked out and immediately mobilized the Prussian police against a possible attack on Berlin. When the other participants left the Chancellery, they had to pass through a police guardpost.[107] The next day the Prussian cabinet issued the following appeal to the citizenry: "The unity of the Reich and its constitution are threatened. . . . Prussia was always famed as the strongest pillar of the Reich. The Prussian government today also stands unconditionally behind the national government in the struggle that has been forced upon it. Citizens! Stand united behind your government, and by doing so, help maintain the unity of the Reich."[108]

Fortunately for the republic, the Bavarian government broke with Hitler on 9 November, and the Bavarian police fired on the Nazi column on Munich's Odeonsplatz, dispersing the Nazi troops and ending the danger of a Nazi takeover of Bavaria. Hitler's move also forced Commissar Kahr and the Bavarian government to back away from their uncompromising stance against the Reich.[109] Of course, Bavaria was more inclined to negotiate with a Reich government in which the SPD was not included.

On 23 November the rump Stresemann government lost a vote of confidence in the Reichstag by a 231–156 margin,[110] which prompted President Ebert to lecture the SPD leaders: "The reasons why you have felled the chancellor will be forgotten in six weeks, but you will feel the effects of your stupidity for the next ten years."[111] The party's prime objective was to end the military state of emergency, but party leaders might have done better to back Stresemann, whose own relationship with General Seeckt was strained. A less decisive chancellor was unlikely to exert substantial pressure on the military.

President Ebert tried repeatedly to get the military to agree to lift the emergency powers, at least in Prussia. Friction between army officers and Prussian administrative officials had become a serious problem. However, General Seeckt firmly opposed Ebert's suggestions, and relations between the two men soured. Seeckt wanted to retain his authority under the state of emergency in order to combat communism, labor disputes, and economic profiteering. He was not willing to see the emergency powers transferred to a civilian.[112]

The army was heavily involved in the political arena. Various officers made it clear that their methods for restoring order and economic stability were tilted to the right. General Friedrich von Lossberg complained that the Prussian administration was effectively controlled by leftists, often union functionaries who allegedly had no qualifications for government work, and who exploited their authority to assist the leftist parties. Lossberg called upon Seeckt and his aide, Major Kurt von Schleicher, to purge the administration, regardless of the reaction of the unions and "their" government representatives.[113] Shortly afterwards Schleicher analyzed the military's objectives and opportunities before his colleagues.[114] He claimed that strengthened state authority in the hands of the Reich, repair of the economy, and restoration of Germany's capacity to wage war were all necessary preconditions for a successful foreign policy. Schleicher argued that these goals could be attained only if the Reich government and the various state interior ministries were occupied by energetic patriots. Complaining that the SPD still controlled the state bureaucracies, Schleicher emphasized the Prussian case, which he called deplorable, but he still hoped for a new coalition in Prussia from which the SPD would be excluded.[115]

Schleicher also left little doubt about the Reichswehr's willingness to throw its weight around to obtain its objectives. If the Reich government that succeeded Stresemann's refused to support expansion of the military, it was finished before it started. If the Reichstag were dissolved and new elections called, army officers could use their authority under the state of emergency to delay the elections for several months on the ground that the campaign would disturb public order. During this period the government would be free from "interference."[116]

High army officials were not eager for a military dictatorship at this time. General Hasse followed Schleicher's speech with the comment that the army could best pursue its aims through legal channels—they were slower but surer.[117] But the SPD was certainly justified in its concern about the military's role during the state of emergency. Kurt Rosenfeld, a spokesman for the SPD's left wing, used a metaphor that was only a slight exaggeration: "The state of emergency has placed the fate of the German republic in the hands of the Reichswehr—an impossible condition."[118] The SPD's problem was to find a way to alter this situation.

Against the military's assertiveness, the politicans held a weak hand. The new government formed by Wilhelm Marx (Center) was a reshuffled version of Stresemann's rump cabinet, with Stresemann remaining as foreign minister and as a major force in the government. The SPD fraction requested Marx to place authority under the state of emergency in the hands of state governments and to take immediate steps against Kahr in Bavaria.[119] But Marx sided with Seeckt on the first matter, and he was not willing to interfere with the slow consolidation of political conditions in Bavaria. It was not until late February 1924 that Seeckt relinquished his authority under Article 48.

Marx needed the SPD's support for another Enabling Law to act independently of parliament on financial matters, since the old law had expired automatically when the SPD exited from the government. President Ebert threatened to use the emergency powers of Article 48 to enact the bill if the Reichstag defeated it and new elections were called. Marx also asked for a provision permitting him to make exceptions to the eight-hour workday. After obtaining one minor concession, the SPD fraction voted its support for the bill by a 73–53 margin.[120] Some fifty deputies then walked out of the Reichstag rather than submit to the majority's view, and one deputy, Wilhelm Hoffmann, broke party ranks to vote against the bill, which promptly led to his ouster from the party.[121]

It may seem paradoxical that the SPD fraction still felt compelled to go along with the government on a bill bound to be unpopular with its working-class constituents. Yet there were more general issues at stake. The fraction majority found the risks of overturning the Marx government too great: disruption of diplomatic progress on a reparations settlement,[122] interference with the stability of the new currency,[123] possible exclusion of the SPD from the Prussian government. Hermann Müller warned the fraction against the last development: "Prussia and Bavaria would then rule the Reich."[124] Eduard Bernstein wrote that it would bring about "the delivery of the Prussian Ministry of the Interior, today ruled by Karl [sic] Severing and constituting the greatest asset of the republic, to the reactionaries."[125] In short, withdrawal from the government had not allowed the SPD to escape unsatisfactory compromises as long as the foundations of the parliamentary republic were shaky.

Given strong opposition to this course within the fraction and among party functionaries, party leaders put the narrowest possible construction on the vote for the Enabling Law. Hermann Müller told the fraction that its vote should not become or be seen as a vote of confidence in the government. Müller urged those impatient to challenge the government to wait until the masses felt the impact of the decree altering the length of the workday. Meanwhile, he said, the executive committee could begin preparations for the election campaign.[126] Müller's line was intended to reconcile the forces within the party opposed to coalition government.

Both sides within the fraction were somewhat disillusioned at the end of 1923. Many of the supporters of coalition government were distraught with the results of Stresemann's Great Coalition and the irresponsible position of the military during the state of emergency.[127] Although the left wing of the party denounced the coalition policy of the party leadership, revelations about Communist plans for revolution and the KPD's subservience to Moscow diminished the appeal of proletarian solidarity as an alternative political strategy. In late November the SPD executive committee won the near-unanimous support of the party council for a resolution rejecting cooperation with the Communist party at any level of government.[128] This move by no means ended all disputes between the party leadership and the Saxon organization,[129] but by drawing sharper lines of division between the SPD and the parties on its right and left, party leaders were able to create a fragile internal equilibrium.

This solution had serious deficiences. Early 1924 elections were not likely to benefit the SPD. Would the voters forget the SPD's vote on the Enabling Law or its participation in Stresemann's Great Coalition? If there was negative sentiment against the government, the SPD was bound to suffer as well. Could the SPD leaders themselves dissociate the procoalition stance maintained by Otto Braun in Prussia (with general party approval) from the anticoalition direction now taken by the Reichstag fraction? Party leaders assumed that a retreat in the Reich and a period of waiting in opposition would automatically serve the party's interest—at least, in the short run. But ever since 1917 the SPD had committed itself not only to the creation and maintenance of parliamentary democracy but also to the practice of coalition and compromise with nonsocialist parties. It could not now leap quickly to high ground to escape a flood of voter discontent.

It was much too late for the SPD leaders to cast the party in its traditional role from the Second Reich: fundamental opposition. Whether the party could play an active role as a temporary opposition and at the same time guard the foundation of the parliamentary republic remained to be seen. The clear danger, however, was that it might be forced into a passive, ineffective position. Party leaders might have done better to seek greater leverage within the system that they supported as the most favorable foundation for the development of socialism.

7. Toward a Clearer Concept of Democracy–Rudolf Hilferding

TH E short-lived Stresemann cabinets were the only governments in which the SPD participated during a period of more than five years. After its brief service in the late summer and fall of 1923, the SPD remained in opposition until the Reichstag elections of May 1928—precisely the period when the Weimar Republic enjoyed its greatest stability and prosperity. How is one to account for this turnabout in coalition policy when the party's main objectives, a foreign policy of reconciliation and a domestic policy aimed at stabilizing the republic, remained unchanged?[1]

In the first place, the election results seemed to dictate a change in strategy. Just as the voters had inflicted a judgment against the Weimar Coalition in June 1920, so they reacted against the Great Coalition in the elections of May 1924. The SPD, which had hoped to make up a great deal of its 1920 losses, particularly after the reunification with the USPD, actually saw its share of the vote decline from 21.6 percent to 20.5 percent, with many former USPD voters preferring the Communists.[2] The Communist party, now firmly under the thumb of Moscow, rose from 2.1 percent to 12.6 percent, despite its disastrous experiments at revolution. The parties of the middle generally suffered at the hands of the DNVP, which became the second largest party. The National Socialists, even with their leader Adolf Hitler in prison for treason, obtained 6.5 percent and thus outstripped the Democrats, who got only 5.7 percent of the vote. Only the Center party held firm at 13.4 percent.

Within the SPD the left-wing opposition had made some headway. Formerly, party leaders had rebutted leftist arguments against coalition governments with a clarion call to defend democracy in time of crisis. Now that the immediate danger seemed over, this justification had diminished effectiveness. Major party figures themselves took a more reserved view of past coalitions and of opportunities for new coalitions. In response to criticism at the SPD congress in 1924, Hermann Müller observed: ''When we review the coalitions of the past years . . . we have been represented in the government only when we have had to be. The reasons that have forced us into it have almost always been based on foreign policy.''[3] This argument was disingenuous. Although foreign-policy considerations were certainly important, the SPD leaders had developed a broader commitment to the parliamentary republic. Müller's statement reflected the growing defensiveness of the party leadership about coalition policy.

The indefatigable Otto Wels and the cautious and conciliatory Hermann Müller both decided to cut the SPD's risks. Wels, a native Berliner, was the son of a restaurateur who himself had been active in the Social Democratic movement. Wels learned the trade of upholsterer, became an active trade unionist, then advanced up the union and party hierarchies. He obtained a seat in the Reichstag in 1912 and was elected to the SPD executive committee in 1913, where he served as Ebert's ally. Despite his orthodoxy on questions of theory and party strategy, Wels too was considered to be favorable toward those groups on the right wing of the party during the prewar period. He was, above all, an effective agitator and organizer; he concentrated upon the practical day-to-day tasks.

During the war he was greatly concerned about the opposition to the party leadership stirred up by the antiwar minority. When the dissidents founded the USPD, Wels wanted to take the offensive against the new rival. The SPD, however, was severely restricted in its maneuverability by its pledge of support for the political truce and for the war effort. Wels simply did his best to tighten the ranks of the organization, to preserve the party's hold on the masses until more favorable circumstances arose.

The party's last-minute decision to abandon the government in November 1918 represented a kind of release for Wels. Because of his influence and experience in the Berlin district, he became one of those Social Democrats most directly involved in the contest for control of the government and the streets that followed the revolution of 9 November. His engagement as city commandant became perilous when he was taken prisoner by a band of mutinous sailors. The December 1918 incident nearly cost him his life,[4] but he emerged intact and with an enhanced reputation. Always a man loyal to his friends and harsh to his enemies, Wels seems to have been strengthened in this respect by his traumatic experience and by the so-called Spartacist uprising against the government in January 1919. Under Wels's direction, the SPD organization carried on vitriolic exchanges of charges and countercharges with its Independent Socialist and Communist rivals, and Wels also remained very suspicious of the left-wing opposition within the SPD throughout the Weimar period. He wanted a unified cohesive movement based upon the strength of the entire working class. Any group that threatened the unity of the party or competed for working-class support was a mortal enemy.

Wels developed a line of policy different from that of Ebert and others such as Eduard David and Wilhelm Sollmann who had consistently championed Social Democratic participation in coalition governments with nonsocialist parties. Sharing power and demonstrating political responsibility during times of crisis could be done only so often. If the SPD alone was continually expected to make sacrifices, it might lose the support of its working-class constituents to its rivals on the left.

It was not Wels but Hermann Müller who was the actual spokesman of the SPD in the Reichstag. Except during those periods in which Müller served in the government, Wels was primarily concerned with managing the party organization, whereas Müller led the fraction. Since the two men were close both personally and politically, this division of functions worked very neatly until 1928 when Müller became chancellor for the second time, and serious differences between the party and government began to emerge. At that point it became clear that Wels was the more influential of the two within the party itself. Wels had the more assertive and emotional personality. He was the man who could arouse working-class audiences with colorful if not always polished rhetoric. Müller's cautious guidance of the party and the government was often insufficient to forge a consensus.

Müller was not willing to bind the fraction to a policy of fundamental opposition, warning that the republic could not be maintained by demonstrations alone, that the SPD must make it possible for republicans to serve in the republic.[5] But after the elections of May 1924 the SPD fraction showed greater willingness to rely on a stance of benevolent neutrality toward minority governments of the middle as a way out of its political dilemma. Müller argued that mere toleration of a nonsocialist government was justifiable, even unavoidable under some circumstances. Müller and other major figures concluded that many of the same foreign-policy results could be obtained without the political sacrifice and intraparty strife caused by participation in coalition government.

From 1924 to 1928 German politics was marked by frequent coalition changes and fragile parliamentary alignments, which was partly the result of the SPD's abstinence.[6] Numerous opportunities arose for the SPD to play a more active political role, and each set off a new debate within the SPD fraction. In the process the SPD leaders began to develop a clearer justification for participation in coalition government. The prime mover during this period was Rudolf Hilferding, who was not personally typical of the men in the higher circles of the SPD. Indeed, his background and political career are unusual enough to warrant a closer look. He derived most of his substantial influence within the party, not from the authority that he exerted directly, but rather from the esteem in which he was held. Hermann Müller and Otto Wels both relied implicitly upon his intellectual talent and his political judgment.[7] Contemporaries regarded him as without question *the* theorist of the SPD,[8] and even the left-wing opposition found it hard to quarrel with his economic analysis, disagreeing only with the political conclusions drawn from it.

Hilferding was born in 1877 in Vienna into a Jewish merchant family. He attended a Gymnasium in Vienna and then proceeded to study medicine. After practicing as a pediatrician for a few years, during which time he was deeply affected by the miserable conditions in the slum sections of Vienna,[9] Hilferding turned his attention to political economy. Already a member of a socialist federation as a university student, he began to write for the socialist journal *Neue Zeit*, which was edited by Karl Kautsky. In 1904 he published an impressive analysis of Böhm-Bawerk's critique of Marx, which advanced his standing within the Social Democratic movement. He moved to Berlin, where he taught at the SPD's party school and was soon promoted to the editorial board of the central SPD newspaper *Vorwärts*.

Hilferding continued to study under Kautsky and to express admiration for the SPD's revered leader August Bebel, but he displayed a tendency toward independence and even stubbornness that made it hard for him to get along with others.[10] His reputation as a first-rank theoretician was firmly established with the publication of his major work, *Das Finanzkapital*, in 1910.[11] In some respects an adaption of Marx's *Das Kapital* to changed economic conditions, Hilferding's book also contained a number of original theories on the relationship between investment banks and industry, the role of cartels in eliminating competition in industrial production and sales, and the importance of new investment opportunities for imperialism. One of his major achievements was to present a more realistic picture of the active involvement of the state in the modern industrial economy of the late nineteenth century—in the form of protective tariffs, sanction of cartels and trusts, trade agreements with other nations, and the acquisition of colonies. He argued that the state's impulse to grow and to dominate went hand in hand with the subordination of the industrial proletariat. The power state—both the image and the reality—distracted and repressed the political aspirations of the working class at home.

During the war Hilferding began to speculate that this "organized capitalism" might be capable of avoiding economic crisis and providing some kind of stability, even if its potential remained inferior to that of a socialist economy. If this were the case, then the victory of socialism was by no means assured; the outcome depended upon a conscious political choice between two alternative conceptions of the proper economic order.[12] Under these circumstances the specific form of state was of considerable importance for the proletariat. Hilferding had previously mentioned in passing that it was easiest for the working class to present socialism as the alternative to imperialism where its political-democratic demands had already been attained.[13] How the workers were to take control of the state and to exercise power he left unspecified. The only certainty was the necessity of a new and more rational economic order built upon the advances of capitalism, but superseding it.

By way of contrast, Lenin argued that imperialism was a more parasitical form of capitalism that was capable of obstructing technological progress and corrupting segments of the working class with the plunder taken from undeveloped areas and colonies.[14] This argument suited Lenin's purpose very nicely, since it could be taken as justification for a more immediate goal of revolution and for a tightly controlled, elitist revolutionary movement such as the Bolshevik party.

Hilferding was both too fatalistic and too democratic to follow Lenin's path.[15] Yet he fought imperialism in his own way. When the war broke out, he was among the editors of *Vorwärts* who protested against the decision by the SPD fraction to vote in favor of military credits. A stint in the Austrian army as a military doctor removed him from Berlin during the most bitter period of strife and schism within the socialist movement, but he returned to Berlin toward the end of the war and joined the USPD, where he quickly assumed a prominent role on the right wing.

Hilferding was favorably impressed by the workers' council movement and tried to incorporate the institution of the factory council into his vision of a socialist economy. He urged the revolutionary government to move cautiously on the issue of nationalization.[16] Agreeing that prosperity was an essential precondition for socialism, he feared the consequences of hasty state takeover of numerous branches of the economy. Nonetheless, he became upset when the revolutionary government and the first Weimar Coalition government took no significant steps to nationalize industries, even on a selective basis. Both Hilferding's ethical concern and his political judgment led him to conclude that a beginning had to be made.[17] He subsequently fought in vain for some sort of nationalization during his service on the first and second Socialization Commissions.

Although his economic views brought him into conflict with the Social Democratic leaders, Hilferding never went so far as to abandon his belief in the legitimacy of parliamentary democracy or its efficacy as the political foundation for socialism. As editor of the central USPD newspaper *Freiheit*, he quickly made clear his displeasure with some of his more radical colleagues, and he openly rejected the idea of a purely revolutionary government as untenable.[18] When Zinoviev, the Russian leader of the Communist International, came to the USPD Congress at Halle in 1920 to persuade the majority to join the Communist movement, Hilferding delivered a brilliant three-hour rebuttal, which did not prevent the party schism but helped to convince a majority of the USPD Reichstag deputies to reject the merger of the USPD with the United Communist party.[19]

In late 1920 Hilferding astutely analyzed the strategy of the SPD leaders during the revolutionary period. He termed the SPD policy of coalition with liberal parties responsible for its failure to pursue a real proletarian economic policy. The failure to nationalize, in turn, brought about a loss in working-class influence within the parliamentary system, as large industrial concerns exploited their economic leverage, and as the political divisions and strife within the working class increased.

Hilferding admitted that he wanted nationalization only if it would raise production. Nationalization resulting in economic disruption was not desirable. However, he thought productivity would increase greatly when workers and employees realized they were working not for the profits of a narrow group of owners but for the benefit of the entire society. The best way to administer nationalized industries was through "industrial parliaments" that would be composed of representatives of workers, employers, consumers, and of the government.[20]

This 1920 speech turned out to be Hilferding's swan song as a leftist critic of the SPD, and even here his tone was far from polemical, merely tinged with regret. He soon went to work building bridges between the SPD and the USPD. Cooperation with the Communist party was out of the question for him. The issue of nationalization gradually receded in his list of priorities. Foreign policy became an important theoretical and practical concern, particularly the connection between foreign relations and economic development. Hilferding served on the German delegation that negotiated the German-Russian treaty at Rapallo in the spring of 1922. With some exaggeration, Count Harry Kessler wrote in his diary that Hilferding and a Foreign Office official, Baron Ago von Maltzan, were the two originators of the Rapallo Pact, which established a basis for trade and military assistance between Germany and the new Soviet state. The surprise treaty aroused anger and suspicion among British and French diplomats who had been negotiating simultaneously with Germany at Genoa. Kessler added to his diary the comment that Hilferding had looked at the diplomatic situation from a purely theoretical angle and lost sight of both reality and timing.[21]

By late 1922 Hilferding had firmly concluded that the state in a capitalist society could not be viewed merely as the enforcement mechanism for an oppressive economic order but rather as the representative of all the groups and interests in society.[22] He later expressly repudiated Marx's definition of the state as the tool of the ruling class, because there were many differences among the different forms of the state.[23] In the German case, the working class itself had created a parliamentary democracy through the revolution of November 1918, which gave the workers a special attachment to the political order. Although there was a great deal of tension between this democratic state and the huge, privately controlled economic organizations,[24] Hilferding implied that the solution was to reassert the supremacy of the state through political action. If the Social Democratic movement were successful, then the gradual expansion of state control in the interests of the entire society would lead to a state-run socialist economy.

The enthusiastic reception that other Social Democratic leaders gave to Hilferding's line of thought demonstrated how much they had earlier lacked a theoretical framework combining economic analysis and political philosophy. The pragmatists in the party leadership had finally found a capable interpreter. Hilferding's expertise as a political economist helped him to gain influence within the upper circles of the reunified party, where most of the former Independent Socialists were mistrusted. Even his preference for comfortable living—lack of sufficient funds was apparently the cause of strain in his marriage[25]—did not damage his reputation within the party, since he defended the policies of the party leadership with a rhetorical elegance that compared favorably with his lifestyle.

As one of the few SPD figures with the economic expertise to comprehend the inflationary spiral, Hilferding assumed an increasingly prominent role in the SPD fraction during the summer of 1923. With the Cuno government on the verge of collapse, *Vorwärts* published Hilferding's plan to halt inflation, which was based on the immediate conversion of all monetary transactions to a gold scale, new taxes and loans to balance the budget, and support for the mark's exchange value.[26] Shortly afterward, he was selected to be minister of finance in the Great Coalition government headed by Gustav Stresemann. Hilferding's tenure in office was brief and unsuccessful, although it remains unclear to what degree he himself was at fault. At first he pushed strongly for government collection of all foreign exchange in private hands, and for a change in the leadership of the Reichsbank, whose policies were the source of much of the trouble.[27] However, the cabinet's authority to influence the Reichsbank was limited by statute, and Economics Minister Hans von Raumer (DVP) was disinclined to use extensive, compulsory measures to collect foreign exchange.[28] A more basic problem was Hilferding's request that drastic budget cutting take place immediately. This in effect required a cessation of passive resistance against the French in the Ruhr and an end to government credits to the Ruhr.[29] Stresemann was eventually forced to do just that, but he was not willing to be pushed into it until he had exhausted all other diplomatic possibilities and had prepared public opinion. Meanwhile, the mark continued its plunge toward worthlessness.

Hilferding held too long to a discredited paper currency, and raised tech-

nical objections to plans for a substitute currency developed by DNVP economist Karl Helfferich without offering a feasible substitute of his own. It was
his nature to think a problem through completely before he acted, and he
delighted in explaining the difficulties with each specific proposal and the differences among the various plans. Chancellor Stresemann finally went to Prussian Minister President Otto Braun and begged him to convince Hilferding to
make a decision quickly. Braun answered that he could persuade Hilferding
to write a wonderful article, but to expect a quick decision was hopeless.[30]
In early October the DVP forced Hilferding's resignation. Although he had
done much preparatory work of value, his successor Hans Luther actually
ushered in the new currency, known as the *Rentenmark* (and later renamed the
Reichsmark), and received most of the credit. As soon as it became clear that
there would be no more unlimited printing of notes, the new currency won
public confidence.

Despite being forced out of office, Hilferding urged the SPD fraction to
remain in Stresemann's Great Coalition government. He depicted the European political scene in stark tones: democracy and the strength of the working
class were crumbling everywhere; only England and Germany were holding
out. He said that withdrawal from the government would weaken the republic's chance of survival against a rightist putsch.[31] It is also likely that he
supported the SPD fraction's decision to tolerate the government headed
by Wilhelm Marx that replaced Stresemann's Great Coalition. Hilferding
placed great emphasis on Germany's diplomatic requirements in 1924, and
the Marx government made progress in this area. Hilferding regarded the
report that became known as the Dawes Plan as a feasible solution of the
reparations problem and stimulant to economic progress—thus, as an essential
precondition for the success of socialism.[32]

Despite his lack of success as finance minister in 1923, Hilferding continued
to gain influence within the Reichstag fraction and the executive committee of
the party. He delivered the main addresses at the SPD national congresses in
1924, 1925, and 1927—there was no congress in 1926. Weaving together a
great many subjects, his speeches focused on the social and political consequences of economic development and their significance for party strategy.
He tried to defend the policies of the party leadership against those critics who
demanded a fundamental opposition to the existing political order, and at the
same time, to clarify the means through which progress could be achieved
toward the final goal of socialism. The result was regarded as a tour de force
by other party leaders,[33] but it was actually more successful as a theoretical
statement than as a guide to practical politics in the immediate future. The left-
wingers, whom Hilferding dismissed publicly and scorned privately, were in
no way convinced by his recommendations on political strategy.[34]

Hilferding argued that the capitalist system continued to evolve away from the old ideal of free competition and toward a monopolistic (oligopolistic) structure marked by industrial concentration, vertical integration, trusts, and cartels. The independent small businessman lost either his business or his independence. Wealth and economic power were controlled by an increasingly small elite, and the managers and owners of the huge economic enterprises strove to dominate the state itself, whose policies had become essential to their welfare. The organized working class became the only significant force whose political, economic, and cultural interest was identical with that of society as a whole, namely, freedom from selfish domination by the interlocking elite of industrialists, merchants, and bankers. Under these circumstances, it was ludicrous for the socialist left-wingers to charge that the class struggle was being abandoned by the SPD leaders. The logic of events continually forced the movement to carry on the class struggle.[35]

The real question, Hilferding continued, was not the existence of the class struggle itself but rather the connection between the class struggle and the Weimar system. While the left wing spoke contemptuously about bourgeois democracy (*bürgerliche Demokratie*), Hilferding recalled that Rosa Luxemburg herself had insisted that the achievement of socialism was only possible within a democratic framework—in complete contrast to bolshevism. To be sure, the socialist opposition claimed that it was willing to defend the political order by means of the "extraparliamentary struggle," especially against monarchist or fascist counterrevolution. But the actual use of the parliamentary system provided the best possible means for the proletariat's capture of power and implementation of its socialist aims.[36] Hilferding thus agreed with Hermann Müller that the SPD required flexible tactics in order to be an effective force within a multiparty, parliamentary system; coalition with nonsocialist parties under the proper conditions could not be ruled out.

Hilferding maintained that in the long run such coalitions would become obsolete when all strata (*Schichten*) of the working class became conscious of their real class interest. Here he referred specifically to the need to win over the salaried workers in industry and commerce, whose share of the work force was increasing at a tremendous rate, and to the small farmers, who had defied previous Marxist predictions and adapted to the needs of the modern economy. The support of both groups was needed for the present political battles as well as for the successful operation of a socialist economy in the future.[37]

The real question of the hour seemed to be: under what circumstances was entrance into a coalition government justifiable and beneficial? Here Hilferding provided no clear answer—at least not publicly. In 1924 he delivered a strong defense of the eight-hour day but concluded that taxation policy had become less important.[38] The next year he argued on behalf of the specific platform contained in the SPD's new Heidelberg Program—a four-page shopping list of political, economic, social, legal, and cultural reforms that did not distinguish priorities.[39] Hilferding himself emphasized that the SPD's participation in government could have direct financial benefits for the working class, because the Ministry of Labor had become a key actor in the process of arbitration and collective bargaining.[40]

In late 1924 Hilferding wrote to his former teacher Karl Kautsky about the German political situation: "We must finish with the political-democratic controversy first, before the social one can be dealt with. Naturally, they are not fully separate, but this nevertheless requires two stages with different tactics for each. Now we must make the German working class conscious of the intrinsic value (*Eigenwert*) of the republic and democracy, which is still grasped insufficiently."[41] The immediate political opportunity for the SPD was limited by the fact that the reliable republicans among the other parties were too few to form a working majority. Hilferding expressed his pleasure that the Democratic party, although shrunken in size, had remained loyal to its democratic ideals, for this made it easier to keep attention on the basic issue of parliamentarism versus authoritarianism, rather than on the material demands of the different classes. He also felt that such a discussion might lead to a schism in the Center party, with the left wing providing the SPD with another trustworthy coalition partner.[42] Two months later he wrote to Kautsky that the December 1924 elections, in which the SPD added 6 percent of the vote to its total and 31 seats to its delegation in the Reichstag, marked a turning point upwards. Apparently satisfied with the results of a sometimes toleration, sometimes opposition tactic, he said that he hoped the SPD would be able to refrain from participating in a coalition government.[43]

In retrospect, Hilferding and other top figures in the SPD fraction were disillusioned with the Great Coalition of 1923, which caused them to decline similar opportunities for a Great Coalition. When Erich Koch-Weser (DDP) tried to form such a government in late 1925 and January 1926, Hilferding helped to persuade the SPD fraction to reject participation on the ground that the DVP had shown insufficient compromise.[44] In a letter to Kautsky, Hilferding added that any Great Coalition would quickly collapse, just as had happened in 1923.[45] A year later Hilferding told a reporter that shortly after the formation of the Stresemann cabinet in August 1923, four of the nonsocialist ministers began to discuss among themselves how to force the SPD out of the coalition. Stresemann allegedly knew nothing of it, but when Hilferding was forced to resign, this was the first stage of a plan designed to get rid of the SPD. Hilferding added that the same political forces, particularly DVP leader Scholz, continued to work against the Great Coalition. Hilferding himself felt that the SPD should only be interested in a Great Coalition that had good prospect of lasting, which seemed unlikely as of early 1927.[46]

He was not prepared to renounce all opportunities to obtain a more favorable government. In mid-1926 he offered the SPD's support for a proposed minority government of the middle parties under the leadership of Konrad Adenauer, but the plan fell through.[47] After the failure of another attempt to form a Great Coalition in December 1926, Hilferding helped to convince the fraction that a minority government of the DDP, DVP, and Center under Wilhelm Marx should be tolerated.[48] He hoped thereby to strengthen the leftist faction ("workers' wing") of the Center party and to prevent it from joining with the DNVP in a conservative government.

Hilferding thus played a key role in the formulation of the SPD's coalition policy from 1923 to 1928. Against the leftist opposition, he defended the principle of coalition government. At the same time, however, he no longer found that the need to defend the democratic system was an immediate and compelling reason for the SPD to join the government. The one thing that the party depended upon above all—the loyalty of rank-and-file members and workers generally—was jeopardized whenever the SPD was forced to take responsibility for unpopular economic decisions. If the SPD remained outside the government, it could await the expected decline of its Communist rivals while maintaining cordial relations with the liberal parties.[49] Improvement of the economy also made it possible for the SPD to adopt a more passive political stance. In the absence of extreme economic crisis, the parliamentary system was not quite so vulnerable. There were also other ways in which it could be protected.

Hilferding placed great faith in the beneficial effects of economic stabilization, yet did not specify how this process could be pushed further in the direction of socialism. He expressed satisfaction with the direction of economic development, because the process of concentration was itself eliminating the adverse effects of free competition. However, he complained at one point that the transformation from capitalism to socialism had been described only in generalizations. He believed that some sort of worker participation in management would have to precede full-scale nationalization; otherwise, workers themselves would not be prepared for their eventual role in a socialist economy.[50]

Carried to its logical conclusion, this idea would suggest a strong emphasis on the need to complete and to expand the provisions of the factory-council legislation. Yet Hilferding by and large relegated the task of formulating a program of "economic democracy" to Fritz Naphtali and to the leaders of the socialist unions, who were in fact quite impressed with his analysis of the stabilization of capitalism.[51] Hilferding concentrated on working out a theoretical justification for the SPD's future participation in coalition government. He wanted to find a way to make the SPD's socialist aims appear compatible with the compromises involved in any coalition with the non-socialist parties. In part this was a matter of choosing the proper circumstances for entrance into a government, of waiting for the other parties to show enough flexibility. It was also necessary to convince SPD voters and party members of the beneficial effect of sharing power.

The highpoint of Hilferding's effort at persuasion was his speech at the 1927 SPD congress held in Kiel, which was entitled, "The Tasks of Social Democracy in the Republic."[52] He began by restating his analysis of the development of greater economic concentration and of interlocking relations among industry, commerce, and finance. This latest stage of capitalism made possible tremendous technological advances, for only large firms had the resources to develop and exploit the new chemical discoveries, the liquification of coal, etc. The large firms relied on planning, research, and scientific management for their success, and this was seen as a better and more rational regulator than the "invisible hand" of free competition. "Organized capitalism in reality means the fundamental replacement of the capitalist principle of free competition by the socialist principle of planned production." However, socialism would not develop automatically out of capitalism. Capitalism in its more rational, organized phase was actually capable of stability through well-calculated state economic policy. Socialism would have to be "the conscious deed of the working class." The workers would have to seize control of the economy by obtaining control of the democratic state, whose powers could then be used to eliminate the privilege of property. The socialist economy would then be a completion of representative democracy. The trade unions would have an essential task—helping to determine the proper form of worker participation in economic decision-making.

Hilferding also argued that, even with a less-than-controlling influence in the state, the working class could exert significant economic influence and reap direct material benefits: "We must hammer it into the head of each worker that the weekly wage is a political wage, that it depends . . . on the strength of the parliamentary representation of the working class."[53] This fact should make it obvious that in the present, as well as in the past and the future, democracy remained the cause (*Sache*) of the proletariat. Those socialist critics who reviled *bourgeois* democracy, Hilferding claimed, were making a very serious mistake. Democracy in the political sense had an intrinsic worth and at all times retained the potentiality of effecting social change. If those with economic privilege resorted to force to protect it, violating the constitution, then it would be time for the Social Democrats to use all means, including force, against their class enemies. But the resulting civil war would be a severe obstacle to the realization of socialism. If political conflict could be kept within the bounds set by the constitution, it would be of the utmost value. "If you have not understood," Hilferding told a critic, "that the main-tenance of democracy and the republic is the most important interest of the party, then you have not grasped the 'ABC' of political thought." Those opposition leaders warning the masses against "democratic illusions" were absolutely wrong; the real danger, which was sadly evident in other countries, was that the proletariat might not perceive the importance of democracy. He warned that without the active support of working-class organizations, any democratic order was doomed to collapse.[54]

The real battle between the party leaders and the left-wing opposition was not for control of the fraction and the party organization, where the former enjoyed the advantage of entrenched bureaucrats. Rather, Hilferding and his colleagues wanted to educate the workers politically, to rally them in support of the democratic state, while the opposition warned that this goal was un-appealing compared to socialism itself. The widespread distrust of coalition with nonsocialist parties even within the ranks of the SPD demonstrated that there was limited support for a political strategy of interclass cooperation in a society plagued by sharp class antagonisms. This problem was compounded by the fact that neither the Weimar Coalition nor the Great Coalition had functioned effectively in the past. Fearful of losing a substantial portion of its following, the party leadership was caught between the principle of parlia-mentary integration and the traditional socialist concept of the class struggle.[55]

The inability to break with the traditional socialist approach was itself a factor that limited the SPD's accomplishments in parliamentary politics—though not the most important factor. Historian Michael Stürmer has shown how the SPD's preference for tolerating minority cabinets from 1924 to 1928 deprived it of the leverage to influence government social and economic policy.[56] Hilferding, who recognized that the SPD had to broaden its social base of support if it were ever to obtain a majority, nonetheless contributed to the problem by maintaining that this was primarily a matter of winning the entire "proletariat." He wanted to make inroads into the working-class sup-port of the Center party, the DNVP, and the Communist party.[57] But it was an illusion to think that all wage and salary earners were members of the same class. Membership is primarily a question of perceived affiliation, and those who supported the DNVP (and some of those supporting the Center) hardly identified with factory workers, whether or not their material interests were the same. Only when the SPD leaders had grasped the difficulty of reaching the average white-collar worker, artisan, small businessman, or farmer did the SPD have any substantial chance of adapting its appeal successfully. It is noteworthy how reluctantly and tardily party leaders consented to draw up special platforms designed to win the support of government employees and farmers.[58] Hilferding did not go far enough in extirpating the attitudes and assumptions that rested on a teleological view of the evolution of capitalist economic and social structure.

Hilferding also did little to provide a set of realistic goals and priorities for a suitable coalition government. Any such platform had to overcome substantial obstacles posed by ideological spokesmen and interest groups. The terms on which the other parties were prepared to reach agreement with the SPD were often one-sided, given the initial disparity. Nonetheless, the SPD leaders did not work out a positive program within the realm of domestic policy, or, in the instance of the Heidelberg Program of 1925, their action program contained a list of undifferentiated goals, which had marginal relevance to practical decisions for the immediate future.[59] No conceivable coalition would have accepted the Heidelberg Program in toto. One assumes that the major SPD politicians were more candid about their expectations for a coalition government in private, but even so, one senses an uncertainty about the purpose of sharing and wielding political power on the national level. If the parliamentary system was to provide the path to democratic socialism, then there was need for a clearer tracing of the route than Hilferding provided. The resolution that Hilferding presented to the 1927 congress for approval merely left all options open for the party leadership: "Participation by Social Democracy in the national government depends solely on the question of whether its strength with the public and in the Reichstag gives assurance that it will be able to achieve specified goals which are in the interest of the working class, or to prevent reactionary dangers, through participation in the government in a given situation. The decision on participation in the government is a tactical question, the answer to which cannot be determined once and for all by a specific formula."[60] Such vagueness was in no way calculated to educate the public and the party's constituency about the uses of political power. Nor was it a suitable response to those critics on the left and right wings of the party who were increasingly disturbed by the oligarchic features in the party organization and the lack of free and serious discussion of basic issues.[61] A rather passive stance of unconditional support for the republic combined with a disinclination to shape its features could not attract a great deal of enthusiasm from the party's constituents.

Hilferding failed to draw the full consequences from his own theory of the stabilization of capitalism. Despite his warning that socialism would not develop by itself out of capitalism, he relied essentially on a view of social structure and class consciousness that assumed unduly favorable results over time, and on a concept of parliamentary democracy that remained abstract and institutional.[62] Although he recognized the need to broaden the social base of the party and to make it a more suitable coalition partner, he did not push hard enough for specific changes designed to accomplish these ends. He lacked both the strength of will to make such choices and the authority to impose them. The novelty of his attempt to relate political theory to political strategy can easily be overrated; he could well have written the following:

> Since Social Democracy has become a political force at a time when other social strata besides the proletariat and the capitalist class exist, it must either remain in political reserve until everything is proletarized, or it must try to bring all democratic elements onto the side of the proletariat. The first appears to be revolutionary in principle, but in reality means passivity, stagnation . . . impotence, and regressive development. The second means development of power and demonstrates the way to victory. Through class stratification (*Klassenabsonderung*) the proletariat thus gains [the way to] a new democracy; it raises democracy on the foundation of its class struggle.[63]

This passage, written in 1908 by socialist intellectual Parvus-Helphand, has much in common with Hilferding's postwar thought. Hilferding too recognized that other strata besides factory workers might be accessible to an appeal on behalf of parliamentary democracy. Weimar democracy was after all designed to promote political stability, economic prosperity, and more harmonious relations with the western powers—all of which were in the general interest of German society. However, other parties and special interest groups did not all agree that the republic was capable of providing a suitable political vehicle, and some repudiated the idea of reconciliation with Germany's wartime enemies. As a result, there was no overwhelming consensus on the form of government. The number willing to give parliamentarism a chance was dangerously close to the minimum required for the system to operate.

In a choice between democracy and authoritarian government, the SPD took the side of "the people." Yet in economic and financial controversies it held to the language of the class struggle and bore the interests of the working class on its standard. Its reluctance to incorporate nonworking-class elements through specific occupational and material appeals left a gap, if not a contradiction, in the party's strategy.

Another omission was the SPD's failure to develop an integrated economic and financial program to promote general economic development. The SPD supported state intervention in the economy for the purpose of introducing social reforms that benefited working-class constituents. Of course, it also championed the principle of nationalization. But while Hilferding and other party economists recognized the key role of macroeconomic state policy upon modern capitalism, they shied away from recommending any clear plan for economic expansion under capitalism.

Even the moderate SPD spokesmen were not willing to bear responsibility for management of the economy. The SPD's legacy as a working-class party opposed to the economic and political order was still too strong.[64]

In actuality, the party's social base had been broadened substantially. Hans Neisser estimated in 1930 that about 40 percent of the SPD's votes came from nonfactory workers.[65] Even if this figure turns out to be exaggerated, it is obvious that the SPD's stance on basic political and foreign policy issues had considerable appeal outside the ranks of the working class.[66] Had the SPD been able to present a general program for economic growth, it might have been able to tap a larger well of support from other classes. Lack of a clear economic policy made it difficult for SPD spokesmen to present the public with convincing and attractive alternatives to the slogans of the nonsocialist parties.

Hilferding assumed that the process of economic development would establish an identity of interest among workers and other strata that did not enjoy the privilege of substantial property. He expected a more homogeneous social structure in the future and therefore worried less about the multiplicity of cleavages that remained in the present. This is not to say that Hilferding alone could have brought about the transformation of German Social Democracy from a class party to a people's party. Certainly there was considerable resistance to each step in this direction within the ranks of the party and union organizations, and Hilferding was in no position to dismiss or override such opposition unilaterally. On the other hand, his persuasive influence extended not only to other party leaders but also into the ranks of the organization. Although not a brilliant speaker, he knew how to express complex theoretical and political issues in a way that the rank and file could understand.[67] Hilferding used his talents ably to promote acceptance of the concept of parliamentary democracy, while he failed to devote similar attention to the methods that the SPD required to increase its leverage within the Weimar system.

Hilferding's interpretation of democratic socialism became the standard SPD line. Without doubt, many party loyalists found that the Weimar Republic compared unfavorably with their vision of a socialist society, but party spokesmen did not lay the blame upon the democratic form of government. Ernst Fraenkel ingeniously made the problems of Weimar democracy seem positively advantageous for democratic socialism. "He who is a democrat and a socialist cannot conceive of a socialist society except as a democratic one. The circumstance that democracy often failed in a class-divided society should not make us pessimistic, but rather optimistic. A form of state that functions without friction in the present society would certainly be unsuitable for the future society."[68]

Gustav Radbruch's charge that the SPD leaders did not make a sufficient effort to convince the masses of the intrinsic worth of democracy seems unfounded.[69] On the fundamental political principle of democratic socialism high party officials and organs were quite explicit: "With regard to the form of the state, Social Democracy knows no goal beyond the democratic republic. In the democratic republic and with all the means of the democratic republic, it represents the interests of the working class and promotes the infusion of collective economic principles into a still predominantly capitalist economy. Certainly it will be a long time before this capitalist economy is fully replaced by a socialist one—the Social Democratic party has no illusions about this—but we can conceive of the last remnant of capitalism disappearing without changing even a single letter of the Weimar Constitution."[70] Party leaders are more vulnerable to the criticism that they did not pursue all methods of expanding the SPD's influence within the parliamentary system, thereby failing to demonstrate the present benefits of parliamentary democracy. Moreover, the SPD's erratic course in coalition policy was not a good way to educate the voters or to establish durable ties with liberal elements hesitant to deal with the SPD in any case. Here Prussian politics provides an interesting contrast with the SPD's conduct in the Reich.

8. The Prussian Strategy

H E Social Democrats who shared power in Prussia continuously from the end of 1921 until the coup that unseated them in July 1932 had a certain amount of independence from the rest of the party. However, their motives were consistent with SPD strategy, even if their coalition policy contrasted with the SPD's behavior in national politics. Carl Severing told the Prussian Landtag in 1925: "My entire activity in state government and in previous public life has been an effort to reduce (*ausgleichen*) the sharp antagonisms within the German populace . . . between the working class and the middle classes."[1] He later wrote to a friend that he felt the SPD should participate in all governments that could help to strengthen the democratic republic and to formulate progressive social legislation.[2] The SPD pursued an active coalition policy in Prussia, a state that contained three-fifths of the population of Germany. What then accounted for the difference in SPD policy in the Reich?

In his memoirs Wolfgang Heine, one-time Prussian interior minister, suggested that the SPD leaders in Prussia were simply more willing to take responsibility for government than were their counterparts in the Reich. In turn, they were given more adequate backing by the SPD fraction in the Prussian Landtag, and they had better relations with their coalition partners. Heine wrote that the SPD Reichstag fraction, more worried about the potential loss of votes to the Communists than about anything else, was unwilling to act similarly.[3]

Ernest Hamburger, former vice-chairman of the SPD fraction in the Prussian Landtag, stressed a number of factors that facilitated successful coalition policy in Prussia: the firm leadership of Otto Braun and Ernst Heilmann; the presence of a huge bureaucracy, making patronage appointments available; and the greater visibility of the old reactionary forces in Prussia, which unified their opponents.[4]

The SPD leaders in Prussia had an emotional attachment to the Prussia that they hoped to reform,[5] and they also believed that the continued existence of a powerful Prussia would be best for the SPD. Prussian Minister President Paul Hirsch had suggested immediately after the revolution that a democratic Prussia could guarantee a democratic Germany. The SPD leaders in the Reich did not share this viewpoint. A unitary state complemented by local self-government and self-administration was the traditional Social Democratic ideal. It was not, however, a high priority for the party elite in 1918–1919. Hermann Müller commented in late 1920 that everyone seemed to agree on the principle of the unitary state, but no one could agree on how to proceed. Müller complained that the Prussian position of waiting until the other states were ready meant inaction.[6] By the time that serious plans for administrative and constitutional reform surfaced in the mid-1920s, the SPD's Prussian leaders had already demonstrated the value of a strong Prussia to the party as a whole. The SPD's achievements in Prussia impressed many contemporaries outside the party and continue to raise debate among historians.[7] In some ways Prussian politics up to the depression illustrate what the SPD might have accomplished in the Reich with a more active coalition policy and with more effective leadership.

Coalition Government in Prussia

Social Democratic acceptance of broad coalition governments was initially no greater in Prussia than it was in the Reich. The Weimar Coalition held a secure majority in the Prussian Landtag through 1920, and the Prussian Social Democrats had little desire to consort with the People's party, whose allegiance to the republic was questionable. But the Prussian elections of February 1921, like the Reichstag elections of June 1920, delivered a blow to the Weimar Coalition. Again the Democrats suffered most, falling from 66 seats to 26, while the People's party got most of the defectors, rising from 21 seats to 58. In the period between the Reichstag and the Landtag elections the USPD had split apart, with its left wing joining the Communist party. This schism may have enabled the SPD to reduce its losses to its left-wing competitors. The SPD dropped 31 seats down to a total of 114; the attenuated USPD captured only 28, and the Communists received 31. The Center party, as usual, was the most stable, losing 13 seats, which gave it a total of 81.

Unlike the situation in the Reichstag, the parties of the Weimar Coalition still held a majority in the Prussian Landtag after the election—221 of 428 seats. However, the Center party refused to continue the existing alignment, proposing instead that the DVP join the Prussian coalition, and that the SPD enter the Reich government. After a long internal debate about the merits of the Great Coalition,[8] the SPD Landtag fraction offered to accept the DVP if the latter would pledge its approval of the republican constitutions in the Reich and in Prussia. The Prussian Social Democrats also demanded the continued democratization of the Prussian administration and the SPD's retention of the cabinet positions of minister president, minister of the interior, and minister of agriculture. When the DVP refused to give the SPD any explicit guarantees, the Social Democrats tried to reestablish the Weimar Coalition. Both the DDP and the Center put up strong resistance, but eventually they agreed on condition that the SPD vacate the office of minister president. Although the Landtag fraction was willing to accept these terms, it was dissuaded by the SPD executive committee—specifically Otto Wels, Hermann Müller, and Franz Krüger—who regarded the bargain as unsatisfactory.[9]

Eventually, a minority government composed of Democrats and Centrists was formed by Adam Stegerwald, the head of the Christian Trade Union Federation. Whereas the Social Democrats had hoped that Stegerwald would look to the left for support, the new minister president was more impressed by the prospect of cooperation among Centrists and Nationalists. There were many conservatives, some ranging as far right as the DNVP, within the Christian unions, and Stegerwald tried to make this alignment the basis for his government in Prussia.[10] His conservative drift became more and more galling to the SPD as the months went by. After the Erzberger assassination in late August 1921, the SPD executive committee reversed its previous policy and pushed for the creation of the Great Coalition both in the Reich and in Prussia. By a 46-41 vote the SPD Landtag fraction authorized Carl Severing to conduct negotiations with Stegerwald about a Great Coalition government. Severing told the minister president that the SPD wanted to enter the coalition, whether or not the DVP was willing to do the same. The SPD fraction also insisted that officials in the Prussian administration support the constitution by acting against disloyal organizations prone to violence. When Stegerwald balked, the Democrats pulled out of the government, which fell on 1 November. Blocked by the DVP from returning to the Agriculture Ministry, where he had previously clashed with the owners of large estates, Otto Braun was elected instead to direct a Great Coalition government on 5 November. Severing again received the Interior Ministry. The third SPD member of the cabinet was Minister of Commerce Wilhelm Siering.[11]

On the surface, there was little to distinguish Braun from his cohorts in the SPD. The son of an unsuccessful shoemaker from Königsberg, Braun was trained as a lithographer and moved into the Social Democratic organization at an early age. As treasurer and member of the SPD executive committee before 1918 Braun showed considerable administrative ability and skill in dealing with his colleagues. He was a tall, imposing figure and possessed a keen mind, but his high-pitched, nonresonant voice and reserved nature detracted from his effectiveness as a public speaker. Adept around the green baize table of a negotiating room, Braun lacked the charisma needed to move the masses emotionally, a deficiency shared by most SPD leaders. In a number of respects, however, Braun was atypical of the SPD elite. Although he had no burning desire for power and often found his official duties to be a personal burden, he nonetheless was comfortable with the use of power in government. In his contacts with nonsocialist colleagues and civil servants he showed no trace of the inferiority complex that marked the behavior of many Social Democrats of working-class origin.[12]

Braun also had a clear sense of the purpose and immediate objectives of SPD participation in coalition governments. He believed not only that the parliamentary republic provided the necessary foundation for progress toward socialism but also that the SPD's highest priority should be the protection of the republic. Braun sought to make Prussia the bastion and guardian of parliamentary democracy. Forestalling a rightist government, reforming the civil service and particularly the police, prosecuting antirepublican organizations for illegal activities, weakening the influence of large landowners in the East Prussian districts, rebuilding the economy (although not necessarily along socialist lines)—these were critical issues for Braun. Compromises with the Democrats, the Center, and the People's party could be struck in other areas to promote these objectives. The SPD leaders in the Reich expressed appreciation for Braun's achievements in Prussia, but often refused to follow his strategy themselves in the Reich, which was a source of continuing exasperation for Braun, who was supreme only within his own political realm.

Although the DNVP exerted constant pressure on the DVP to break away from the Prussian coalition, Braun consciously made sacrifices to the latter in order to avoid a confrontation.[13] His government survived the remainder of the Landtag's term (through 1924), in remarkable contrast to the recurring cabinet crises and shifting coalitions in the Reich. The Landtag election at the end of 1924 added to Braun's difficulties, for the parties of the Weimar Coalition no longer held half the seats, and the DVP refused to remain in the government. After a prolonged period of uncertainty and political bargaining among the SPD, DDP, and Center involving not only the minister presidency of Prussia, but also the vacant presidency of the Reich, Braun was reelected head of the Prussian government on 3 April by a slim margin over a DNVP candidate.[14] This result looked all the better to the SPD when Field Marshal von Hindenburg edged out Wilhelm Marx (Center) in the second round of the Reich presidential election.[15]

Braun's base of support from 1925 on remained dangerously thin, but his government survived because of the fact that the DVP, the Communists, and a small party called the Economic Association all feared the possibility of new elections. Braun quipped, "My majority is half [of the Landtag] minus four plus the fear of my opponents."[16] Characteristically, Braun helped to make the Weimar Coalition tenable for the DDP and the Center by giving the former two, and the latter three ministries. The link between the SPD and the Center was reinforced by warm personal relationships among Braun, Ernst Heilmann, chairman of the SPD fraction, and Josef Hess, the leader of the Centrist fraction. Hess and Heilmann gave Minister President Braun their firm support and warned him whenever the independently minded cabinet put too great a strain upon interparty relations in the Landtag. Trained as a lawyer, Heilmann was particularly adept at running the fraction and negotiating with the other parties.[17]

Hess, who had been a member of the Prussian House of Deputies before 1914, had seen the arrogance and recklessness of the Prussian Conservatives at first hand. This experience, combined with the discrimination against Catholics during the Second Reich, made a powerful impression upon him. He never lost his intense dislike for the Junkers or their politics. In 1929 Hess made a trip to East Prussia, the first time in his life that he had been there. He stared at the barren countryside and the poor farmers and agricultural laborers in amazement, exclaiming to his companion in the train compartment, Ernest Hamburger (SPD): "Hamburger, where are the people who governed us for one hundred years?"[18] The sense of having been outsiders in the old Prussia united both Centrists and Social Democrats.

The SPD and the Center in Prussia directed their fire primarily at the National People's party, the party par excellence of the Junkers and the Prussian monarchy.[19] This hostility toward the right also influenced Prussia's attitude toward the Reich during the mid-1920s. Braun consistently resisted encroachments by the Reich against the administrative authority of Prussia.[20] Officially, he maintained that Prussia would ultimately be dissolved into a unitary Reich, but only after all preconditions were met. In the meantime, the best way to make progress was to merge the small states and enclaves into the larger ones, such as Prussia.[21] Braun's aide Herbert Weichmann argued that Prussia would grow organically into a unified Reich—as soon as the Reich understood how to perform its functions.[22] Severing told a politically reliable journalist that Prussia was not about to subordinate itself to the Reich as long as there was a possibility of a right-wing government in the latter.[23] The idea of a right-wing government in Prussia was apparently inconceivable.

The significance of Prussia for the SPD was partly that it offered the party greater opportunities than did national politics. In many ways a state whose administration covered nearly two-thirds of Germany was a more important prize than any number of Reich ministries. The SPD's highest political priority, the defense of the parliamentary republic, could not be pursued with any likelihood of success without reliance upon the power of the Prussian administration.

The Prussian Administration

In 1928 the Prussian administration consisted of about 156,000 officials, dwarfing the national administration and that of the other states.[24] The Prussian Ministry of Justice and the Ministry of Culture were substantial agencies in their own right, but the head of the largest bureaucracy in Germany was the Prussian minister of the interior. Serving under him were the state secretaries in charge of the various divisions of the ministry and their staffs. Below them were some 540 general-purpose, field officials in the so-called political offices—*Oberpräsidenten* (provincial governors), *Regierungspräsidenten* (roughly, "district officers"), and *Landräte* (county councilors). Each of these positions was serviced by deputies and/or staff. The *Landrat* served as the link between the state administration and the independent communal government. Also included in the category of political official (which meant that occupants were appointable and removable on political grounds) were the chiefs of police of the major cities. The Oberpräsidenten and the Regierungspräsidenten initially had to satisfy technical requirements through university training in law and administration, or through experience as a Landrat.[25] The rest of the huge civil service, also subject to training prerequisites, was guaranteed substantial job security, and officials could be removed only after an extensive disciplinary procedure had proved due cause.

During the Second Reich the political officials were not only the general field administrators of the state ministry, they were also the government's eyes, ears, and mouthpiece throughout the country. Max Weber described their essential function as the maintenance of existing power relations.[26] It was no accident that members of the Social Democratic party were ineligible for appointment to these positions according to state law, or that Catholics, Jews, and liberals were few.

This official policy of discrimination during the Second Reich, plus the educational and class barriers that kept the lower classes out of the universities, created a serious problem for the SPD in November 1918. Party leaders by and large believed that a professional, technically qualified civil service was indispensable to meet the problems of the postwar period. Yet the existing bureaucracy, especially in Prussia, was predominantly antirepublican. There were also very few republicans who could meet the technical prerequisites and serve as replacements. Only a handful of Social Democrats had been able to obtain high-level administrative experience during the war. The SPD leaders decided quickly about the nonpolitical officials, who represented an overwhelming proportion of the total; those who wished to retire on grounds of political conviction were allowed to do so on generous terms, but there was to be no purge. The Social Democrats tried instead to win the loyalty of state officials. They were largely unsuccessful in this effort,[27] but it nonetheless serves as another example of Social Democratic willingness to retreat from traditional socialist demands. Renouncing for the time being its traditional goal of elected officials, the SPD made its peace with a pluralistic society.

With regard to the political offices, where discrimination had been more blatant, the Social Democrats initiated some changes in 1919. Some 10 percent of the existing political officials took advantage of an option to resign on grounds of political conscience and to receive a pension at three-fourths the level of their former salaries. Minister President Hirsch and Interior Minister Heine also removed the previous eligibility requirements for the post of Landrat—university training and state examination, or ownership of a large estate and four years' experience in communal administration. This alteration enabled them to appoint Social Democrats and Catholics to some of the vacancies. However, the state government quickly prohibited local workers' and soldiers' councils from removing officials whom they considered reactionary, and Heine himself was not particularly inclined to force antirepublican political officials out of office.[28] The lack of progress toward "democratization" of the political posts, i.e., representation of social and religious groups according to their political strength and/or percentage of the population, not only raised the ire of delegates to the SPD congress in 1919,[29] it also proved dangerous for the republic during the Kapp Putsch, when many political officials in the eastern provinces sided with the insurgents.

Severing came into the Prussian Ministry of the Interior in April 1920 convinced that antirepublican officials were a political liability and a danger to state security. He maintained that all new appointees had to be reliable supporters of the republican order, regardless of party affiliation. Personnel policy became another means to help secure the republic.[30] Severing soon won the state government's approval for a policy that allowed "outsiders"—those who did not satisfy the previous technical requirements—to be appointed to all the political posts, as long as the interior minister and the finance minister both agreed to each such appointment. A wave of outsiders entered the bureaucracy after the Kapp Putsch, and another group was installed to take the place of those civil servants removed after the Rathenau assassination in 1922.[31] Shortly thereafter, the circle of state officials subject to removal solely on political grounds was extended to include many of the staff members attached to the political offices, but the juristic requirements for these jobs remained unaltered.[32] During the rest of Severing's term as interior minister, the turnover in the political offices lessened, and no actual purge ever took place. When Severing left office in 1926, 43 percent of the Oberpräsidenten, 16 percent of the Regierungspräsidenten, and only 10 percent of the Landräte were outsiders.[33]

The difficulties that an outsider faced were formidable. In the areas politically dominated by the conservative parties and administered by monarchist civil servants, the hostility to outsiders reached ludicrous proportions. Ferdinand Friedensburg, a member of the Democratic party, arrived to take office as Landrat in the East Prussian county of Rosenberg only to find that the county had already sent county officials and employees on indefinite vacation, sold the Landrat's automobile, and rented the Landrat's residence to Friedensburg's predecessor, who had been dismissed because of his monarchist convictions. Friedensburg, who had previous experience in the state mining administration as well as juristic training, was able to outmaneuver his antagonists. Nonetheless, he described the magnitude of the outsider's task as follows: "In an atmosphere filled with fervent hate . . . with incessant attacks in the press, interpellations in parliament, complaints to higher authorities when one of the inevitable foul-ups occurred, he [the outsider] had to go through hell, and only too easily lost his nerves. Therefore, I do not venture to criticize the Prussian government, in particular Severing, the interior minister for many years, if it hesitated to send outsiders into areas where they could not count on a majority of local followers—exactly where they were actually needed the most"[34]

Severing's successor as interior minister, Albert Grzesinski (SPD), was also convinced that a loyal republican administration was indispensable, and he was much more willing than Severing to resort to the use of outsiders.[35] The number of outsiders appointed to the office of Landrat increased by 15 percent during Grzesinski's tenure as interior minister (1926–1930).[36] In October 1930 there were also 4 SPD Oberpräsidenten out of a total of 12, 8 SPD Regierungspräsidenten out of 32, 64 SPD Landräte out of 408.[37] In 1929 a DVP member complained to a colleague who himself held the post of Regierungspräsident: "Before 1918 we [our student society] had two members who were Regierungspräsidenten, perhaps fifteen as Landräte, and some twenty in other administrative positions. Now, except for a few who lean toward the Center party, they have all disappeared. The Severing-Grzesinski system has indeed cleaned them out maliciously."[38] The results were even more dramatic with the position of chief of police in the major cities. In 1925 there was only one SPD member in the group of 44 men; in 1929 there were some 24. Prussian Finance Minister Hermann Höpker-Aschoff (DDP) once complained that the police-chief office was becoming the exclusive preserve of the SPD.[39]

Grzesinski later wrote that his highest priority was the struggle against the enemies of the republic. His specific objectives—the strengthening of state authority, especially through the police, the removal of reactionary officials, the elimination of the remaining legal privileges that the owners of large estates enjoyed, and administrative reform—were all related to his basic goal.[40] In his campaign to strengthen the authority of Prussia against anti-republican forces, Grzesinski gave several speeches and wrote a number of articles suggesting that the SPD had in the past overemphasized the legislative aspect of democracy.[41] The execution of law, he held, outranked legislation in importance. Grzesinski was trying to correct a political error of omission that had resulted (at least in part) from inexperience with the democratic form of government. The majority of the German people (and the Social Democrats in particular) had erroneously believed that the introduction of universal and equal suffrage and the establishment of a parliamentary system sufficed to create a democracy. If Germany really was to become a government of and by the people, then the citizens had to be confident that they would receive fair, equal, and effective treatment from the administration.

The Braun-Severing-Grzesinski line in Prussia contrasted with the SPD's reluctance to join the national government. Only the Labor Ministry, the agency with the greatest immediate impact upon the daily lives of German workers,[42] represented a major prize for the SPD in the Reich cabinet. In other departments the SPD's traditional socialist orientation was unacceptable to its potential coalition partners, and no one came forth with mutually satis-factory compromises. The political costs of coalition government outweighed the benefits of directing ministries and having a voice in the Reich cabinet, in the eyes of the SPD leaders in the Reich.

Braun and other leading Social Democrats in Prussia feared that the SPD's stance in the Reich would adversely affect Prussian politics. The leaders of the Center party in the Reich, particularly Wilhelm Marx, were moving visibly to the right, and they might have dragged Hess in Prussia with them.[43] Braun and Severing agreed that it was unwise for Prussia to be drawn into controversial issues in the Reich. The Prussian government was prepared to abstain on controversial votes in the Reichsrat rather than endanger its own narrow coalition.[44]

A second, and potentially greater Prussian concern about politics in the Reich was that the parliamentary process might break down entirely. If the parties were unable to form a government, President Hindenburg might employ his emergency powers under Article 48 with unforeseeable conse-quences. According to one report passed on to Prussian Interior Minister Severing in late 1925, some members of the National Association of German Industry were prepared to put pressure on Chancellor Luther and President Hindenburg to resort to presidential rule in the event of a parliamentary deadlock.[45] The bypassing of parliament might have led to Reich intervention

against Prussia, just as the Reich had intervened against the Saxon government in 1923. Only this time the target would not have been an SPD-KPD
government but rather the Weimar Coalition government in Prussia.

The threat may well have been a factor in Braun's decision to campaign in
favor of SPD participation in the Reich government at that time.[46] Hermann
Müller specifically warned the Reichstag fraction that there was a possibility
of a "Luther dictatorship." Hans Vogel referred to the delicate position of the
Weimar Coalition in Prussia. But the Reichstag fraction remained suspicious
of the DVP and the Great Coalition after its experience in 1923 and drew up
an unrealistic list of preconditions for SPD participation. On the other hand,
the potential danger of rule through Article 48 apparently induced the fraction
to abstain from a vote of no confidence against the minority Luther government, thereby allowing the motion to fail.[47] During one meeting of the SPD
Reichstag fraction Rudolf Breitscheid gave Severing a ringing endorsement:
"I am for abstention, but I support (folge) Severing. Severing is the last pillar:
the armed position of power. He has prevented the worst consequences of the
misdirected leadership in the Reich. I support Severing!"[48] Although this
praise undoubtedly pleased Severing, it did nothing to eliminate the possibility
of future parliamentary crises and the potential misuse of Article 48.

During the summer of 1926 there were highly confidential talks about what
preventive measures might be taken. Severing thought seriously about proposing a law specifying the procedure to be used when Article 48 was employed. One provision would have required the Supreme Court to give its
opinion before the Reich could intervene against a state government with
armed force. Another would have required a civilian deputy to supervise the
activity of the military under a state of siege.[49] Severing recognized that this
law would be hard to get through the Reichstag, and President Hindenburg
later denounced any attempt to restrict the presidential emergency powers.[50]
Wolfgang Heine, Severing's predecessor as Prussian interior minister, hesitated to spell out any details of his plan for restrictions on the use of Article
48. But he followed up on a conversation with Severing by writing that the
plan's realization would depend on unforeseeable circumstances. Specifically,
there was no chance until new elections produced a sufficiently strong republican front and a more committed attitude on the part of the SPD (in the
Reich). Heine also claimed that a precondition of the plan was that Severing
remain in office. He suggested that the interior minister discuss the plan with
Braun but otherwise keep it confidential.[51]

Severing actually was eager to take a rest, having been in a very difficult
post almost continuously since March 1920. Plagued by bad nerves, exhaustion, and migraine headaches, he took a long vacation in the late spring and
summer of 1926. The Communist newspaper Rote Fahne then published an

article about confidential discussions in the SPD fraction on the subject of Severing's successor; the first choice seemed to be Robert Leinert.[52] But Minister President Braun chose Albert Grzesinski to take Severing's place. With the full support of Braun and fraction leader Heilmann, Grzesinski bypassed the maze of procedural, financial, and political obstacles that had so often held up Severing. When a matter that he considered politically important was at stake, Grzesinski stood his ground stubbornly and usually got his way. He overrode the objections raised by Finance Minister Höpker-Aschoff to the dissolution of the estate districts (*Gutsbezirke*), where the owners of large estates had preserved complete control of local government. On another occasion he urged Braun to threaten the DDP with new elections, predicting that it would then end its talk of leaving the government.[53] His efforts to curb the activity of right-wing paramilitary groups have been described at length elsewhere.[54]

The SPD ministers were rewarded for their performance in office by the election of 20 May 1928, in which the SPD picked up 23 seats in the Landtag. Meanwhile, the DDP and the Center suffered substantial declines in Prussia, but the Weimar Coalition now held a slim majority—228 out of 449 seats. Under these circumstances Minister President Braun saw an opportunity to hold onto his present office and to become chancellor as well, a form of governmental coordination used previously only by Bismarck.

During the election campaign Braun had been mentioned as the most likely SPD choice for the chancellor's office.[55] However, he felt that he needed the strength provided by his Prussian post to be an effective leader in the national government. Combining the two jobs was a huge task to which Braun reacted ambivalently. His wife had been partially paralyzed since 1927, and he himself had suffered from insomnia and nervous tension for years.[56] In conjunction with the SPD executive committee, he invited leading party and union members to his residence one evening shortly after the elections to discuss the idea. The meeting convinced him that he could get the party's nomination, but there was opposition: the executive committee leaned toward Hermann Müller. Among the objections to Braun's plan were the concern that President Hindenburg would create obstacles, and fear that the other parties would not accept Braun as a self-styled Bismarck—specifically, that the Center party would insist on one of its own members as head of the Prussian government.[57] Forced to choose between the two offices, Braun preferred the one he already held. Braun's failure to attain the chancellor's post may have been a sign of his cool personal relations with Otto Wels, the increasingly powerful co-chairman of the executive committee.[58] But there was little dispute within the SPD elite about the success of the Prussian coalition policy, as a number of comments at the 1927 party congress showed.

Hermann Müller: I believe that no one in the party is willing to give up voluntarily the positions in Prussia that have been held up until now. *Rudolf Hilferding*: Thanks to Otto Braun and Karl (*sic*) Severing, the waves of bolshevism and fascism have broken themselves against Prussia (*lively agreement*). That was a world-historical achievement (*renewed lively agreement*). Only history will recognize what this short metalworker from Bielefeld has done for central Europe, yes, even for all Europe (*stormy agreement*).
Rudolf Breitscheid: We can thank above all the active and successful work of our friends in the Prussian government for the fact that the republic can be seen as temporarily secure. . . . We therefore urge our comrades in Prussia not only to defend their positions of power, but also where possible, to extend them, for they are the securest anchor of the German republic.[59]

Hermann Müller also showed that he understood the thrust of the Prussian strategy: "I believe that specifically this system that is tied to the name Severing is the system of summoning the democratic parties of the center to common work with the SPD. It is the system under which we can guarantee that democracy will be carried out in Germany."[60]

Even the spokesmen for the SPD left opposition were not fundamentally hostile to the Prussian coalition. Ernst Eckstein worried only that the SPD's stake in Prussia might restrict its tactics in the Reichstag.[61] Thus, Braun, Severing, and Grzesinski were only rarely subject to serious criticism from the left for their Prussian policies. The sacrifices that the SPD made in order to stay in power in Prussia in the areas of education, church-state relations, and even partial compensation of the Hohenzollerns for the seizure of royal property were less galling to the left than the party's retreats on nationalization, factory councils, taxation, and its inability to reform the military, which were all in the sphere of national politics. The intraparty truce regarding Prussia and the durable Prussian coalition provided the SPD leaders in the Reich with a kind of safety net. If the SPD chose not to take an active role in the Reich government, the Prussian government would at least ensure that the republic would not be unprotected.

In a peculiar way the SPD strategy in Prussia made it easier for the SPD leaders in the Reich to withdraw from the national government or to refrain from entering it when abstinence seemed to be in the party's short-term interest.[62] This tactical approach to politics in the Reich was not at all what Braun, Severing, and Grzesinski wanted from their colleagues, but they lacked the influence to gain their own way in the Reichstag fraction.

The SPD's relatively harmonious relationship with the DDP and the Center in Prussia was facilitated by the fact that the most acrimonious interparty disputes were carried out in the Reichstag.[63] Even so, all three parties in Prussia showed themselves willing to risk unpopular compromises in order to shore up the Weimar Coalition. Consensus was achieved partly because the fraction leaders and cabinet ministers were granted enough leeway to reach arrangements among themselves, partly because the SPD's goals in Prussia were mostly democratic rather than socialist. The SPD leaders stressed the importance of protecting the republic against violent overthrow or subversion, and of ensuring fair treatment of all social groups, religious groups, and economic interests. They were fortunate to find two other parties sharing or at least accepting these objectives in part. To be sure, the three parties fought over patronage and policies, but they did not contest the need to use the parliamentary process and to cooperate with each other.

The SPD's control of the police, the largest governmental administration in Germany, and the largest delegation in the Reichsrat seemed to be an effective way to assure the preservation of parliamentary democracy. The Prussian strategy, acceptable to all factions of the party (although not equally so), served as compensation for the SPD's unsuccessful adaptation to national politics. The party's ineffectiveness on the national level was partly the result of the uncompromising stance of the other parties (and the persistence of class cleavages), partly the result of less decisive leadership, partly also the consequence of the SPD's lack of clarity about the purpose of exercising political power in a capitalist economy.

The SPD leaders in the Reich thus came to depend on Prussia to guarantee a smooth political evolution toward socialism within the framework of parliamentary democracy. Obviously, they assumed too much about the direction and inevitability of political and economic *Entwicklung*. The Prussian stronghold, however, gave the SPD its greatest leverage within Weimar democracy. The Prussian strategy protected the parliamentary republic well enough that the SPD leadership was left without an alternative when Braun and Severing themselves began to have doubts about it during the depression.

9. The Last Unsuccessful Coalition

TH E "golden years" of the mid-1920s did not solidify Germany's precarious social and political equilibrium. The installation of the new currency, the acceptance of the Dawes Plan as a provisional settlement of reparations disputes,[1] and the influx of foreign loans revived the economy and stimulated real growth. But agriculture and handiwork did not share in the industrial boom. Free trade, low prices, and a general tendency toward economic concentration accelerated long-term declines in both of these sectors. Meanwhile, business and labor continued to quarrel over their respective shares of national income. The arbitration functions of the Ministry of Labor on the whole served to protect the position of the labor unions, which had suffered severely from the inflation, but business spokesmen responded with virulent criticism of state interference in the economy. Finally, disputes over revaluation, or compensation of those who had lost assets through the virtual destruction of the old currency, added new interest groups and splinter parties to an already crowded parliamentary arena.[2] Diverse middle-class voters resented the superior cohesion, organization, and political influence of both big business and labor, and many such individuals eventually sought their salvation in the Nazi party. The pressure upon the nonsocialist parties to resist Social Democratic demands was intense even before the depression.

The Reichstag elections of May 1928, held simultaneously with the Prussian Landtag elections, masked the republic's forthcoming difficulties. Reacting against a conservative and often clumsy government headed by Wilhelm Marx, German voters tilted the political balance somewhat to the left. The SPD picked up almost 1.3 million additional votes, despite a lower turnout rate than in December 1924. With 29.8 percent of the votes, the Social Democrats obtained 153 out of 491 seats in the Reichstag. The Communists made substantial gains as well. With nearly 3.3 million votes and 54 seats, the KPD was quite close to the level of the Center party. Given the vituperation between the two Marxist parties, however, the voters' judgment could not easily be translated into added parliamentary influence for the left. The parties of the middle, with whom the SPD had cooperated in the past, fared poorly. The Democrats fell from 32 to 25 mandates, the DVP dropped from 51 to 45, and even the Center declined from 69 to 62 seats. The far right was not the beneficiary, since both the DNVP and the Nazis lost votes, although the

144

former remained the second largest party with 73 seats. New interest group parties such as the Economic party and the *Landbund* took up some of the slack. The fact remained that the left had prospered, while the middle suffered—an unnerving result for bourgeois party officials. Moreover, the KPD's prominent stance to the left of the SPD in no way enthused Social Democratic supporters of coalition government.

Vorwärts Editor Friedrich Stampfer privately expressed unhappiness that there were no alternatives to the Great Coalition, because he felt that the SPD would be unable to extract specific economic and social benefits for the masses from such a government. He approved of the experiment only because the party really had no choice; its election campaign slogan had been "Away with the rightist government (Bürgerblock)!"[3] Theodor Leipart, chairman of the ADGB, claimed publicly that the socialist unions supported SPD participation in a Great Coalition, believing that the working class would gain more in this way than through dogmatic opposition.[4] Within a short time, however, the unions found that the economic benefits of such participation consisted at most of warding off retrogressive developments. The socialist union leaders then began to assert themselves against both the party and the government. The SPD fraction leaders also distanced themselves from the coalition government. By January 1930 Otto Wels responded to union complaints against the party's role in the government with the remark that the party and the government had recently been confused with one another.[5]

The rise of Rudolf Breitscheid as fraction leader reinforced Wels's own dissatisfaction with the Great Coalition. Rudolf Breitscheid was born in 1874 in the city of Cologne, the only child of a bookstore employee. His father died when he was nine years old, but his mother nonetheless managed to put him through the Gymnasium, which enabled him to qualify for university training at Munich and Marburg. As his financial background and circumstances were quite modest, he was forced to take a job while in college. Nonetheless, his education later set a substantial class barrier between himself and most party functionaries. In proposing Breitscheid for election to the executive committee in 1931, Otto Wels found it necessary to explain the circumstances of Breitscheid's family and education to delegates at the party congress.[6]

Breitscheid's first venture in politics was in support of Friedrich Naumann's prewar National Social Association, a liberal attempt to transcend the class barriers in German politics. He then worked as a newspaper reporter for the left-liberal Democratic Union. It was not until just before the war that Breitscheid, more and more upset with foreign-policy developments, joined the SPD. Yet his obvious talents as a speaker and writer quickly made him a figure to be reckoned with, and his antiwar views impelled him to join the party dissidents on the left. Because he was drafted in 1916, he was unable to attend the founding congress of the USPD. After the revolution in November 1918 he served briefly as Prussian interior minister, but he departed along with the other Independent Socialists from the revolutionary government at the end of December.

Breitscheid remained surprisingly conciliatory toward the SPD, disagreeing openly with the left wing of his own party. His efforts to bring about a rapprochement between the two socialist parties stood him in good stead after their reunification in 1922. Although he was elected to the executive board of the SPD fraction only in 1926, he began to play a prominent role in parliamentary affairs as early as 1923. In 1928 he became one of the three cochairmen of the SPD fraction, and, as noted earlier, he was successfully proposed for membership on the SPD executive committee in 1931. It was at the party congress of that year that Breitscheid gave what might be called a repentance speech, admitting that the founding of the USPD during the war had been a mistake. This concession, at a time when the party was again threatened by schism, was a boost to the morale of the party faithful.[7]

Breitscheid was the best SPD speaker in the Reichstag and a man with enough experience in foreign affairs to be entrusted with semiofficial negotiating tasks abroad by Foreign Minister Stresemann. But he could not have achieved such prominence within the party without the backing of Wels and Müller. Breitscheid had no base in the party organization. His personal manner was somewhat diffident despite his wit and intelligence. He did not relate comfortably to many colleagues from working-class backgrounds. There were those in the upper ranks of the organization who resented his role, and one official said of him: "His speaking ability is dangerous."[8] Still, Breitscheid reflected the center of gravity in the Reichstag fraction during the depression. He could not countenance the abandonment or dilution of social reforms benefiting the working class.

Rudolf Hilferding, the other high-ranking SPD intellectual (and former Independent Socialist) considered the political situation from a different perspective. Hilferding related what his thoughts immediately after the May 1928 elections were:

> I decided in favor of entrance into the government, because throughout my life I have represented the view . . . that it was the duty of Social Democrats, true to the word of Marx, to represent not the momentary interests or the interests of individual strata (*Schichten*), but the collective interests (*Gesamtinteresse*) of the proletariat. What were at that time and still are today the lasting and permanent interests which make it our duty to participate in the government. . . . First, the interest in the maintenance of democracy. The greater the political experience in

democracy I gained, . . . the more I can state as a fact that democracy is actually the precondition for the achievement of socialism, and that socialism cannot suddenly develop out of fascism or absolutism, because it would not have the huge treasury of experience which the proletariat can only obtain in democracy. Democracy is the indispensable precondition for the realization of socialism.[9]

Hilferding felt that the SPD's presence in the government was necessary to stabilize the parliamentary system and to exert a positive influence upon foreign policy. But the tug of war between those Social Democrats who looked for concrete economic benefits from coalition policy and those who sought to stabilize the republic continued from mid-1928 until March 1930.

After Hermann Müller was entrusted with the formation of a government, he encountered one difficulty after another with the SPD, the Center, and the DVP.[10] At one point the chancellor-designate tried to draw up a compromise platform that five parties could agree upon as a basis for a coalition.[11] The section on economic policy, although rather vague, went surprisingly far in the direction of the DVP's thinking. One sentence read: "The development and expansion of German production from its own resources is a precondition of German economic reconstruction." Tax policy was also to be used to encourage the use of savings and investment as capital for industry and agriculture.[12]

Nonetheless, the DVP fraction remained obdurate. Gustav Stresemann finally called a halt, stating in a telegram to Müller that any attempt to get the parties to agree upon a common program beforehand was unlikely to succeed. He suggested instead the solution that was eventually adopted, namely, that Müller select a cabinet from the coalition parties and that the ministers themselves then unite upon a program which could be presented to the Reichstag.[13] Even this form of indirect coalition met strenuous resistance from the DVP fraction, and Stresemann was able to quell the rebellion only by threatening to resign.[14]

Although Müller was able to select ministers from the five parties from which he needed support and to present a program to the Reichstag in early July,[15] his government was widely viewed as a "vacation cabinet" that would not last long beyond the summer recess. In response to such skepticism, the new Reich Minister of the Interior Carl Severing overconfidently predicted a four-year vacation from governmental crisis.[16] The five participating parties finally committed themselves to support Müller's government in April 1929; it then became no longer a cabinet of personalities but a formally constituted Great Coalition. But the ministers were no more able than before to impose decisions reached in the cabinet upon the party fractions. Instead, each political controversy brought lengthy negotiations among the fraction leaders of the coalition parties, which more often frustrated than promoted responsible settlement. Whereas the parties were at least somewhat in agreement on immediate foreign-policy concerns—reduction of reparations prescribed by the Dawes Plan and early removal of French troops from the Rhineland—a dispute over the construction of new battleships almost torpedoed the government in late 1928.

Pocket Battleship A

The Treaty of Versailles permitted Germany to construct six new battleships to replace its few remaining heavy cruisers, which were outmoded even in 1919. However, these ships were restricted to a displacement of 10,000 tons, thus limiting Germany's offensive capacity against the Entente navies. Although the Defense Ministry frequently pushed for appropriations for new ships in the early years of Weimar, only one light cruiser was approved up until 1928. At that point the navy came forward with a new design for a cruiser that was light and agile enough to evade more powerful attackers, but which offered enough firepower to inflict substantial damage upon enemy ships. Navy officials claimed that such ships were essential to defend the eastern portion of Germany, cut off from the rest of the country by the Polish Corridor.[17] The conservative government headed by Wilhelm Marx accepted the navy's view and proposed an initial appropriation of 9.3 million marks in fiscal 1928 for the first ship, Pocket Battleship A. On 27 March 1928 the Reichstag passed the navy budget over the heated opposition of the KPD, SPD, and DDP.[18]

The Prussian government then pulled off what appeared to be a very clever maneuver. Arnold Brecht, state secretary to Minister President Braun, successfully proposed to the cabinet that Prussia instruct its representatives in the Reichsrat to strike the appropriation for the ship. Enough delegates from the other states joined the Prussians to defeat the proposed ship. This decision was not in itself binding, but the Reichsrat threatened to reject the entire budget if the 9.3 million mark appropriation were included. To override the Reichsrat, the Reichstag needed a two-thirds margin, which was politically unattainable. Moreover, the dates for the dissolution of the Reichstag and for new elections had already been set. Finally, the Marx government agreed to a compromise with Prussia. It pledged that work on the ship would not begin before 1 September, by which time the new government would decide whether construction was still financially possible.[19]

The SPD exploited the controversy during the election campaign. Fact sheets compiled for SPD speakers stressed that the government and right-

wing parties had passed this unnecessary bill for a battleship but had refused
to appropriate five million marks for a program to feed needy children. "First
bread, then battleships," rang one slogan.[20] When the elections brought large
SPD gains, opponents of the ship were strengthened in their resolve not to
permit construction. Most of the left-wing SPD deputies had consistently
opposed virtually any military appropriations: some because of pacifist convictions, some because of their perception of the armed forces as an enforcement mechanism for a still repressive economic order. Other SPD deputies
resented the antirepublican episodes in which the navy had been involved,
doubted the military value of a small fleet unsupported by aircraft and sub-
marines (which were prohibited by the Versailles Treaty), and in any case
gave social programs a higher priority.

Nevertheless, Chancellor Müller was unable to persuade the other coalition
parties to drop the project. Publicly, he said that he was bound by the previous
government's decision unless budgetary considerations intervened.[21] According to cabinet rules of procedure, an appropriation bill required either the
support of the finance minister or that of a majority of the ministers with the
chancellor voting with the majority.[22] This meant that Finance Minister Hilferding and Müller together held veto power within the government over any
spending measure. On 20 July, however, Defense Minister Groener informed
Hilferding that, owing to savings effected in other parts of the military budget,
the 9.3 million marks were already available. When the cabinet considered
the matter on 10 August, Hilferding indicated that savings in all departments
were desirable because of the impending budget deficit. When Severing asked
if the ship was really needed now, Groener firmly answered yes. The decision
to go ahead with construction was made without a formal vote.[23]

There are indications that both Groener and President Hindenburg exerted
extreme pressure behind the scenes to get construction approved.[24] Müller
concluded that he had to give in to create a more solid foundation for his
coalition. It was also difficult for him to use the excuse of financial difficulty,
he said to Braun, when the government was increasing its spending on unemployment benefits.[25] But his prime concern was the impact of the decision
upon his coalition and future ones. He later wrote to a Dutch acquaintance:
"The defense issue cannot be viewed in isolation. Defense questions are
general political questions of the highest rank. If the German Social Democratic party were to take an absolutely negative attitude on questions of
defense, following the views of the pacifists, that would necessarily have the
practical consequence that it could never participate in the national government."[26] Severing too warned that the SPD could not simply be a "guest"
within the Weimar political system.[27]

The SPD ministers in Prussia were outraged by the decision. Braun wrote

Müller directly, telling him that the Prussian government had been "disavowed," that the military budget had been too high to start with, that Hilferding was to blame for not objecting to the spending, and that the future of the coalition in the Reich now looked dim.[28] Grzesinski was even more caustic in a letter to Braun, accusing the SPD ministers in the Reich of lacking the character to stand up to the military experts.[29]

Local SPD assemblies throughout the country also issued accusations and resolutions of protest.[30] The left-wing opposition knew how to exploit this sentiment. Paul Levi argued that this betrayal of socialist tradition and election promises was an inevitable consequence of the SPD leadership's ill-advised coalition policy.[31] This charge was most painful to the Prussian Social Democrats, supporters of coalition participation, since they felt that the whole crisis could have been avoided with more skillful direction on the part of Chancellor Müller. Now they began to worry that disillusioned party members and voters would repudiate the strategy of cooperation with the nonsocialist parties.[32]

In view of all the protest, party authorities felt compelled to restate their opposition to the ship. At a meeting of the executive committee and the fraction leadership on 15 August, Philipp Scheidemann proposed a resolution regretting the fact that the SPD ministers had not voted against the appropriation. The party council and the entire fraction ratified this resolution on 18 August.[33] At the same time, the party council also concluded that continued SPD participation in the government was in the interests of the working class.[34] When the Communists decided to take advantage of the SPD's embarrassment by pushing for a popular referendum, Paul Löbe persuaded the SPD authorities that the party had to take further action.[35] The SPD then introduced a bill in the fall to cease construction on the pocket battleship. Although the move failed, it brought about another tense battle between the SPD and its coalition partners.[36]

Hilferding ultimately concluded that the matter had to be settled formally. Otherwise its constant recurrence with each subsequent appropriation would rupture the government and create an impossible situation for the party.[37] Hilferding suggested that a party congress in early 1929 establish an official position on the general issue of national defense. The SPD executive committee then appointed a defense commission entrusted with the task of presenting a program to the congress. Although the commission's members were selected to reflect and balance the divisions within the party, the executive committee hedged a bit by choosing leftists regarded as reasonable.[38] Franz Künstler, Toni Sender, and Paul Levi were not fundamental opponents of the concept of national defense like some on the left. Rather, they resented the antirepublican spirit of the officer corps and felt that the armed forces as constituted were unsuited to the task of defending the republic.[39]

Spokesmen for the center-right majority on the commission chose to do battle on precisely this ground. Severing pointed out that the SPD could only influence the composition and policies of the armed forces by entering the government and remaining there. Then workers and other hitherto excluded elements could be encouraged to enter the military with some prospect of success.[40] A more positive attitude toward national defense would also benefit the party politically, Wilhelm Dittmann argued, since many workers presently supporting the nonsocialist parties might vote for a more patriotic socialist party.[41] Theodor Haubach stressed that it was in the workers' own interest to strengthen the existing state, and that the armed forces could still play a role in this process (even if they had not yet done so).[42]

The SPD's defense program cautiously approved the concept of national defense. The armed forces were needed to defend German neutrality against dangers brought about by fascism and imperialism. The republic, which had brought many gains for the workers, required military protection. The program also contained a list of ten specific demands to ensure that the military remained within the bounds of its proper functions: most importantly, closer parliamentary supervision of the military, and a ban on secret and illegal armaments.[43] This move was perhaps intended to bring together critics of the armed forces with those convinced that the SPD's coalition policy dictated a more positive attitude.

The defense program did not sail easily through the congress. One leftist-sponsored resolution against the battleship and the Great Coalition was defeated 254 to 139. The program was approved by 242 to 147, after a motion to postpone the issue until the next congress failed, 225 to 166.[44] The results reflected the fact that a number of delegates not aligned with the left-wing opposition, e.g., Paul Hertz and Kurt Schumacher, felt that the matter was too controversial for the party to act upon immediately.[45] One can also sense a lingering resentment that the guidelines had been proposed to give ex post facto justification to the cabinet decision on Pocket Battleship A.

The two most obvious lessons for the SPD were the need for better coordination between the executive committee (which had supervised the election campaign) and the party's ministers, and the danger involved in moves perceived as a deviation from socialist tradition. The party elite was uncertain about its willingness to make sacrifices to stabilize coalition government and worried about the political costs of doing so. The crisis rested, as *Vorwärts* itself noted, not only on disagreements about national defense, but on the difficulty in transforming the SPD from an opposition party into a governing one.[46] This same problem would assert itself even more forcefully in the controversy over unemployment insurance.

Unemployment Insurance and Interest-Group Politics

The Unemployment Insurance Law of 1927 was the most significant social reform since the revolutionary period. The law provided support payments for workers and employees who were involuntarily out of work, without requiring that they demonstrate financial need.[47] Payments to workers were in proportion to the level of wages or salaries previously earned. A male worker who was married but without children, for example, who had earned 33 marks per week in Berlin, received 14.85 marks while unemployed. In the same situation a worker with a wife and two children would be paid 18.15 marks.[48] The average weekly wage of an industrial worker in 1927, according to one recent tabulation, was just over 37 marks. However, ten percent of his gross weekly earnings was withheld to cover taxes, and unemployment and accident-insurance contributions. Thus, the net weekly earnings of the average worker in 1927 amounted to 33.6 marks.[49] When unemployed, he could subsist on benefit payments that ranged upward from 45 percent of his take-home pay, depending upon his place of residence and on the size of his family.

Support payments could continue for 26 weeks, or, when unemployment was widespread, up to 39 weeks. Seasonally unemployed workers, such as those in the construction industry, were initially excluded from coverage, but a later amendment provided for some benefits for six weeks in cases of need. There were separate insurance funds for workers and for white-collar employees. Each was financed by a 3 percent payroll tax upon employers and an equal premium deducted from the wages and salaries of workers and employees. Original estimates were that this rate would provide enough income for the funds to support some 800,000 unemployed. The whole program was administered by an independent Reich Unemployment Insurance Agency.[50]

From the very beginning, the calculation of the Agency's revenue and expenses appeared optimistic. The onset of the depression and the creation of massive unemployment wrecked all hopes that the Agency could be financially independent. The government was forced to step in with a subsidy of 260 million marks in fiscal 1928. For fiscal 1929 the government thought to impose a limit of 150 million marks on its subsidy, technically categorizing it as a loan, but Labor Minister Wissell (SPD) fought strenuously against any act that might lead to reducing benefits to the growing number of unemployed.[51] Finance Minister Hilferding preferred to make changes in the law to restore the Agency's secure financial basis, but this provoked a confrontation between business and labor over the fundamental premises of the legislation.

Prominent businessmen complained loudly about unemployment insurance during 1929. Most representatives of large-scale industry were not only opposed to any step to increase the income of the Unemployment Agency, they also felt that the support payments had a pernicious effect upon the economy and upon the mentality of the labor force, propping up wages to an artificially high level and destroying the laborer's incentive to work. They suggested a reduction in benefits and a return to the means test as a criterion for determining who was to receive them. The employers' campaign was directed against the whole concept of state intervention in the economy for the purpose of social reform.[52]

Conversely, the socialist trade unions regarded social reform as the normal function of a state that was democratic. The Unemployment Insurance Law was particularly important to them, because it attacked one of the real evils of capitalism—the effect of the "reserve army of the unemployed" described by Marx. With widespread unemployment and without effective social legislation, the worker had no bargaining power and was forced to sell his labor at whatever price the employer offered. A few labor leaders also mentioned a general economic justification for unemployment insurance; the benefits were said to increase the buying power of the masses and thereby provide a stimulus to the economy.[53] The socialist trade unionists recognized that the opposition of many businessmen to the insurance was part of a more fundamental attack against the labor movement and the democratic form of government.[54] Heavy industry in particular had only granted recognition to organized labor and accepted substantial reforms in 1918–1919 under duress, and many of labor's gains had evaporated in the course of 1923. The question now arose whether industrial interests could use their influence within the nonsocialist parties to weaken or destroy the only major social reform adopted since.

The SPD fraction decided in the spring of 1929 that it would support an increase in employer-worker contributions to the insurance fund to balance income and expenditures, but that it could not tolerate a reduction in benefits.[55] Breitscheid emphasized the party's determination to maintain unemployment benefits at the 1929 party congress, mentioning the possibility of SPD withdrawal if the government refused to cooperate. Even outside the government, he said, the SPD could always defend the constitution through mass action.[56] Several months later, party chairman Wels wrote Chancellor Müller that he was convinced the insurance issue was a vital matter (*Lebensfrage*) for the party.[57] The ADGB newspaper also warned in October 1929 that the working class would turn against a state that robbed it of its most important social reform.[58]

The unenviable task of drawing up a financial program that would meet the conflicting desires and objections of the SPD and the DVP fell to Finance Minister Hilferding. Hilferding's main objective was clear: to maintain the Great Coalition and the stability of parliamentary democracy.[59] He took dubious financial steps and delayed urgently needed financial remedies in order to satisfy the coalition parties. Lacking an innovative approach to macroeconomic policy in a capitalist society, Hilferding was dependent upon some of the same classical economic assumptions expressed by many businessmen and nonsocialist politicians.[60] Above all, business interests wanted to reduce their costs; they called for a tax policy which would promote capital formation. Government spending was seen as unproductive, government interference regarded as stifling.

Hilferding initially suggested a financial program that included a rise in the tobacco, beer, and luxury-goods taxes, combined with a reduction in income-tax rates to take effect after reparations payments were lowered through the newly negotiated Young Plan. A separate bill to raise premiums paid to the unemployment insurance fund to 3.5 percent (through 31 March 1930) made it through the Reichstag in October 1929 only after Foreign Minister Stresemann spent his dying breath convincing the DVP fraction not to break up the coalition over this issue.[61] But various objections delayed the financial program until December, when it became clear that even the proposed tax increases would not balance the budget.

Reichsbank President Hjalmar Schacht then upset Hilferding's delicately balanced calculations with a sharp note on 6 December, which he released to the press. Essentially, Schacht criticized the government's sloppy finances and demanded that it begin immediately a sinking fund to reduce the national debt.[62] Since Schacht's approval was virtually indispensable to the government's hope of borrowing money abroad,[63] it was impossible to ignore his proposal. Schacht's move blocked the proposed reduction in income and property taxes for fiscal 1930, which Hilferding had offered to business interests and to the DVP in order to win their support for his other measures.

Meanwhile, the SPD fraction reacted sharply to the campaign waged against unemployment insurance by the National Association of German Industry.[64] The fraction leaders and union spokesmen had refused to bind the party to the unpopular reductions in income and property taxes envisioned by Hilferding.[65] Hilferding took his package of sales-tax increases and direct tax cuts to the floor of the Reichstag anyway. On 10 December SPD fraction cochairman Breitscheid told a journalist that the fraction was thinking of voting against the proposal.[66] The party stepped back from such a move when the Müller government made the emergency tax increases a matter of confidence, and when Hilferding was forced to drop his proposal for reduction in direct taxes. Breitscheid nonetheless remarked publicly that the Finance Minister's program was closer to the DVP's ideas than the SPD's.[67] The DVP finally gave its assent to the bill, because the imminent conference in The Hague on reparations made it a most inopportune moment to have a cabinet crisis. The

SPD fraction was mollified by an extension of the increase in unemployment insurance premiums. But the financial outlook remained bleak.[68]

Hilferding's position had become completely untenable. All sides in the dispute were convinced of his incompetence.[69] But the pressure of circumstances contributed to Hilferding's inability to find a solution. The two previous finance ministers had raised the salaries of civil servants and cut taxes. Needing to borrow money to meet deficits they had created, Hilferding found himself in a real bind when the depression increased welfare expenditures and cut tax income.[70] He did not want to pay the political penalty of taking unpopular measures to reduce spending drastically. State Secretary Popitz encouraged him to hopscotch from one payment deadline to the next, borrowing money at high interest when necessary. Schacht put an end to this maneuvering, and both Hilferding and Popitz resigned in late December.

The success of Hilferding's approach had depended upon too many "ifs": the government's ability to borrow sufficient funds at home and abroad to cover operating deficits; a quick upturn in the economy to balance the budget and reduce the strain on the unemployment insurance funds; the SPD's willingness to countenance income-tax reduction in the face of rising sales taxes.[71] In the cabinet Labor Minister Wissell said to Hilferding's successor, former Economics Minister Moldenhauer (DVP), that Hilferding had been conducting the DVP's policy—which Moldenhauer strenuously denied.[72]

Moldenhauer found the budget outlook for fiscal 1930 to be deeply in the red. The unanticipated fund for the retirement of debt, the shortfall in tax revenue owing to the worsening economy, and the need for a subsidy of 250 million marks to the Unemployment Insurance Agency created the prospect of a deficit of at least 750 million marks even without any cut in income-tax rates—this despite the reduction in German reparations payments specified in the Young Plan.[73] The experts in the SPD fraction drew up a tax package avoiding any hike in consumer taxes beyond the rise in alcohol and tobacco taxes already proposed. The bulk of the increased revenue was to come from heavier taxation of industry, accelerated collection of back taxes, and a one-year surtax of 10 percent on the income and wealth taxes, which affected only those in the upper income levels.[74] This solution was rejected not only by the DVP but also by the Center party fraction leader Heinrich Brüning.[75]

Brüning told Breitscheid that he had learned from reliable DVP sources that this party intended to break up the Müller government and to create a minority government of the four nonsocialist coalition parties.[76] This decision by the DVP to cross the Rubicon coincided more or less with preparations being made by General Schleicher and others close to President Hindenburg for the ouster of the Great Coalition and the establishment of a new government resting upon presidential authority rather than on a precarious parliamentary majority.[77] The presidential emergency powers might then become the means for the destruction of parliamentary government.

Müller's government found itself in a truly critical situation in early March 1930. When the coalition parties could not agree upon a package of increased taxes and higher unemployment insurance premiums, Interior Minister Severing suggested to the chancellor that he ask the president for an order to dissolve the Reichstag. With Hindenburg's support, Müller could then have issued decrees under the authority of Article 48 during the election campaign. Such power would have allowed him to impose a solution to the deadlock over unemployment insurance and the budget. Müller doubted, however, that the president would consent to such a scheme. He thought instead about resignation.[78]

The political crisis deepened when the Center party persisted in its demand that the financial issues be settled before the Reichstag voted to ratify the Young Plan for reparations payments. There is some evidence (but of questionable quality) that Müller then reconsidered Severing's suggestion about Article 48. A decade later Heinrich Brüning wrote that Müller had pledged to President Hindenburg that, if the latter signed the Young Plan, Müller would make cuts in unemployment benefits by decree, even against the opposition of his own party.[79] Whether or not this version is entirely accurate, it is certainly not outlandish. The chancellor had a relatively good relationship with President Hindenburg. Notes taken by General Schleicher's adjutant sometime in January or February make it clear that the president was originally prepared to offer Müller the power to dissolve the Reichstag and to govern under Article 48. The Field Marshal was also inclined to use this assurance of support for the chancellor to get the Center party's support for the Young Plan and to prevent the People's party from withdrawing from the coalition. Schleicher dissuaded the President and promoted the alternative of a Brüning chancellorship backed by Article 48.[80]

A financial compromise devised earlier by Finance Minister Moldenhauer and discarded because of protests by the parties, was given new life at this point. The tax package was neatly balanced—increases in all categories for 1930, combined with a legally binding commitment to reduce income taxes by 600 million marks for fiscal 1931. There were also cuts in government spending in several ministries. The key to the proposal was the section on unemployment insurance. The Insurance Agency would be given the proceeds of the sale of 150 million marks worth of preferred stock in the (nationalized) railroads, as well as 50 million marks from general tax revenues. If the 200-million-mark subsidy in 1930 was not enough, the Agency's governing board would be permitted to raise the premiums paid by employers and workers to 4 percent, or to propose to the Reichstag changes (that is, reductions) in the benefit structure.[81]

The cabinet unanimously approved Moldenhauer's proposal on 5 March, but the DVP fraction quickly rebuffed its own finance minister.[82] As the Reichstag finally approved the Young Plan, the four other coalition parties (who possessed a slim majority without the DVP) began talks on how to maintain the government. Chancellor Müller, however, was dubious about Hindenburg's willingness to accept what was essentially a Weimar Coalition government, and the Center party had also ruled out such an arrangement in the recent past.[83] So Müller placed his hopes on the fact that both DVP ministers, Moldenhauer and Foreign Minister Curtius, continued to support the program accepted by the rest of the cabinet, despite the DVP fraction's position.[84] Would the DVP fraction remain adamant if confronted in the Reichstag by a united cabinet and the four other coalition parties?

Müller had long since recognized that the collapse of the Great Coalition would likely result in the formation of a government without the support of parliament but backed by the president's emergency powers. In February 1929 he had written to party chairman Wels: "If we do not secure government relations in the Reich, that will be the bankruptcy of parliamentarism based on the Weimar Constitution."[85] At the 1929 party congress Breitscheid had also warned that the fall of the Müller government might be exploited by "political desperadoes" using the nonparliamentary provisions of the constitution to give the president power that was clearly undemocratic. Breitscheid called a presidential government a "concealed dictatorship."[86] In December 1929 Müller again told the SPD fraction that failure to reach a compromise on finance and unemployment insurance might lead to a government under Article 48.[87]

But perhaps because of their past success in combating autocratic government, the Social Democratic leaders were not totally averse to this outcome in March 1930. Breitscheid claimed in *Vorwärts* on 21 March that the DVP undoubtedly wanted to create a rightist government, perhaps by way of a minority government supported by Article 48. He wrote as if the outcome were already determined, remarking that if the coalition collapsed it would not be the SPD's doing.[88]

However, Brüning was unwilling to let the showdown take place as the battle lines then were drawn up. With all the parties aware that he had the president's blessings,[89] the Center party leader held more leverage than most mediators. In late March he offered a new compromise on the unemployment-insurance issue. The government could continue to subsidize the insurance fund, but there would be a legally binding limit placed on the subsidy each year. For fiscal 1930 the limit was to be 150 million marks. If the Agency was still in the red after efforts to economize administration, the government could then propose means for further savings, raise payment premiums to 3.75 percent, or balance the Agency's expenses with its income. In effect, the first and third alternatives were euphemisms for a reduction in unemployment benefits.[90]

Brüning's motives remain disputed. It has been suggested that the compromise was designed so as to force the SPD to reject it.[91] Although Brüning did not want a confrontation with the DVP, it does seem he would have preferred the Müller government to continue in office for some months. Brüning apparently hoped to take over the chancellorship in the fall—after some of the unpopular decisions to cut social programs had already been taken.[92] The most likely interpretation of Brüning's move is that it was a way to delay the governmental crisis.

No one seriously thought that the Insurance Agency could get along with a subsidy of only 150 million marks and maintain current benefit levels, or that it could suddenly discover a way to make huge administrative savings. But the plan won the reluctant approval of the DVP fraction, because it at least did not entail an immediate half-percent increase in employer-worker premiums. Chancellor Müller was willing to consent to the arrangement as long as the coalition parties all agreed, but Labor Minister Wissell's outspoken opposition foreshadowed the negative response of the SPD fraction. Moldenhauer, having finally swung the DVP fraction over to the new compromise, was now unwilling to defend the compromise that he himself had proposed earlier in the month. The cabinet could no longer present a united front on behalf of the Moldenhauer compromise, and Müller refused to take it to the floor of the Reichstag. The weary chancellor preferred resignation to defeat in open battle.[93]

He was immediately replaced by Heinrich Brüning, who formed a minority government without the SPD within two days. No succeeding government ever enjoyed a majority in the Reichstag until Hitler took power and then coerced both the voters and the other parties into giving him full authority. Normal parliamentary government was not restored until after the Second World War.

How did the SPD fraction arrive at a decision that was recognized in advance as one with potentially grave consequences? The fraction leaders, Breitscheid and Wels, felt that the party had made a substantial concession by agreeing to the tax package proposed by Moldenhauer in early March, after fraction negotiators had rejected the first Moldenhauer compromise in mid-February.[94] Their main reason for going along had been to strengthen the unemployment-insurance fund through the increase in premiums.[95] The Brüning compromise, on the other hand, did not increase the premiums sufficiently.

When it was first discussed in a meeting of the coalition parties on 25 March, Breitscheid pronounced it unacceptable. The SPD delegates—Breitscheid, Wels, Wilhelm Keil, Paul Hertz, and Siegfried Aufhäuser—took the same position during interparty negotiations on the next two days.[96]

After Müller made a final appeal on 27 March for the parties to reach agreement, the SPD fraction held a brief but heated session. Labor Minister Wissell called the Brüning compromise unacceptable, and he was supported by the left wing in the fraction. Hermann Müller-Lichtenberg (not to be confused with the chancellor), an SPD deputy and a member of the ADGB executive, threatened that the unions would conduct a public campaign against the government if the SPD consented to the compromise.[97] The three SPD ministers and former Finance Minister Hilferding argued that Brüning's proposal did not threaten the level of benefits, since the SPD ministers could veto any attempt by the government to reduce benefits. Their posts in the cabinet should not be abandoned.[98] But the extremely tough language used by Müller-Lichtenberg was apparently decisive.[99] Otto Wels urged the fraction to avoid giving even the appearance that benefits might be reduced. Wels may also have been influenced by a threat from the ADGB leadership or from Müller-Lichtenberg that the unions were prepared to break relations with the SPD if the party opposed the union position. A large majority then voted to stick with the Moldenhauer compromise, which no longer had a chance. The opponents may have numbered only five.[100]

The balance of power within the SPD fraction shifted away from its "governmental wing" as a result of the defection of two groups: the trade unionists who had initially supported the Great Coalition experiment, and a group of key organization men and financial experts headed by Wels, Breitscheid, Hertz, and Keil. In the past both the trade-union elements and the group of "centrists" had most often accepted Hermann Müller's judgment on major decisions in the realm of coalition policy, if not always on tactics. Now it appeared that among its other effects, the depression weakened Müller's hand by making economic and social issues the party's foremost concern. The dominant perspective within the higher ranks of the SPD on such issues was still that of an interest group for the industrial workers. However, the party system in Weimar Germany did not allow the SPD much scope for successful interest-group politics, and the economic crisis virtually eliminated the chance of reasonable compromise in parliament.

Can the SPD leaders be accused of responsibility for the collapse of the Great Coalition, and by implication, that of parliamentary democracy itself? The real responsibility lay with those who consciously intended to destroy not only the Müller government but the whole system of parliamentary government as well.[101] Social Democratic representatives, who had so long been forced into the position of choosing the lesser evil, now chose not to delay the crisis any further. Certainly it is likely that the Müller government would have collapsed after the insurance fund ran dry, if not sooner. But Hilferding himself likened the logic of the SPD fraction's decision to that of a man driven to suicide by his fear of death.[102] Despite all the obvious factors contributing to the SPD fraction's decision—anger at the abandonment of the government's bill, fear of Communist gains among the workers, concern about the relationship between the SPD and the ADGB—there is still something mysterious about the move. A party trying to maximize its effectiveness within the parliamentary system would not behave in the same way.

German Social Democracy retained an ambivalent attitude, not toward parliamentary democracy per se, but toward its own role within the Weimar system with its multiparty structure. Even in a nonrevolutionary socialist party there were strong traces of the philosophical traditions that had shaped the thinking of SPD leaders in the late nineteenth century. Many members of the party elite confidently expected capitalism to develop toward socialism and other social groups to join forces with the proletariat (or to disappear entirely), which justified an SPD stance of political opposition, particularly in time of economic crisis. The Social Democratic leaders wished to emphasize their dissatisfaction with the existing economic order and with government economic policies, even though they lacked a well-developed alternative.

Ambivalence toward governmental responsibility was not solely the product of socialist tradition. The SPD leaders had not appreciated the political repercussions of previous coalition governments. Rank-and-file disenchantment may have been even stronger, but figures such as Otto Wels and Rudolf Breitscheid also took a pessimistic view of what the party might accomplish through participation in government. The depression only intensified a tendency within the SPD elite that had been growing since 1923. But the extraordinary events of the early 1930s demonstrated that withdrawal into opposition was no panacea for the SPD.

10. Prussia and the Reich, 1930–1931

Y 1930 international economic collapse and inadequate government policy smashed the already delicate foundation of Weimar democracy. An economic depression of uncharted depth and duration threw three million Germans out of work. The withdrawal of foreign loans added to the severity of the German economic tailspin. Chancellor Heinrich Brüning's deflationary policy aimed at balancing the budget and promoting German exports required new taxes and cuts in welfare programs, both of which set the political parties and interest groups against each other.[1] Rather than struggle endlessly with parliament, the new chancellor preferred to govern by means of the presidential emergency powers.

The resurgence of the Nazi movement actually preceded the depression but intensified during 1930. The Nazis strove to gain power through many of the same methods that Mussolini had employed in Italy in 1922: a combination of propaganda and organization, parliamentary obstructionism, street violence against unpopular foes, and skillful political bargaining with conservative elements. Of course, Hitler had learned from his own failure as well as from Mussolini's example. The Beer Hall Putsch in November 1923 had demonstrated the risk of a Nazi attempt to seize power by armed force. But the aftermath was equally revealing. Put on trial for high treason in a Munich court, Hitler managed to seize control of the proceedings when the judges allowed him to speak to his own purposes. Admitting responsibility for the Putsch, Hitler justified any act of treason against the Weimar Republic as true patriotism. Bavarian Commissar Kahr, General Otto von Lossow, and Police Chief Hans von Seisser, who appeared as prosecution witnesses, found it hard to quarrel with Hitler's nationalistic and authoritarian objectives. Even the state prosecutor came to adopt an approving attitude toward Hitler during the course of the trial.[2] The graphic demonstration of antirepublican sentiment within the ranks of government and judiciary revealed the opportunities for an effectively organized political movement making use of legal (as well as illegal) methods. In the reorganized Nazi party, Hitler confined the storm troopers to a limited political role rather than a military one.[3] While the SA attacked Communists and other targets on the streets during the early 1930s, Hitler strode to the chancellery by way of the Kaiser Wilhelm Memorial Church.

In the past the SPD had relied upon Prussia to combat antirepublican extremism. As early as 1926 Prussian Minister President Braun had expressed concern about a right-wing campaign to alarm the public about the menace of communism. If the citizens were sufficiently frightened, then a conservative government in the Reich could resort to a state of siege, under which the rightist paramilitary forces, with or without the help of the Reichswehr, could crush their opponents.[4] Berlin police raided the houses of a number of suspects in one alleged rightist plot in May 1926, but did not find sufficient evidence to prosecute.[5] The move created a political furor after the residence of prominent industrialist Albert Vögler was searched, which Braun afterwards admitted was unwise. Prussian Interior Minister Grzesinski felt satisfied, however, that the police action had intimidated the right, although he told Prussian officials that the right-wing organizations still bore watching.[6] Prussian officials thus anticipated a political-military operation from the far right.

Prussian Interior Minister Grzesinski made frequent and effective use of the Disarmament Law of 1921 (which the Entente powers had forced the Reichstag to pass) against the rightist paramilitary forces. This law placed strict limitations on the authorized supply of weapons and the training of forces. The government could ban organizations possessing weapons and conducting military activities illegally.[7] But the more prominent nationalist organizations enjoyed official protection and not only from the Reichswehr. When in 1929 Grzesinski ventured to ban the Rhenish-Westphalian division of the Stahlhelm, the largest veterans organization, for conducting military exercises, President Hindenburg himself complained. Hindenburg, an honorary member of the Stahlhelm, refused to dissociate himself from the organization just to please the Prussian government, and after a year of maneuvering he had Grzesinski's decision reversed.[8]

A second Prussian weapon against right-wing extremism was the Law for the Protection of the Republic. Passed in 1922 and extended once, the law had lapsed in July 1929. Not until March 1930 did the Reichstag pass a new and somewhat weaker version, which was a sign that the law had fallen into disfavor among some of its former supporters. SPD spokesmen complained that officials and judges had applied the law against Communists beyond the point of stringency, while they had overlooked more serious violations by right-wing radicals.[9] There was a great deal of truth to this charge. By 1924 the special tribunal established under the law had imposed 75 percent of its total sentences against members of the Communist party, and the Communist share was even higher in some subsequent years. Reich prosecutors also allowed many offenses involving right-wing extremists to be handled by regular state courts, where the defendants often received lenient treatment.[10]

This judicial double standard created a backlash in the SPD Reichstag fraction, where some SPD deputies proposed to reduce the scope of the law. Prussian Interior Minister Grzesinski and Reich Interior Minister Severing were forced to intervene in late 1929 and early 1930, telling their party colleagues that the law was needed to meet the danger posed by the Nazis. One deputy told Grzesinski, however, that the SPD had to consider conditions in other states besides Prussia. In some places officials allegedly applied the law in such a distorted way that it might be used against members of the SPD.[11] After a considerable struggle, Grzesinski and Severing were able to salvage the provisions of the law that they regarded as essential.[12] But the internal conflict exacted a psychological toll. When *Rheinische Zeitung* Editor Wilhelm Sollmann chided Grzesinski for the Prussian government's passivity in the face of libelous criticism from Nazi leaders, Grzesinski responded with sarcastic comments about those "friends of the republic" who had allowed the law to lapse.[13]

When the new version of the law passed the Reichstag on 18 March, 1930 Grzesinski was no longer in office. His marital problems had placed Braun's coalition government in a sticky situation, as some members of the Center party were sensitive on this issue. So Grzesinski removed an irritant between the two major coalition parties by resigning.[14] Nonetheless, he was still actively involved in major political discussions. Braun wrote to Grzesinski (who was away on a trip) to assure him that the Prussian government would now move energetically against the Nazis. Grzesinski responded that the government should use this opportunity to ban both the Nazi party and the Communist party. He proposed that the Disarmament Law be employed against the Nazis and the Law for the Protection of the Republic against the Communists.[15] In this way the Prussian government's actions were less likely to be reversed by the courts. Yet the hope that Reich and Prussian policy against the extremist forces could be coordinated suffered a blow when the Great Coalition government in the Reich collapsed in March 1930.

Otto Braun regarded the SPD fraction's decision to pull out of the Müller government as an irrational move that could have been avoided if Müller had clamped down earlier on Wissell's insubordination, and if cooler heads had prevailed in the SPD fraction. On 1 April 1930 he told Grzesinski that the SPD Reichstag deputies "are now going around somewhat disconcerted and broken."[16] With reference to the fall of the Müller government, Braun declared to one of his aides: "You don't work for years to get into the saddle in order to jump off the horse the instant you see a thorn in your path."[17] In an extremely rare move, the SPD fraction in the Prussian Landtag passed a resolution criticizing the decision by the SPD Reichstag fraction to withdraw from the government.[18]

The minority government headed by Heinrich Brüning (Center) was unlikely to support any anti-Nazi course, although Brüning was certainly no
Nazi sympathizer. Pious, self-disciplined, reserved by nature to the point of
coldness, the new chancellor had little in common personally with the leader
of the Nazi movement. But both Brüning and Hitler were deeply influenced
by one experience—military service on the front lines during World War I.
The impact of war upon Hitler's thinking and subsequent career is well-
known; the declassé, aimless young Austrian found a home and began to
discover his political cause.[19] Brüning certainly did not absorb Hitler's un-
bounded militarism, but as a young officer, Brüning was moved by the unity,
sacrifice, and patriotism his troops showed. His feeling of loyalty to the
Reich, the Kaiser, and to Field Marshal von Hindenburg influenced his subsequent political undertakings. One of his contemporaries described him per-
ceptively: "His first profession was that of soldier, and in essence he remained
a soldier when his Field Marshal entrusted him with the business of the Reich
chancellor. He formed a government allegedly independent of parties, a presidential cabinet, which he called a cabinet of those who fought on the front.
When the war was lost and the revolution broke out at the end of 1918, the
world came to an end for the soldier, and internally he was never able to come
to terms with it. As a politician, he sought to revive in the people the sentiment that had inspired him as a soldier during the World War."[20] Although
Brüning had little regard for the talent and political maturity of most nationalist politicians, he saw them as engaged in a similar quest—even Hitler. In his
first interview with the Nazi leader, Brüning referred to their common experience on the front.[21] He was to learn the hard way that this was not a sufficient
basis for political cooperation.

Brüning's immediate priorities as chancellor were a balanced budget and an
end to German reparations obligations. Assured of the president's support,
which meant that he could govern around parliament with the use of Article
48 if necessary, he did not feel the need to make concessions to the parties.
Minister President Braun now had to contend with the problem of coordinat-
ing policies with a Reich government that was substantially more conservative than its predecessor. The SPD fraction in the Reichstag found Brüning
extremely difficult to get along with, but Braun believed that the alternatives
to a Brüning government were much worse. The rising tide of National
Socialism and the continuing friction between the military and the Prussian
government convinced Braun that the SPD could not risk making additional
enemies. He thus laid out a course of cooperation with Brüning that the party
accepted—with reservations, qualifications, and great reluctance.

After Brüning had formed his cabinet, Braun wanted the SPD Reichstag
fraction to refrain from voting for a motion of no confidence. It did not;

Breitscheid even castigated Brüning and the Center party for their role in the fall of the Müller government. However, twenty-odd deputies absented themselves on this vote, which Brüning survived because of the support of the rightist parties.[22]

As a general rule, Braun felt it necessary to achieve a certain amount of coordination between the Reich and Prussia.[23] In this particular situation his own political fate in Prussia was potentially linked to that of Brüning in the Reich. In April Severing's replacement as Reich interior minister, Joseph Wirth (Center), warned Braun's state secretary Robert Weismann that if the SPD overthrew Brüning, the Center party would have to reconsider its position on the Prussian coalition.[24] Thus, Braun's government was put in a position where it had to mediate between the chancellor and the SPD leaders in the Reich.[25] Prussia was reluctant to oppose the rigorous budget cuts and the new taxes that Brüning presented, despite the danger posed to its own budget by the Reich's reduced transmission of tax revenues to the states.[26]

When Brüning suggested to Braun that the two men remain in close contact with regard to the financial program of the chancellor, Braun responded that this was not necessary, as the Prussian government would support the Reich fully. Braun warned, however, that he could not guarantee how the SPD fraction in the Prussian Landtag (not to mention the Reichstag fraction) would react. He also suggested to Brüning that he seek an Enabling Law which would allow the chancellor to impose his financial program.[27] Brüning disregarded the advice and saw the SPD vote against the part of his tax package that included a poll tax on each citizen; the SPD wanted a small graduated income tax. When the SPD's opposition caused the measure to fail,[28] Brüning resorted to the use of Article 48. At that point the SPD fraction introduced a motion to lift the emergency ordinance, a move within the prerogatives of the Reichstag. Supported by most of the antigovernment forces, the SPD motion passed by a 236–221 margin. In defiance, Brüning got the president to dissolve the Reichstag and to issue new emergency ordinances. Braun described this decision as the beginning of the end of parliamentarism.[29]

Braun had always opposed excessive use of Article 48. Even under Ebert's presidency, Braun had been concerned about the far-reaching presidential emergency powers. He had feared that the Reich intervention in Saxony in late 1923 under Article 48 might set a dangerous precedent.[30] Subsequently, he complained to Chancellor Marx (Center) when the latter, with Ebert's support, used Article 48 to lower taxes in late 1924: "It is the task of the Reich and state governments to apply the constitution strictly. The future consequences of such an extensively generous interpretation of Article 48 appear to be too dangerous for the existence of the German republic."[31] In August 1930, during the election campaign, Braun issued similar warnings in public. Once parliamentarism was abandoned, there was no telling where the republic would end up.[32]

The campaign was marked by numerous incidents of violence, which were to proliferate during the next two years.[33] Nazi mass meetings and marches led to street fights, vandalism, and beatings of innocent bystanders as well as of members of opposition parties. Police usually did their best to punish those who disturbed public order, but violence did not seem to cost the Nazis votes. If anything, political violence won support for the Nazis! Many Germans who did not share Nazi aims or respect Adolf Hitler did share Nazi animosities. The fact that the Communist paramilitary forces frequently served as the opposition in the streets did nothing to damage the NSDAP politically. Hitler had promised he would deal mercilessly with his enemies, and the SA provided supporting evidence. With violence itself an element of Nazi propaganda, the party did not have to rely on demagogic rhetoric alone.

Both the SPD and the Center survived the 14 September elections in decent shape, particularly the Center. The SPD fell from 29.8 percent of the popular vote and 153 seats to 24.5 percent and 143 seats. The Center's number of deputies actually rose from 62 to 68. Nonetheless, the results were a catastrophe for the advocates of parliamentary government. The decline of the Protestant middle-class parties, evident throughout much of the Weimar period,[34] now accelerated, while the Communists raised their holding from 54 to 77 seats. The clear victor, however, was the Nazi party, which went from a modest 12 seats to a phenomenal 107, thereby becoming the second strongest party in the Reichstag. The so-called negative majority (KPD plus NSDAP) of the two extremes was not yet a reality, but it was not far off. The parties formerly composing the Great Coalition (including the Bavarian People's party) no longer commanded a majority.

On the day after the Reichstag election a correspondent from United Press interviewed Minister President Braun, who refused to concede the political arena to the extremists of the left and right. He suggested a Great Coalition of all reasonable elements, concentration on the fight against unemployment, and an end to government by decree. Braun may have intended the interview as an oblique appeal to Brüning to demonstrate his willingness to cooperate.[35] The minister president followed with a more specific offer. Through an intermediary, Braun informed the chancellor that he was interested in becoming vice-chancellor in the Reich, which would facilitate a joint effort by the Reich and Prussia against the extremist forces. Brüning did not respond.[36] The chancellor's own preference for presidential government—government by means of Article 48—made him less sensitive to the immediate political problem posed by the Nazi electoral triumph.

In a face-to-face meeting in early October Braun presented Brüning with the following options: either the Reich join Prussia in the fight against Nazism, or the chancellor allow the NSDAP to enter his government at a time when this party was still too weak to dominate it.[37] A number of experienced political observers backed the second course, arguing that the voters would soon discover the hollowness of Nazi promises.[38] Such a situation might even have induced prominent Nazi officials to break with a recalcitrant Hitler, who was still not a German citizen and was therefore ineligible to hold national office. But Braun made it clear that he preferred the first option.[39]

Neither the chancellor nor the SPD leaders in the Reich were particularly interested in formal ties, but a second meeting among Brüning, Hermann Müller, and Otto Wels produced a tentative consensus. The SPD leaders were prepared to recommend that the SPD fraction "tolerate" the Brüning government in order to avoid further political crises.[40] Seeing his hope for government by parliamentary majority disappear, Braun reversed his longstanding position against the use of Article 48 to bypass parliament. This switch was undoubtedly the result of his pessimism about the political outlook. According to one report, he told one of his state secretaries at the time, "Prepare yourself for civil war."[41]

There was considerable resistance within the SPD Reichstag fraction to the toleration policy. A worried Hermann Müller wrote to Braun, off on a brief vacation, to ask his assistance: "The meeting of the party council has demonstrated that the opinion is widespread outside, more so than one could assume, that the right must be allowed to govern—so that it, including the National Socialists, ruins itself. I have sharply countered such opinions, but it is to be assumed that this reasoning will gain added popularity in the Reichstag fraction." After pointing out that a second attempt to topple Brüning would be disastrous, Müller urged the ailing Braun to come to the fraction meeting: "whenever government participation is discussed in assemblies and in the press, your name is mentioned again and again. You are seen from the socialist side as the strongest unconsumed force."[42] With Braun's assistance, the Reichstag fraction leaders got their way. The fraction approved a resolution setting preservation of the constitution and parliamentarism as the SPD's highest goals.[43] By 10 October Brüning could be confident that the SPD would not try to oust him. On 12 October Braun announced in a column in *Vorwärts* that the SPD was ready and able to adopt an unpopular policy in order to protect the republic against fascism.[44]

As if to underscore the danger, the Nazis held a march through the streets of Berlin on 13 October that resulted in attacks on bystanders and smashing of windows in Jewish-owned stores. Another illuminating incident occurred in December when the American-made film *All Quiet on the Western Front*, based on Erich Remarque's German novel, was given its premier in Berlin.

Angered by the pacifist sentiments of German soldiers in the novel, a group of Nazis led by Joseph Goebbels released white mice and set off stinkbombs in the theater, forcing the evacuation of the building and creating a riot outside. Instead of clamping down on such behavior, the Reich government urged Prussia to ban showings of the film in order to avoid provocations. When Braun refused, the Reich presented its arguments to the national film review board, which prevented exhibition of the film.[45] Such an outcome did nothing to discourage the Nazis from further use of violent and disruptive methods.

By this time Braun had resorted to the reappointment of trusted men to the Prussian offices responsible for protecting public order. Interior Minister Heinrich Waentig was dismissed, and since the Center party was still reluctant to accept Grzesinski in the cabinet, Braun appointed Severing to his old post, and Grzesinski to the office of chief of police of Berlin. Braun and Ernst Heilmann both were concerned that Severing might not act decisively enough, but he seemed to be the best politically acceptable candidate.[46]

Severing did appear to hesitate before potential obstacles. He raised doubts in a private meeting of the SPD executive committee whether Prussia alone could withstand a coup, complaining that the Nazis and Communists both were infiltrating and disrupting the Prussian security police. Although he did not expect any high army officers to support a Nazi coup, he forecast that in the lower ranks of the Reichswehr there would at least be benign neutrality. Severing was further concerned that the Communists, eager to destroy the Social Democratic stronghold in Prussia, would use a general strike or military force to sabotage any Prussian resistance to a coup.[47]

Prussian Ministerial Director Arnold Brecht suggested that the government remove the threat of a Nazi coup by banning the Nazi paramilitary forces. But Severing replied that the Reich government and the Supreme Court might disavow such a move.[48] Even more than Braun, Severing felt capable of proceeding against the extremists only in conjunction with the Reich. He urged the national government to assert its authority against those engaged in lawlessness and demagogy, asking for measures giving police and government officials stronger regulatory powers throughout the Reich.[49]

The Reich did issue a new package of emergency ordinances in March 1931, requiring police permits for all indoor and outdoor political meetings. Any gathering considered a threat to public order could be banned. Controversial posters and handbills were prohibited, and violators were to be severely fined.[50] This substantial curtailment of civil liberties did not resolve the problems of maintaining order, however, and it also raised the questions of who would wield these powers and for what purposes.

After the Nazis and Communists both scheduled June sport festivals in Berlin, Police Chief Grzesinski banned them under the new ordinances. Severing and his aide Hans Hirschfeld then decided to remove the bans. Grzesinski was away on vacation, but his assistants were not pleased with the "unalterable" decision taken by the Prussian Interior Ministry. One of them wrote to Grzesinski: "A republic . . . should not avail itself of weak-kneed liberalism . . . that disapproves of harsh but just treatment of the radical wings."[51] The Nazi reaction to Severing's authorization was so provocative that the interior minister soon changed his mind and reimposed the ban on the Nazi festival.

After Severing went off to Frankfurt to attend an official function, President Hindenburg made known through a telegram his strenuous objection to the differential treatment of the Nazis and the Communists. Hindenburg threatened to use Article 48 and put through a new ban; Severing responded with a threat to resign; and Brüning was forced to mediate in the dispute to protect his own government. Severing finally agreed to forbid the Communist festival if the organizers violated any of the stipulations laid down. After Communists were alleged to have been involved in a 30 June incident in which a policeman was killed, the Prussian interior minister again banned the Communist festival.[52]

Severing's vacillation was largely the result of the delicate political situation in mid-1931. The Stahlhelm had pressed the idea of a referendum to force the dissolution of the Prussian Landtag and new elections, and the DNVP and the NSDAP joined the campaign. Severing was apparently concerned that hostile action against the Communists would drive them to make common cause with the far right (as in fact occurred). Yet he found that his attempt to reconcile the Communists by lifting the ban on their festival had adverse repercussions in the Reich.[53]

President Hindenburg could exert leverage upon Chancellor Brüning, who of course had some influence with his Center party colleagues in Prussia. Given a dispute of sufficient virulence, the Prussian coalition might collapse. Another dangerous possibility was that a right-wing government in the Reich might be formed. It could declare a state of siege and wrest control of the Prussian police from the Prussian government. In that situation the Braun government would no longer represent a major force. Severing was eager to protect his authority over the Prussian police,[54] but he could not hoard Prussian strength, concentrate on the Nazi menace, and maintain amicable relations with the Reich simultaneously.

With the Communists and the parties of the far right urging the voters to oust the Prussian government, the referendum had to be taken seriously. The Prussian government intensified use of its powers over the press, forcing all newspapers to print an announcement on 6 August denouncing the unholy alliance of Bolsheviks and fascists, condemning the attempt to overthrow "the last great bulwark, the citadel of democracy and the republic in Germany: Prussia." Should the extremist effort succeed, it was stated, all citizen rights achieved since 1918 would be destroyed.[55]

The outcome of the referendum was not particularly encouraging for the Prussian government in view of its strong campaigning tactics. While the almost 9.8 million positive votes fell more than 3 million short of the necessary margin for approval, the total was another testimony to the vote-pulling ability of the extremist parties during the economic crisis. Furthermore, the DVP and the DNVP protested vigorously to the Reich government about how Prussia was using its powers over the press.[56] Brüning, who had finally been forced to oppose the referendum after first taking no position, was angry with Braun, who he felt had created difficulties for him with the aggressive methods against the referendum.[57] The chancellor's drift to the right now became increasingly obvious, and the SPD leaders in the Reich began to find the policy of toleration more and more uncomfortable. The chancellor's economic policies and his method of dealing with the parties in the Reichstag were both coming under fire.

SPD Misgivings with Brüning

At a time when the unemployment level was approaching five million, party and union leaders were under extreme pressure to obtain relief for their constituents. Yet Brüning's deflationary economic policy aggravated the unemployment situation, and his budget cuts came at the expense of the social programs and benefits that represented the most tangible achievement of the Weimar system for the average worker. By mid-1932, for example, a worker who originally would have received 14.85 marks per week in unemployment benefits, based on previous weekly earnings of 33 marks, was now receiving 10.2 marks.[58] The level of employment, the level of wages, and the level of benefits given constant wages were all declining throughout 1930–31.

Under these circumstances, SPD leaders in the Reich were sorely tempted to express their opposition to the chancellor, whose intransigence did nothing to smooth the situation. On 15 June 1931 Breitscheid, Hilferding, and Wels requested Brüning to allow the Budget Committee of the Reichstag (which was in recess) to be recalled in order to discuss his latest financial ordinances. Brüning threatened to resign if this were done. Braun and Severing, who were also present, reluctantly supported the chancellor.[59] On this and similar occasions the SPD leaders in the Reich shied away from drawing the "final consequence."

Braun had made the case for continuing the party's toleration policy several months earlier in a meeting of the Reichstag fraction. He first noted that a rebuff of Brüning would have repercussions on the Prussian coalition. He then said he would refuse to carry out the ordinances issued by a (subsequent) Reich government composed of forces from the extreme right, implying that he would rather resign than stay in office in that case. At another meeting of the fraction leaders there was a sharp clash between Severing and Breitscheid. After Paul Hertz had grudgingly consented to Brüning's latest emergency ordinance, he warned that the party could not put up with anything worse. He then asked how relations stood in Prussia. Severing replied that the SPD still held influence through its position in the Prussian government. To preserve its hold, the party had to tolerate Brüning and conduct the struggle against fascism until the last moment. Breitscheid retorted: "When is that? [We cannot afford to] lose the masses!"[60]

Left-wing opponents of the SPD's past coalition policy were even more outspoken in their opposition to Brüning and to toleration, mounting a shrill campaign in the press. When several prominent leftists decided to violate fraction discipline, however, the executive committee moved ruthlessly against them. The leftists then responded by founding a new party, the Socialist Workers' party (SAPD).[61] But even party members with serious reservations about the passive stance of the party leadership had no stomach for another schism within the socialist movement. The SAPD weakened the SPD substantially in Saxony and among socialist youth organizations, but party leaders generally did not consider it a serious electoral rival.[62] The elections of 1932 bore out this judgment.

Of greater consequence was the growing union discontent with the party's toleration policy. Had the various dissidents been able to unite upon an alternative economic policy to Brüning's deflationary measures, they might have carried the day within the fraction. However, the ADGB was only gradually developing a program to stimulate the economy through public works projects, and the SPD's foremost economic experts, Hilferding and Hertz, remained concerned about the danger of inflation.[63] Hence there was no consensus on what course to pursue even if the SPD had the opportunity to influence government policy. Although extremely angry with Brüning, most union leaders did not demand that the party draw the final consequence. The prospect of Brüning's resignation and unforeseeable political consequences following the formation of a rightist government was intimidating to party and union leaders alike.[64]

Reichsreform

By mid-1931 the impending Prussian elections and the state's increasing financial dependence upon the national government made the Prussian ministers pessimistic about their future independence. A number of Prussian officials showed new interest in plans for administrative reform and political coordination. A realignment of authority between Prussia and the Reich might have created a more effective and unified government. It also would have served to broaden parliamentary support for Brüning, perhaps making him less dependent upon the president's backing.

The main architects of a new proposal were a few leading figures in the State party, which was essentially a renamed version of the shrunken Democratic party, and Prussian State Secretary Arnold Brecht. One version of the reform involved appointing Prussian Minister President Braun as vice-chancellor in Brüning's cabinet, naming Severing as Reich interior minister, merging the Prussian and Reich Ministries of the Interior, and selecting the Reich minister of justice as Prussian minister of justice also.[65] This plan went beyond Braun's earlier proposal in establishing links between the Reich and Prussia.

Braun consented to indirect and confidential discussions with the Reich on this subject, but he thought it unwise to force the plan upon Brüning. Brüning's initial reaction had been to delay consideration until after the conclusion of reparations negotiations in early 1932.[66] Nonetheless, the chancellor was attracted by the idea of ending the dualism between the Reich and Prussia. In mid-August he was willing to consider bringing Severing into his cabinet, but only if it could be done so that he was not compelled to lean to the left. One possibility was to appoint a strong conservative as economics minister at the same time.[67] Whether he was deterred by negative reaction to the publication of the proposal or by the arguments of chancellery aide Erwin Planck and General Schleicher against any cooperation with the SPD cannot be determined.[68] In any case, on 29 August Brüning told Württemberg State President Eugen Bolz (Center party) that he would not use Article 48 to restructure relations between the Reich and Prussia, and that he wanted to delay consideration of their relations until after the financial needs of the next few months were dealt with. Braun himself declared publicly that he had no intention of entering the Reich government.[69]

When Prussian Finance Minister Hermann Höpker-Aschoff resigned on 13 October, Brüning let Braun know that he would like Reich Finance Minister Hermann Dietrich (State party) to have the vacant Prussian post. In a meeting with the chancellor on 3 November, Braun countered with a more extensive proposal. Telling Brüning that he had planned to resign after the Prussian elections scheduled for 1932, Braun offered to step down immediately and to use his influence within the SPD to secure Brüning's election as minister president. The simultaneous occupation of the Prussian post and the chancellorship, which Braun had sought for himself three years earlier, would have strengthened Brüning substantially. But Braun's offer was rejected, allegedly owing to the opposition of President Hindenburg.[70]

Braun and Brüning had essentially different motives for their consideration of *Reichsreform*. The minister president, long opposed to Reich interference in the states' affairs, now saw reform as a means to increase Brüning's reliance upon the SPD and to strengthen the republican forces against Nazism. It might even have led to a restoration of parliamentary government. Brüning, on the other hand, was primarily interested in the technical and financial advantages of the reform. The strongest argument that he and Defense Minister Groener found in its favor was that once it was accomplished, a government which leaned more to the right could be established later, inheriting the advantages of the plan.[71] Brüning's ultimate objectives, unknown to contemporaries, were even more removed from Prussian hopes: greater power for the executive through constitutional change and reintroduction of the monarchy after the death of Hindenburg.[72] Even if he was the "lesser evil," Brüning was a most unreliable source of support for Weimar democracy.

The real problem with the SPD's toleration policy was that the party used it to justify inaction. This was certainly not Braun's intention, but his hopes for a rapprochement with the chancellor went unfulfilled. Party leaders had no contingency plans for deterring or responding to the establishment of a far-right government in the Reich. A more potent republican paramilitary organization working in conjunction with the Prussian police might conceivably have given the party some leverage. But the Prussian government and the SPD organization did not pursue this alternative, partly because the chancellor and the military objected, partly because Severing was opposed in principle.[73] If Prussia alone could no longer preserve the Weimar Republic, the SPD leaders needed a substitute strategy. The events of 1932 demonstrated that they had none.

11. The Collapse of the Prussian Strategy

H E Reich and Prussian governments, having failed to consolidate their political influence and policies in 1930–31, faced the massive problems of 1932 in a weak and divided condition. Unemployment passed the six million mark, and per capita income showed a decline of roughly 25 percent from its 1929 level.[1] Meanwhile, a torrent of violence swept through the streets. An American observer wrote in astonishment: "The country is more exclusively and intensively organized for domestic conflict than any other on earth. . . . It is like a village with four gangs [Reichsbanner, SA, Stahlhelm, and Red Front], each ready at the drop of a hat to sally forth to slaughter the others. It is like no other country in the world."[2] With the government's capacity to handle economic and law-enforcement problems at a minimum, the position of the president and the army became all the more important. Control of the emergency powers of Article 48 rested not with Chancellor Brüning, but with an eighty-four year-old field marshal who had never lost his distaste for politics.[3] In the event of open civil war, control of the country lay with the Reichswehr, which had successfully resisted civilian control and pursued its own interests throughout the Weimar Republic.

Wilhelm Groener, the retired general who had cooperated with Friedrich Ebert during the November revolution, had been defense minister since 1928. In October 1931 Groener assumed the position of Reich interior minister as well. His new post brought him into contact with officials who had a nonmilitary perspective, but it also caused him to rely even more heavily upon his close advisor and friend General Kurt von Schleicher, the man Groener called his "adopted son." Schleicher became the effective head of the Defense Ministry.[4] Since he had contributed earlier to the collapse of Hermann Müller's government and had complained bitterly about the Prussian government's anti-military policies, Schleicher's rise was ominous for the SPD.[5] When the Defense Ministry issued new regulations that opened the way for Nazi members to join the Reichswehr, the SPD press denounced Schleicher as a manipulator who was seeking to drive a wedge between the SPD and the Brüning government.[6] Schleicher (and Groener) actually had little regard for Nazism as an independent political force. What they appreciated was the Nazis' capacity to inspire popular support for nationalistic and promilitary goals. In March 1932 Schleicher remarked to Groener regarding the Nazis: "If they did not exist, one would really have to invent them."[7]

The chancellor disillusioned the SPD with another turn to the right. In late 1931 Brüning came up with the idea of extending President Hindenburg's term of office, due to expire in the spring, through legislative action, avoiding the rigors of a bitter reelection fight. But Brüning needed the support of the DNVP and the NSDAP to get the bill through the Reichstag. As an inducement, he held out the prospect of a coalition government that would include the right-wing parties.[8] Although Brüning's efforts eventually proved unsuccessful, a worried Minister President Braun complained to his state secretary: "For four months I have been advising the chancellor to denounce the attempts to extract the poisonous fangs of the Nazis."[9]

Nonetheless, Prussia's policy, and to a lesser extent that of the SPD leaders generally,[10] was to hold fast to Brüning, Groener, and Hindenburg as the best hope of outlasting the rising tide of support for Nazism. Two days before his sixtieth birthday Braun wrote to Severing that the SPD could not force the chancellor into making specific concessions. Brüning was well aware that the Social Democrats would suffer more from the overthrow of his government than the Center.[11] Braun was also conscious of the delicate situation of the Prussian coalition with elections coming up. The death of Josef Hess, leader of the Centrist fraction in the Landtag, on 4 February increased the fragility of Braun's government; he could no longer count on a good friend and loyal supporter in a key political position.[12]

Braun resisted the urging of his colleagues in the Reich to run as the SPD's candidate in the presidential election. Despite the fact that his relations with Hindenburg, once good on the personal level, had been chilly ever since 1930,[13] he lobbied strenuously within the party for an early endorsement of the president. The main opposition was, after all, Adolf Hitler. Braun helped to mobilize SPD support for Hindenburg even before the runoff election made the choice an absolute necessity.[14] Hindenburg fell just short of a majority on the first round, competing against numerous candidates including Hitler and Stahlhelm leader Theodor Duesterberg. On the second round the president collected more than nineteen million votes to defeat Hitler, who had more than thirteen million. Yet Hindenburg was in no way grateful to the SPD, which delivered its voters solidly to him. Wanting a government oriented toward the "patriotic" right, the president was ashamed to owe his victory to the "Marxists," and he hoped to bring about the formation of a rightist government in Prussia after the elections there.[15].

In a letter to Karl Kautsky that was filled with comments about his personal and political suffering, Braun observed that the presidential election and subsequent Prussian elections could be decisive not only for the German people, but for all Europe: "We will summon all forces to rescue the last for the republic that is still possible under the given confusion. . . . As pleasant as it would be personally, one cannot follow the advice of those party friends who state that one must leave the government and transfer the odium for dismantling the revolution's achievements to the nonsocialists. Certainly one can reach a limit beyond which one can no longer retreat without inflicting irremediable damage to the movement. But until then one must remain inside and fight tenaciously for every inch of territory."[16] Despite his ill health, the partial paralysis and illness of his wife, and his fatigue with constant political battles, Braun was not yet willing to surrender his position and influence.

Prussia continued to exert pressure upon the Reich government with regard to the handling of the Nazi paramilitary forces. In November 1931 Brüning complained to SPD representatives that some Prussian officials were trying to instigate armed conflict between the Nazi SA and the Reichswehr, an allegation that the Social Democrats denied.[17] Brüning later claimed that Berlin Chief of Police Grzesinski had discussed with Severing a plan to provoke a battle between the Nazis and Communists, then to use this conflict as justification for banning both parties. Allegedly, their telephone conversation in the Reichstag was overheard by a DVP member, who informed both the Nazis and the Reichswehr.[18] Brüning's testimony is often unreliable, but Grzesinski had a previous record of trying to prohibit the Nazis and Communists. Moreover, subsequent events demonstrated that he had not changed his mind.

In December 1931 an official in the Reich Interior Ministry alerted Grzesinski that Hitler intended to hold a press conference in the Hotel Kaiserhof in Berlin. This gathering might have been considered a political assembly, which required prior police authorization. With this opening, Grzesinski sent Minister President Braun a list of evidence that Hitler had maintained a private army for subversive purposes. He urged Hitler's arrest and imprisonment or exile. Braun and Severing felt compelled to check on the potential reaction of the Reich government, which demurred.[19] President Hindenburg may even have threatened to use the army against the Prussian police if the latter arrested Hitler.[20] Another version was that Hindenburg had spoken of blocking Prussian action against Hitler with a special emergency ordinance.[21] Shortly afterwards, Severing told a friendly journalist: "He [Severing] would have preferred to have had Hitler . . . arrested and deported, but he couldn't, since Hitler had been received by Hindenburg and had breakfasted with Schleicher. Prussia therefore had to fear disavowal by the Reich. But now it would seize the opportunity. Until 3 January there would be a truce, but then there would be all sorts of action. I asked, What? He, laughingly, I can't tell you anything about that today."[22]

As it turned out, nothing dramatic occurred immediately after 3 January.

Grzesinski gave a speech on 7 February that may have indicated his frustration over thwarted plans. He declared, "How humiliating that this foreigner, Hitler, who interferes with the conduct of our foreign affairs and discusses vital problems of Germany's future with foreign correspondents, is not immediately driven out [of the country] with a dog whip."[23] This comment was rich material for press columnists and cartoonists alike, and it seems to have incensed Hitler, who was to recall it some thirteen months later when political conditions were quite different.[24] Groener found Grzesinski's remark offensive too and sent a threatening note to the Prussian Interior Ministry, inquiring whether this speech might not be seen as an incitement to violence.[25]

Severing was trying more tactfully to gain Reich cooperation against Nazi disruption of public order, but his problems were multiplying. There were rumors and stories in the press that the Prussian police had established secret links with the army, and that the force was no longer loyal to the Prussian government.[26] Severing met secretly with Bavarian Interior Minister Karl Stützel in mid-February, hoping to get other states to join Prussia in pressuring the Reich to ban the Nazi SA force. But the Reichswehr learned of this meeting from its spies within the Prussian Interior Ministry,[27] and the news was leaked to the press. The Bavarians then backed off, saying that the time was not yet ripe.[28] At a conference on 27 February with Prussian *Regierungspräsidenten* and *Oberpräsidenten*, Severing emphasized the importance of the struggle against Nazism but admitted that the Reich and Prussia had serious differences on this issue. Shortly afterwards, Braun sent Brüning a huge mass of documents on the illegal intentions of the Nazis and urged that the SA and the Nazi party itself be outlawed through a presidential ordinance. Brüning did not answer the letter and ordered some of the documents destroyed.[29]

Groener and Schleicher themselves began to adopt a zigzag course after receiving threatening reports in mid-March about Nazi plans for a coup. When the defense minister passed along the information to Prussia, Severing then authorized a police raid on Nazi headquarters, where some incriminating documents were seized. When Severing met with Groener to discuss the evidence, however, Groener discounted its significance.[30] The defense minister also reacted angrily when the Prussian government announced in court that the Reich had initiated the police action. Prussia proceeded to make skillful use of the captured documents, displaying them to other state governments and to the press. The Nazi desire to sabotage the frontier defense program was stressed. When Hitler confirmed publicly that his men would not fight to defend the republic against Polish attack, Braun responded at a mass rally in Berlin by attacking Hitler's lack of patriotism. Even Schleicher now agreed that the Nazi forces should be banned.[31]

The interior ministers of nearly all the states met on 5 April and again on 10

April, strongly favoring a ban of the Nazi paramilitary forces throughout the Reich.[32] The Bavarian government had presented its own demand even earlier, threatening to act unilaterally if the Reich procrastinated. Up until this point Groener and Schleicher had been in agreement on each shift of stance. But while Groener wished to go ahead with the ban, at the last minute Schleicher expressed reservations. The major states, united behind Prussian leadership, warned that they would go ahead without the Reich, which forced Groener's hand. The defense/interior minister issued a ban of the SA and the SS throughout the Reich on 13 April. As a gesture of appeasement to the right, Groener insisted that the republican defense organization, the Reichsbanner, dissolve its own combat formations a couple of days later.[33] But this move did not placate President Hindenburg, who expressed misgivings before signing the ordinance banning the Nazi forces. Groener's standing with the president was shaken.[34]

The Prussian Elections

By April 1932 the Prussian government had a problem of its own. The state constitution stipulated that elections were to be held at least once every four years. The government had delayed the moment of reckoning as long as possible, but its four-year term expired without any letup in the depression. A skillful parliamentary maneuver by the SPD fraction in the Prussian Landtag just before the election gave the Braun government a chance to maintain power even with unfavorable election results. At the suggestion of Ernest Hamburger,[35] vice-chairman of the Landtag fraction, the coalition parties changed the rules of procedure for election of the minister president, so that only an absolute majority would suffice. Their aim was to prevent the election of a Nazi candidate by a mere plurality. If the Nazis wished to enter or capture the government, they would now have to bargain not only with the DNVP but also with the Center. The Prussian Social Democrats felt that the Center could be trusted to impose restraints upon the Nazis, if it was willing to negotiate with them at all. If, however, the combined votes of the Nazis and the Communists reached the level where they could block election of a new minister president by a majority, then the Braun government could continue in office in a caretaker status.[36]

The election results were worse than expected. The SPD fell from 137 seats to 94; the State party (formerly the Democratic party) plunged from 21 seats to 2. The Center held steady with 67, but the Nazis rose from 6 seats to a stunning total of 162, and only a little more than half of their gains came at the expense of the DNVP and the DVP. Nonetheless, the three parties of the right still needed the support of the Center party (or the Communist party) to obtain a majority.

At this point Braun and Severing apparently shifted their stance and abandoned the strategy of holding power in Prussia that they had so long championed. On 26 April the Braun government decided to resign by 24 May, although, under the constitution, it did not have to do so.[37] In an interview with a correspondent from United Press, Severing observed that the SPD and Center were now more inclined to allow the Nazis to join a coalition government in Prussia. He added that the other parties joining the NSDAP in a coalition would have to guarantee the integrity of the constitution.[38] According to one conservative newspaper, the SPD had nothing against a coalition between the Center and the NSDAP, as long as the Nazis did not get either the Minister Presidency or the Ministry of the Interior.[39] Friedrich Stampfer later wrote that Braun had become convinced of the need to experiment with NSDAP participation in a coalition.[40] Finally, State party member Theodor Heuss wrote to friends on 29 April that, from what he had been able to learn in discussions, Braun would foresake the attempt to carry on a caretaker government.[41]

In his discussion with Brüning in the fall of 1930 Braun had raised the alternative of bringing the Nazis into the (Reich) government at a time when they were still unable to dominate it. Now he reluctantly concluded that this option should be tried in Prussia, so that the SPD might have a chance to recover its strength in opposition. But other advocates of the SPD's Prussian strategy reacted strongly against Severing's comments in the United Press interview, which may have been intended as a trial balloon. Berlin Police Chief Grzesinski issued what in effect was a rebuttal in the SPD press, arguing that the SPD had to avoid driving the Center party toward the Nazis. Finally, Severing was forced to issue a denial, which Grzesinski regarded as tardy and insufficient.[42]

On 4 May 1932 the SPD party council met to discuss the election and the political situation. Although the minutes of that meeting have not survived, Rudolf Hilferding gave the main report, which was later printed and distributed to the party's district executives.[43] It can be assumed that his views were shared by the majority of the executive committee and party council members. Hilferding began by putting the best possible face on the Prussian election results, calling them rather good, considering the circumstances. He also saw the reelection of President Hindenburg as a stabilizing factor, even though increasing concentration of power in the president's hands was a danger. Hilferding felt that Brüning himself was unlikely to form a rightist government. But the Reichswehr and the circle around the president clearly disapproved of the behavior of Reichswehr Minister Groener (partly as a result of his ban of the Nazi paramilitary forces). Hilferding mentioned the possibility that Schleicher was angling to displace Groener. If either the NSDAP or the DNVP could elect one of its members minister president of Prussia, he would then have the right to select the other ministers, including the minister of the interior. With these two posts either party could effectively control Germany, conducting a purge of government administration. The Prussian deadlock therefore was extremely dangerous. Hilferding concluded that the SPD had to work to keep both Brüning and Braun in office. He recommended concluding an explicit agreement with the Center to prevent the election of a DNVP or NSDAP member as Prussian minister president. Hilferding's position in May 1932 was essentially the same as it had been in October 1931; the SPD had to avoid all action that might alienate the president or the Center—the two main barriers to a rightist government.[44]

An article by the influential chairman of the SPD Landtag fraction, Ernst Heilmann, outlined the options in Prussia similarly. If the Nazis refused to work with the Center, which would undoubtedly insist on a pledge to respect the constitution and maintain domestic order, then the Braun government would have to continue in its unpleasant caretaker role. Heilmann wrote: "Social Democracy must not decline this painful mission, since it will not deliver the state to fascism without a fight to its utmost capacity."[45]

Only three weeks later Heilmann began to retreat. "We wrote here two weeks ago regarding our Prussia that, presuming [normal] constitutional developments, the task of the Braun-Severing government has not yet reached its immediate end. How necessary it was to make that express reservation of constitutional developments has been shown in the meantime by the fall of Groener. . . . Whether . . . politics in Prussia and in the Reich maintains its previous direction, the defense of the state against the fascist criminals who would use force, will no longer be directly or primarily determined by Social Democracy."[46] The increasing pressure from right-wing groups, culminating with an ultimatum from Schleicher for Groener's resignation, achieved the desired goal by mid-May. Almost immediately Heilmann and other Social Democratic observers came to the conclusion that Brüning's days were numbered.[47] The prospects for carrying on the battle in Prussia now looked even bleaker than before. Even Braun's last hope—that Brüning might finally pull off a merger of Prussian functions with the Reich—now seemed extinguished. If the Reich intervened in Prussia, Brüning would not be at the helm.[48]

As expected, Brüning's forced resignation came quickly (30 May).[49] The president then chose Franz von Papen to head the new government in the Reich. An aristocrat from the extreme right of the Center party, Papen had little political skill and no prospect whatever of obtaining substantial parliamentary support. Hindenburg equipped him with the power to rule by decree and the power to dissolve the Reichstag, which the new chancellor immediately exploited. Although Papen tried to bring about the formation of a coalition in Prussia of the Center, DNVP, and NSDAP, he failed completely. The Nazis insisted on naming one of their own as minister president, and the Center was angry at Brüning's ouster.[50]

With the Prussian political situation still at a stalemate, Minister President Braun could no longer restrain his discontent and exhaustion. One of his colleagues, Ernest Hamburger, later wrote:

> . . . it can be assumed that Otto Braun decided that the resignation of Heinrich Brüning as chancellor was a good opportunity to take his vacation from office. This, however, does not mean that Braun's decision . . . [to take sick leave] came as late as in June 1932. Immediately after the electoral defeat of the coalition government in Prussia, headed by Braun, he took the firm decision . . . [to withdraw], and only the timing remained to be determined. Not only Ernst Heilmann and I considered Braun's intention as a grave error, but also the party chairman Otto Wels and many other important members of the party . . . in the Reichstag and in the Prussian Diet. Braun knew that, but it was impossible to convince him.
>
> We all knew, of course, that the result of the elections of April 1932 was a serious blow to the survival of democracy, but, in any case, we had to think of our tactics even thereafter, whereas Braun concentrated on the defeat he had suffered after twelve years of successfully governing. This was to him a psychological shock which he could not overcome.[51]

Despite renewed efforts by Otto Wels to persuade Braun to remain in office, he left on 6 June for an indefinite vacation, declaring that the department ministers could carry on. He wrote in his memoirs that he fully intended not to return to office. On 30 May, the same day on which Brüning resigned, Braun had filled out a passport application. Under the heading "occupation" he wrote "without profession."[52]

Welfare Minister Heinrich Hirtsiefer, the senior cabinet minister, became acting head of the Prussian government, although his advanced age and unassertive personality made him unsuitable for what was bound to be a very difficult role. The rumor that had circulated earlier, that the Reich government would use Article 48 to install a commissar to govern Prussia, now began to gain more credence. Severing, who remained as interior minister, knew of the rumors that Papen intended to use Article 48 to oust the caretaker Prussian government. He asked Reich Interior Ministry officials whether the Prussian government was on firm legal ground. They responded that the Landtag's change in the procedure for electing the minister president had been legal.[53]

The parties' attempt to reverse the change in the procedural rules was blocked when the Communists surprisingly came to the rescue of the caretaker government—after having proposed their own motion of no confidence. A high official in the Prussian Interior Ministry sounded out two Communist deputies on the KPD's willingness to tolerate the government in the face of the right-wing threats, but Communist policy toward the SPD by and large remained hostile.[54]

Severing met privately with Reich Interior Minister Wilhelm von Gayl in mid-June to inquire about Papen's intentions. Gayl avoided a direct answer when asked whether the Reich intended to install a commissar in Prussia, but he implied that it would not do so for the time being. Severing then told Gayl that he expected the Reichstag elections scheduled for 31 July to produce a deadlock, and that he could well imagine the Reich government would find it necessary to unite its powers with those of Prussia. He said this should not be done through a commissar, however, but through personal unification of the various ministries.[55] Gayl subsequently reported back to the Reich cabinet that Severing had recommended the use of a Reich commissar in Prussia, but there is good reason to doubt this account.[56]

Nonetheless, Severing's remarks were unlikely to deter Papen. Remarkably, the governments of Baden, Württemberg, and Bavaria took a more active stance in favor of states' rights and against the unlawful use of a Reich commissar than the Prussian ministers themselves did. The south German governments were naturally more concerned about their own positions than about Prussia, but they all had reason to fear the lifting of the ban on the Nazi SA, elimination of the ban on uniformed demonstrations, and another precedent for Reich intervention against the states.[57]

Berlin Chief of Police Grzesinski criticized Severing's passive attitude. Immediately after a conference of the south German state representatives with the chancellor on 12 June, Grzesinski wrote an article denouncing the idea of a Reich commissar for Prussia. He directed his argument more to the Prussian government than to the Reich or the public. Grzesinski wrote that Prussia should not allow the impression to arise that the south German states cared more about defending Prussian rights than Prussia itself did. He called for the Prussian government to state its firm opposition to the plan for a commissar. Finally, he expressed the hope that Minister President Braun would soon recover from his illness, and that his government would carry on, whether on the offensive or on the defensive, until a new government was formed. This barely disguised attack against Severing was not published, however. Ernst Heilmann dissuaded Grzesinski from submitting it to the SPD press on the ground that it would hurt the SPD during the election campaign.[58]

But Grzesinski did not hold his tongue. On 26 June he gave a speech in

Magdeburg in which he warned that there were individuals around the president who exerted a bad influence. He added that the Prussian government and the Iron Front, the republican antifascist cartel, would strike down any attempt by the Nazis to obtain their goals by force.[59] Severing found this speech objectionable, particularly the section about the president. He may have gone so far as to threaten Grzesinski with dismissal.[60] Severing's strategy of wooing the support of the Reich had now been transformed into one of avoiding offense to the Reich. The first approach had very limited prospect of success under Brüning; the second had no chance whatever with Papen.

The Reich was now clearly committed to winning the support of the Nazis. Papen and Schleicher may even have reached an explicit agreement with the NSDAP, that if the Reich was unable to bring about the formation of a Nazi-led coalition government in Prussia, then it would displace the caretaker government and install a commissar.[61] Meanwhile, the Reich lifted the ban on the Nazi paramilitary forces in mid-June, despite the heated atmosphere of the election campaign, greatly adding to the difficulties of the police and state interior ministries in maintaining order. The south German states responded by issuing their own bans on uniformed demonstrations, but President Hindenburg countered on 28 June with a Reich ordinance preventing any general prohibitions of this nature. During the next three weeks 99 people were killed and 1,125 were wounded in street clashes.[62]

The one initiative taken by Severing was a meeting of the Prussian ministers (except Braun) with various ministers from the other state governments on 27 June. The purpose of the meeting was to form a delegation that would confer with the president and demand a Reich ban of all political demonstrations. However, Bavarian Interior Minister Stützel, having clashed sharply with the president only two weeks earlier, suggested that this idea be held in reserve, and the others agreed.[63]

A credible republican defense force might have made the Papen-Schleicher government hesitate to oust the Prussian government. Even the die-hard conservatives might have shunned the risk of civil war. Yet there was no reconsideration of the old idea of arming the combat formations of the Reichsbanner and attaching them to the Prussian police.[64] To be sure, this solution would have been a gamble, as the military still would have had far superior strength. Another contingency plan once considered was the declaration of a state of emergency in Prussia as a response to (or in anticipation of) the Reich's use of Article 48. Bavaria had set a precedent for this action in September 1923. The plan, however, needed for success a strong and unified Prussian government,[65] which was no longer the case in July 1932. Finally, Ministerial Director Badt suggested to Severing that he counter the rumors about a commissar by issuing a statement that Prussia would take legal action against it. But Severing declined on the ground that it would have given the Reich ideas.[66] In any case, it might not have been an effective deterrent.

By July there was so much talk about the plan to send a Reich commissar to Prussia that, as Grzesinski later wrote, only the date and the pretext were uncertain.[67] On 17 July there was a bloody clash between Nazi demonstrators and the inhabitants of a working-class quarter of the city of Altona. Severing then sent a telegram to all *Oberpräsidenten, Regierungspräsidenten*, and police chiefs to ensure that they would be at their posts in the days ahead. Severing refused to declare a state of siege for Prussia, because he said that the Reich would have insisted that it be lifted immediately.[68]

On 18 July an important SPD discussion took place. According to party Chairman Wels (who wrote an account of the meeting in 1933 that is more reliable than the version in Severing's memoirs[69]), Severing came to the office of the executive committee to brief Wels, Hans Vogel, and Paul Hertz on the Prussian situation. Severing raised the possibility that the SPD might want to withdraw from the Prussian government, an idea that startled Wels. Severing explained that the government's ability to act was becoming ever more limited, and the Reich was clearly trying to create a conflict with Prussia. Wels immediately telephoned a contact in the chancellery to inquire, among other things, whether the Reich intended to act against Prussia. He was told "not for the time being." Wels, Vogel, and Hertz then agreed that the SPD should not voluntarily abandon a position of power which was of value to the working class. Wels added that Severing's resignation would have brought forth an angry reaction within the party. He suggested a formal consideration of the matter by relevant party authorities.

Events were moving too fast for that. On the same day Chancellor Papen asked Severing, Hirtsiefer, and Prussian Finance Minister Otto Klepper to come to the chancellery on 20 July for a conference. On the morning of 20 July the press was full of stories that a commissar would be installed that very day. Klepper claims to have predicted such a move just before the meeting with Papen, but Hirtsiefer and Severing allegedly doubted that Papen would make a move without first specifying his complaints against Prussia and without giving the Prussian government an opportunity to effect remedies. Klepper also claims to have suggested armed resistance by the Reichsbanner and the working class. Severing and Hirtsiefer again were said to be opposed.[70] Whatever suggestions were made, no action was prepared.

The Twentieth of July

On the morning of 20 July the three Prussian ministers went to see the chancellor as requested. Papen announced that he was removing Braun and Severing from office under the provisions of Article 48, sections 1 and 2, because Prussia could no longer guarantee public security and order against Communist disturbances. The Prussian government's contacts with Communists were cited subsequently as indications that Prussia lacked the necessary independence to fulfill its duties. Papen announced the appointment of himself as commissar for Prussia and of Franz Bracht, mayor of Essen, as his representative. Severing denied the legality of the move and rejected the Reich's claims. After further disagreement, Severing declared that he would yield only to force. Papen closed the meeting with the remark that the intervention was an act of raison d'etat.

A state of siege for Berlin and the province of Brandenburg was quickly proclaimed, one division of the Reichswehr having been alerted for action. Military officials sent a small force of infantry to Braun's Berlin office to prevent him from entering it. Hirtsiefer, Klepper, and Severing went to the Prussian Interior Ministry to discuss their response, all agreeing with Ministerial Director Hermann Badt's suggestion of an immediate appeal to the Supreme Court—he had worked out the legal argument months before. After the other Prussian ministers failed to cooperate with Papen, they too were ousted.[71]

Alarmed by the reports in the morning newspapers, Berlin Police Chief Grzesinski had been trying unsuccessfully to reach Severing. At 11:20 General von Rundstedt telephoned Grzesinski to inform him of the state of siege and of his removal from office as well. Grzesinski then finally got through to Severing, who had come back from the meeting with Papen. Severing said that he also had been dismissed, but he was unwilling to discuss the matter further on the phone. When Grzesinski asked what should be done, Severing replied that bloodshed must be avoided.[72]

Before getting through to Severing, Grzesinski had called Otto Wels, who was then attending a meeting of the ADGB executive. Notified about the state of siege (and subsequently, about the appointment of a commissar), Wels called Severing to arrange a meeting after the ADGB leaders had had a chance to discuss the matter. The trade-union officials were dispirited and largely without ideas. Wels pointed out to them that, because of probable Communist opposition, the masses would not support an SPD appeal for resistance with the same cohesiveness that they had shown in 1920 in response to the Kapp Putsch. A general strike had to be considered, he said, but the Reich government might be looking to provoke a working-class uprising in order to crush it and then to tear up the constitution. Wels suggested that one solution might be to call for the protection of the Reichstag elections set to take place on 31 July. When the leaders of the individual unions present were reluctant to make commitments to strike, ADGB Chairman Leipart and Reichsbanner head Karl Höltermann agreed to Wels's line.[73]

About 1 p.m. Wels left in order to meet with Severing, reporting that the unions were not prepared to strike. Severing discouraged any further consideration of a strike, warning that it would bring about a military dictatorship and civil war. Nor could he rely upon the police to fight the Reichswehr; they would not obey such an order from him. Severing fully agreed with the slogan of securing the elections. When Wels brought Severing's views back to the ADGB leaders, all the participants reached the same conclusion.[74]

Meanwhile, Grzesinski's aides convinced him that his ouster would be illegal. He checked again with Severing, who responded that he personally would yield only to force, but that he felt that Grzesinski's ouster was legal under the state of siege. Grzesinski disagreed and refused to leave, which led to his arrest by a subordinate of General Rundstedt. As the soldiers escorted him away from police headquarters, police officials flocked to the overlooking windows and shouted, "Freedom," "Hail to the republic," and "Hail to our chief."[75] Grzesinski was released from Moabit prison that evening. Severing also was forced out of his office by his successor and by newly appointed police officials. Despite his statement that he would yield only to force, he gave them no difficulty in order to avoid provoking mass unrest.[76]

Two days after the coup d'etat the Berlin correspondent for United Press sent Severing a number of questions about the background to the Reich's move. Severing's response had a listless tone:

> In previous years the rightist parties in the Reich had already raised the demand for homogeneous governments in the Reich and in Prussia. This wish was expressed with special vigor when the Nationalists temporarily had influence in the Reich government. There was talk of discrepancies between the Reich and Prussia that never were present to the extent that was maintained. Fulfillment of the demand for homogeneous governments was inconceivable as long as the Prussian government was supported by a majority of the Prussian Landtag. After the elections of 24 April of this year removed this majority for the Prussian government, however, the Reich government, in my view, took advantage of this situation to install a Reich commissar in order to produce this "coordination" (*Gleichschaltung*) between the Reich and Prussia. The military state of siege for Berlin and Brandenburg was declared . . . to break any resistance against its measures by means of military force.[77]

Severing concluded that a restoration of the monarchy was unlikely, but the future course of events remained to be seen.

Historians have raised the possibility that Braun and Severing actually welcomed the installation of a Reich commissar,[78] but this seems to be a misreading of their behavior and motives. Braun's bitterness over the way in which he was thrown out of office and over the charge that the Prussian government had not fulfilled its duties was quite evident in August 1932.[79] On the other hand, the two SPD ministers apparently shared the desire to go into parliamentary opposition. They were both unwilling and unprepared to call for violent resistance against the ouster of the caretaker Prussian government, which they felt had lost its legitimacy and effectiveness. On 20 July they were convinced that violence and the general strike were bound to fail. The Prussian government's appeal of Papen's intervention to the Supreme Court was not really intended to restore the ministers in office but rather to rehabilitate the government's reputation against Papen's smears.[80] In short, Braun and Severing objected to the illegal and damaging coup, but they would have welcomed an unobjectionable way to go into parliamentary opposition. With Prussia no longer capable of protecting the republic alone, the cost of continued political responsibility seemed too high.

A few months later Ernst Heilmann told the SPD party council: "For twelve or thirteen years we [in Prussia] always made decisions conscious of our responsibility. Each time we asked ourselves what would come afterwards, or whether we could replace what existed with something better. Since the 20th of July of this year we are free."[81] This comment was more than an attempt to make the best of a bad situation. It reflected a longstanding desire in the SPD to return to the simplicity of political opposition. The irony of the situation was that Braun, Severing, and Heilmann had consistently fought this view in the past, while the SPD leaders in the Reich made concessions to it from 1923 on. In the months before July 1932, however, the positions were almost reversed. The SPD leaders in the Reich (as well as Grzesinski) wanted the Prussian ministers to hold on, whereas the latter were weary of political responsibility. The behavior of Braun and Severing caused consternation in the upper ranks of the party hierarchy, because the Social Democratic movement had no alternative means of defending the republic.

The Kapp-Lüttwitz Putsch had convinced the SPD leaders of the danger as well as the power of mass action. With the Communists much stronger in 1932 than in 1920, Social Democratic officials feared that the workers would not rally behind a call for the defense of a parliamentary democracy that no longer functioned.[82] The SPD leaders in the Reich had come to rely on Prussia to protect the republic against its enemies. When a weakened Prussian government no longer felt capable of fulfilling that role, the SPD was at a loss for a response to Papen's coup. It seemed safest to protect the party and union organizations from possible repression, to refrain from rash action, to await a more favorable opportunity to carry on the struggle for democracy and socialism. Such a decision was in keeping with the long Social Democratic tradition of working within the existing legal and constitutional framework.

The political cost of 20 July 1932 for the SPD was devastating in several respects. Rank-and-file party members had regarded Braun and Severing as the party's most decisive and least "bureaucratic" leaders. Their decision to yield to military force without resistance was a shattering blow to the party's morale. Shortly after the coup a high ADGB official wrote in his diary: "The day was such a severe defeat for us, that the electoral struggle, even if it turns out . . . favorable, is predetermined. The fall of the Prussian government without a real struggle, without the use of force, this inglorious disintegration of the 'fortress' is a fundamental destruction of illusions. If Social Democracy should maintain its parliamentary strength on 31 July, it would not be thanks to any courage that party, union, and Reichsbanner leaders maintained in the critical hour, but only to the common man's patience, willingness to accept sacrifice, discipline, and belief in the cause."[83] The twentieth of July 1932 discredited not only the Prussian government but also the SPD's Prussian strategy.

Despite some union hopes for a working arrangement with General Schleicher,[84] the Social Democratic movement returned to the role of opposing authoritarian government in the months that followed. However, the Papen and Schleicher governments in the Reich now discounted the SPD's potential to interfere with their plans. The warnings of SPD spokesmen[85] could not even deter the president from his fatal decision on 29 January 1933 to entrust Adolf Hitler with the chancellorship of Germany. The course of events in late 1932 and in January 1933 only emphasized the limitations of the SPD's parliamentary influence in a nonparliamentary system of government. Hitler gained power not through direct elections, but by way of the smoke-filled rooms around the president, to which the Social Democrats lacked entry. The Social Democratic leaders had long since recognized the dangers of presidential government through Article 48, but they hoped that Weimar democracy would return with the ebbing of the depression and the decline of Nazi strength. From their stance of passive political opposition, however, the SPD leaders could gain neither the enthusiasm of the voters nor leverage within the upper levels of government. At least one, and perhaps both, would have been required to prevent the Nazi triumph.

Conclusion

IFFICULTIES with the repressive and undemocratic features of the Second Reich gave the Social Democratic elite an appreciation of the value of parliamentary government. Because parliamentary democracy was not a concept originating with socialism but a bourgeois invention, leading Social Democrats believed that it could serve as a mechanism for cooperation between the SPD and nonsocialists. Whether such cooperation was necessary or desirable remained a disputed issue within the Social Democratic movement. At first only a small group of revisionists and reformists advanced the notion of establishing links with nonsocialists. The war helped to break down many of the barriers among Social Democrats, Catholics, and liberals, and from 1917 on, substantial parliamentary links existed between the SPD and the parties of the middle.

Within the SPD even many nonrevisionists forecast that the postwar situation would be unsuitable for the creation of a socialist society. The destructive impact of the war itself and the specter of political and social polarization to the point of civil war diminished the appeal of a revolutionary socialist solution. To avoid the kind of violence, widespread misery, and dictatorial rule reported in Russia, the SPD leaders were eager to share power with a variety of existing interests. In 1932 Ernst Fraenkel called this solution "parity"; today we would be more likely to call it pluralism.[1]

Was Germany forced to choose between bolshevism or a pluralistic Weimar Republic with all of its limitations?[2] Too many of the preconditions for a Bolshevist type of revolution were absent to make the first a realistic possibility. In recent years many western scholars have also concluded that a "third way" might have been pursued in 1918–1919.[3] Even if the shortage of food made expropriation of large estates infeasible, the SPD leaders might have reformed the army, government administration, and parts of the industrial economy with the aid of the revolutionary councils. The last two decades of scholarship have tremendously increased our awareness and understanding of the events and options of the German revolution. But recent scholarship is less successful in explaining why the SPD leaders perceived such a limited range of choices. There is still too much of a tendency to ascribe their actions to a passion for order and correct procedure, distrust of mass action, and disdain for the violent and dictatorial tactics of their "primitive" Russian comrades. Even less adequate is the notion that the SPD leaders were simply buffeted by events, that they improvised their responses without any guiding principle.

The SPD leaders limited the revolution of November 1918 because its more radical manifestations threatened the links that they had already established with representatives of nonsocialists parties and economic interests. None of the revolutionary government's objectives were purely socialist ones. The achievement of a quick and equitable peace settlement, the enactment of overdue social reforms, the rebuilding of the war-torn economy, and above all, the establishment of a parliamentary system based on equal suffrage and proportional representation enabled the Social Democratic leaders to present their party to the public as the guardian of the national interest during a time of extreme crisis. Only the SPD could have played this role. Party leaders sought to use their leverage to reconcile their working-class constituents with other German citizens in a temporary social partnership. The Weimar Republic was designed to convert the negative integration of the working class into a more positive one.

Yet the SPD did not renounce its ultimate socialist objectives founded on nationalization of the means of production and aimed at a class-conscious proletariat. In fact, parliamentary democracy was regarded as the only secure pathway to socialism. One SPD deputy to the Constituent Assembly described the optimism in high party circles during Weimar's first ten years: "We saw no reason to doubt democracy based on equal suffrage. Previously we were subjected to the plans of a government hostile toward us; we had freed ourselves from that. Equal suffrage and the liberal principles now secured freedom of political activity for the worker, which he had never possessed before. There had been great progress from the time when we could only protest, organize, and agitate."[4] The belief in constant progress toward socialism, drawn from the SPD's organizational and electoral success in the past as well as from its ideological determinism, added immeasurably to the attractiveness of parliamentary democracy. At the same time, however, it left the SPD elite prone to certain errors in political strategy.

First of all, the SPD leaders underestimated the difficulties that they faced. The status quo of late 1918 did not favor interclass cooperation. The political parties represented in the Constituent Assembly and later in the Reichstag reflected the multiple fissures that remained in German society. The Center party had a firm hold over a large Catholic minority seared by the experience of Bismarck's campaign against the Catholic Church. Whereas industrialists expected state cooperation and assistance, the preindustrial *Mittelstand* resented many aspects of urban industrial society. The landed aristocracy retained effective control over millions of agricultural workers, while small farmers in many areas resisted modern methods of agricultural production. Precariously poised above the industrial workers in the status hierarchy were the white-collar employees, a rapidly expanding group that did not consider itself part of the proletariat. Many upper-middle-class professionals regarded partisan politics with disdain. The workers organized in the socialist and Communist movements remained something of a pariah group to all the other social strata.

If the early years of Weimar had been prosperous and crisis-free, social tension and political conflict might have sunk to manageable levels. But the Treaty of Versailles and the German reparations bill aggravated all the social and political problems, and the hyperinflation imposed new tension and psychological strain. Social Democratic officials had failed to anticipate how fragmented German society was and how difficult it would be to maintain social and political cohesion.

Nationalization of a few key industries during the revolutionary period, combined with a concerted SPD effort to maintain a presence in the Reich government, might have given Weimar democracy a better chance of survival. Nationalization would have limited the economic power and thereby the potential political influence of a business elite sometimes neutral, sometimes hostile toward the new German state. Such action would have served a political purpose even if it did not aid economic recovery, and it would have equipped the state with more powerful tools to counteract the hyperinflation and, later, the depression.

Instead, Social Democratic leaders postponed nationalization to an indefinite date in the future because it did not fit in with their strategy of interparty and interclass cooperation. This nonsolution did not create a genuine social partnership between business and labor. Despite the initiatives of some progressive industrialists, business interests as a whole did not recognize the legitimacy of a socialist labor movement and agreed to its short-term social welfare goals only under duress. Social Democratic leaders failed to perceive the fundamental tension between their ideal of social and political integration and their desire to advance toward socialism gradually.

Moreover, Social Democratic confidence that the natural process of economic development would eventually bring about socialism had another negative consequence. Social Democratic strategists failed to work out and promote alternative economic models after nationalization had been postponed. More than a decade after party leaders grounded the Wissell-Moellendorff "common economy," they also put up resistance to a general program to stimulate the economy and reduce unemployment advanced by union economist Wladimir Woytinsky and accepted by the ADGB.[5] The party was suspicious of programs designed to guide and direct a capitalist economy.

The SPD sought to achieve only traditional labor goals such as the eight-hour day, compulsory arbitration, and unemployment insurance. But on these narrow issues the party had limited leverage in parliament and within coalition governments. Occasionally, it could work successfully with the Center party, which had a sizable working-class constituency, to advance the material interests of labor, but all too often the nonsocialists lined up against the SPD en bloc.

SPD leaders nonetheless found three basic reasons to participate in coalition governments: maintenance of parliamentary democracy, promotion of a foreign policy of reconciliation with Britain, France, and the United States, and establishment of a reliable republican administrative apparatus.[6] These goals were compatible with the SPD's decision in 1918–1919 to promote social and political integration, but they required the party to exploit its opportunities to obtain political power and to broaden its social base. The assumption that the working class alone could defend parliamentary democracy and advance the cause of socialism[7] served to deter any major campaign to diversify the SPD's constituency. Concern about the appeal of its left-wing rivals, internal dissent, and lack of compromise on the part of the nonsocialist parties induced the SPD to adopt a defensive strategy after 1922 in the Reich. The party's reliance upon its Prussian stronghold was some compensation, but ultimately, the strain upon Prussia proved to be too great.

Opposed to revolution, consciously committed to uphold the constitutional framework of Weimar democracy, the SPD and the socialist unions faced hostile governments in the Reich from late 1930 on. Brüning's practice of government by decree and his desire to keep his distance from the SPD frustrated the latter's efforts to take part in the formulation of government policy. The Prussian government became increasingly incapable of conducting an independent course during the depression, and Brüning's policies were extremely disadvantageous to labor interests. Papen's government intensified the trend and made the SPD its prime political target. Still, the SPD did not carry its opposition to particular policies or particular governments so far as to abandon the constitution or to force the collapse of the regime. The working class was urged to maintain its support of the parliamentary republic.

The Social Democratic elite accepted a form of negative integration[8] at the end of the Weimar Republic because the alternatives, mass action and/or cooperation with the Communists, were both highly risky and highly unpopular within the upper ranks of the Social Democratic organizations.[9] By avoiding approaches that would intensify middle-class fears of Marxism, the SPD leaders also hoped to escape the consequences of an alliance between conservatives and the Nazis, and to outlast the worst phase of the depression. The bureaucratic background of party and trade-union leaders certainly conditioned their choice of political strategy, but it is not sufficient explanation for their behavior or for the failure of their strategy.

During the last few months before Adolf Hitler became chancellor and stamped out all opposition, party authorities made some effort to come to grips with what had gone wrong. Whenever calls for a new direction in the party's agitation touched upon the concept of democratic socialism, however, party leaders adamantly resisted criticism:

> *Dietrich* (Weimar): If one were to raise the question . . . Potsdam or Weimar, at the moment one must say, "Potsdam, no, but Weimar also no." For the time being it is smashed to bits.
> *Breitscheid*: We must not fall into the error of saying that the Weimar Constitution is nothing, that it is outmoded. I also feel that it is not completely good. I hold it for bad, because it presents a dualistic division between the power of the Reichstag and that of the Reich president. We must return to the foundation of the Weimar Constitution, which expressed the idea that state power is derived from the people. We must not allow the impression to arise that we want to overthrow the edifice of the Weimar Constitution. It is threatened because we ourselves have also discredited it through the slogan: "Republic—that is too lame; socialism is our aim." Social Democratic agitation has prospects of success only if it sticks to a democratic foundation. The task of the fraction in the near future is to take care that democracy does not go down the drain.
> *Böchel* (Chemnitz): With certain justification Breitscheid has criticized the slogan "Republic—that is too lame; socialism is our aim." This slogan first stemmed from the youths. We know that youths are often too quick to make a judgment. . . . But this is an entirely sound and welcome reaction.
> *Hilferding*: More reaction(ary) than welcome.
> *Wels*: It has been stressed that there are indications of opposition to the republic and democracy everywhere. I don't believe that trees grow in the sky. I also don't believe that the concept of democracy suffers serious damage, because those who are now in power hardly represent democracy (*einer des anderen Teufel sind*).[10]

Despite undeniable errors of judgment and strategy, the leading figures in the SPD never wavered in their commitment to achieve democratic socialism by means of the parliamentary system. Their consolation for the failure of pluralistic democracy in the Weimar Republic was the older Social Democratic conviction that "democracy is the only rock upon which the working class can build the house of the German future."[11]

Given the unfavorable circumstances in which the Weimar Republic was born, and the succeeding economic and diplomatic crises, it may well have been impossible for the SPD to achieve the objective of social and political integration. Certainly, it would be hard to find a political party less responsible for the many failures of the Weimar Republic than the SPD. But the SPD's decisions of 1918–1919 should have led the party to a more concerted effort to bring about political and social cooperation.

The very combination of assets that made parliamentary democracy so attractive to the SPD leaders made it difficult for them to arrive at a clear political strategy. It was too easy for party leaders to revert to the older socialist belief that parliamentary democracy provided a secure pathway to socialism. That belief helped to rationalize political passivity. In politics as in life generally, there are few guarantees. Awareness of that fact allows one to make the most of available opportunities.

Appendix A
The Social Democratic Organization

For present purposes, the SPD elite during the Weimar Republic consisted of those individuals prominent in national and state politics or in the SPD's own hierarchy. These persons spoke at party congresses, meetings of the parliamentary fractions,[1] Reichstag or Landtag debates, cabinet sessions, and meetings of high party organs. The term "leadership" is reserved for the most powerful individuals within the elite. However, the names of party leaders cannot simply be read off a single organizational chart.

The SPD executive committee (*Parteivorstand*), usually headed by three cochairmen (*Parteivorsitzenden*), served as the managing body of the entire organization. The annual or biennial party congresses in theory represented the highest authority. The party congress could confirm or reject decisions of the executive committee, and the congress also elected the members of the committee. Moreover, the congress elected a control commission and a party council (*Parteiausschuss*), the former to supervise the executive committee, the latter to keep the executive committee informed of sentiment throughout party ranks and throughout the country. But the executive committee, whose members rarely faced challenge in elections, usually prevailed over all these bodies. In addition to many other powers, the executive committee exerted substantial influence over the party's regional organizations (which corresponded to the national election districts), partly through its right to participate in the hiring of regional executives.[2] Some members of the regional executive committees, however, were elected by regional party congresses and held independent influence.[3]

Despite its formal and informal authority, the executive committee did not dictate parliamentary policy. The SPD fraction in the Reichstag and the state parliamentary fractions could act independently. Some members of the executive committee held prominent posts in the Reichstag fraction, but only at the very beginning and toward the end of the Weimar Republic did a single individual hold a preeminent position on both institutions simultaneously. In the early period the man was Friedrich Ebert, at the end Otto Wels.

The SPD ministers in the national and state governments represented another force independent of the executive committee. Recent documentary publications[4] have provided evidence of frequent disagreement between SPD ministers and the Reichstag fraction. The Prussian wing of the party, buoyed by its success in retaining the leading positions in the Prussian government for many years, gained high prestige and substantial autonomy from 1923 on. Prussian Minister President Otto Braun, who was not a member of the executive committee, represented the only prominent challenger to Otto Wels in the last years of the republic.[5]

Finally, the General Federation of German Trade Unions (ADGB) and to a lesser extent, the General Free Federation of Salaried Employees (AfA) as well as the General Federation of German Civil Servants gave socialist trade unionists their own centralized organizations. The ADGB was by far the most powerful of these federations. Its salaried officials numbered roughly six thousand, a relatively small figure compared with the estimated twenty to thirty thousand SPD officials and leading functionaries.[6] But in terms of membership size and financial resources the ADGB dwarfed the SPD. Membership in ADGB affiliated unions ranged from four million to eight million during the Weimar years, compared with the SPD's roughly one million members. Obviously, SPD officials sought whenever possible to maintain the goodwill of their union counterparts, and union leaders did not hesitate to lobby within the party organization for their own objectives.[7]

Richard N. Hunt has described the SPD leadership during the Weimar period as an interlocking directorate.[8] The phrase is useful as long as one recognizes that, despite their overlapping membership and personal ties, the directors of the various Social Democratic institutions often locked horns with each other. When sharp disagreements erupted within the party elite, the perceived sentiments of voters, party members, and lower-level functionaries were likely to carry some weight. Despite the narrowness and longevity of the party leadership, the Social Democratic organization responded to strong rank-and-file feelings, although not necessarily in the way that the average members wanted. The expected reaction of the "masses" influenced several key leadership decisions on participation in coalition governments.

Since the present focus is on the parliamentary activity of the SPD, a few words about the Reichstag fraction are in order. Headed by its own executive board (*Vorstand der Reichstagsfraktion*) consisting of up to twenty persons, and by one or more chairmen, the fraction ranged from about one hundred to one hundred sixty-five deputies during the Weimar period. The number of candidates elected depended upon the SPD's vote in each electoral district—one deputy was elected for every sixty thousand votes for the party in the district. The accumulated remainder votes from each district served to elect candidates from a national list, again with each sixty thousand votes electing one deputy. The executive committee chose the SPD's national list; the regional executives, subject to the approval of regional congresses, selected the district lists. Radical, moderate, and centrist tendencies in the various regional organizations resulted in some political diversity in the fraction. The national list usually produced six to nine deputies reflecting the preferences of the executive committee. The ADGB leaders also pushed for their share of Reichstag candidacies on both the national and regional lists.[9]

Most SPD deputies had originally been skilled workers of one type or another, but the majority had since taken jobs in the Social Democratic organizations.[10] Under the Second Reich prominent Social Democrats constantly risked loss of their jobs and were barred entirely from many forms of state employment. This discrimination affected university graduates as well as factory workers.[11] The only solutions for loyal party members were to find an independent occupation (private legal or medical practice, tavernkeeping, or small business) or to make one's living within the Social

Democratic organization. As the size and resources of the organization grew, the latter practice became increasingly common. Naturally, those who dedicated themselves to the Social Democratic cause aspired to the distinctions that the movement could offer them. However, the predominance of Social Democratic careerists had certain disadvantages.

Despite some exceptions, party and trade-union bureaucrats rarely became striking or noteworthy figures in the Reichstag. One SPD deputy wrote in her memoirs about a particular union secretary elected to the Constituent Assembly in 1919: "Thurow could not accomplish much in parliament, but the executive committee and the fraction leadership had in him a member whom they could rely on. What they overlooked . . . was the fact that, although men such as Thurow were known within the organization and enjoyed the trust of its officials, they possessed nothing that would attract wider circles of voters in election campaigns."[12] In this sense Thurow was typical of SPD's backbenchers. The party's failure to select candidates who might attract broad voting support reflects an insular frame of mind within the organization, which was a product of the SPD's past political experience. This mentality restricted the SPD's ability to exploit the opportunities offered by parliamentary democracy. *Rheinische Zeitung* Editor Wilhelm Sollmann observed at the very end of the republic: "We would have been spared many a surprise, the sudden onset of the brown flood of Nazism being not the last, if our eyes and ears had reached far enough outside the ranks of our organization and our loyal followers."[13]

Appendix B
Reichstag Elections of 1919–1932

PARTY	National Assembly 19 January 1919			6 June 1920			4 May 1924			7 December 1924		
	Total Votes	%	No. Deputies	Total Votes	%	No. Deputies	Total Votes	%	No. Deputies	Total Votes	%	No. Deputies
No. eligible voters	36,766,500		423	35,949,800		459	38,375,000		472	38,987,300		493
No. valid votes cast	30,400,300	82.7		28,196,300	78.4		29,281,800	76.30		30,290,100	77.69	
Social Democrats (SPD)	11,509,100	37.9	165	6,104,400	21.6	102	6,008,900	20.5	100	7,881,000	26.0	131
Independent Socialists (USPD)	2,317,300	7.6	22	5,046,800	17.9	84	—	—	—	—	—	—
Communists (KPD)	—	—	—	589,500	2.1	4	3,693,300	12.6	62	2,709,100	9.0	45
Center	5,980,200	19.7	91	3,845,000	13.6	64	3,914,400	13.4	65	4,118,900	13.6	69
Bavarian People's party (BVP)	—	—	—	1,238,600	4.4	21	946,700	3.2	16	1,134,000	3.7	19
Democrats (DDP)	5,641,800	18.6	75	2,333,700	8.3	39	1,655,100	5.7	28	1,919,800	6.3	32
People's party (DVP)	1,345,600	4.4	19	3,919,400	13.9	65	2,694,400	9.2	45	3,049,100	10.1	51
Wirtschaftspartei	275,100	0.9	4	218,600	0.8	4	693,600	2.4	10	1,005,400	3.3	17
Nationalists (DNVP)	3,121,500	10.3	44	4,249,100	14.9	71	5,696,500	19.5	95	6,205,800	20.5	103
Christlich-soz. Volksdienst	—	—	—	—	—	—	—	—	—	—	—	—
Landbund	—	—	—	—	—	—	574,900	1.9	10	499,400	1.6	8
Christlich-natl. Bauern u. Landvolk	—	—	—	—	—	—	—	—	—	—	—	—
Deutsch-Hannov. Partei	77,200	0.2	1	319,100	0.9	5	319,800	1.0	5	262,700	0.8	4
Deutsche Bauernpartei	—	—	—	—	—	—	—	—	—	—	—	—
National Socialists (NSDAP)	—	—	—	—	—	—	1,918,300	6.5	32	907,300	3.0	14
Other parties	132,500	0.4	2	332,100	1.6	—	1,165,900	4.0	4	597,600	2.0	—

| 20 May 1928 | | | 14 September 1930 | | | 31 July 1932 | | | 6 November 1932 | | |
Total Votes	%	No. Deputies	Total Votes	%	No. Deputies	Total Votes	%	No. Deputies	Total Votes	%	No. Deputies
41,224,700		491	42,957,700		577	44,226,800		608	44,373,700		584
30,753,300	74.60		34,970,900	81.41		36,882,400	83.39		35,471,800	79.93	
9,153,000	29.8	153	8,577,700	24.5	143	7,959,700	21.6	133	7,248,000	20.4	121
—	—	—	—	—	—	—	—	—	—	—	—
3,264,800	10.6	54	4,592,100	13.1	77	5,282,600	14.6	89	5,980,200	16.9	100
3,712,200	12.1	62	4,127,900	11.8	68	4,589,300	12.5	75	4,230,600	11.9	70
945,600	3.0	16	1,059,100	3.0	19	1,192,700	3.2	22	1,094,600	3.1	20
1,505,700	4.9	25	1,322,400	3.8	20	371,800	1.0	4	336,500	1.0	2
2,679,700	8.7	45	1,578,200	4.5	30	436,000	1.2	7	661,800	1.9	11
1,397,100	4.5	23	1,362,400	3.9	23	146,900	0.4	2	110,300	0.3	1
4,381,600	14.2	73	2,458,300	7.0	41	2,177,400	5.9	37	2,959,000	8.8	52
—	—	—	868,200	2.5	14	405,300	1.1	3	412,500	1.2	5
199,500	0.6	3	194,000	0.5	3	96,900	0.2	2	105,200	0.3	2
581,800	1.8	10	1,108,700	3.0	19	90,600	0.2	1	46,400	0.1	—
195,600	0.5	3	144,300	0.4	3	46,900	0.1	—	64,000	0.2	1
481,300	1.5	8	339,600	1.0	6	137,100	0.3	2	149,000	0.4	3
810,100	2.6	12	6,409,600	18.3	107	13,745,800	37.4	230	11,737,000	33.1	196
1,445,300	4.8	4	1,073,500	3.1	4	342,500	0.9	1	749,200	2.2	—

Adapted from: Koppel S. Pinson, *Modern Germany: Its History and Civilization*
New York: Macmillan, 1962.

Notes

Introduction

1. V. I. Lenin, *Imperialism: The Highest Stage of Capitalism*, pp. 107–8, 126. Lenin, *Left-Wing Communism: An Infantile Disorder*, p. 568.
2. Robert Michels, *Political Parties*, espec. pp. 81, 170, 270–80.
3. See Charles S. Maier, *Recasting Bourgeois Europe*, pp. 22–87.
4. Gerhard Beier, "Das Problem der Arbeiteraristokratie im 19. und 20. Jahrhundert," pp. 9–71, includes a review and critique of recent east European literature on the subject.
5. For example, see J. P. Nettl, "The German Social Democratic Party 1890–1914 as a Political Model," pp. 79–81.
6. Harvey Mitchell and Peter Stearns, *Workers and Protest*, pp. 214–17.
7. See my review essay, "Negative Integration and Parliamentary Politics," pp. 175–97.
8. Aviva Aviv, "The SPD and the KPD at the End of the Weimar Republic," p. 172.
9. Richard N. Hunt, "Friedrich Ebert and the German Revolution of 1918," pp. 333–34.
10. The only party more democratic than the SPD in terms of party organization was the Independent Social Democratic party of Germany (USPD), which, however, suffered severely from internal divisions. See the fine study of the USPD by David W. Morgan, *The Socialist Left and the German Revolution*. For an interesting comparison between the structure of the SPD and that of the Center party, see Ursula Mittmann, *Fraktion und Partei*.
11. In a sample of 1,838 upper-level SPD officials during the Weimar period, 81.7 percent had only a primary-school education. The vast majority of this group was composed of former factory workers and artisans. Joachim Siemann, "Der sozialdemokratische Arbeiterführer in der Zeit der Weimarer Republik," pp. 21–26. According to official party statistics in 1930, 60 percent of the SPD's members were workers, 10 percent employees, and 7 percent civil servants. SPD, *Jahrbuch der deutschen Sozialdemokratie für das Jahr 1930*, p. 194.
12. One useful documentary collection about the ties between a Reichstag deputy (Ebert) and his constituency is Dieter K. Buse, ed., *Parteiagitation und Wahlkreisvertretung*.
13. For a more specific discussion of the terms *elite* and *leadership*, as well as an overview of the party organization, consult Appendix A.
14. Mittmann, *Fraktion und Partei*, p. 139.
15. Hartmut Schustereit, *Linksliberalismus und Sozialdemokratie in der Weimarer Republik*, p. 215. Karl Dietrich Bracher, *Die Auflösung der Weimarer Republik*, pp. 72–73.

Chapter One: Parliamentarism and Progress

1. On the SPD's experience under Bismarck's antisocialist laws, see Vernon L. Lidtke, *The Outlawed Party*.
2. Friedrich Engels, "Zur Kritik des sozialdemokratischen Programmentwurfs [1891]," p. 347.
3. Karl Kautsky to Eduard Bernstein, 18 Feb. 1898, *Nachlass* Kautsky C 180.
4. Hans-Josef Steinberg, *Sozialismus und deutsche Sozialdemokratie*, p. 67.
5. Ibid. See also Dieter Groh, *Negative Integration und revolutionärer Attentismus*, pp. 57, 185–90.
6. Guenther Roth, *The Social Democrats in Imperial Germany*, espec. pp. 315–19.
7. Groh, *Negative Integration*, pp. 36–37, 45.
8. Ibid., pp. 17–21, 33–57, 81–106. See also Klaus Saul, *Staat, Industrie, Arbeiterbewegung im Kaiserreich*.
9. Groh, *Negative Integration*, pp. 53–54, 66–69.
10. Steinberg, *Sozialismus*, pp. 109–19; Groh, *Negative Integration*, pp. 56–79.
11. Eduard Bernstein, *Evolutionary Socialism*, pp. 54–72, 95–108.
12. ". . . the desirable object would be that no class, and no combination of classes likely to combine, shall be able to exercise a preponderant influence in the government (to the lasting detriment of the whole)." John Stuart Mill, *Considerations on Representative Government*, p. 141. "We shall . . . define democracy as an absence of class government, as an indication of a social condition where political privilege belongs to no one class as opposed to the whole community." Bernstein, *Evolutionary Socialism*, p. 142. On Bernstein's concept of democracy, see also Peter Gay, *The Dilemma of Democratic Socialism*, espec. pp. 244–47.
13. Karl Kautsky, "Ein sozialdemokratischer Katechismus," p. 368. On the decline of socialist interest in direct democracy, see Peter Domann, *Sozialdemokratie und Kaisertum unter Wilhelm II*, pp. 48–50.
14. A dispute between the German military and the population of Zabern (in Alsace) led to a major political debate within Germany. See Hans-Ulrich Wehler, *Krisenherde des Kaiserreichs 1871–1918*, pp. 65–83, and Martin Kitchen, *The German Officer Corps 1890–1914*, pp. 186–220.
15. Peter Domann, *Sozialdemokratie und Kaisertum unter Wilhelm II*, pp. 219–20.
16. Ibid., pp. 91–100, 223–24.
17. Groh, *Negative Integration*, pp. 289–96. Still a valuable treatment of the left, although in disagreement with Groh on a number of points, is Carl Schorske, *German Social Democracy 1905–1917*.
18. Groh, *Negative Integration*, pp. 129–60, 476–502.
19. Hedwig Wachenheim, *Vom Grossbürgertum zur Sozialdemokratie*, p. 47.
20. Groh, *Negative Integration*, pp. 185–95, 499–500.
21. Susanne Miller, *Burgfrieden und Klassenkampf*, pp. 40–43, 69–70; Groh, *Negative Integration*, pp. 624–75.
22. Hedwig Wachenheim, ed., *Ludwig Frank*, p. 133, quoted by Miller, *Burgfrieden*, p. 72.
23. Miller, *Burgfrieden*, pp. 71–72, 241–42.
24. Susanne Miller, ed., *Das Kriegstagebuch des Reichstagsabgeordneten Eduard David 1914 bis 1918*, 11 Aug. 1914, pp. 14–16.
25. Miller, *Burgfrieden*, pp. 75–122.
26. Morgan, *Socialist Left*, pp. 42–52; Miller, *Burgfrieden*, pp. 91, 133–77.

27. Gerald D. Feldman, *Army, Industry, and Labor in Germany 1914–1918*, espec. pp. 197–249.

28. Miller, *Kriegstagebuch David*, pp. 24, 137–38, 233; Reinhard Patemann, *Der Kampf um die preussische Wahlrechtsreform im Ersten Weltkrieg*, pp. 18–96.

29. Miller, *Kriegstagebuch David*, pp. 64, 210.

30. Morgan, *Socialist Left*, pp. 37–39.

31. J. P. Nettl, *Rosa Luxemburg*, 2: 615.

32. Not all representatives on the interparty committee were willing to push for the rapid establishment of a parliamentary system, however. See the discussion by Udo Bermbach, *Vorformen parlamentarischer Kabinettsbildung in Deutschland*, pp. 83–92.

33. Feldman, *Army, Industry, and Labor*, pp. 337–39. See also Gerald Feldman, Eberhard Kolb, and Reinhard Rürup, "Die Massenbewegungen der Arbeiterschaft in Deutschland am Ende des Ersten Weltkrieges (1917–1920)," pp. 88, 93.

34. Miller, *Burgfrieden*, pp. 290–98.

35. *Reichstag: Stenographische Berichte*, 15 May 1917, 310: 3, 394–95.

36. Bermbach, *Vorformen*, p. 59.

37. Miller, *Burgfrieden*, pp. 303–9.

38. *Reichstag: Sten. Ber.*, 26 Oct. 1916, 308: 1, 814.

39. SPD, *Protokoll über die Verhandlungen des Parteitages der SPD . . . 1917*, pp. 406–7 (hereafter cited in the following form: SPD *Parteitag* 1917).

40. Ibid., pp. 137–38.

41. See, for example, Peter Kritzer, *Die bayerische Sozialdemokratie und die bayerische Politik in den Jahren 1918 bis 1923*, pp. 30–33.

42. Robert Sigel, "Die Lensch-Cunow-Haenisch Gruppe," pp. 421–36. On Rudolf Hilferding, see chapter seven below.

43. SPD *Parteitag* 1917, p. 408.

44. Wilhelm Mommsen, ed., *Deutsche Parteiprogramme*, pp. 391–97.

45. See Morgan, *Socialist Left*, pp. 68–79 for a discussion of the USPD's strongholds. Morgan estimates USPD membership at 100,000 at this time—about 25–33 percent of the SPD's total. The SPD's one million members in 1914 had dwindled because of the military mobilization and the political truce.

46. Bermbach, *Vorformen*, pp. 222–44.

47. Erich Matthias and Rudolf Morsey, eds., *Die Regierung des Prinzen Max von Baden*, pp. xiv–xvi; Gerhard Ritter, "Die Niederlage des Militärs," pp. 44–62.

48. Erich Matthias and Eberhard Pikart, eds., *Die Reichstagsfraktion der deutschen Sozialdemokratie 1898 bis 1918*, 23 Sept. 1918, 2: 429–60.

49. This assessment is made by Miller, *Burgfrieden*, pp. 133–35, 155–56. On Ebert's career until 1918, see Georg Kotowski, *Friedrich Ebert*. At this writing, Dieter K. Buse is engaged in a full biography of Ebert.

50. Quoted in D. K. Buse, "Ebert and the German Crisis, 1917–1920," p. 241.

51. Gerald Feldman, "German Business between War and Revolution," pp. 312–41; Feldman, "The Origins of the Stinnes-Legien Agreement," pp. 45–102.

52. Protokoll der Konferenz der Vertreter der Verbandsvorstände, 3 Dec. 1918, Restakten des Allgemeinen Deutschen Gewerkschaftsbundes, August-Bebel-Institut, NB 1 0011. (Hereafter cited: ADGB Restakten (ABI) I/0011).

53. ADGB, *Protokoll der Verhandlungen des zehnten Kongresses der Gewerkschaften Deutschlands . . . 1919*, p. 553.

54. Koch-Weser Diary, 13 Oct. 1919, *Nachlass* Koch-Weser.

55. SPD *Parteitag* 1920, p. 105.
56. Susanne Miller, *Die Bürde der Macht*, pp. 35–36.
57. Miller, *Kriegstagebuch David*, pp. 113, 191 (Ebert's and Scheidemann's comments).
58. Nettl, "German Social Democratic Party," p. 66.
59. Morgan, *Socialist Left*, pp. 52–53. Miller, *Bürde*, p. 44.
60. Feldman, Kolb, and Rürup, "Die Massenbewegungen," p. 88.

Chapter Two: The Limited Revolution

1. For detailed descriptions of the uprisings, see Eberhard Kolb, *Die Arbeiterräte in der deutschen Innenpolitik 1918/19*, pp. 56–113, and Ulrich Kluge, *Soldatenräte und Revolution*, pp. 24–125.
2. Morgan, *Socialist Left*, pp. 112–13.
3. For an assessment of the government of Prince Max, see Wolfgang Sauer, "Das Scheitern der parlamentarischen Monarchie." pp. 77–99, and Patemann, *Kampf*, pp. 220–23.
4. See n. 1 above.
5. Theodor Eschenberg, *Die improvisierte Demokratie*, p. 28. See the critical discussion of this interpretation in Miller, *Bürde*, pp. 62–69.
6. Prince Maximilian von Baden, *Erinnerungen und Dokumente*, p. 593; Ernst Feder, *Heute sprach ich mit . . .* , p. 169.
7. Matthias and Pikart, *Reichstagsfraktion*, 2: 514.
8. Hans Peter Hanssen, *Diary of a Dying Empire*, p. 349.
9. Erich Matthias and Susanne Miller, eds., *Die Regierung der Volksbeauftragten*, 1: 3–9.
10. Dieter K. Buse, "The Trustee, or Ebert as Reich President," p. 2.
11. Waldemar Besson, "Friedrich Ebert's Political Road from the Kaiserreich to the Republic," p. 79.
12. The SPD executive committee put out a printed notice on 9 Nov. 1918 that Ebert had become chancellor of the Reich. See the document reprinted in Charles Burdick and Ralph Lutz, eds., *The Political Institutions of the German Revolution 1918–1919*, p. 44.
13. Wilhelm Dittmann, "Erinnerungen," pp. 864–66.
14. Philipp Scheidemann, *The Making of New Germany*, 2: 262–64.
15. Miller, *Bürde*, p. 96.
16. *Vorwärts*, 10 Nov. 1918, reprinted by Matthias and Miller, *Regierung*, 1: 20–21.
17. Kolb, *Arbeiterräte*, pp. 115–16. Dittmann, "Erinnerungen," p. 870.
18. *Vorwärts*, 11 Nov. 1918, reprinted in Matthias and Miller, *Regierung*, 1: 30–31.
19. Kolb, *Arbeiterräte*, p. 119; Miller, *Bürde*, pp. 97–98.
20. Morgan, *Socialist Left*, p. 122.
21. Miller, *Bürde*, p. 168.
22. Dittmann, "Erinnerungen," p. 872.
23. The agreement, converted into an ordinance of the Council of People's Deputies, is reprinted in *Verfassunggebende deutsche Nationalversammlung: Anlagen*. vol. 335, no. 215, Anlage, p. 4.
24. *Reichsgesetzblatt*, 12 Nov. 1918, pp. 1, 303–4, reprinted in Matthias and Miller, *Regierung*, 1: 37–38.

25. Wolfgang Elben, *Das Problem der Kontinuität in der deutschen Revolution*, p. 33.
26. *Vorwärts*, 11 Nov. 1918, reprinted in Matthias and Miller, *Regierung*, 1: 34.
27. Emil Barth, *Aus der Werkstatt der Revolution*, p. 34.
28. Elben, *Problem*, pp. 34, 37.
29. Wolfgang Runge, *Politik und Beamtentum im Parteienstaat*, pp. 17–18.
30. Matthias and Miller, *Regierung*, 1: 127–30.
31. Wolfgang Sauer, "Das Bündnis Ebert-Groener," p. 46.
32. Kolb, *Arbeiterräte*, p. 121.
33. Kluge, *Soldatenräte*, pp. 136–44.
34. Numerous documents regarding these contacts, including some transcripts, are reprinted in Lothar Berthold and Helmut Neef, eds., *Militarismus und Opportunismus gegen die Novemberrevolution*, pp. 158–62.
35. Karl Kautsky, *Demokratie oder Diktatur*, pp. 9–10. Further citations of contemporary literature on nationalization, and a discussion of the significance of nationalization for the SPD may be found in Michael William Honhart, "The Incomplete Revolution," pp. 6–33. For the recent scholarly works on this subject, see Hans Dieter Hellige, "Die Sozialisierungsfrage in der deutschen Revolution 1918/19," pp. 91–100.
36. Henryk Skrzypczak, "From Carl Legien to Theodor Leipart," p. 31.
37. Protokoll der Konferenz der Vertreter der Verbandsvorstände, 3 Dec. 1918, ADGB Restakten (ABI) I/0011.
38. ADGB, *Auszug aus dem Protokoll der Verhandlungen der Konferenz der Vertreter der Vorstände der gewerkschaftlichen Zentralverbände vom 25. April 1919*, p. 28.
39. Barth, *Aus der Werkstatt*, pp. 66–68.
40. The term *socialization* implied state control, but not necessarily state ownership; its exact meaning varied from speaker to speaker. For further discussion, see Honhart, "Incomplete Revolution," pp. 44–45.
41. Elben, *Problem*, p. 83.
42. *Allgemeiner Kongress der Arbeiter- und Soldatenräte . . . 1918*, pp. 21–22; Dittmann, "Erinnerungen," pp. 889, 920.
43. *Allgemeiner Kongress*, pp. 21–22.
44. Kautsky, *Demokratie oder Diktatur*, pp. 42–51.
45. Ibid., pp. 41–42; *Allgemeiner Kongress*, pp. 106, 109–11.
46. *Allgemeiner Kongress*, pp. 156–61, 171–72.
47. *Bericht der Sozialisierungskommission über die Frage der Sozialisierung des Kohlenbergbaues vom 31. Juli 1920: Anhang; Vorläufiger Bericht vom 15. Februar 1919*.
48. *Vorwärts*, 14 Nov. 1918, cited in Kolb, *Arbeiterräte*, p. 170.
49. Reichskonferenz der Länderregierungen, 25 Nov. 1918, reprinted in Matthias and Miller, *Regierung*, 1: 156, 161, 165, 167.
50. Ibid., p. 215. More generally, Miller, *Bürde*, pp. 104–15.
51. Cabinet meeting of 29 Nov. 1918 in Matthias and Miller, *Regierung*, 1: 227.
52. Richard Müller, *Vom Kaiserreich zur Republik*, p. 85.
53. Peter Lösche, *Der Bolschewismus im Urteil der deutschen Sozialdemokratie 1903–1920*, pp. 166, 239–44; Kolb, *Arbeiterräte*, p. 184. Arno Mayer, *The Politics and Diplomacy of Peacemaking*, pp. 97–102.
54. Reichskonferenz, 25 Nov. 1918, in Matthias and Miller, *Regierung*, 1: 92. Also cabinet meeting of 7 Dec. 1918, ibid., 1: 294. Mayer, *Politics and Diplomacy*, pp. 104, 114.

55. *Allgemeiner Kongress*, pp. 2, 106–12.
56. Ibid., pp. 8, 114–17.
57. Ibid., pp. 127–28, 135.
58. Kolb and Rürup, eds., *Der Zentralrat*, pp. xxvii–xxviii.
59. Kluge, *Soldatenräte*, pp. 160–204.
60. Cabinet meetings of 3 and 12 Dec. 1918 in Matthias and Miller, *Regierung*, 1: 247, 369. Kluge, *Soldatenräte*, pp. 247–50.
61. Kluge, *Soldatenräte*, pp. 205–11.
62. Groener to Dear Friend [Ebert], 1 Dec. 1918, *Nachlass* Schleicher xiii/15, cited by Buse, "Ebert and the German Crisis," p. 249n66.
63. Reprinted in Berthold and Neef, *Militarismus und Opportunismus*, pp. 158–62.
64. Even as late as 26 Dec. Groener reported to a conference of high military officials that Ebert was reluctant to impose his will with military backing. See the minutes in Heinz Hürten, ed., *Zwischen Revolution und Kapp Putsch*, pp. 31–33.
65. E. O. Volkmann, *Revolution über Deutschland*, p. 128. Oberkommando des Heeres, Kriegsgeschichtliche Forschungsanstalt, *Die Wirren in der Reichshauptstadt und im nördlichen Deutschland 1918–1920*, pp. 21, 31. (Hereafter cited as OKH, *Wirren*.)
66. Ibid., pp. 28–29; Hagen Schulze, *Freikorps und Republik 1918–1920*, p. 11; Morgan, *Socialist Left*, pp. 186–88.
67. Jens Flemming, "Parlamentarische Kontrolle in der Novemberrevolution," p. 120; Kluge, *Soldatenräte*, pp. 264, 290–93.
68. On this episode, see H. H. Herwig, "The First German Congress of Workers' and Soldiers' Councils and the Problem of Military Reform," pp. 150–65.
69. *Allgemeiner Kongress*, pp. 64–66, 90.
70. Reprinted in Berthold and Neef, *Militarismus und Opportunismus*, p. 184.
71. Morgan, *Socialist Left*, p. 193.
72. Minutes reprinted in Kolb and Rürup, *Zentralrat*, pp. 25–43. See also, Flemming, "Parlamentarische Kontrolle," pp. 114–30; Kluge, *Soldatenräte*, pp. 250–60.
73. Kluge, *Soldatenräte*, pp. 273–76. Excerpts from the regulations are reprinted in F. L. Carsten, *The Reichswehr and Politics 1918–1933*, pp. 25–26, 32–33.
74. *Allgemeiner Kongress*, pp. 88, 126, 144–51, 184. Kolb and Rürup, *Zentralrat*, pp. 22–23.
75. Arthur Rosenberg, *A History of the German Republic*, pp. 31–32.
76. Kolb, *Arbeiterräte*, pp. 209, 233; Flemming, "Parlamentarische Kontrolle," pp. 98–99.
77. Rosenberg, *History of the German Republic*, pp. 59–60. But there is some evidence that the Naval Division council preferred working with Haase, rather than Ebert, if the coalition broke up. See Anton Fischer, *Die Revolutionskommandatur Berlin*, pp. 33–34.
78. OKH, *Wirren*, p. 36.
79. Morgan, *Socialist Left*, p. 194; Kluge, *Soldatenräte*, p. 263n277.
80. Cabinet meeting of 24 Dec. 1918, in Matthias and Miller, *Regierung*, 2: 35.
81. Fischer, *Revolutionskommandatur*, pp. 42–46.
82. Cabinet meeting of 28 Dec. 1918, in Matthias and Miller, *Regierung*, 2: 97 (quote), 128; Dittmann, "Erinnerungen," pp. 941–46.
83. For details of the conflicts within the USPD, see Morgan, *Socialist Left*, pp. 198–211.
84. For the discussion, see Hermann Weber, ed., *Der Gründungsparteitag der KPD–Protokoll und Materialien*.

85. Eric Waldman, *The Spartacist Uprising of 1919 and the Crisis of the German Socialist Movement*, pp. 171–78.

86. Kolb, *Arbeiterräte*, p. 233.

87. Gustav Noske, *Von Kiel bis Kapp*, pp. 67–68.

88. Sessions of 7 and 11 Jan. 1919, in Matthias and Miller, *Regierung*, 2: 200, 210–13; Morgan, *Socialist Left*, pp. 213–16.

89. Waldman, *Spartacist Uprising*, pp. 187–90; Nettl, *Luxemburg*, 2: 755–56.

90. See Lösche, *Bolschewismus*, pp. 170, 171, 249, who maintains that the uprising was the turning point of the revolution.

91. Hermann Heidegger, *Die deutsche Sozialdemokratie und der nationale Staat 1870–1920*, p. 309.

92. Kaul (Hessen) in *Allgemeiner Kongress*, p. 134.

93. See Heinrich Muth, "Die Entstehung der Bauern- und Landarbeiterräte im November 1918 und die Politik des Bundes der Landwirte," pp. 1–38.

94. This interpretation is developed by Reinhard Rürup, "Problems of the German Revolution, 1918–1919," pp. 109–36, and Flemming, "Parlamentarische Kontrolle," pp. 70–76.

Chapter Three: A Shaky Beginning

1. Protokoll der SPD Fraktionssitzung, 4 Feb. 1919; see also chapter one.

2. Protokoll der SPD Fraktionssitzung, 4 Feb. 1919.

3. Reprinted in SPD *Parteitag* 1919, p. 56.

4. The SPD leaders apparently never considered the idea of a minority government of the two socialist parties. See Walther Oehme, *Die Weimarer Nationalversammlung 1919*, pp. 85–86.

5. Protokoll der SPD Fraktionssitzungen, 5, 17 Feb. 1919; *Nationalversammlung: Sten. Ber.*, vol. 326, p. 373, 28 Feb. 1919; *Nationalversammlung: Anlagen*, vol. 336, no. 391, pp. 252, 274–75. Also Heinrich Potthoff, "Das Weimarer Verfassungswerk und die deutsche Linke," pp. 437, 456–57, 465.

6. Scheidemann, *Making*, 2: 614–16. General Groener also pushed for the establishment of a strong presidency and t rejection of English-style parliamentarism. See Hürten, ed., *Zwischen Revolution und Kapp Putsch*, p. 54.

7. Buse, "The Trustee," pp. 2, 14.

8. *Nationalversammlung: Sten. Ber.*, vol. 326, p. 44, 13 Feb. 1919.

9. Newspaper clipping "Scheidemann über das Rätesystem," found in *Nachlass Grzesinski* I ₁ II/409. Also Oehme, *Nationalversammlung*, p. 15.

10. Peter Kuckuk, ed., *Revolution und Räterepublik in Bremen*. There are good brief descriptions of the clashes in Morgan, *Socialist Left*, pp. 219–22, and Miller, *Bürde*, pp. 236–41.

11. Jürgen Kocka, *Klassengesellschaft im Krieg*, pp. 33–57; Peter von Oertzen, "Die grossen Streiks der Ruhrbergarbeiterschaft im Frühjahr 1919," pp. 185–217; Erhard Lucas, "Ursachen und Verlauf der Bergarbeiterbewegung in Hamborn und im westlichen Ruhrgebiet," pp. 37–64. Some of the most recent research is presented by Reinhard Rürup, ed., *Arbeiter- und Soldatenräte im rheinisch-westfälischen Industriegebiet*.

12. Hans Mommsen, "Die Bergarbeiterbewegung an der Ruhr 1918–1933," pp. 291–92.

13. Oertzen, "Die grossen Streiks," p. 191.

14. Richard Müller, *Der Bürgerkrieg in Deutschland*, p. 129.
15. Oertzen, "Die grossen Streiks," p. 192.
16. Joint meeting of cabinet and *Zentralrat*, 28 Jan. 1919, Matthias and Miller, *Regierung*, 2: 344; Honhart, "Incomplete Revolution," p. 99.
17. Neunerkommission, *Die Sozialisierung des Bergbaues und der Generalstreik im rheinisch-westfälischen Industriegebiet*, pp. 8–9.
18. This point is stressed by Oertzen, "Die grossen Streiks," pp. 201–2.
19. Copy of a report from Dr. Buberine, Essen, to an unidentified captain, 17 Feb. 1919, *Nachlass* Severing VII/173.
20. Mommsen, "Bergarbeiterbewegung," pp. 291–92.
21. The union leaders had already come out strongly against the Ruhr movement, which was regarded at least in part as a revolt against the unions by younger, less experienced workers. Honhart, "Incomplete Revolution," pp. 111–13, 132. Free Union Federation Chairman Carl Legien virulently denounced the institution of the factory council: Protokoll der SPD Parteikonferenz in Weimar, 22–23 Mar. 1919, pp. 31–35. Most SPD leaders took a more moderate stance, and Labor Minister Bauer said that he hoped to find a middle position between Legien's and that of the left.
22. Neunerkommission, *Sozialisierung*, pp. 14–17.
23. Peter von Oertzen, *Betriebsräte in der Novemberrevolution*, pp. 140–41.
24. Ulrich Kluge, "Essener Sozialisierungsbewegung und Volkswehrbewegung im Rheinisch-Westfälischen Industriegebiet 1918/1919," pp. 55–65; Kluge, "Militärrevolte und Staatsumsturz," pp. 39–82.
25. Kolb and Rürup, eds., *Zentralrat*, p. 691.
26. Neunerkommission, *Sozialisierung*, pp. 23–29. Oertzen, *Betriebsräte*, pp. 116–17.
27. Oertzen, *Betriebsräte*, p. 143; Morgan, *Socialist Left*, pp. 229–31.
28. *Vorwärts*, no. 105, 26 Feb. 1919 charged that the aim of the strike movement was the collapse of the government and the overthrow of the Constituent Assembly.
29. Cabinet meeting of 28 Feb. 1919 in *Akten der Reichskanzlei Weimarer Republik: Das Kabinett Scheidemann* (hereafter cited as *Akten: Scheidemann*), p. 10; Oehme, *Nationalversammlung*, pp. 242–47.
30. *Nationalversammlung: Anlagen*, vol. 335, p. 73.
31. Kolb and Rürup, eds., *Zentralrat*, p. 752n3. For the list of strike demands see Sozialistische Einheitspartei Deutschlands, Institut für Marxismus-Leninismus, *Dokumente und Materialien zur Geschichte der deutschen Arbeiterbewegung*, 7/1, p. 45. On the background to the Berlin movement, see Morgan, *Socialist Left*, pp. 232–34.
32. Hans Schieck, "Der Kampf um die deutsche Wirtschaftspolitik nach dem Novemberumsturz 1918," p. 168.
33. *Nationalversammlung: Anlagen*, vol. 335, p. 74, 4 Mar. 1919.
34. R. Müller, *Bürgerkrieg*, pp. 159–60; Oertzen, *Betriebsräte*, pp. 145–46.
35. Morgan, *Socialist Left*, pp. 234–35.
36. OKH, *Wirren*, pp. 80–84. Noske, *Von Kiel*, pp. 103–4.
37. Robert G. L. Waite, *Vanguard of Nazism*, p. 72.
38. OKH, *Wirren*, p. 83.
39. *Dokumente und Materialien*, 7/1, p. 7; Kolb, *Arbeiterräte*, pp. 312–16.
40. Lösche, *Bolschewismus*, pp. 170–74, 280–81.
41. Protokoll der SPD Parteikonferenz, 22–23 Mar. 1919, pp. 2 (Hermann Müller), and 4 (Wels).

42. *Dokumente und Materialien*, 7/1, p. 58.
43. Enno Eimers, *Das Verhältnis von Preussen und Reich in den ersten Jahren der Weimarer Republik (1918–1923)*, p. 150, maintains that the state of siege cost the SPD substantial support in all areas where it was used.
44. Stenographischer Bericht über die Konferenz der revolutionären Bergarbeiter am 17. April im 'Kölnischen Hof' zu Dortmund, copy in *Nachlass* Severing VII/181.
45. Oertzen, "Die grossen Streiks," p. 194; *Nachlass* Severing VII/181.
46. Cabinet meeting of 11 Apr. 1919, *Akten: Scheidemann*, p. 154.
47. Carl Severing, *1919–1920: Im Wetter- und Watterwinkel*, pp. 31–34. Cabinet meetings of 7 and 11 Apr. 1919, *Akten: Scheidemann*, pp. 142–43, 154. Food rations were denied to strikers also. Cabinet meeting of 31 Mar. 1919, *Akten: Scheidemann*, p. 119.
48. Elben, *Problem*, pp. 46–48. See also Gerhard Schulz, *Zwischen Demokratie und Diktatur*, 1: 21–173; Reinhard Rürup, "Entstehung und Grundlagen der Weimarer Verfassung," pp. 218–43.
49. Cabinet meeting of 14 Jan. 1919, Matthias and Miller, *Regierung*, 2: 240–41, 246.
50. Schulz, *Zwischen Demokratie*, 1: 146–47.
51. Wolfgang Mommsen, *Max Weber und die deutsche Politik, 1890–1920*, pp. 328–30. On Preuss and other liberals, see Ernst Portner, *Die Verfassungspolitik der Liberalen, 1919*, especially pp. 93–115, 153–59.
52. Potthoff, "Weimarer Verfassungswerk," pp. 437, 456–57.
53. *Nationalversammlung: Anlagen*, vol. 336, no. 391, p. 252, 5 Apr. 1919 (Davidsohn). Also Potthoff, "Weimarer Verfassungswerk," p. 465.
54. Schulz, *Zwischen Demokratie*, 1: 133.
55. Protokoll der SPD Fraktionssitzung, 26 Feb. 1919.
56. Ebert to Branting, 16 Apr. 1920, reprinted by Agnes Blänsdorf, "Friedrich Ebert und die Internationale," pp. 425–26.
57. Gustav Radbruch, "Goldbilanz der Reichsverfassung," pp. 60–62.
58. Heinrich August Winkler, *Mittelstand, Demokratie, und Nationalsozialismus*, p. 73; *Nationalversammlung: Anlagen*, vol. 336, no. 391, p. 392 (Simon Katzenstein).
59. Protokoll der SPD Fraktionssitzungen, 12 Mar. 1919; *Nationalversammlung: Sten. Ber.*, vol. 327, p. 747, 13 Mar. 1919.
60. *Nationalversammlung: Sten. Ber.*, vol. 329, p. 2, 111, 30 July 1919 (Haas amendment). One SPD deputy had complained about the emergency powers even before the amendment: "I am astounded that we want to create absolutism in this way." Ibid., *Anlagen*, vol. 336, no. 391, pp. 459–60.
61. Reinhard Schiffers, *Elemente direkter Demokratie im Weimarer Regierungssystem*, pp. 130–33.
62. *Nationalversammlung: Sten. Ber.*, vol. 328, p. 2,075, 29 July 1919; ibid., vol. 329, p. 2,195.
63. Protokoll der Sitzung des Parteivorstandes, des Parteiausschusses, und der Parteiredakteure, 27 Jan. 1920, p. 1.
64. SPD, *Handbuch für sozialdemokratische Wähler 1920*, pp. 58, 144–46. SPD *Parteitag 1920*, p. 91 (Hildenbrand); SPD *Parteitag 1921*, p. 131 (Wels); SPD *Parteitag 1922*, p. 4 (Müller), p. 63 (Wels).
65. See below, chapter seven, for a more extended discussion.
66. Ernst Fraenkel, "1919–1929—Verfassungstag," p. 230.

67. Protokoll der SPD Fraktionssitzung, 19 June 1919.
68. Quoted by Erich Eyck, *A History of the Weimar Republic*, 1: 97–98.
69. Wachenheim, *Vom Grossbürgertum*, p. 101.
70. Protokoll der SPD Fraktionssitzung, 21 June 1919; Scheidemann, *Making*, 2: 316–17.
71. Arnold Brecht, *Aus nächster Nähe*, p. 296.
72. Besprechung am 23. Juni 1919 im Grossen Hauptquartier, *Nachlass* Schleicher XII/113a. Also Johannes Erger, *Der Kapp-Lüttwitz Putsch*, pp. 23–35.
73. A series of articles in *Vorwärts* on developments in the Reichswehr caused the Reichswehr officials and the Defense Ministry to submit written protests to the SPD. The relevant clippings and protest notes are in *Nachlass* Schleicher XV/33–40. On Noske, see Wachenheim, *Vom Grossbürgertum*, p. 110.
74. *Nationalversammlung: Sten. Ber.*, vol. 330, pp. 2,886–88, 7 Oct. 1919; Scheidemann, *Making*, 2: 327–28.
75. Protokoll der SPD Fraktionssitzung, 21 Nov. 1919; Wilhelm Keil, *Erlebnisse eines Sozialdemokraten*, 2: 190–91.
76. Protokoll der Sitzung des Parteiausschusses, 13 Dec. 1919, pp. 2–4, 22, 26–28.
77. See chapter four.
78. Protokoll der Sitzung des Parteivorstandes, des Parteiausschusses und der Parteiredakteure, 27 Jan. 1920, p. 20.
79. Erger, *Kapp-Lüttwitz Putsch*, pp. 85–101.
80. Ibid., pp. 116–22.
81. [Wolfgang Heine], "Aufzeichnungen über den Kapp-Putsch und Vorgeschichte," typewritten manuscript in *Nachlass* Otto Braun III/118 and in *Nachlass* Heine XXXVI/7.
82. Erger, *Kapp-Lüttwitz Putsch*, pp. 135, 142, 146.
83. Ibid., pp. 147–49, 322–23.
84. Reich Chancellery Press Secretary Ulrich Rauscher (SPD) prepared and distributed this proclamation. Noske and possibly other ministers saw it before they left. Erger, *Kapp-Lüttwitz Putsch*, pp. 193–94, cites a multitude of sources for this version. Brecht, *Aus nächster Nähe*, p. 302 also relates that he received the proclamation directly from Rauscher. Wolfgang Heine wrote in a memo on 24 March that Otto Wels had told him that Rauscher had composed the text at the request of the SPD ministers and signed it for them. *Nachlass* Heine XXXVI/8.
85. Friedrich Stampfer, *Die ersten vierzehn Jahren der deutschen Republik*, p. 166.
86. Erger, *Kapp-Lüttwitz Putsch*, pp. 177–91, 194–95.
87. *Korrespondenzblatt des Allgemeinen Deutschen Gewerkschaftsbundes*, vol. 30, nos. 12–13, 27 Mar. 1920, p. 150.
88. Ibid. Also Erger, *Kapp-Lüttwitz Putsch*, pp. 195–97. The term *workers' government* could be interpreted either as a minority socialist government or as a broader coalition that included the SPD, USPD, and workers' representatives from the Center party.
89. Protokoll der Sitzung des Parteiausschusses, 30 Mar. 1920, p. 2 (Wels).
90. *Dokumente und Materialien*, 7/1, pp. 211–13.
91. Erger, *Kapp-Lüttwitz Putsch*, pp. 200–203; George Eliasberg, "Der Ruhrkrieg 1920," p. 304.
92. *Korrespondenzblatt*, 27 Mar. 1920, p. 151.
93. Hermann Pünder, *Von Preussen nach Europa*, pp. 55–56.

94. Document in *Nachlass* Severing VIII/9, 14 Mar. 1920.
95. Brecht, *Aus nächster Nähe*, pp. 304–5.
96. Gerald Feldman, "Big Business and the Kapp Putsch," p. 106.
97. See the description of Gustav Stresemann's maneuvers in Henry Ashby Turner, Jr., *Stresemann and the Politics of the Weimar Republic*, pp. 49–63.
98. Statement made later by DNVP leader Hergt, who was present during the negotiations. *Reichstag: Sten. Ber.*, vol. 341, p. 545, 2 Aug. 1920.
99. Ebert, technically only the provisional president, had been elected by the Constituent Assembly. The constitution called for direct popular election, and Field Marshal Hindenburg was expected to be a formidable rightist candidate.
100. Erger, *Kapp-Lüttwitz Putsch*, pp. 282–83.
101. Wilhelm Koenen, "Zur Frage der Möglichkeit einer Arbeiterregierung nach dem Kapp Putsch," pp. 347–49.
102. Minutes of the three-day meeting between union leaders, Schiffer, Prussian Minister President Hirsch, and representatives of the coalition parties are in *Nachlass* Südekum 121. Excerpts are reprinted in Erger, *Kapp-Lüttwitz Putsch*, pp. 350–52. The nine union demands are listed in *Korrespondenzblatt*, 27 Mar. 1920, p. 153, and reprinted in Hartmut Schustereit, *Linksliberalismus und Sozialdemokratie in der Weimarer Republik*, pp. 85–87.
103. *Korrespondenzblatt*, 27 Mar. 1920, p. 155.
104. *Nachlass* Südekum 121.
105. Cabinet meeting of 20 Mar. 1920, U.S. National Archives microfilm T-120, 3438/1668/744153–154; *Korrespondenzblatt*, 27 Mar. 1920, p. 153.
106. Wels's account is in Protokoll der Sitzung des Parteiausschusses, 30 Mar. 1920, pp. 6–7.
107. Notes of Haussmann's meeting with Ebert, 23 Mar. 1920, *Nachlass* Haussmann XLIII, cited in Schustereit, *Linksliberalismus*, p. 94n101.
108. Meeting of the chancellor, representatives of the unions, and the two socialist parties, 22 Mar. 1920, (BA Koblenz) R 43I/2664/52.
109. Cabinet meeting of 22 Mar. 1920, 4 p.m. No official minutes of this meeting exist, but Erich Koch-Weser has extensive notes on it. Koch-Weser Diary, *Nachlass* Koch-Weser.
110. Schustereit, *Linksliberalismus*, pp. 88–89.
111. Protokoll der Sitzung des Parteiausschusses, 30 Mar. 1920, p. 31.
112. Koch-Weser Diary, 22 Mar. 1920, *Nachlass* Koch-Weser. Notes of DDP fraction meeting, apparently 22 Mar. 1920, *Nachlass* Gothein XLII/6.
113. Koch-Weser Diary, 23 Mar. 1920, *Nachlass* Koch-Weser. The proclamation of the SPD executive committee is reprinted in Fritz Krause, ed., *Arbeitereinheit rettet die Republik*, p. 122. See also Müller's remarks, Protokoll über die Verhandlungen der Reichskonferenz der SPD, 5–6 May 1920, pp. 54–55.
114. Günter Arns, "Friedrich Ebert als Reichspräsident," pp. 19–21. Hans Biegert, "Gewerkschaftspolitik in der Phase des Kapp-Lüttwitz Putsches," p. 203.
115. Koch-Weser Diary, 23 Mar. 1920, *Nachlass* Koch-Weser.
116. *Nachlass* Eugen Schiffer II cited in, *Akten der Reichskanzlei Weimarer Republik: Das Kabinett Müller I* (hereafter cited as *Akten: Müller I*), p. xii.
117. Braun to Gessler, 1 May 1920, and Gessler to Braun, 18 May 1920, *Nachlass* Braun V/165.
118. *Nationalversammlung: Sten. Ber.*, vol. 332, p. 4,949, 29 Mar. 1920.

119. Recent research on these events includes: Eliasberg, "Der Ruhrkrieg 1920," pp. 291–378; Lucas, *Märzrevolution im Ruhrgebiet*, 1: 147–310; Schulze, *Freikorps*, pp. 304–18.
120. *Akten: Müller I*, pp. 47n2, 49–55, 308–9; *Korrespondenzblatt*, no. 15, 10 Apr. 1920, p. 182.

Chapter Four: The Failure of Structural Economic Reform

1. Gerald Feldman, "Economic and Social Problems of the German Demobilization 1918–1919," pp. 1–23.
2. Protokoll der SPD Parteikonferenz, 22–23 Mar. 1919, p. 30.
3. Charles S. Maier, "Between Taylorism and Technology," pp. 27–62.
4. On Wissell, see David E. Barclay, "Social Politics and Social Reform in Germany."
5. Walther Rathenau, *Von kommenden Dingen*. For a more extensive discussion of Moellendorff, see David E. Barclay, "A Prussian Socialism," pp. 52–58.
6. *Nationalversammlung: Sten. Ber.*, vol. 326, p. 542, 7 Mar. 1919.
7. Barclay, "Social Politics," pp. 130–75; Honhart, "Incomplete Revolution," pp. 192–229.
8. *Nationalversammlung: Anlagen*, vol. 335, Drucksache 105.
9. *Akten: Scheidemann*, pp. 72–75, 103–4, 131–32. The final version is in *Nationalversammlung: Anlagen*, vol. 335, pp. 227–31.
10. Cabinet meeting of 20 Mar. 1919, *Akten: Scheidemann*, p. 73. Bauer was himself influenced by Hugo Sinzheimer, the SPD's expert on the councils. See the discussion of Sinzheimer's theories in Ernst Fraenkel, *Deutschland und die westlichen Demokratien*, pp. 93–99.
11. *Akten: Scheidemann*, pp. 131–32.
12. Schieck, "Kampf," p. 169, is mistaken about the timing of Wissell's move.
13. Heinz Josef Varain, *Freie Gewerkschaften, Sozialdemokratie und Staat*, p. 150.
14. See Wissell's own description of this organizational structure, "Zur Räte-Idee," pp. 195–207.
15. Varain, *Freie Gewerkschaften*, p. 149; Oertzen, *Betriebsräte*, p. 153.
16. Wissell, "Zur Räte-Idee," p. 195.
17. Program reprinted in *Akten: Scheidemann*, pp. 284–88; Wissell to Scheidemann, 7 May 1919, *Akten: Scheidemann*, p. 270. For the provenance of this letter, see Honhart, "Incomplete Revolution," p. 154n2.
18. "Denkschrift," reprinted in *Akten: Scheidemann*, pp. 272–83.
19. Excerpt from an unpublished work by Treasury Minister Gothein (DDP), reprinted in *Akten: Scheidemann*, p. 264n1.
20. Schieck, "Kampf," p. 175.
21. Ibid., pp. 246–49. Schieck may overestimate the impact of the treaty on the fate of the common economy, because the original goal of economic autarky was no longer the main purpose of the plan. Wissell himself emphasized that it provided a less rocky path to socialism than nationalization. SPD *Parteitag* 1919, p. 369.
22. Denkschrift des Reichsernährungsministers, 7 May 1919, *Akten: Scheidemann*, pp. 297–303.
23. Denkschrift des Schatzministers, 7 May 1919, *Akten: Scheidemann*, pp. 297–303.
24. Varain, *Freie Gewerkschaften*, p. 136.

25. Wissell to Scheidemann, 7 May 1919, *Akten: Scheidemann*, p. 271.
26. Schieck, "Kampf," p. 175. Wissell was later to claim that an aide had leaked the information without authorization. Honhart, "Incomplete Revolution," p. 169.
27. Cabinet meeting of 24 May 1919, *Akten: Scheidemann*, p. 372.
28. SPD *Parteitag* 1919, pp. 363–69, 373.
29. Ibid., pp. 376, 383.
30. Müller's judgment was probably correct. The USPD party program of March 1919 explicitly repudiated the concept of a mixed economy with public controls. USPD *Parteitag* (March) 1919, pp. 3–4. However, many USPD members would likely have been pleased if the government had adopted any economic reforms. SPD *Parteitag* 1919, pp. 396, 404.
31. Cabinet meeting of 8 July 1919, Anlage zum Protokoll, U.S. National Archives film T-120, 3438H/1666/742726–31 (hereafter cited as USNA).
32. Protokoll der SPD Fraktionssitzungen, 8, 10–11, 31 July 1919.
33. Ibid., 26 Nov. and 9 Dec. 1919.
34. For an analysis, see Barclay, "Prussian Socialism," pp. 72–73, 79–82.
35. Eimers, *Verhältnis*, pp. 177–78.
36. Protokoll über die Verhandlungen der Reichskonferenz der SPD, 5–6 May 1920, p. 30.
37. SPD *Parteitag* 1919, pp. 113, 126–27, 406–54.
38. Cabinet meeting of 5 Aug. 1919, USNA T-120, 3438H/1666/742899–900.
39. See above, pp. 60–61.
40. *Reichstag: Anlagen*, vol. 338, no. 928, Anlage 19.
41. Varain, *Freie Gewerkschaften*, p. 154.
42. Protokoll der SPD Fraktionssitzungen, 30 Sept., 10 Oct., 21 and 25 Nov. 1919.
43. Gothein in the *Berliner Tageblatt*, 30 Oct. 1919, cited by Maier, *Recasting Bourgeois Europe*, p. 161.
44. Protokoll der SPD Fraktionssitzung, 26 Nov. 1919.
45. Ibid., 25 Nov. 1919. For a different version of the negotiations related to the DDP fraction by DDP negotiators, see Lothar Albertin, *Liberalismus und Demokratie am Anfang der Weimarer Republik*, pp. 181–88, 359–60.
46. Maier, *Recasting Bourgeois Europe*, pp. 161–62.
47. Varain, *Freie Gewerkschaften*, p. 155.
48. Protokoll der SPD Fraktionssitzungen, 15–16 Dec. 1919.
49. Protokoll der Sitzung des Parteiausschusses, 13 Dec. 1919, p. 21.
50. Maier, *Recasting Bourgeois Europe*, pp. 162–63; Albertin, *Liberalismus*, p. 185.
51. Walther Grosch, "Der Reichswirtschaftsrat in seiner jetzigen und künftigen Ausgestaltung," pp. 50–51.
52. *Korrespondenzblatt*, no. 19, 7 May 1919, pp. 263–65. Ludwig Preller, *Sozialpolitik in der Weimarer Republik*, p. 264.
53. Ernst Fraenkel, "Zehn Jahre Betriebsrätegesetz," p. 122.
54. Ibid., pp. 117–18, 128.
55. Protokoll über die Verhandlungen der Reichskonferenz der SPD, 5–6 May 1919, p. 10.
56. Varain, *Freie Gewerkschaften*, p. 135; Preller, *Sozialpolitik*, p. 240.
57. Reichskonferenz der SPD, 5–6 May 1920, p. 31.
58. *Korrespondenzblatt*, nos. 12/13, 27 Mar. 1920, p. 155. At a meeting of the ADGB executive committee on the same day, Chairman Carl Legien specified that the unions wanted only the right to help select the persons chosen for the new

governments, not the authority to oust the governments with a vote of no confidence. He wanted assurance that individuals chosen would pursue the goals sought by the unions. ADGB Restakten (ABI) 227/017.

59. Otto Hue, *Die Sozialisierung der Kohlenwirtschaft*.

60. Compare Hilferding's December 1918 speech, *Allgemeiner Kongress*, pp. 159–60, with his October 1920 speech, reprinted as *Die Sozialisierung und die Machtverhältnisse der Klassen*, pp. 3–5, 13–15.

61. SPD *Parteitag* 1920, p. 39.

62. Ibid., p. 91 (Karl Hildenbrand).

63. *Verhandlungen der Sozialisierungskommission* 1920, 1: vi (hereafter cited as *Sozialisierungskommission* 1920).

64. *Nationalversammlung: Sten. Ber.*, vol. 333, p. 5,451, 26 Apr. 1920; pp. 5,495–96, 27 Apr. 1920 (Riesser).

65. *Reichsgesetzblatt* 1919, pp. 661–82.

66. Maier, *Recasting Bourgeois Europe*, pp. 213–14.

67. *Sozialisierungskommission* 1920, 1: 179–207, 223–45.

68. Ibid., 2: 395–440.

69. Peter Wulf, "Regierung, Parteien, Wirtschaftsverbände und die Sozialisierung des Kohlenbergbaues 1920–1921," p. 654.

70. *Reichstag: Sten. Ber.*, vol. 344, pp. 272–73.

71. *Bericht der Sozialisierungskommission*, pp. 6–7, 13–16, 21–24.

72. For more details, see Maier, *Recasting Bourgeois Europe*, pp. 218–20.

73. BA Koblenz, R 43I/2114/188, 27 Sept. 1920.

74. Maier, *Recasting Bourgeois Europe*, pp. 219–22.

75. Sozialisierungsausschuss der Deutschen Demokratischen Partei, 20 Oct. 1920, *Nachlass* Gothein LXIX/73.

76. Maier, *Recasting Bourgeois Europe*, pp. 221–23.

77. Cabinet meeting of 7 Dec. 1920, *Akten: Fehrenbach*, pp. 336–37.

78. Cabinet meeting of 20 Jan. 1921, ibid., p. 421.

79. Ibid., p. 451nn5, 4.

80. The ADGB leaders concluded in January 1921 that new elections alone might bring action. *Korrespondenzblatt*, no. 2, 8 Jan. 1921, p. 17.

81. SPD *Parteitag* 1920, p. 152 (Hoch).

82. Protokoll der Sitzung des Parteiausschusses, 8 Dec. 1920, p. 22. Hildenbrand also rejected Löbe's suggestion that the SPD cease its toleration of the government.

83. Protokoll der USPD Fraktionssitzung, 26 Jan. 1921.

84. SPD *Parteitag* 1921, pp. 263, 269.

85. These drafts are to be found in *Nachlass* Bernstein N/2–9.

86. SPD *Parteitag* 1921, p. 359.

87. Ibid., pp. 359, 366.

88. Ibid., pp. 299–303.

89. Ibid., pp. 303–4.

90. Ibid., p. 112.

Chapter Five: Defense of the Republic 1920–1922

1. On the SPD's contribution to fulfillment policy, see William H. Maehl, "The German Socialists and the Foreign Policy of the Reich from the London

Conference to Rapallo,'' pp. 35–54. Also Peter Pistorius, ''Rudolf Breitscheid 1874–1944,'' pp. 245–46. More generally, Reimund Klinkhammer, ''Die Aussenpolitik der sozialdemokratischen Partei Deutschlands in der Zeit der Weimarer Republik.''

2. Interview with Ernest Hamburger, 3 Feb. 1976.

3. Müller to Austrian State Secretary Dr. Ellenbogen, 21 Apr. 1920, BA Koblenz R 43I/2662/108.

4. Protokoll der Sitzung des Parteiausschusses, 4 May 1920, pp. 2, 11, 13, 15–16.

5. Reichskonferenz der SPD, 5–6 May 1920, p. 29.

6. Ibid., pp. 7, 10.

7. Turner, *Stresemann*, pp. 74–76.

8. Arnold Brecht, *The Political Education of Arnold Brecht*, p. 187.

9. SPD, Reichstagsfraktion, *Bericht der sozialdemokratischen Fraktion des Reichstages*, June–Oct. 1920, pp. 8–9.

10. Comment by Hermann Müller, meeting of SPD fraction and party council 13 June 1920, notes in *Nachlass* Giebel II/210.

11. SPD, *Bericht der SPD Fraktion* 1920, pp. 6–7.

12. *Nachlass* Giebel II/210–16.

13. Koch-Weser Diary, 18 and 25 June 1920, *Nachlass* Koch-Weser. Rudolf Morsey, *Die Deutsche Zentrumspartei 1917–1923*, p. 331. Already on 24 June Gustav Bauer told Chancellor Fehrenbach that the SPD would oppose any vote of no confidence based on the government's foreign policy. USNA T-120, 3438H/5744/K642738–39.

14. Stampfer, *Ersten vierzehn Jahren*, p. 202.

15. SPD *Parteitag* 1920, p. 25.

16. See Turner, *Stresemann*, pp. 75–82.

17. Texts of the resolution and amendment, SPD *Parteitag* 1920, pp. 319, 321 (nos. 324 and 338); Wels's failure to mention the latter, p. 83; voting results, p. 85. Protokoll der Sitzung des Parteiausschusses, 8 Dec. 1920, pp. 3–7.

18. Ernst Laubach, *Die Politik der Kabinette Wirth 1921/22*, pp. 9–13. For a new look at the whole reparations dispute, see Sally Marks, ''The Myth of Reparations,'' pp. 231–55.

19. Koch-Weser Diary, 10 May 1921, *Nachlass* Koch-Weser; Morsey, *Deutsche Zentrumspartei*, p. 382; fragmentary minutes of SPD fraction, 10 May, *Nachlass* Giebel II/216; voting results in *Vorwärts*, no. 217, 10 May 1921.

20. For a discussion of the schism, see Morgan, *Socialist Left*, pp. 341–80.

21. Protokoll der USPD Fraktionssitzung, 10 May 1921.

22. *Reichstag: Sten. Ber.*, vol. 349, p. 36.

23. Koch-Weser Diary, 13 May 1921, *Nachlass* Koch-Weser; Protokoll der USPD Fraktionssitzung, 10 May 1921.

24. Koch-Weser Diary, 4 June 1921, *Nachlass* Koch-Weser.

25. Pistorius, ''Rudolf Breitscheid,'' p. 194.

26. Feldman, *Army, Industry, and Labor*, pp. 52–64, 349–404.

27. Bry, *Wages in Germany*, pp. 209–12.

28. Both Stinnes and Rathenau seem to have concurred on this view. See Fritz Ringer, *The German Inflation of 1923*, pp. 90–93. Also Maier, *Recasting Bourgeois Europe*, pp. 209–17.

29. Maier, *Recasting Bourgeois Europe*, pp. 358, 361. Maier (p. 358) is explicit on the causes of the hyperinflation, the most controversial phase of the long

inflationary spiral: "The frantic resort to the printing press was a form of taxation imposed by the powerful industrial forces upon the weaker elements and lent a degree of public approval because of prevailing bewilderment about the causes of inflation and general acceptance of the right's thesis that ultimately the Allies were to blame." Karsten Laursen and Jørgen Pedersen, *The German Inflation 1918– 1923*, pp. 10, 81–85, take the view that up through mid-1923 the inflation promoted economic expansion.

30. Maier, *Recasting Bourgeois Europe*, pp. 300–301.
31. Preller, *Sozialpolitik*, pp. 255–95.
32. Peter-Christian Witt, "Finanzpolitik und sozialer Wandel in Krieg und Inflation 1918–1924," pp. 413–19.
33. Cabinet meeting of 17 May 1921 and Denkschrift des Reichswirtschaftsministers zur Erfüllung des Londoner Zahlungsplanes, 19 May 1921, *Akten: Wirth*, pp. 4–5, 7–13.
34. Rathenau, the third DDP minister, had entered the cabinet belatedly on 29 May.
35. Cabinet meetings of 24 and 29 June 1921, *Akten: Wirth*, pp. 88–90, 115–18.
36. Maier, *Recasting Bourgeois Europe*, pp. 249–55.
37. Laubach, *Politik*, pp. 73–79.
38. Klaus Epstein, *Matthias Erzberger and the Dilemma of German Democracy*, pp. 379–90; John G. Williamson, *Karl Helfferich 1872–1924*, pp. 217–38, 291–302, 312–29.
39. Gotthard Jasper, *Der Schutz der Republik*, p. 35.
40. Besprechung mit Vertretern der politischen Parteien, 26 Aug. 1921, BA Koblenz R 43I/1020/26; Jasper, *Schutz*, p. 37.
41. *Reichsgesetzblatt* 1921, p. 1,239.
42. Jasper, *Schutz*, pp. 40–43.
43. Memo of 30 Aug. 1921, Otto Wels to the SPD district secretariats, marked "For information only!" ADGB Restakten (ABI) 468/001; Jasper, *Schutz*, pp. 35, 38.
44. Jasper, *Schutz*, p. 38. Wirth's speech did not win him any plaudits within the Center party. After taking heavy criticism, he explained that he was merely making a hypothetical statement. Morsey, *Deutsche Zentrumspartei*, pp. 411–12.
45. SPD *Parteitag* 1921, p. 326.
46. Ibid., pp. 147, 181.
47. Jasper, *Schutz*, p. 40; Albert Grzesinski to Philipp Scheidemann, 16 Sept. 1921, *Nachlass* Grzesinski A/II/304.
48. Grzesinski to Scheidemann, 16 Sept. 1921, *Nachlass* Grzesinski A/II/304.
49. Besprechung mit dem Interfraktionellen Ausschuss, 13 Sept. 1921; Besprechung mit Vertretern der Banken und der Industrie, 14 Sept. 1921, *Akten: Wirth*, pp. 254–58, 265–69; Lothar Albertin, "Die Verantwortung der liberalen Parteien für das Scheitern der Grossen Koalition im Herbst 1921," pp. 580–82.
50. Repeated by Hermann Müller and Philipp Scheidemann, SPD *Parteitag* 1921, pp. 112, 176.
51. Ibid., pp. 148–49 (Krüger).
52. SPD *Parteitag* 1921, p. 182.
53. See above, pp. 18–19, 72–73.
54. SPD *Parteitag* 1921, p. 389. See also, ibid., pp. 113–14, 178–79, 182, 195.
55. Ibid., pp. 160–62, 164–65, 169, 172–73 (Marckwald, Eckstein, Brosswitz, Biester, and Kiess).
56. Grzesinski to Scheidemann, 16 Sept. 1921, *Nachlass* Grzesinski A/II/304; Protokoll der USPD Fraktionssitzung, 26 Sept. 1921.

57. Text of resolution SPD *Parteitag* 1921, pp. 576–77; reaction of USPD in Morgan, *Socialist Left*, pp. 406–7; quote from USPD *Parteitag* 1922, p. 107, reprinted in Morgan, *Socialist Left*, p. 407.
58. SPD *Parteitag* 1921, p. 131.
59. On the lack of a specific party program for civil servants, see Gabrielle Hoffmann, *Sozialdemokratie und Berufsbeamtentum*, pp. 123–37.
60. *Vorwärts*, no. 159, 21 Sept. 1921.
61. Vorbesprechung zwischen Vertretern der Koalitionsparteien, 28 Sept. 1921, *Akten: Wirth*, pp. 292–93; a careful analysis of the minutes of this meeting appears in Albertin, "Verantwortung," pp. 587–88.
62. *Die Freiheit*, no. 461, 2 Oct. 1921.
63. Protokoll der USPD Fraktionssitzung, 1 Oct. 1921.
64. Besprechung mit Parteiführern, 3 Oct. 1921, *Akten: Wirth*, pp. 301–2.
65. *Vorwärts*, no. 471, 6 Oct. 1921.
66. Besprechung mit Parteiführern, 3 Oct. 1921, *Akten: Wirth*, pp. 298–300.
67. The USPD fraction took the view that after an imperialist war one had to expect an imperialist peace. It also felt that the right-wing parties were inciting a strong emotional reaction to the settlement in order to force Wirth's resignation. Protokoll der USPD Fraktionssitzung, 20 Sept. 1921.
68. Cabinet meeting of 12 Oct. 1921, *Akten: Wirth*, pp. 313, 317.
69. Besprechung mit dem Interfraktionellen Ausschuss, 18 Oct. 1921, *Akten: Wirth*, pp. 325–29; Albertin, "Verantwortung," pp. 594–95.
70. This conclusion can be drawn from Hermann Müller's remarks in Besprechungen mit dem Interfraktionellen Ausschuss, 17 and 20 Oct. 1921, *Akten: Wirth*, pp. 324, 331.
71. Cabinet meeting of 22 Oct. 1921, *Akten: Wirth*, pp. 335–37; Albertin, "Verantwortung," pp. 599–601; Erkelenz to Rathenau, 3 Nov. 1921, *Nachlass* Erkelenz 17/111–14.
72. Albertin, "Verantwortung," pp. 607–9.
73. *Akten: Wirth*, p. 411n1.
74. Wels in Besprechung mit Vertretern der Regierungsparteien, 11 Nov. 1921, *Akten: Wirth*, p. 386.
75. Scheidemann in Besprechung, 11 Nov. 1921, *Akten: Wirth*, pp. 385–86. *Vorwärts*, no. 533, 12 Nov. 1921.
76. Der ADGB an den Reichskanzler, 21 Nov. 1922, *Akten: Wirth*, pp. 415–18; quote from Besprechung mit Vertretern der Gewerkschaften, 22 Nov. 1922, *Akten: Wirth*, p. 423.
77. *Vorwärts*, no. 17, 11 Jan. 1922.
78. Laubach, *Politik*, p. 146.
79. *Vorwärts*, no. 42, 25 Jan. 1922.
80. Protokoll der USPD Fraktionssitzung, 24 Jan. 1922.
81. *Vorwärts*, no. 505, 4 Feb. 1922.
82. Eduard David Diary, 25 Jan. 1922, *Nachlass* David.
83. SPD *Parteitag* 1921, pp. 134, 149, 174, 178 (Krüger, Scheidemann, Müller).
84. Scheidemann to Otto Landsberg, 19 Apr. 1922, *Nachlass* Landsberg II/2/66–67. For Scheidemann's more restrained public criticism, see *Vorwärts*, no. 81, 17 Feb. 1922.
85. Besprechung mit dem Interfraktionellen Ausschuss, 16 Feb. 1922, *Akten: Wirth*, pp. 566–68; *Vorwärts*, no. 226, 14 May 1922.
86. Albertin, "Verantwortung," p. 627.

87. *Vorwärts*, no. 266, 8 June 1922.
88. *Vorwärts*, no. 295, 24 June 1922.
89. *Reichstag: Sten. Ber.*, vol. 355, pp. 7,988–8,001.
90. Grotjahn, *Erlebtes*, pp. 225–27; Löbe, *Weg*, pp. 102–4.
91. *Reichstag: Sten. Ber.*, vol. 355, pp. 8,033–34; 8,054–58.
92. Ibid., pp. 8,037–39; *Reichsgesetzblatt* 1922, p. 532.
93. Hugo Sinzheimer to Rudolf Wissell, 5 July 1922, Korrespondenz Wissell, ADGB Akten (DGB) xxviii/200–201.
94. Protokoll der USPD Fraktionssitzung, 24 June 1922; *Vorwärts*, no. 298, 27 June 1922.
95. Protokoll der USPD Fraktionssitzung, 24 June 1922.
96. Ibid., 26 June 1922.
97. *Vorwärts*, no. 297, 26 June 1922.
98. Ibid., no. 302, 29 June 1922; Jasper, *Schutz*, pp. 63–64.
99. Protokoll der USPD Fraktionssitzung, 28 June 1922.
100. Morsey, *Deutsche Zentrumspartei*, pp. 464, 464n38.
101. Erkelenz to Wilhelm Cohnstaedt, 6 July 1922, *Nachlass* Erkelenz 1/20/54.
102. Besprechung mit Vertretern der Parteien und Gewerkschaften, 1 July 1922, *Akten: Wirth*, p. 926; *Vorwärts*, no. 317, 7 July 1922.
103. Jasper, *Schutz*, pp. 62–63, 76–83.
104. Protokoll der USPD Fraktionssitzung, 10 July 1922.
105. Notes of SPD Fraktionssitzung, 10 July 1922, *Nachlass* Giebel ii/218.
106. The SPD fraction's decision was almost unanimous according to *Vorwärts*, no. 330, 15 July 1922. Among the opponents were Eduard David and Alfred Grotjahn. David Diary, 14 July 1922, *Nachlass* David. Grotjahn, *Erlebtes*, p. 240.
107. Turner, *Stresemann*, pp. 97–100.
108. Jasper, *Schutz*, pp. 84–87; *Reichsgesetzblatt* 1922, pp. 585ff., reprinted in ibid., pp. 292–300.
109. Jasper, *Schutz*, pp. 88–89.
110. Ibid., pp. 92–97.
111. Adolf Braun to Karl Kautsky, 2 Aug. 1922, *Nachlass* Kautsky D/iv/402. On the activities of the Bavarian right-wing associations, see James M. Diehl, *Paramilitary Politics in Weimar Germany*, pp. 100–109, 121–30.
112. Gustav Radbruch, *Der innere Weg*, pp. 161–62.
113. *Vorwärts*, no. 452, 24 Sept. 1922.

Chapter Six: The Crises of 1923

1. SPD *Parteitage* 1922, pp. 131, 173. See also Toni Sender, *Autobiography of a German Rebel*, pp. 189–90.
2. SPD *Parteitage* 1922, pp. 134–36.
3. Hunt, *German Social Democracy*, pp. 204–10.
4. Günter Arns, "Die Linke in der SPD-Reichstagsfraktion im Herbst 1923," p. 202.
5. Hermann Molkenbuhr Diary, 11 Apr. 1923, *Nachlass* Molkenbuhr.
6. SPD *Parteitage* 1922, resolution 337, p. 106.
7. *Vorwärts*, no. 437, 15 Sept. 1922.
8. SPD *Parteitage* 1922, pp. 5, 67.

9. Major figures in the SPD opposition are discussed by Hanno Drechsler, *Die Sozialistische Arbeiterpartei Deutschlands (SAPD)*, pp. 1–32.
10. Toni Sender, *Grosse Koalition?*, pp. 8–9.
11. *Vorwärts*, nos. 505–6, 508, 25–27 Oct. 1922.
12. Laubach, *Politik*, pp. 303–6.
13. Cabinet meeting of 23 Oct. 1922, *Akten: Wirth*, pp. 1,136–37; Besprechung mit den Parteiführern, 23 Oct. 1922, ibid., p. 1,137n2.
14. *Akten: Wirth*, p. 1,139n4.
15. *Vorwärts*, no. 514, 31 Oct. 1922.
16. Kessler, *Diaries*, 7 Nov. 1922, p. 196; Hagen Schulze, *Otto Braun oder Preussens demokratische Sendung*, p. 424.
17. *Vorwärts*, no. 532, 10 Nov. 1922. See also Stinnes's text of the program, reprinted in George W. F. Hallgarten, *Hitler, Reichswehr und Industrie*, pp. 50–55.
18. The arrangement to allow exceptions to the eight-hour day was apparently a compromise worked out by business and labor representatives. See Maier, *Recasting Bourgeois Europe*, p. 300n157. The SPD refused to make further concessions in part because it wished to maintain a record of support for the eight-hour day that would be suitable for subsequent election campaigns. *Handbuch für sozialdemokratische Wähler 1924*, p. 101.
19. Maier, *Recasting Bourgeois Europe*, pp. 298–302. For an extended discussion of heavy industry's positions, see Gerald D. Feldman, *Iron and Steel in the German Inflation 1916–1923*, pp. 327–32.
20. *Vorwärts*, no. 536, 12 Nov. 1922.
21. Ibid., no. 538, 14 Nov. 1922.
22. Klügmann to Hasselmann, 27 Nov. 1922, BA Koblenz R 43I/2662/227–34. Klügmann, a DVP deputy in the Reichstag, discussed a recent conversation with Breitscheid regarding the SPD's moves of the preceding two weeks. See also notes of SPD fraction meeting, 13 Nov. 1922, *Nachlass* Giebel II/219–22, and Kessler, *Diaries*, p. 196.
23. Stampfer, *Ersten vierzehn Jahren*, pp. 306–7.
24. Hagen Schulze, "Ein Briefwechsel zwischen Otto Braun und Joseph Wirth im Exil," pp. 160–63, 173, 176–79, 181–82; Buse, "The Trustee," pp. 21–23.
25. Klügmann to Hasselmann, 27 Nov. 1922, R 43I/2662/227–34.
26. *Vorwärts*, no. 541, 15 Nov. 1922, and no. 545, 17 Nov. 1922.
27. Stampfer, *Ersten vierzehn Jahren*, pp. 310–11.
28. The Ruhr crisis has been described in detail by Jean-Claude Favez, *Le Reich devant l'occupation franco-belge de la Ruhr en 1923*. Maier, *Recasting Bourgeois Europe*, pp. 289–304, provides a succinct description and analysis.
29. Constantino Bresciani-Turroni, *The Economics of Inflation*, p. 35.
30. Maier, *Recasting Bourgeois Europe*, p. 358.
31. Bry, *Wages in Germany*, p. 227.
32. *Frankfurter Zeitung*, no. 534, 29 July 1923.
33. Carl Severing, "Das Gebot der Stunde," pp. 2–3; Sender, *Grosse Koalition?*, pp. 3, 10. Notes of SPD fraction, 10 June 1923, *Nachlass* Giebel II/237.
34. Sinzheimer to Sollmann, 30 May 1923, *Nachlass* Sollmann II/18/16.
35. *Frankfurter Zeitung*, no. 568, 3 Aug. 1923; *Vorwärts*, no. 359, 3 Aug. 1923.
36. Text in *Nachlass* Giebel II/223.
37. Ibid., II/224. For a well-informed interpretation, see *Frankfurter Zeitung*, no. 570, 4 Aug. 1923.

38. Notes of SPD fraction, 13 Aug. 1923, *Nachlass* Giebel II/243–44. Prussian Minister President Otto Braun was not given the additional function of Reich minister without portfolio, which the fraction had sought for him. Four Social Democrats were appointed to the cabinet: Hilferding (finance), Sollmann (interior), Radbruch (justice), and Schmidt (reconstruction). The most difficult bargaining occurred over the tax-financial program, according to Severing, *Mein Lebensweg*, 1: 424–25.

39. Arns, "Linke," pp. 195–96.

40. Meeting of the chancellor with party leaders, 22 Aug. 1923, minutes in *Nachlass* Erkelenz 1/27/141–43.

41. Cabinet meetings of 30 Sept. and 1 Nov. 1923, USNA T-120, 3491/1748/756881 and 756909–11. See also Turner, *Stresemann*, p. 121.

42. *Frankfurter Zeitung*, nos. 729 and 731, 2–3 Oct. 1923. Turner, *Stresemann*, pp. 132–34.

43. *Reichstag: Sten. Ber.*, vol. 361, p. 11,949, 8 Oct. 1923 (Breitscheid); *Vorwärts*, no. 461, 3 Oct. 1923. The DVP's demands had also included the reduction of the coal tax, the passage of an Enabling Law, the resignation of Hilferding, and a serious attempt to bring the DNVP into the government. Even years later the SPD's parliamentary leaders showed rancor over this brusk action by the DVP. See Feder, *Heute*, p. 76, 16 Sept. 1926; ibid., p. 100, 24 Jan. 1927.

44. Cabinet meetings of 2–3 Oct. 1923, USNA T-120, 3491/1748/756957; 1749/757005–6.

45. Ibid., 756993–95.

46. Notes of SPD fraction, 5 Oct. 1923, *Nachlass* Giebel II/251.

47. Gustav Stresemann, *Vermächtnis*, 1: 158.

48. Cabinet meeting of 3 Oct. 1923, USNA T-120, 3491/1749/756998.

49. Notes of SPD fraction, 5–6 Oct. 1923, *Nachlass* Giebel II/251–54. Also *Vorwärts*, no. 461, 3 Oct. 1923, and no. 473, 10 Oct. 1923.

50. Arns, "Linke," pp. 196–99.

51. *Reichstag: Sten. Ber.*, vol. 361, pp. 12,152–54, 10 Oct. 1923, and p. 11,955, 8 Oct. 1923.

52. Braun to Ebert, 24 Aug. 1922, *Nachlass* Braun V/492.

53. Niederschrift über vertrauliche Mitteilung—Streng geheim! 19 Oct. 1922, *Nachlass* Severing XII/31.

54. Severing's official justification is reprinted by Jasper, *Schutz*, pp. 301–4.

55. Diehl, *Paramilitary Politics*, pp. 100–107, 121–30; Harold J. Gordon, Jr., *Hitler and the Beer Hall Putsch*, pp. 168–74.

56. Aussprache über die politische Lage in Bayern, 5 Nov. 1922, ADGB Restakten (ABI) LXIV/0007a; also Donald L. Niewyk, *Socialist, Anti-Semite and Jew*, p. 59.

57. ADGB Restakten (ABI) LXIV/0007–13.

58. Leipart to Braun, 3 Oct. 1922, and Braun to Leipart, 20 Oct. 1922, *Nachlass* Braun V/499 and 496.

59. Besprechung in der Reichskanzlei, 16 June 1923, ADGB Restakten (ABI) LXIV/0051; Carsten, *Reichswehr and Politics*, p. 158.

60. *Akten: Cuno*, pp. 207–8.

61. Abegg to Severing, 31 May 1947, reprinted in part by Thilo Vogelsang, *Reichswehr, Staat und NSDAP*, p. 407.

62. Carsten, *Reichswehr and Politics*, pp. 162–63.

63. Severing to Gessler, 23 Apr. 1923 and 14 June 1923, *Nachlass* Severing XIX/124–25.

64. *Akten: Cuno*, pp. 567–68n29; for disputes, see for example: Severing to Gessler, 9 May 1925, *Nachlass* Braun (FES) I/I; Grzesinski to Severing, 3 Nov. 1926, and Severing to Grzesinski, 23 Nov. 1926, *Nachlass* Severing xxxii/86–87; Otto-Ernst Schüddekopf, ed., *Das Heer und die Republik*, pp. 114–17.

65. Braun to Severing, 21 Aug. 1929, *Nachlass* Severing I/15; Schulze, *Otto Braun*, pp. 610–13.

66. Abegg to Severing, 31 May 1947 in Vogelsang, *Reichswehr*, p. 407.

67. Diehl, *Paramilitary Politics*, pp. 133–36. On political developments in Saxony, see Angress, *Stillborn Revolution*, pp. 382–86, and Donald B. Pryce, "The Reich Government versus Saxony, 1923," pp. 113–20.

68. Hermann Weber, *Die Wandlung des deutschen Kommunismus*, p. 44.

69. *Frankfurter Zeitung*, no. 221, 24 Mar. 1923; Severing, *Mein Lebensweg*, I: 386–87.

70. Telephone message from Hermann Müller to Chancellor Cuno, 19 July 1923, BA Koblenz, R 43I/677/15; also, Reich Commissar Ernst Mehlich to Cuno, 19 July 1923, copy in *Nachlass* Severing xiv/29.

71. Reich Interior Minister Oeser (DDP) was among those pressing Cuno for equal treatment of left and right. Cuno urged the Bavarian government to take action of its own against the paramilitary forces, but he was not willing to intervene. See Pryce, "Reich Government," pp. 122–23.

72. Severing, *Mein Lebensweg*, I: 369, 386–89.

73. *Frankfurter Zeitung*, nos. 716 and 726, 27 Sept. and 1 Oct. 1923. On Kahr's previous relations with the paramilitary groups, see Diehl, *Paramilitary Politics*, pp. 71–73, 100–101, 121.

74. *Frankfurter Zeitung*, no. 718, 28 Sept. 1923.

75. Wilhelm Hoegner, *Der schwierige Aussenseiter*, p. 27.

76. *Vorwärts*, nos. 456 and 457, 29–30 Sept. 1923.

77. Carsten, *Reichswehr and Politics*, pp. 173–82; Turner, *Stresemann*, pp. 124–25.

78. Cabinet meetings of 1, 22, and 23 Oct. 1923, USNA T-120, 3491/1749/756901–905, 757285, 757304.

79. Ibid., 30 Sept. and 22–23 Oct. 1923, 1748/756882, 1749/757285, 1749/757304.

80. For a list of Zeigner's accusations and the Reichswehr's responses, see *Nachlass* Schleicher xxiv/53–54.

81. Pryce, "Reich Government," pp. 128–32.

82. Angress, *Stillborn Revolution*, pp. 397–406, 427–35.

83. Pryce, "Reich Government," p. 134.

84. *Vorwärts*, no. 490, 19 Oct. 1923.

85. Cabinet meeting of 17 Oct. 1923, USNA T-120, 3491/1749/757227.

86. Cabinet meetings of 17 and 27 Oct. 1923, ibid., 757226–27, 757443–51.

87. Dittmann, "Erinnerungen," p. 1,316. Hans Meier-Welcker, *Seeckt*, p. 387.

88. *Vorwärts*, no. 505, 28 Oct. 1923.

89. Cabinet meeting of 29 Oct. 1923, USNA T-120, 3491/1749/757513.

90. Stresemann regarded any government that included the Communists as unconstitutional. Cabinet meeting of 27 Oct. 1923, ibid., 757443–51. The text of Stresemann's ultimatum is reprinted in Stresemann, *Vermächtnis*, I: 186–87.

91. According to Dittmann, "Erinnerungen," pp. 1,317–18, Zeigner had informed the SPD Landtag fraction on 23 Oct. that he could no longer work with the Communists. He said that he planned to resign on 30 Oct.

92. Comments by Hermann Müller, notes of SPD fraction 31 Oct. 1923, *Nachlass* Giebel II/258, 266. See also, *Vorwärts*, no. 513, 2 Nov. 1923.

93. Pryce, "Reich Government," pp. 140–42.
94. Cabinet meeting of 29 Oct. 1923, USNA T-120, 3491/1749/757512–13. Also, Pryce, "Reich Government," p. 142.
95. Dittmann, "Erinnerungen," p. 1,318.
96. Ibid., pp. 1,319–23; quote p. 1,323.
97. Angress, *Stillborn Revolution*, pp. 444–51.
98. Notes in *Nachlass* Giebel II/257–67. Alfred Kastning, *Die deutsche Sozialdemokratie zwischen Koalition und Opposition 1919–1923*, pp. 123–24, also deciphers these notes, but there are certain differences between Kastning's reading and my own. Given the fact that the handwriting is nearly illegible at points, this difference is understandable.
99. The words "certain conditions" appear in Giebel's notes with a blank space afterward. There is every indication that the conditions Müller set forth were the ones that the fraction approved. *Vorwärts*, no. 511, 1 Nov. 1923; ibid., no. 509, 31 Oct. 1923.
100. USNA T-120, 3491/5744/K643049.
101. Cabinet meeting of 1 Nov. 1923, ibid., 1749/757563–66.
102. Meier-Welcker, *Seeckt*, pp. 394–95.
103. Cabinet meeting of 2 Nov. 1923, (11 a.m.), USNA T-120, 3491/1749/757579–86.
104. Hans Luther, *Politiker ohne Partei*, p. 110, describes this incident without dating it. The cabinet minutes do not contain Schmidt's outburst.
105. *Vorwärts*, no. 515, 3 Nov. 1923.
106. Meier-Welcker, *Seeckt*, pp. 400–404, 409–10, 413–15. The emergency executive authority given to Defense Minister Gessler in late September was transferred to Seeckt on 9 November.
107. Severing, *Mein Lebensweg*, I: 446–47. Unsupported, self-serving accounts are always a bit suspect. However, *Vorwärts*, no. 525, 9 Nov. 1923, at least confirms that Severing was present at the meeting.
108. Protokoll der Sitzung des preussischen Staatsministeriums, 9 Nov. 1923, *Nachlass* Braun V/278.
109. See Gordon, *Hitler and the Beer Hall Putsch*, espec. pp. 313–65, and pp. 455–56.
110. *Reichstag: Sten. Ber.*, vol. 361, pp. 12,292–94.
111. Stresemann, *Vermächtnis*, I: 245, cited in Turner, *Stresemann*, p. 153.
112. Meier-Welcker, *Seeckt*, pp. 410–15, 422–23.
113. Memo by General Lossberg, 17 Nov. 1923, *Nachlass* Schleicher XIX/46–49a.
114. Truppenamts-Vortrag, 7 Dec. 1923, ibid., XIX/25–26.
115. This evidence contradicts Meier-Welcker, *Seeckt*, pp. 421–22, who claims that Schleicher favored cooperation with the SPD.
116. Truppenamts-Vortrag, 7 Dec. 1923, *Nachlass* Schleicher XIX/25–26.
117. Ibid.
118. *Reichstag: Sten. Ber.*, vol. 361, p. 12,270, 22 Nov. 1923. Hermann Müller later wrote with exasperation that the SPD had less trouble arranging public meetings in the areas under French control than in those where the German military possessed emergency powers. Müller to Sollmann, 10 Jan. 1924, *Nachlass* Sollmann II/19/11.
119. Notes of SPD fraction, 30 Nov. 1923, *Nachlass* Giebel II/274.
120. The government was to send its ordinances to a Reichstag committee for a prior

hearing. The committee could at least raise objections, although the government was not forced to take them into account. *Vorwärts*, no. 567, 5 Dec. 1923.

121. Arns, "Linke," pp. 197–99.

122. Hugo Sinzheimer found the foreign-policy situation to be sufficient cause for the SPD to support a reasonable minority government. He was quite aware, however, that many SPD deputies felt differently. Sinzheimer to Sollmann, *Nachlass* Sollmann II/18/37.

123. Keil, *Erlebnisse*, 2: 278–79, claims to have reversed an earlier fraction decision with this argument.

124. Notes of SPD fraction, 30 Nov. 1923, *Nachlass* Giebel II/273.

125. Undated, handwritten manuscript in *Nachlass* Bernstein A/60.

126. Notes of SPD fraction, 4 Dec. 1923, *Nachlass* Giebel II/277.

127. On the subject of control of the military, see Jürgen Schmädeke, *Militärische Kommandogewalt und parlamentarische Demokratie*.

128. *Vorwärts*, no. 555, 28 Nov. 1923.

129. For a summary of further political developments in Saxony, see Hunt, *German Social Democracy*, pp. 216–21.

Chapter Seven: Toward a Clearer Concept of Democracy—Rudolf Hilferding

1. Siegfried Marck, "Sozialdemokratie," p. 30.

2. The extent of the setback is revealed more clearly by the loss of Reichstag seats—from 171 (SPD plus former USPD) down to 100.

3. SPD *Parteitag* 1924, p. 83.

4. See above, p. 35. On Wels generally, see Hans J. L. Adolph, *Otto Wels und die Politik der deutschen Sozialdemokratie 1894–1939*.

5. SPD *Parteitag* 1924, p. 85.

6. The best study of this period is by Michael Stürmer, *Koalition und Opposition in der Weimarer Republik 1924–1928*.

7. On Hilferding's relation to Wels, see Adolph, *Wels*, p. 113. Hilferding seems to have been even closer to Müller, who chose him as finance minister in 1928 over considerable opposition.

8. Marck, "Sozialdemokratie," p. 30.

9. Lutz Graf Schwerin von Krosigk, *Es geschah in Deutschland*, p. 80.

10. Luise Kautsky to Eduard Bernstein, 10 May 1926, *Nachlass* Kautsky C/256. Other biographical details taken from Wilhelm Gottschalch, *Strukturveränderungen der Gesellschaft und politisches Handeln in der Lehre von Rudolf Hilferding*, pp. 13–18.

11. Rudolf Hilferding, *Das Finanzkapital*.

12. Gottschalch, *Hilferding*, pp. 189–92; Heinrich August Winkler, "Einleitende Bemerkungen zu Hilferdings Theorie des Organisierten Kapitalismus," pp. 9–10.

13. Hilferding, *Finanzkapital*, 2: 500–503.

14. Lenin, *Imperialism*, pp. 99, 126.

15. Hilferding's fatalism is stressed by Wachenheim, *Vom Grossbürgertum*, p. 44.

16. See chapter two: Nationalization.

17. *Allgemeiner Kongress*, p. 161.

18. *Die Freiheit*, 10 Dec. 1919.

19. Dittmann, "Erinnerungen," p. 1,203.

20. Hilferding, *Sozialisierung*.
21. Kessler, *Diaries*, p. 169.
22. *Frankfurter Zeitung*, no. 937, 31 Dec. 1922 ("Wandel in der Politik," von Rudolf Hilferding).
23. SPD *Parteitag* 1927, p. 170.
24. Rudolf Hilferding, "Probleme der Zeit," pp. 12–13.
25. Paul Hertz to Luise Kautsky, 5 June 1925, *Nachlass* Kautsky D/xii/416.
26. *Vorwärts*, no. 370, 9 Aug. 1923.
27. Cabinet meeting of 20 Aug. 1923, USNA T-120, 3491/1748/756423–30.
28. Cabinet meeting of 7 Sept. 1923, ibid., 756597–600.
29. Cabinet meetings of 30 Aug. 1923, ibid., 756496–97, 7 Sept. 1923, 756593–95; joint Reich-Prussian cabinet meeting of 15 Sept. 1923, ibid., 756724.
30. Otto Braun, *Von Weimar zu Hitler*, pp. 126–27. This incident was also recounted to me by Ernest Hamburger in an interview on 3 Feb. 1976. Hamburger, an influential member of the SPD fraction in the Prussian Landtag, heard the story from Braun himself in 1923.
31. These remarks are recorded, unattributed, by Carl Giebel, fraction meeting of 2 Oct. 1923, *Nachlass* Giebel ii/246. Other evidence indicates that Hilferding made these comments. See SPD *Parteitag* 1924, p. 196. Stampfer, *Ersten vierzehn Jahren*, p. 352.
32. SPD *Parteitag* 1924, pp. 169–71.
33. Ibid., p. 189 (Adolf Braun). SPD *Parteitag* 1927, pp. 190 (Scheidemann), 196 (Löbe), 200 (Severing), and 211 (Müller); Dittmann, "Erinnerungen," p. 1,414.
34. SPD *Parteitag* 1924, p. 166; Hilferding to Kautsky, 19 July 1924, *Nachlass* Kautsky D/xii/636; SPD *Parteitag* 1927, pp. 184–88, 198–200 (Sender and Aufhäuser). See also Drechsler, *SAPD*, pp. 10–20.
35. SPD *Parteitag* 1924, pp. 165–66.
36. SPD *Parteitag* 1925, p. 275.
37. Ibid., pp. 276–77.
38. SPD *Parteitag* 1924, pp. 174–75.
39. For the text of the program, the first part of which was written by Kautsky and edited by Hilferding, see SPD *Parteitag* 1925, pp. 5–10. Hilferding did point out during the congress that the defense and broadening of the democratic republic had been put at the head of the list of aims. SPD *Parteitag* 1925, p. 276.
40. SPD *Parteitag* 1924, pp. 175–76. For a brief analysis of the Ministry of Labor, see Barclay, "Social Politics," pp. 259–68.
41. Hilferding to Kautsky, 19 Oct. 1924, *Nachlass* Kautsky D/xii/638.
42. Ibid.
43. Hilferding to Kautsky, 29 Dec. 1924, *Nachlass* Kautsky D/xii/640.
44. Undated notes of SPD fraction, *Nachlass* Severing xxix/1.
45. Hilferding to Kautsky, 8 Jan. 1926, *Nachlass* Kautsky D/xii/642.
46. Feder, *Heute*, p. 100, 24 Jan. 1927.
47. Stürmer, *Koalition und Opposition*, p. 153.
48. Notes of SPD fraction, 18 Jan. 1927, *Nachlass* Giebel ii/297; Stürmer, *Koalition und Opposition*, pp. 185–86.
49. Hilferding regarded the decline of the KPD as disappointingly slow, but inevitable nonetheless. He expected the SPD to regain its losses to the KPD in the Rhineland-Westphalia area with the return of economic prosperity. Hilferding to Kautsky, 29 Dec. 1924 and 8 Jan. 1926, *Nachlass* Kautsky D/xii/640 and 642.
50. Hilferding to Kautsky, 19 July 1924, *Nachlass* Kautsky D/xii/636.

51. ADGB *Kongress* 1928, pp. 170-90; Robert A. Gates, "The Economic Policies of the German Free Trade Unions and the German Social Democratic Party 1930-1933," pp. 85-104.
52. SPD *Parteitag* 1927, pp. 162-72, quotation on p. 168.
53. Ibid., p. 170.
54. Ibid., pp. 172-74.
55. Sigmund Neumann, *Die Parteien der Weimarer Republik*, p. 37.
56. Stürmer, *Koalition und Opposition*, pp. 254-57.
57. SPD *Parteitag* 1927, pp. 183, 265.
58. Hoffmann, *Sozialdemokratie und Berufsbeamtentum*, espec. pp. 123-37, stresses that the few party figures interested in the Beamten were generally ignored by party leaders. Dr. Fritz Baade wrote a new agrarian program for the 1927 congress, but it was referred back to committee for further changes. SPD *Parteitag* 1927, pp. 114-36.
59. SPD *Parteitag* 1925, pp. 7-10.
60. SPD *Parteitag* 1927, pp. 265-66.
61. Hunt, *German Social Democracy*, pp. 221-40; Hans Mommsen, "Die Sozialdemokratie in der Defensive," pp. 117-31.
62. For a similar view, see Stürmer, *Koalition und Opposition*, pp. 256-57.
63. Parvus [Alexander Helphand], *Der Klassenkampf des Proletariats*, p. 18.
64. This point is developed by Robert Gates and Gerald Feldman in the discussion reprinted in Hans Mommsen, et al., eds., *Industrielles System und politische Entwicklung in der Weimarer Republik*, pp. 358-59.
65. Hans Neisser, "Sozialstatistische Analyse des Wahlergebnisses," p. 658. This figure is cited inaccurately and, I believe, interpreted wrongly in Hunt, *German Social Democracy*, pp. 140-41.
66. A computerized analysis of Reichstag elections now being conducted by Thomas Childers tends to support Neisser's estimate. Considering its working-class image, the SPD did fairly well with white-collar workers and small businessmen.
67. Interview with Ernest Hamburger, 3 Feb. 1976.
68. Fraenkel, "1919-1929—Verfassungstag," p. 231.
69. Radbruch, *Der innere Weg*, p. 178.
70. *Vorwärts*, no. 139, 23 Mar. 1930.

Chapter Eight: The Prussian Strategy

1. *Preussischer Landtag: Sitzungsberichte*, vol. 3, p. 4,365, 14 Oct. 1925.
2. Severing to Berthold Heymann, 30 July 1926, *Nachlass* Severing XXXII, cited by Hans-Peter Ehni, "Zum Parteienverhältnis in Preussen 1918-1932," p. 284.
3. Wolfgang Heine, "Politische Aufzeichnungen," p. 122, *Nachlass* Heine.
4. Interview with Ernest Hamburger, 3 Feb. 1976.
5. Ibid. Hamburger related the following story. Erich Kuttner, an SPD journalist who wrote a short biography of Braun, once composed a brief poem that he read at a *Bierabend* for the leading figures in the SPD's Prussian wing. The substance of the poem was that Artur Crispien had erred in making his famous (prewar) statement about the German proletariat having no fatherland. ("Wir kennen kein Vaterland, das Deutschland heisst.") The German workers did have a fatherland—Prussia! The SPD's Prussian leaders were proud of what they had accomplished in Prussia

since 1918. They felt that the onetime bastion of reaction had become the bastion of democracy.

6. Protokoll der Sitzung des Parteiausschuss, 8 Dec. 1920, p. 10.

7. For a positive assessment of Prussia's achievements supported by a wealth of evidence, see Schulze, *Otto Braun*. For a different interpretation, see Hans-Peter Ehni, *Bollwerk Preussen?* and Erich Dave Kohler, "Otto Braun, Prussia, and Democracy. 1872–1955."

8. See Schulze, *Otto Braun*, pp. 330–36.

9. SPD, Vorstand, *Handbuch für sozialdemokratische Wähler: Der Preussische Landtag 1921–1924*, pp. 8–9; Grzesinski to Scheidemann, 16 Sept. 1921, *Nachlass* Grzesinski A/II/304.

10. Interview with Ernest Hamburger, 3 Feb. 1976.

11. For detailed description, see Schulze, *Otto Braun*, pp. 341–49.

12. This sketch is drawn primarily from Schulze, *Otto Braun*, espec. pp. 31–38, 488–98, and from my interview with Ernest Hamburger, 3 Feb. 1976.

13. Braun to Severing, 5 Aug. 1924, *Nachlass* Severing I/9. See also the broader discussion in Schulze, *Otto Braun*, pp. 384–96.

14. For details, see Schulze, *Otto Braun*, pp. 466–74.

15. Fraction leader Ernst Heilmann later expressed great satisfaction at this deal. SPD, *Preussentag der SPD 1928*, p. 29. The unexpected outcome of the presidential election was largely the result of the abandonment of the Catholic candidate Wilhelm Marx by the Bavarian People's party.

16. Stampfer, *Ersten vierzehn Jahren*, p. 444. There is a similar but slightly varying quote in Braun, *Von Weimar*, pp. 174–75. After a while, a Communist deputy left his party and joined the SPD, and the two Polish deputies became dependable allies of the government, which gave Braun 225 votes—exactly half of the Landtag, SPD, *Preussentag der SPD 1928*, p. 30.

17. Interview with Ernest Hamburger, 3 Feb. 1976; Wachenheim, *Vom Grossbürgertum*, p. 111.

18. Ibid.

19. On Braun's feelings toward the Junkers, see Schulze, *Otto Braun*, espec. p. 365.

20. Feder, *Heute*, p. 147, 7 Dec. 1927; Albert Grzesinski, "Der Verwaltungsunfug im Reich," *Das Freie Wort*, no. 38, 21 Sept. 1930.

21. Ehni, *Bollwerk Preussen?*, pp. 103–5, 111–13, 115–16.

22. *Vossische Zeitung*, no. 618, 31 Dec. 1927.

23. Feder, *Heute*, p. 196, 5 Oct. 1928. This remark came at a time when the SPD was participating in a Great Coalition government in the Reich.

24. This total is cited by Prussian Interior Minister Grzesinski. SPD, *Preussentag der SPD 1928*, p. 9.

25. For a description of the origins and operation of this system during the Second Reich, see Lisbeth Walker Muncy, *The Junker in the Prussian Administration under Wilhelm II, 1888–1914*.

26. Max Weber, "Politics as a Vocation," in H. H. Gerth and C. Wright Mills, eds., *From Max Weber*, p. 91.

27. Hoffmann, *Sozialdemokratie und Berufsbeamtentum*, pp. 45–80.

28. Heine surprisingly dismissed the importance of having Social Democrats in the political offices, regarding them neither as a mark of influence for the party nor as a means to conduct agitation more effectively. Heine to Sollmann, 21 Sept. 1919, *Nachlass* Sollmann II/13/70. See also, Runge, *Politik und Beamtentum*, pp. 18,

47, 57–66, 109–20; Herbert Jacob, *German Administration since Bismarck*, pp. 96–97.

29. SPD *Parteitag* 1919, pp. 140, 145, 269–70.
30. Severing, *Mein Lebensweg*, 1: 352. For a general discussion and analysis, Schulze, *Otto Braun*, pp. 299–309, 562–74.
31. Runge, *Politik und Beamtentum*, pp. 66–74, 121–42; Severing, *Mein Lebensweg*, 1: 285.
32. Eberhard Pikart, "Preussische Beamtenpolitik, 1918–1933," p. 123.
33. Runge, *Politik und Beamtentum*, p. 146. The Landrat was in part a state official, in part a county official who worked with communal assemblies. The latter had the right to nominate candidates for the office of Landrat. Although the state government held the final decision on such appointments, it was not easy to overcome strong local opposition.
34. Ferdinand Friedensburg, *Lebenserinnerungen*, pp. 110–11, quotation on 120.
35. Runge, *Politik und Beamtentum*, p. 75; Pikart, "Preussische Beamtenpolitik," p. 136.
36. Runge, *Politik und Beamtentum*, pp. 155–56.
37. Data (incomplete) in *Nachlass* Grzesinski B/III/743.
38. Friedrich Carl Rode to Regierungspräsident Johannsen, 12 Jan. 1929, *Nachlass* Grzesinski A/III/363.
39. Runge, *Politik und Beamtentum*, p. 201; Höpker-Aschoff to Grzesinski, 15 Mar. 1928, *Nachlass* Grzesinski A/I/72.
40. Albert Grzesinski, "Im Kampf um die deutsche Republik," p. 182, *Nachlass* Grzesinski 2547.
41. "Verwaltungsreform und demokratische Republik," copy in *Nachlass* Grzesinski B/IX/1281; "Staatsverwaltung einst und jetzt," *Berliner Morgenpost*, no. 72, 24 Mar. 1929, copy in *Nachlass* Grzesinski B/IX/1281. See also SPD, *Preussentag der SPD 1928*, p. 10.
42. Barclay, "Social Reform," pp. 259–60.
43. Severing to Braun, 30 July 1925, and Braun to Severing, 1 Aug. 1925, *Nachlass* Severing xxv/4 and I/12. Excerpts are quoted by Ehni, *Bollwerk Preussen?*, pp. 86–87.
44. Braun to Severing, 1 and 5 Aug. 1925, *Nachlass* Severing I/12 and I/9.
45. Stelling to Severing, 23 Dec. 1925, *Nachlass* Severing LXXII/34; Michael Stürmer, "Der unvollendete Parteienstaat," pp. 119–26, mentions a number of schemes of this nature, but not the one in Stelling's letter.
46. See the discussion in Schulze, *Otto Braun*, pp. 485–86.
47. *Vorwärts*, no. 17, 12 Jan. 1926, and no. 47, 29 Jan. 1926; undated notes of SPD fraction (early Jan. 1926), *Nachlass* Severing xxix/1.
48. Notes of SPD fraction, 28 Jan. 1926, *Nachlass* Severing xxix/1.
49. Severing revealed his own role in 1932. Protokoll des Parteiausschusses, 10 Nov. 1932, reprinted in Hagen Schulze, ed., *Anpassung oder Widerstand?*, pp. 34–35.
50. BA Koblenz R 43I/1870, 14 Aug. 1926.
51. Heine to Severing, 10 Aug. 1926, *Nachlass* Severing I/50.
52. *Die Rote Fahne*, no. 158, 10 July 1926. Severing to Leinert, 16 July 1926, *Nachlass* Severing xxvi/69. See also the discussion in Schulze, *Otto Braun*, pp. 510–13.
53. Grzesinski to Braun, 1 Aug. 1928, *Nachlass* Grzesinski B/IX/1153; Grzesinski to Braun, 21 Mar. 1930, ibid. A/II/204.

54. Ehni, *Bollwerk Preussen?*, pp. 138–59; Anthony Glees, "Albert Grzesinski and the Politics of Prussia, 1926–1930," pp. 827–34.

55. *Akten der Reichskanzlei Weimarer Republik: Das Kabinett Müller II*, p. viii; Braun, *Von Weimar*, p. 245; Dittmann, "Erinnerungen," p. 1,422. Braun's picture was featured on the front page of *Vorwärts*, no. 237, 21 May 1928, the day after the elections.

56. Feder, *Heute*, p. 179, 18 May 1928; Braun, *Von Weimar*, p. 240.

57. Braun's account, *Von Weimar*, pp. 245–46, is supported in part by Grzesinski's handwritten notes of a meeting with Braun on 23 May 1928, *Nachlass* Grzesinski B/IX/705. However, Braun's assertion that Müller wanted the chancellor's post seems wrong. See Müller's remarks to Severing and Karl Renner, reprinted in *Akten: Müller II*, p. 1n2; Dittmann, "Erinnerungen," p. 1,422; Müller to Braun, 20 Aug. 1928, *Nachlass* Müller VI/60.

58. Schulze, *Otto Braun*, p. 541.

59. SPD *Parteitag* 1927, pp. 11, 180, 210.

60. SPD *Parteitag* 1924, p. 88.

61. SPD *Parteitag* 1927, p. 189. The leftists, however, did oppose Braun's advocacy of the Great Coalition in the Reich. See Schulze, *Otto Braun*, p. 542.

62. For example, Adolf Bartels commented to the SPD party council that the SPD could leave the Reich government because it still had Braun, Severing, and Haenisch in their Prussian posts. Protokoll des Parteiausschusses, 13 June 1920, p. 18, quoted by Schulze, *Otto Braun*, p. 315.

63. Ehni, *Bollwerk Preussen?*, p. 45.

Chapter Nine: The Last Unsuccessful Coalition

1. On the negotiation of the Dawes Plan, see Stephen A. Schuker, *The End of French Predominance in Europe*. On the German political debate, see Maier, *Recasting Bourgeois Europe*, pp. 455–58, 487–88.

2. Ibid., pp. 444–50, 513–15.

3. Stampfer to Kautsky, 28 May 1928, *Nachlass* Kautsky D/XXI/304.

4. ADGB *Kongress* 1928, pp. 79–80.

5. Besprechung zwischen Fraktionsvorstand, Parteivorstand, Vorständen des ADGB und AfA-Bundes, 21 Jan. 1930, ADGB Restakten (ABI) 468/0217.

6. Pistorius, "Breitscheid," p. 237n.

7. Interview with Ernest Hamburger, 3 Feb. 1976. For the text of the speech, SPD *Parteitag* 1931, pp. 169–77.

8. Theodor Leipart, chairman of the ADGB, said at one point that his colleagues felt that Breitscheid should be removed as the foreign-policy expert of the party. Leipart to Wilhelm Keil, 8 Jan. 1932, ADGB Vorstands-Korrespondenz (DGB) VI/390. Quotation attributed to Kurt Baake in Friedrich Stampfer, *Erfahrungen und Erkenntnisse*, p. 132. See also, Wachenheim, *Vom Grossbürgertum*, p. 43.

9. SPD *Parteitag* 1929, p. 195.

10. For further details, see *Akten: Müller II*, pp. 1–3.

11. The parties were the SPD, DDP, Center, DVP, and the Bavarian People's party.

12. Drafts in *Nachlass* Müller II/13–14, dated 20 June 1928.

13. Original telegram, 23 June 1928, *Nachlass* Müller II/32.

14. See Turner, *Stresemann*, pp. 241–44.

15. *Reichstag: Sten. Ber.*, vol. 423, pp. 38–47. Müller's program closely resembled his original draft to which the parties had failed to agree. However, the section that had hinted at a laissez faire, probusiness approach to economic policy was removed, perhaps because of the DVP's refusal to agree to a formal coalition.

16. Severing, *Mein Lebensweg*, 2: 149.

17. Gaines Post, *The Civil-Military Fabric of Weimar Foreign Policy*, pp. 241–49, 253–54, discusses naval strategy.

18. See Wolfgang Wacker, *Der Bau des Panzerschiffes "A" und der Reichstag*, pp. 1–53.

19. Brecht, *Mit der Kraft*, p. 49; Wacker, *Der Bau*, pp. 62–77.

20. Wacker, *Der Bau*, pp. 87, 90, 99.

21. SPD *Parteitag* 1929, p. 82; *Reichstag: Sten. Ber.*, vol. 423, pp. 91–92, 5 July 1928.

22. Wacker, *Der Bau*, p. 84n4.

23. Cabinet meeting of 10 Aug. 1928, in *Akten: Müller II*, pp. 62–64.

24. Koch-Weser Diary, 15 Aug. 1928, reprinted in *Akten: Müller II*, p. 64n13. At a later stage both Groener and Hindenburg threatened to resign if the decision were reversed. Cabinet meetings of 14 and 15 Nov. 1928, in ibid., pp. 225, 228; Dittmann, "Erinnerungen," p. 1,429; Wacker, *Der Bau*, pp. 100–102.

25. Müller to Braun, 20 Aug. 1928, *Nachlass* Müller IV/60.

26. Müller to J. W. Albarda, 9 Oct. 1928, *Nachlass* Müller IV/3.

27. Quoted in Wacker, *Der Bau*, p. 101n87.

28. Braun to Müller, 15 Aug. 1928, *Nachlass* Müller I/6.

29. Grzesinski to Braun, 16 Aug. 1928, *Nachlass* Grzesinski A/II/204.

30. Wacker, *Der Bau*, pp. 85–86. Even *Vorwärts*, no. 383, 15 Aug. 1928, conceded that many party members were upset.

31. *Sozialistische Politik und Wirtschaft*, 17 Aug. 1928. The most comprehensive extreme statement of the left-wing view came in a pamphlet, *Panzerkreuzer und Sozialdemokratie*.

32. Grzesinski to Braun, 16 Aug. 1928, *Nachlass* Grzesinski A/II/204; Toni Jensen to Grzesinski, 20 Aug. 1928, *Nachlass* Grzesinski A/I/77.

33. *Panzerkreuzer und Sozialdemokratie*, p. 7.

34. Dittmann, "Erinnerungen," p. 1,429; *Vorwärts*, nos. 385 and 391, 16 and 19 Aug. 1928.

35. Löbe to Severing, 2 Sept. 1928, *Nachlass* Severing I/70; Wacker, *Der Bau*, pp. 106–9; *Panzerkreuzer und Sozialdemokratie*, p. 25.

36. For further details, see Wacker, *Der Bau*, pp. 129–67; Adolph, *Otto Wels*, pp. 166–69; Feder, *Heute sprach ich mit . . .* , pp. 197, 200–203.

37. Hilferding to Müller, undated (late 1928), *Nachlass* Müller I/40.

38. Dittmann, "Erinnerungen," pp. 1,434–35; Keil, *Erlebnisse eines Sozialdemokraten*, 2: 346–48. Wacker, *Der Bau*, p. 121n51, lists the members of the commission but inaccurately categorizes their political leanings.

39. Toni Sender, "Kritik an den Richtlinien zur Wehrpolitik," pp. 113–24.

40. Carl Severing, "Randbemerkungen zu den Richtlinien," p. 205; SPD *Parteitag* 1929, pp. 141–43.

41. SPD *Parteitag* 1929, pp. 105–6.

42. Theodor Haubach, "Der Sozialismus und die Wehrfrage," p. 121; Haubach, "Die Richtlinien zur Wehrfrage," pp. 108–10.

43. SPD *Parteitag* 1929, p. 106.

44. These votes are analyzed in some detail in Hunt, *German Social Democracy*, pp. 78–83, 228–30, and Drechsler, *Die SAPD*, pp. 49–50.
45. SPD *Parteitag* 1929, pp. 150, 272.
46. *Vorwärts*, no. 403, 26 Aug. 1928, "Die tieferen Ursachen: Woher der Panzerschiff-Konflikt." This unsigned article was attributed to Julius Deutsch in Hilferding's letter to Müller (undated, *Nachlass* Müller 1/40). Hilferding remarked that his own thoughts were similar.
47. A previous relief ordinance intended as a temporary measure (Erwerbslosenfürsorgeverordnung 13 Dec. 1918) required a demonstration of financial need.
48. Data compiled by the ADGB, Restakten (ABI) 463/061. Changes in the law during the Brüning government discriminated against married female workers.
49. Bry, *Wages in Germany*, p. 58.
50. Helga Timm, *Die deutsche Sozialpolitik und der Bruch der grossen Koalition im März 1930*, pp. 23–25.
51. Ilse Maurer, *Reichsfinanzen und grosse Koalition*, pp. 50, 80–85.
52. Timm, *Deutsche Sozialpolitik*, pp. 124–26, 129–30, 151; Maurer, *Reichsfinanzen*, p. 83.
53. Ursula Hüllbüsch, "Die deutschen Gewerkschaften in der Weltwirtschaftskrise," p. 133; Werner Conze, "Die politischen Entscheidungen in Deutschland 1929–1933," p. 185.
54. Siegfried Aufhäuser, "Der politische Kampf um die Arbeitslosenversicherung und ihre sozialpolitische Bedeutung," p. 393.
55. SPD, Vorstand, *Der Kampf um die Arbeitslosenversicherung*, p. 5. For an extended treatment of the early discussion of unemployment insurance within the SPD, see Barclay, "Social Reform," pp. 270–310.
56. SPD *Parteitag* 1929, pp. 160, 165, 170.
57. Wels to Müller, 23 Sept. 1929, *Nachlass* Müller 1/123.
58. Hüllbüsch, "Deutsche Gewerkschaften," p. 140.
59. Maurer, *Reichsfinanzen*, pp. 91, 144; Timm, *Deutsche Sozialpolitik*, p. 160. Gustav Noske wrote in his diary that he had run into Hilferding on 7 May 1929. Hilferding had complained about the lack of leadership in the SPD fraction, adding that it was willing to let democracy and the republic go to the devil over thirty pennies more or less for the unemployment insurance fund. Noske, *Aufstieg und Niedergang der deutschen Sozialdemokratie*, p. 309.
60. On Hilferding's economic orthodoxy, see Robert A. Gates, "German Socialism and the Crisis of 1929–33," pp. 343, 348.
61. Turner, *Stresemann*, pp. 258–61; Eyck, *History*, 2: 228–30. The DVP fraction ultimately abstained.
62. Hjalmar Schacht, *Das Ende der Reparationen*, p. 108.
63. Statement by Chancellor Müller at a briefing given to SPD fraction leaders, 10 Dec. 1929, handwritten notes by ADGB representative Peter Grassmann, ADGB Restakten (ABI) 471/0091.
64. Timm, *Deutsche Sozialpolitik*, p. 151.
65. ADGB Restakten (ABI) 471/0091. Grassmann's notes include the following comments: "Intentional attack by the capitalists. Party and unions have become too influential for the propertied. Long-term commitment of the party. Do we want the masses to desert us?"
66. Feder, *Heute*, p. 233.
67. *Reichstag: Sten. Ber.*, vol. 426, p. 3,561, 13 Dec. 1929.

68. Martin Vogt, "Die Stellung der Koalitionsparteien zur Finanzpolitik 1928–1930," pp. 456–57.

69. Among the Social Democrats Löbe, Breitscheid, and Otto Braun disapproved of Müller's appointment of Hilferding in the first place. Feder, *Heute*, p. 186, 29 June 1928; p. 233, 12 Dec. 1929. Schacht said that the average man in the street would make a better finance minister than Hilferding, ibid., p. 231, 5 Dec. 1929.

70. Krosigk, *Es geschah*, pp. 82–83.

71. Maurer, *Reichsfinanzen*, pp. 101, 107.

72. Cabinet meeting of 21 Dec. 1929, *Akten: Müller II*, pp. 1,299–301 and 1,297–98n1. The SPD fraction had nominated Paul Hertz to take over Hilferding's post, but Müller had disapproved. Instead, Moldenhauer moved over from the Economics Ministry, and Robert Schmidt took the vacant spot there.

73. Maurer, *Reichsfinanzen*, p. 114.

74. Erich Rinner to Müller, 4 Feb. 1930, *Nachlass* Müller II/2–7. The key figures involved with this proposal were Rinner and Paul Hertz. They were responding to a Finance Ministry plan that depended heavily upon increased taxation of beer and a higher general sales tax.

75. Breitscheid to Müller, 1 Feb. 1930, *Nachlass* Müller II/113. Brüning felt that a rise in the sales and beer taxes was necessary, but he did not support the DVP's demand for a cut in the income tax for fiscal 1931.

76. State Secretary Pünder to Müller, 1 Mar. 1930, *Nachlass* Müller II/271.

77. Vogelsang, *Reichswehr*, pp. 69–93. Conze, "Politische Entscheidungen in Deutschland," pp. 202–3, 209–10; Maurer, *Reichsfinanzen*, pp. 121–28.

78. Cabinet meeting of 3 Mar. 1930, *Akten: Müller II*, p. 1,519.

79. Brüning to Wilhelm Sollmann, 29 Sept. 1940, *Nachlass* Sollmann I/6/11b.

80. "Gedanken um eine Sturz der Regierung H.M. und dessen Folgen: Absichten des Reichspräsidenten," undated notes by Schleicher's aide Nöldechen, *Nachlass* Schleicher XXIX/1b–5a reprinted in part in Vogelsang, *Reichswehr*, pp. 414–15; ibid., p. 73.

81. Cabinet meeting of 5 Mar. 1930, *Akten: Müller II*, pp. 1,535–36 and 1,535–37n2. See also the discussion in Maurer, *Reichsfinanzen*, p. 117.

82. Maurer, *Reichsfinanzen*, p. 119; *Vorwärts*, no. 115, 9 Mar. 1930.

83. Maurer, *Reichsfinanzen*, pp. 119–20; State Secretary Pünder to Müller, 22 Mar. 1929, *Nachlass* Müller V/9.

84. Maurer, *Reichsfinanzen*, p. 120; Timm, *Deutsche Sozialpolitik*, p. 176.

85. Müller to Wels, 12 Feb. 1929, *Nachlass* Müller IV/558.

86. SPD *Parteitag* 1929, p. 170.

87. Fraction meeting of 10 Dec. 1929, ADGB Restakten (ABI) 471/0091.

88. *Vorwärts*, no. 135, 21 Mar. 1930.

89. Maurer, *Reichsfinanzen*, pp. 129–30; Conze, "Politische Entscheidungen," pp. 200–201.

90. Timm, *Deutsche Sozialpolitik*, pp. 180–81; *Akten: Müller II*, pp. 1,604–5.

91. Vogt, "Stellung der Koalitionsparteien," pp. 456–57.

92. Heinrich Brüning, *Memoiren, 1918–1934*, p. 160; Gottfried Reinhold Treviranus, *Das Ende von Weimar*, pp. 114–16.

93. Cabinet meeting of 27 Mar. 1930, *Akten: Müller II*, pp. 1,607–10; Severing, *Mein Lebensweg*, 2: 239; *Vorwärts*, no. 147, 28 Mar. 1930.

94. Conference of ministers and fraction leaders, 15 Feb. 1930, ADGB Restakten (ABI) 471/0111.

95. Rudolf Hilferding, "Der Austritt aus der Regierung," p. 388.
96. *Akten: Müller II*, pp. 1,595, 1,600–603.
97. *Vorwärts*, no. 147, 28 Mar. 1930; Braun, *Von Weimar*, p. 292; Stampfer, *Ersten vierzehn Jahren*, p. 562.
98. Hilferding, "Austritt aus der Regierung," p. 388.
99. Treviranus, *Ende von Weimar*, p. 111. However, Stampfer, *Ersten vierzehn Jahren*, p. 562, disagrees with this judgment.
100. Adolph, *Otto Wels*, p. 172n242, found this union threat mentioned in an account written by Wels and left among his papers. *Vorwärts*, no. 147, 28 Mar. 1930, reports the voting.
101. Bracher, *Auflösung*, pp. 298–303, singles out the DVP and the leaders of business. Vogelsang, *Reichswehr*, pp. 69–74, stresses the role of General Schleicher and others in influencing President Hindenburg.
102. Hilferding, "Austritt aus der Regierung," p. 389.

Chapter Ten: Prussia and the Reich 1930–1931

1. Gates, "Economic Policies," and Michael Schneider, *Das Arbeitsbeschaffungsprogramm des ADGB*, present good descriptions of the economic-political dynamics of the Brüning period.
2. A published translation of the trial is now available. *The Hitler Trial*, 3 vols.
3. Diehl, *Paramilitary Politics*, pp. 276–81. On the structure of the Nazi organization generally, see Dietrich Orlow, *The History of the Nazi Party 1919–1933*.
4. Braun to Severing, 27 May 1926, *Nachlass* Severing 1/13.
5. Friedensburg, *Lebenserinnerungen*, pp. 162–67; Jasper, *Schutz*, pp. 156–60.
6. Notizen, 18 Feb. 1927, *Nachlass* Grzesinski B/IX/1329.
7. Schulze, *Otto Braun*, pp. 609–13. Detailed information about Prussia's use of the Disarmament Law against right-wing organizations and its conflicts with the Reich over the use of this law may be found in Grzesinski's undated memo, *Nachlass* Grzesinski B/IX/1224.
8. Ehni, *Bollwerk Preussen?*, pp. 138–39, 154–55; Schulze, *Otto Braun*, pp. 613–16, 631–33.
9. Jasper, *Schutz*, pp. 184, 283.
10. Ibid., pp. 139–46, 178, 188–89.
11. Grzesinski to the executive committee and the executive board of the SPD Reichstag fraction, 2 Jan. 1930, *Nachlass* Grzesinski B/IX/1298; Grzesinski to Braun, 3 Jan. 1930, *Nachlass* Grzesinski, A/II/204; Kurt Rosenfeldt to Grzesinski, 6 Jan. 1930, *Nachlass* Grzesinski B/IX/1302.
12. Compare the original SPD proposal, *Reichstag: Anlagen*, vol. 440, Drucksache 1641, with the final version of the law, *Reichsgesetzblatt* 1930, pp. 91–93.
13. Wilhelm Sollmann to Grzesinski, 3 Oct. 1929, and Grzesinski to Sollmann, 14 Oct. 1929, *Nachlass* Grzesinski B/X/1502 and 1491.
14. Grzesinski's own account of this episode is presented in a short manuscript, "Mein Ausscheiden als Minister des Innern 1930," *Nachlass* Grzesinski B/IX/1332.
15. Braun to Grzesinski, 18 Mar. 1930, and Grzesinski to Braun, 21 Mar. 1930, *Nachlass* Grzesinski A/I/18 and A/II/204.
16. Tagebuch Aufzeichnungen, 1 Apr. 1930, *Nachlass* Grzesinski B/IX/1332.

17. Kohler, "Otto Braun," p. 360, based on an interview with Herbert Weichmann.
18. Ernest Hamburger, "Betrachtungen über Heinrich Brünings Memoiren," p. 28.
19. Adolf Hitler, *Mein Kampf*, tr. Ralph Manheim, pp. 166–69, 175.
20. Hamburger, "Betrachtungen," pp. 20–21.
21. Brüning, *Memoiren*, p. 195.
22. Braun, *Von Weimar*, p. 295; *Reichstag: Sten. Ber.*, vol. 427, pp. 4,732–34, 2 Apr. 1930.
23. Interview with Ernest Hamburger, 3 Feb. 1976.
24. Tagebuch Aufzeichnungen, 1 Apr. 1930, *Nachlass* Grzesinski B/IX/1332.
25. Brüning to Joseph Hess, 7 May 1930, BA Koblenz R 43I/2663/96. Hess to Braun, 20 July 1930, *Nachlass* Braun V/241. For a general discussion, see Schulze, *Otto Braun*, pp. 627–34.
26. Ehni, *Bollwerk Preussen?*, pp. 171–76, 185–86.
27. Niederschrift über die Ministerbesprechung, 24 June 1930, BA Koblenz R 43I/1444.
28. Schulze, *Otto Braun*, p. 634, describes the SPD's decision as a response to an inaccurate rumor that Brüning had collaborated with President Hindenburg in sending a hostile presidential letter to Braun regarding the Stahlhelm affair.
29. Eyck, *History*, 2: 267–74; Braun, *Von Weimar*, p. 306.
30. Braun, *Von Weimar*, p. 133.
31. Braun to Marx, 9 Dec. 1924, copy in *Nachlass* Braun V/563; Ehni, *Bollwerk Preussen?*, p. 181; Schulze, *Otto Braun*, pp. 635–36.
32. Speech by Braun, 8 Aug. 1930, reprinted in part in the *Königsberger Zeitung*, 11 Aug. 1930, quoted by Ehni, *Bollwerk Preussen?*, p. 181. Two weeks later Braun gave a similar speech. *Vorwärts*, no. 391, 22 Aug. 1930.
33. See Hsi-Huey Liang, *The Berlin Police Force in the Weimar Republic*, pp. 109–12, and Erich D. Kohler, "The Crisis in the Prussian Schutzpolizei 1930–1932," pp. 131–50.
34. On this well-researched topic, see in particular Larry E. Jones, "The Dying Middle," pp. 23–54. For a guide to other literature, see James C. Hunt, "The Bourgeois Middle in German Politics 1871–1933," pp. 83–106.
35. Interview in the *New York Herald Tribune*, 16 Sept. 1930. Braun's move is so interpreted by Erich Matthias, "Die Sozialdemokratische Partei Deutschlands," p. 104.
36. Matthias, "SPD," pp. 113–15. Herbert Weichmann, "Kritische Bemerkungen Herbert Weichmanns zu den Briefen Brünings an Sollmann," p. 459.
37. Braun, *Von Weimar*, pp. 309–10.
38. Ministerial Councilor Schomer to Braun, 30 Sept. 1930, *Nachlass* Braun V/435, cited in Kohler, "Otto Braun," p. 387. See also Feder, *Heute*, p. 270.
39. Braun, *Von Weimar*, p. 309.
40. Hermann Pünder, *Politik in der Reichskanzlei*, p. 63; Matthias, "SPD," pp. 104–5.
41. Feder, *Heute*, p. 271; Ehni, *Bollwerk Preussen?*, p. 194.
42. This letter is reprinted without date in Braun, *Von Weimar*, p. 308.
43. *Vorwärts*, no. 465, 4 Oct. 1930. The original draft prepared by Otto Wels was amended slightly and passed against about fifteen dissenting votes. ADGB Restakten (ABI) 471/0130–31.
44. Pünder, *Politik in der Reichskanzlei*, p. 66; *Vorwärts*, no. 479, 12 Oct. 1930.
45. Eyck, *History*, 2: 290–91, 295–96.

46. Tagebuch Aufzeichnungen, 13 Oct.–5 Nov. 1930, *Nachlass* Grzesinski B/x/ 2017; Ehni, *Bollwerk Preussen?*, p. 195; Schulze, *Otto Braun*, pp. 641–43.
47. *Die Rote Fahne*, no. 293, 16 Dec. 1930.
48. Arnold Brecht, *Mit der Kraft des Geistes*, p. 140.
49. Severing to Braun, 18 Dec. 1930, *Nachlass* Braun v/457.
50. *Reichsgesetzblatt* 1931, p. 79.
51. Theodor Haubach to Grzesinski, 25 June 1931, *Nachlass* Grzesinski B/x/1443.
52. Hans Hirschfeld to Grzesinski, 30 June and 1 July 1931, *Nachlass* Grzesinski A/1/70 and B/x/1444.
53. Ehni, *Bollwerk Preussen?*, pp. 207–8.
54. Severing to Rudolf Hilferding, 4 Dec. 1931, *Nachlass* Severing II, cited in Ehni, *Bollwerk Preussen?*, p. 235.
55. *Schulthess' Europäischer Geschichtskalendar*, 1931, p. 176. According to Schulze, *Otto Braun*, pp. 667–68, Braun's press secretary sent the text to the newspapers without clearing it with Braun.
56. Ehni, *Bollwerk Preussen?*, p. 210.
57. State Secretary Planck to General Schleicher, 11 Aug. 1931, *Nachlass* Schleicher XVII/3 reprinted in part in Vogelsang, *Reichswehr*, pp. 427–28.
58. ADGB Restakten (ABI) 463/061.
59. Niederschrift über eine Parteiführerbesprechung, 15 June 1931, BA Koblenz R 43I/1020/171–87.
60. Notes of SPD fraction, 18 Mar. 1931, ADGB Restakten (ABI) 471/0169, and 21 May 1931, ADGB Restakten (ABI) 471/0174.
61. Notes of SPD fraction, 28 May 1931, ADGB Restakten (ABI) 471/0174. On the founding of the SAPD, see Drechsler, *SAPD*, pp. 64–119.
62. Stampfer to Kautsky, 6 Oct. 1931, and Hilferding to Kautsky, 2 Oct. 1931, *Nachlass* Kautsky D/xxi/310 and D/xii/653.
63. Gates, "Economic Policies," pp. 182–263.
64. Sitzung des Bundesvorstandes des ADGB, 10 June 1931, ADGB Restakten (ABI) III/0131. Breitscheid, Wels, Hilferding, Hertz, and Stampfer represented the SPD at this meeting, and Breitscheid was the one who cautioned the unions about the consequences of Brüning's fall.
65. Matthias, "SPD," p. 116; Matthias and Rudolf Morsey, "Die Deutsche Staatspartei," pp. 44–45.
66. On Braun, see a detailed discussion in Schulze, *Otto Braun*, pp. 695–96; on Brüning, see Matthias and Morsey, "Deutsche Staatspartei," pp. 45–46.
67. Planck to Schleicher, 11 Aug. 1931, reprinted in Vogelsang, *Reichswehr*, p. 428.
68. Both possibilities are mentioned in Matthias and Morsey, "Deutsche Staatspartei," p. 47n42. Schulze, *Otto Braun*, p. 699, argues that Schleicher's role was critical.
69. This information was brought to Brecht by Bolz and then relayed to Braun. Brecht to Braun, 29 Aug. 1931, *Nachlass* Braun v/472; Schulze, *Otto Braun*, p. 698.
70. Weichmann, "Kritische Bemerkungen Herbert Weichmanns," p. 459; Braun, *Von Weimar*, pp. 354–55; Brüning to Sollmann, 29 Sept. 1940, *Nachlass* Sollmann, I/6/12. Brüning's account in his memoirs varies considerably and is less credible: Brüning, *Memoiren*, pp. 482–84.
71. Planck to Schleicher, 18 Aug. 1931, reprinted in Vogelsang, *Reichswehr*, p. 429.
72. Brüning's claim to have advised the SPD leaders of his goal is not credible, Hamburger, "Betrachtungen," p. 36; Brüning, *Memoiren*, pp. 278, 461–63.
73. Rohe, *Reichsbanner*, pp. 369–79; Ehni, *Bollwerk Preussen?*, p. 196.

Chapter Eleven: The Collapse of the Prussian Strategy

1. Statistics are discussed by Schneider, *Arbeitsbeschaffungsprogramm*, pp. 22–28.
2. H. R. Knickerbocker, *The German Crisis*, p. 132, quoted by Diehl, *Paramilitary Politics*, p. 288.
3. On Hindenburg, see Andreas Dorpalen, *Hindenburg and the Politics of the Weimar Republic*.
4. Kurt Caro and Walther Oehme, *Schleichers Aufstieg*, pp. 217–20.
5. Notes by Nöldechen early 1930, *Nachlass* Schleicher xxix/5a.
6. Vogelsang, *Reichswehr*, p. 161, *Vorwärts*, no. 71, 12 Feb. 1932; *Der Abend*, no. 72, 12 Feb. 1932.
7. Schleicher to Groener, 23 Mar. 1932, reprinted in Jeremy Noakes and Geoffrey Pridham, *Documents on Nazism, 1919–1945*, p. 128.
8. Brüning, *Memoiren*, pp. 461, 466.
9. Braun to Weismann, 19 Jan. 1932, *Nachlass* Severing, 1/19.
10. Rudolf Hilferding to Kautsky, 2 Oct. 1931, *Nachlass* Kautsky D/xii/653. Braun occasionally complained about Wels's attempts to use pressure. (See n. 11 for one example of Braun's disagreement with Wels.)
11. Braun to Severing, 26 Jan. 1932, *Nachlass* Severing 1/21.
12. Schulze, *Otto Braun*, p. 715.
13. Braun, *Von Weimar*, pp. 298–304, 368.
14. Paul Hertz to Kautsky, 22 Feb. 1932, *Nachlass* Kautsky D/xii/437; Keil, *Erlebnisse*, 2: 433–35; Braun, *Von Weimar*, p. 372; Schulze, *Otto Braun*, pp. 718–19.
15. Vogelsang, *Reichswehr*, pp. 185–86.
16. Braun to Kautsky, 19 Feb. 1932, *Nachlass* Kautsky vi/590, reprinted in Erich Matthias, "Hindenburg zwischen den Fronten," pp. 82–84.
17. Prussian cabinet meeting of 17 Nov. 1931, Deutsches Zentralarchiv Merseburg 90a/B/iii/2b/6, cited in Ehni, *Bollwerk Preussen?*, p. 233.
18. Brüning to Sollmann, 29 Sept. 1940, *Nachlass* Sollmann 1/6/12.
19. Grzesinski to Braun, 9 Dec. 1931, and memo of 11 Dec. 1931, *Nachlass* Grzesinski B/x/1575 and 1555. Also Grzesinski, *Inside Germany*, pp. 136–37; Ehni, *Bollwerk Preussen?*, p. 234.
20. Braun mentioned this incident to journalist Immanuel Birnbaum, who recounted it to author Hagen Schulze in a letter of 6 Aug. 1973. Birnbaum did not recall the date of Hindenburg's threat. Schulze conjectures that it occurred in late 1929 or early 1930—see Schulze, *Otto Braun*, pp. 618, 982n672. The additional evidence presented here indicates that an early 1932 date is far more likely.
21. Ibid., p. 720.
22. Feder, *Heute*, p. 307.
23. Quoted in Grzesinski, *Inside Germany*, p. 137.
24. See Hitler's Reichstag speech of 23 Mar. 1933. *Reichstag: Sten. Ber.*, vol. 457, p. 36.
25. Ehni, *Bollwerk Preussen?*, p. 237n47.
26. Kohler, "Crisis in the Prussian Schutzpolizei," pp. 145–47.
27. Bemerkungen des Herrn Ministers [Groener], 17 Feb. 1932, *Nachlass* Schleicher xci/30.
28. This at least was Severing's subsequent explanation. Protokoll des Parteiausschusses, 10 Nov. 1932, reprinted in Schulze, ed., *Anpassung oder Widerstand?*, p. 35.

29. Schulze, *Otto Braun*, p. 721.
30. Vogelsang, *Reichswehr*, pp. 162–66. Severing met with Groener on 2 April 1932 to discuss the evidence. Notizen, *Nachlass* Schleicher XCI/72.
31. Vogelsang, *Reichswehr*, pp. 167–68; Ehni, *Bollwerk Preussen?*, pp. 240–41; Schulze, *Otto Braun*, pp. 722–23; Caro and Oehme, *Schleichers Aufstieg*, p. 224.
32. Waldemar Besson, *Württemberg und die deutsche Staatskrise 1928–1933*, pp. 393–96.
33. Vogelsang, *Reichswehr*, pp. 172–77.
34. See Groener's account reprinted by Vogelsang, *Reichswehr*, p. 453.
35. Hamburger's letter to the author, 27 Mar. 1976.
36. Jürgen Bay, "Der Preussenkonflikt 1932/33," pp. 22–24.
37. Only a vote of no confidence required a government to resign. Even then it normally continued to function until its successor was elected.
38. Text is in *Nachlass* Severing LIV/90.
39. *Der Ring*, no. 287, cited in Bay, "Preussenkonflikt," p. 63.
40. Stampfer, *Ersten vierzehn Jahren*, p. 629.
41. Heuss (State party) to Albert Hopf, Reinhold Maier, and Peter Bruckmann, 29 Apr. 1932, reprinted in Modris Eksteins, *Theodor Heuss und die Weimarer Republik*, p. 171.
42. *Sozialdemokratische-Partei-Korrespondenz*, 29 Apr. 1932 ("Festbleiben"); Franz Arczynski and W. Allai to Grzesinski, 29 and 30 Apr. 1932, *Nachlass* Grzesinski A/1/3 and B/XII/2019; Grzesinski's answer to the former A/II/194. Also Severing, *Mein Lebensweg*, 2: 333–34.
43. *Nach den Wahlen: Referat des Genossen Dr. Hilferding vor dem Parteiausschuss am 4. Mai 1932*.
44. Hilferding to Kautsky, 2 Oct. 1931, *Nachlass* Kautsky D/XII/653.
45. *Das Freie Wort*, 1 May 1932 ("Ihr siegenden Geschlagenen," signed by Illo, a pseudonym for Heilmann).
46. Ibid., 22 May 1932 ("Das Spiel der Generäle," signed E. H.).
47. For details, Vogelsang, *Reichswehr*, pp. 188–92. Lothar Erdmann, a member of the ADGB executive, wrote in his diary on 30 May: "Fourteen days ago I said, 'The first shot hits Groener; the second will hit Brüning.'" Aus Aufzeichnungen von Lothar Erdmann 1932 und 1933, p. 2, DGB.
48. Schulze, *Otto Braun*, pp. 731–32.
49. For details, see Vogelsang, *Reichswehr*, pp. 180–202, and Bracher, *Auflösung*, pp. 481–526.
50. Bay, "Preussenkonflikt," pp. 75, 97–98.
51. Hamburger's letter to the author, 28 Oct. 1975.
52. Otto Wels, "Um den 20. Juli," manuscript written in early 1933 and reprinted in Schulze, *Anpassung oder Widerstand?*, p. 4; Braun, *Von Weimar*, p. 396; Schulze, *Otto Braun*, p. 733.
53. Bay, "Preussenkonflikt," pp. 47–68, 75, 86–87.
54. Ehni, *Bollwerk Preussen?*, pp. 248, 259–60. Vogelsang, *Reichswehr*, p. 237. On the divisions within the KPD, see Siegfried Bahne, *Die KPD und das Ende von Weimar*, pp. 23–25.
55. Severing, *Mein Lebensweg*, 2: 340–41.
56. Cabinet meetings of 21 and 25 June 1932, discussed in Bracher, *Auflösung*, p. 578; in support of Severing's version, see Brecht, *Mit der Kraft*, p. 217. Another indication was the behavior of the Prussian government when Papen's government withdrew a promised subsidy to Prussia, making the latter legally responsible for

the amount. The Prussian government hastily imposed unpopular new taxes on the slaughtering of cattle and a cut in the salaries of civil servants—in an effort to avoid giving Papen any legal pretext for intervention. Bay, ''Preussenkonflikt,'' pp. 87–90; Schulze, *Otto Braun*, p. 737.

57. Besson, *Württemberg*, pp. 274–81.

58. ''Was tut die preussische Staatsregierung?'' *Nachlass* Grzesinski B/XII/2023, with Grzesinski's penciled notation at the top on why the article was not published.

59. Text in *Nachlass* Grzesinski B/XIII/2154. Newspaper report of the speech in *Nachlass* Grzesinski B/XII/2027.

60. Severing to Grzesinski, 29 June 1932, *Nachlass* Grzesinski B/XIII/2191. See also Grzesinski to Ministerial Director Badt, 29 Aug. 1932, *Nachlass* Grzesinski B/XII/2058. Grzesinski, ''Im Kampf um die deutsche Republik,'' p. 286, *Nachlass* Grzesinski 2457.

61. Bay, ''Preussenkonflikt,'' p. 75; Bracher, *Auflösung*, pp. 571–91.

62. Bay, ''Preussenkonflikt,'' pp. 78–82; Schulze, *Otto Braun*, p. 739.

63. Schulze, *Anpassung oder Widerstand?*, pp. 36–37n70; Besson, *Württemberg*, pp. 280, 285.

64. Rohe, *Reichsbanner*, p. 375.

65. This plan was revealed by a Social Democratic official in the Reich Interior Ministry to a friendly journalist—it had been drawn up as early as 1926. Feder, *Heute*, p. 267, 30 Sept. 1930.

66. Ibid., p. 316, 5 Oct. 1932.

67. Grzesinski, ''Im Kampf,'' p. 286.

68. Friedensburg, *Lebenserinnerungen*, p. 206. Feder, *Heute*, p. 316, 5 Oct. 1932.

69. The Wels manuscript is reprinted in Schulze, *Anpassung oder Widerstand?*, pp. 3–14. On its probable date of writing, see Schulze's comments, ibid., p. xvii; Severing, *Mein Lebensweg*, 2: 347. See also, Matthias, ''SPD,'' pp. 144–45. Severing dated this meeting on 16 July in his memoirs, but in a letter written to Arnold Brecht on 8 Feb. 1950 Severing said only that the meeting took place a few days before 20 July. In all probability, Severing's 16 July meeting is Wels's 18 July meeting. See Brecht, *Mit der Kraft*, p. 436.

70. Otto Klepper, ''Das Ende der Republik,'' pp. 20–22, is the sole source for this version, which Severing, *Mein Lebensweg*, 2: 350–53, strenuously denies. Although there is no confirming evidence for Klepper's account, it is clear that Severing had repelled other pressures for resistance by force. Bay, ''Preussenkonflikt,'' pp. 120–22.

71. Bay, ''Preussenkonflikt,'' pp. 5–10; Feder, *Heute*, p. 316, 5 Oct. 1932; Severing, *Mein Lebensweg*, 2: 350–53; Brecht, *Mit der Kraft*, p. 211.

72. Tagebuch Aufzeichnungen, 20–22 July 1932, *Nachlass* Grzesinski B/XII/2045.

73. Wels, ''Um den 20. Juli,'' in Schulze, *Anpassung oder Widerstand?*, pp. 8–11. The concurrence of high party, union, and Reichsbanner officials in this decision is confirmed by Lothar Erdmann, a high ADGB official and a very reliable source. He wrote in his diary: ''Unforgettable and unforgotten [is] the unanimous passivity of Wels, Leipart, and Höltermann on that day [20 July].'' Aus Aufzeichnungen von Lothar Erdmann 1932 and 1933, 10 Aug. 1932, DGB.

74. Wels, ''Um den 20. Juli.'' Adolph, *Otto Wels*, p. 245.

75. Tagebuch Aufzeichnungen, 20–22 July 1932, *Nachlass* Grzesinski B/XII/2045.

76. Bay, ''Preussenkonflikt,'' p. 12; Severing, *Mein Lebensweg*, 2: 352; Brecht, *Mit der Kraft*, p. 211.

77. *Nachlass* Severing LVI/23–24.

78. Most direct in his remarks has been Karl Dietrich Bracher. See his inquiry to former State Secretary Arnold Brecht and Brecht's response in Brecht, *Mit der Kraft*, pp. 216–17. Also Bracher, "Der 20. Juli 1932," pp. 243–51.
79. Braun's letter to Brecht, 29 Aug. 1932, reprinted in Brecht, *Mit der Kraft*, pp. 437–39.
80. Bay, "Preussenkonflikt," p. 126. Brecht to Braun, 27 Aug. 1932, *Nachlass* Braun VI/626.
81. Protokoll des Parteiausschusses, 10 Nov. 1932, in Schulze, *Anpassung oder Widerstand?*, p. 31.
82. Hilferding to Kautsky, 12 Apr. 1933, *Nachlass* Kautsky D/XII/655.
83. Erdmann Aufzeichnungen, 27 July 1932. For a similar interpretation, see Matthias, "SPD," pp. 142–45.
84. For detailed treatment of this period, see Richard Breitman, "On German Social Democracy and General Schleicher 1932–33," pp. 352–78.
85. Schulze, *Anpassung oder Widerstand?*, pp. 133n11, 134n14.

Conclusion

1. Ernst Fraenkel, "Abschied von Weimar," pp. 109–10. Fraenkel himself later adopted the term pluralism in *Deutschland und die westlichen Demokratien*.
2. East German scholarship has focused on the first possibility. For an introduction to the literature, see "Die Novemberrevolution in der Sicht der kommunistischen Geschichtswissenschaft," pp. 369–85; and Alexander Decker, "Die November-revolution und die Geschichtswissenschaft in der DDR," pp. 269–99.
3. Grebing, "Konservative Republik oder soziale Demokratie?" pp. 386–403.
4. Wachenheim, *Vom Grossbürgertum*, p. 103.
5. See Schneider, *Arbeitsbeschaffungsprogramm*.
6. Hilferding, "Austritt aus der Regierung," p. 385; Severing in SPD *Parteitag 1929*, p. 143; Fraenkel, "1919–1929—Verfassungstag," p. 231.
7. Hermann Müller in SPD *Parteitag 1921*, p. 181.
8. On the origin and meaning of this term, see above, chapter one.
9. The best evidence of the sentiments of the SPD elite toward mass action and cooperation with the Communists can be found in Schulze, *Anpassung oder Widerstand?*
10. Protokoll des Parteiausschusses, 19 Nov. 1932, reprinted in ibid., quotations from pp. 43, 47, 54, 92.
11. *Allgemeiner Kongress*, p. 2 (Ebert).

Appendix A: The Social Democratic Organization

1. The term *fraction*, an Anglicized version of the German *Fraktion*, is generally used in this study in preference to party delegation or caucus.
2. See Richard N. Hunt, *German Social Democracy 1918–1933*, pp. 63–74, for a detailed discussion.
3. For a case study (of the SPD's Baden organization), see Jörg Schadt, ed., *Im Dienst an der Republik*, espec. pp. 22–24, 27–29.

4. *Akten der Reichskanzlei Weimarer Republik*. Edited by Karl Dietrich Erdmann and Wolfgang Mommsen. (See Bibliography, Section B.)

5. On Braun and Wels, see Schulze, *Otto Braun*, pp. 644–58.

6. Gerard Braunthal, *Socialist Labor and Politics in Weimar Germany*, p. 93; Hunt, *German Social Democracy*, p. 57.

7. Braunthal, *Socialist Labor*, pp. 121–41, 155–82, surveys union lobbying.

8. Hunt, *German Social Democracy*, p. 86.

9. Braunthal, *Socialist Labor*, pp. 132–39.

10. Wilhelm Heinz Schröder, "Die Sozialstruktur des sozialdemokratischen Reichstagskandidaten 1898–1912," pp. 75, 85–87.

11. Ibid., p. 83.

12. Wachenheim, *Vom Grossbürgertum*, p. 69.

13. *Rheinische Zeitung*, 27 Nov. 1932, "Positive Parteikritik."

Bibliography

Section A: Archival Sources

1. OFFICIAL MINUTES

The records of high party institutions suffered losses as a consequence of the Nazi takeover of power in 1933, just as the party organization itself was decimated. Only a small portion of the minutes of the executive committee, party council, and Reichstag fraction meetings have survived. The following list of proceedings may be found in the International Institute of Social History, Amsterdam (hereafter IISH), and in the Archiv der sozialen Demokratie at the Friedrich-Ebert-Stiftung, Bonn-Bad Godesberg (hereafter FES).

> Protokoll der Parteikonferenz in Weimar, 22–23 March 1919.
> Sitzung des Parteiausschusses, 28–29 Aug. 1919.
> Protokoll der Sitzung des Parteiausschusses, 13 Dec. 1919.
> Protokoll der Sitzung des Parteivorstandes, des Parteiausschusses, und der
>   Parteiredakteure, 27 Jan. 1920.
> Sitzung des Parteiausschusses, 30–31 Mar. 1920.
> Sitzung des Parteiausschusses, 4 May 1920.
> Protokoll über die Verhandlungen der Reichskonferenz der SPD, 5–6 May 1920.
> Protokoll der Sitzung des Parteiausschusses, 8 Dec. 1920.

The minutes of the party council meetings during the latter half of 1932 and January 1933 have also survived and been published in a collection edited by Hagen Schulze—see Section B.

The official handwritten minutes of the Reichstag fraction during the Weimar Republic originally were contained in five volumes, but only the minutes from 4 Jan. 1919 to 18 Jan. 1920 have survived. Along with the slightly more extensive minutes of the USPD Reichstag fraction, they are held at the IISH. They are cited herein as Protokoll der SPD Fraktionssitzung.

Individual members of the fraction also kept notes of some of the meetings. The papers of Carl Giebel, Carl Severing, Eduard David, contain such unofficial minutes. (See below for the location of these collections.) The ADGB records in the August-Bebel-Institut (in notes and hereafter, ABI) also contain Peter Grassmann's notes of some fraction meetings in 1929–32.

2. COLLECTIONS OF PRIVATE PAPERS (*Nachlässe*)

The following list, organized by the location of the collections, indicates the collections that I made use of and found valuable. It should be noted that I was denied permission to use collections in the archives of the German Democratic Republic.

IISH, Amsterdam
  Eduard Bernstein
  Otto Braun (*Teilnachlass*)
  Albert Grzesinski
  Wolfgang Heine
  Paul Hertz
  Carl Herz
  Karl Kautsky
  Kleine Korrespondenz

FES, Bonn-Bad Godesberg
  Emil Barth
  Otto Braun (*Teilnachlass*)
  Wilhelm Dittmann
  Carl Giebel
  Wilhelm Keil
  Paul Levi
  Hermann Molkenbuhr
  Hermann Müller-Franken (*Teilnachlass*)
  Gustav Noske
  Carl Severing
  Friedrich Stampfer
  Otto Wels

Bundesarchiv (BA) Koblenz
  Eduard David
  Anton Erkelenz
  Georg Gothein
  Erich Koch-Weser
  Albert Südekum
  Rudolf Wissell
  Kleine Erwerbungen—Otto Landsberg

Bundesarchiv-Militärarchiv Freiburg
  Kurt von Schleicher

Archiv des Deutschen Gewerkschaftsbundes (DGB) Düsseldorf
  Lothard Erdmann
  Franz Josef Furtwangler

The Leo Baeck Institute, New York
  Julie Braun-Vogelstein
  Ernst Feder
  Ernest Hamburger
  Hans Schäffer

The Swarthmore College Peace Collection
  Wilhelm Sollmann

3. UNION RECORDS

The files of the ADGB that have survived also contain valuable information about the SPD. Some of the records are in the ABI, Historische Kommission zu Berlin. Others are held at the DGB, Düsseldorf.

The university library of the Free University of Berlin also possesses some union documents and some party records, particularly of regional organizations.

4. GOVERNMENT FILES

The most essential government files for this study were the records of the Reich Chancellery: BA Koblenz, R 43I/411–23, 583–86, 676–79, 1020–21, 1028–29, 1304–9, 1940–44, 2111–15, 2127–28, 2284–90, 2653, and 2662–64.

The U.S. National Archives also possesses microfilms of some material from German government files. Of particular value was USNA film T-120, Reels 1664–68 and 1748–50.

Many other German government documents have now been published in the Akten der Reichskanzlei Weimarer Republik series—see Section B for listings under the names of the individual cabinets.

5. UNPUBLISHED MEMOIRS

Wilhelm Dittmann (IISH)   Wolfgang Heine (BA Koblenz)
Lothar Erdmann (DGB Düsseldorf)   Philipp Loewenfeld (Baeck)
Albert Grzesinski (IISH)   Rudolf Wissell (BA Koblenz)

Section B:
Published Documents and Documentary
Collections; Government Institutions,
Party and Union Proceedings

Akten der Reichskanzlei Weimarer Republik: Das Kabinett Cuno, 22. November 1922 bis 12. August 1923. Edited by Karl Heinz Harbeck. Historische Kommission bei der Bayerischen Akademie der Wissenschaften und das Bundesarchiv. Boppard am Rhein: Boldt, 1971.

Akten der Reichskanzlei Weimarer Republik: Das Kabinett Fehrenbach, 25. Juni 1920 bis 4. Mai 1921. Edited by Peter Wulf. Historische Kommission bei der Bayerischen Akademie der Wissenschaften und das Bundesarchiv. Boppard am Rhein: Boldt, 1972.

Akten der Reichskanzlei Weimarer Republik: Die Kabinette Luther I und II, 15. Januar 1925 bis 20. Januar 1926; 20. Januar 1926 bis 17. Mai 1926. Edited by Karl Heinz Minuth. Historische Kommission bei der Bayerischen Akademie der Wissenschaften und das Bundesarchiv. Boppard am Rhein: Boldt, 1977.

Akten der Reichskanzlei Weimarer Republik: Die Kabinette Marx, 30. November 1923 bis 3. Juni 1924; 3. Juni 1924 bis 15. Januar 1925. Edited by Günter

Abramowski. Historische Kommission bei der Bayerischen Akademie der Wissenschaften und das Bundesarchiv. 2 volumes. Boppard am Rhein: Boldt, 1973.

Akten der Reichskanzlei Weimarer Republik: Das Kabinett Müller I, 27. März 1920 bis 21. Juni 1920. Edited by Martin Vogt. Historische Kommission bei der Bayerischen Akademie der Wissenschaften und das Bundesarchiv. Boppard am Rhein: Boldt, 1970.

Akten der Reichskanzlei Weimarer Republik: Das Kabinett Müller II, 3. Juli 1928 bis 27. März 1930. Edited by Martin Vogt. Historische Kommission bei der Bayerischen Akademie der Wissenschaften und das Bundesarchiv. 2 volumes. Boppard am Rhein: Boldt, 1970.

Akten der Reichskanzlei Weimarer Republik: Das Kabinett Scheidemann, 13. Februar 1919 bis 20. Juni 1919. Edited by Hagen Schulze. Historische Kommission bei der Bayerischen Akademie der Wissenschaften und das Bundesarchiv. Boppard am Rhein: Boldt, 1971.

Akten der Reichskanzlei Weimarer Republik: Die Kabinette Wirth I und II, 10. Mai 1921 bis 26. Oktober 1921; 26. Oktober 1921 bis 22. November 1922. Edited by Ingrid Schulze-Bidlingmaier. Historische Kommission bei der Bayerischen Akademie der Wissenschaften und das Bundesarchiv. 2 volumes. Boppard am Rhein: Boldt, 1973.

ADGB (or Generalkommission der Gewerkschaften Deutschlands). *Auszug aus dem Protokoll der Verhandlungen der Konferenz der Vertreter der Vorstände der gewerkschaflichen Zentralverbände vom 25. April 1919.* Berlin: Generalkommission, 1919.

————. *Protokoll der Verhandlungen des zehnten Kongresses der Gewerkschaften Deutschlands abgehalten zu Nürnberg, 30. Juni–5. Juli 1919.* Berlin: Generalkommission, 1919.

————. *Protokoll der Verhandlungen des 13. Kongresses der Gewerkschaften Deutschlands abgehalten in Frankfurt am Main vom 3. bis 7. September 1928.* Berlin: ADGB, 1928.

Allgemeiner Kongress der Arbeiter- und Soldatenräte, 16. bis 21. Dezember 1918. Berlin: Zentralrat, 1919.

Bericht der Sozialisierungskommission über die Frage der Sozialisierung des Kohlenbergbaues vom 31. Juli 1920: Anhang; Vorläufiger Bericht vom 15. Februar 1919. Berlin: Engelmann, 1920.

Berthold, Lothar; and Neef, Helmut, eds. *Militarismus und Opportunismus gegen die Novemberrevolution: Das Bündnis der rechten SPD-Führung mit der Obersten Heeresleitung November und Dezember 1918; eine Dokumentation.* Berlin: Rütten und Loening, 1958.

Burdick, Charles; and Lutz, Ralph, eds. *The Political Institutions of the German Revolution 1918–1919.* Hoover Institution on War, Revolution, and Peace. New York: Praeger, 1966.

Buse, Dieter K., ed. *Parteiagitation und Wahlkreisvertretung: Eine Dokumentation über Friedrich Ebert und seinen Reichstagswahlkreis Elberfeld-Barmen 1910–1918.* Archiv für Sozialgeschichte, Supplement 3. Bonn-Bad Godesberg: Neue Gesellschaft, 1978.

Deutscher Sozialistentag: Protokoll der Konferenz für Einigung der Sozialdemokratie . . . zu Berlin vom 21. Juni bis 23. Juni 1919. Berlin: Zentralstelle für Einigung der Sozialdemokratie, n.d. [1919].

Feig, J.; and Sitzler, F., eds. *Das Betriebsrätegesetz vom 4. Februar 1920 nebst Wahlordnung, Ausführungsbestimmungen und Verordnungen verwandten Inhalts.* Berlin: Dahlen, 1920.

The Hitler Trial. Translated by H. Francis Frenier. Washington, D.C.: University Publications of America, 1978.

Huber, E. R. *Dokumente der Novemberrevolution und der Weimarer Republik.* Dokumente zur deutschen Verfassungsgeschichte, vol. 3. Stuttgart: Kohlhammer, 1966.

Hürten, Heinz, ed. *Zwischen Revolution und Kapp Putsch: Militär und Innenpolitik 1918–1920.* Quellen zur Geschichte des Parlamentarismus und der politischen Parteien: Zweite Reihe, Militär und Politik, vol. 2. Düsseldorf: Droste, 1977.

Kolb, Eberhard; and Rürup, Reinhard, eds. *Der Zentralrat der deutschen Republik, 19. Dezember 1918 bis 8. April 1919: Vom ersten zum zweiten Rätekongress,* Quellen zur Geschichte der Rätebewegung in Deutschland 1918/1919, vol. 1. International Institute of Social History and Kommission für Geschichte des Parlamentarismus und der politischen Parteien. Leiden: Brill, 1968.

Krause, Fritz, ed. *Arbeitereinheit rettet die Republik: Dokumente und Materialien zur Niederschlagung des Kapp Putsches im März 1920.* Frankfurt am Main: Marxistische Blätter, 1970.

Matthias, Erich, ed. *Der Interfraktionelle Ausschuss 1917/18.* 2 vols. Quellen zur Geschichte des Parlamentarismus und der politischen Parteien, vol. 1. Düsseldorf: Droste, 1969.

————; and Miller, Susanne, eds. *Die Regierung der Volksbeauftragten.* 2 vols. Quellen zur Geschichte des Parlamentarismus und der politischen Parteien, vol. 6. Düsseldorf: Droste, 1966.

————; and Morsey, Rudolf, eds. *Die Regierung des Prinzen Max von Baden.* Quellen zur Geschichte des Parlamentarismus und der politischen Parteien: Erste Reihe, vol. 2. Düsseldorf: Droste, 1962.

————; and Pikart, Eberhard, eds. *Die Reichstagsfraktion der deutschen Sozialdemokratie 1898 bis 1918.* 2 vols. Quellen zur Geschichte des Parlamentarismus und der politischen Parteien, vol. 3. Düsseldorf: Droste, 1966.

Miller, Susanne, ed. *Das Kriegstagebuch des Reichstagsabgeordneten Eduard David 1914 bis 1918.* Quellen zur Geschichte des Parlamentarismus und der politischen Parteien, vol. 4. Düsseldorf: Droste, 1966.

Mommsen, Wilhelm, ed. *Deutsche Parteiprogramme: Deutsches Handbuch für Politik.* Vol. 1. Munich: Olzog, 1964.

Morsey, Rudolf, ed. *Die Protokolle der Reichstagsfraktion und des Fraktionsvorstands des Zentrums 1926–1933.* Veröffentlichungen der Kommission für Zeitgeschichte bei den Katholischen Akademie in Bayern, vol. A 9. Mainz: Matthias-Grunewald, 1969.

Nach den Wahlen: Referat des Genossen Dr. Hilferdings vor dem Parteiausschuss am 4. Mai 1932. Berlin: SPD, 1932.

Nationalversammlung: see *Verfassunggebende Deutsche Nationalversammlung.*

Noakes, Jeremy; and Pridham, Geoffrey. *Documents on Nazism, 1919–1945.* New York: Viking, 1974.

Preussische Landesversammlung: Sitzungsberichte 1919–1920.

Preussischer Landtag: Sitzungsberichte 1920–1932.

Reichsgesetzblatt 1918–1932.

Reichstag: Stenographische Berichte und Anlagen, 1914–1918, 1920–1932.

Ritter, Gerhard A.; and Miller, Susanne, eds. *Die deutsche Revolution 1918–1919*. Frankfurt am Main: Fischer, 1968.

Schadt, Jörg, ed. *Im Dienst an der Republik: Die Tätigkeitsberichte des Landesvorstands der Sozialdemokratischen Partei Badens 1914–1932*. Veröffentlichungen des Stadtarchivs Mannheim, vol. 4. Stuttgart: Kohlhammer, 1977.

Schüddekopf, Otto-Ernst, ed. *Das Heer und die Republik: Quellen zur Politik der Reichswehrführung 1918 bis 1933*. Hanover: Norddeutsche Verlagsanstalt, 1955.

Schulthess' Europäischer Geschichtskalendar, Neue Folge, 1918–1932.

Schulze, Hagen, ed. *Anpassung oder Widerstand? Aus den Akten des Parteivorstands der deutschen Sozialdemokratie 1932/33*. Archiv für Sozialgeschichte, Supplement 4. Bonn-Bad Godesberg: Neue Gesellschaft, 1975.

Sozialdemokratische Partei Deutschlands. *Preussentag der SPD am 14. Februar 1928 in Berlin*. Berlin: SPD, 1928.

————. *Protokoll über die Verhandlungen des Parteitages der SPD abgehalten in Würzburg, 14. bis 20. Oktober 1917*. Berlin: Vorwärts, 1917.

————. *Protokoll über die Verhandlungen des Parteitages der SPD abgehalten in Weimar vom 10. bis 15. Juni 1919*. Berlin: Vorwärts, 1919.

————. *Protokoll über die Verhandlungen des Parteitages der SPD abgehalten in Kassel vom 10. bis 16. Oktober 1920*. Berlin: Vorwärts, 1920.

————. *Protokoll der sozialdemokratischen Parteitage in Augsburg, Gera, und Nürnberg . . . 1922*. Berlin: Dietz, 1923.

————. *Sozialdemokratischer Parteitag 1924 in Berlin: Protokoll. . . .* Bonn-Bad Godesberg: Dietz, 1974, originally 1924.

————. *Sozialdemokratischer Parteitag 1925 in Heidelberg: Protokoll. . . .* Bonn-Bad Godesberg: Dietz, 1974, originally 1925.

————. *Sozialdemokratischer Parteitag 1927 in Kiel: Protokoll. . . .* Bonn-Bad Godesberg: Dietz, 1974, originally 1927.

————. *Sozialdemokratischer Parteitag 1929 in Magdeburg: Protokoll. . . .* Bonn-Bad Godesberg: Dietz, 1974, originally 1929.

————. *Sozialdemokratischer Parteitag 1931 in Leipzig: Protokoll. . . .* Bonn-Bad Godesberg: Dietz, 1974, originally 1931.

Sozialdemokratische Partei Sachsens. *Protokoll über die Verhandlungen der Landesversammlung abgehalten am 12. und 13. Januar 1929 in Leipzig*. Dresden: Landesarbeitsausschuss der SPD, 1929.

Sozialdemokratische Partei Württembergs. *Protokoll über die Verhandlungen der Landesversammlung der Sozialdemokratischen Partei Württembergs am 13. und 14. Juli 1925 . . . in Stuttgart*. Stuttgart: Landesvorstand, 1925.

————. *Protokoll über die Verhandlungen der Landesversammlung der Sozialdemokratischen Partei Würtembergs am 24. und 25. Oktober 1925 in Stuttgart*. Stuttgart: Landesvorstand, 1925.

————. *Protokoll über die Verhandlungen der Landesversammlung der Sozialdemokratischen Partei Württembergs am 9. und 10. April 1927 in Stuttgart*. Stuttgart: Landesvorstand, 1927.

Sozialistische Einheitspartei Deutschlands, Institut für Marxismus-Leninismus. *Dokumente und Materialien zur Geschichte der deutschen Arbeiterbewegung*. Vol. 7, no. 1. Berlin: Dietz, 1966.

Unabhängige Sozialdemokratische Partei Deutschlands. *Protokoll der Reichskonferenz vom 1. bis 3. September 1920 zu Berlin*. Berlin: Freiheit, 1920.

———. *Protokoll über die Verhandlungen des ausserordentlichen Parteitages in Berlin vom 2. bis 6. März 1919*. Berlin: Freiheit, 1919.
Verhandlungen der Sozialisierungskommission über den Kohlenbergbau. Vol. 1, *1918–1919*. Vol. 2, *1920*. Berlin: Engelmann, 1919–1920.
Verfassunggebende Deutsche Nationalversammlung: Stenographische Berichte und Anlagen 1919–1920.
Vorschlag der Sozialisierungskommission vom 24. September 1920 für ein Kommunalisierungsgesetz. Berlin: Engelmann, 1920.
Weber, Hermann, ed. *Der Gründungsparteitag der KPD—Protokoll und Materialien*. Frankfurt am Main: Europäischer Verlag, 1969.

Section C: Newspapers and Periodicals

Die Arbeit: Zeitschrift für Gewerkschaftspolitik und Wirtschaftskunde
Der Arbeiter-Rat: Wochenschrift für praktischen Sozialismus
Archiv für Sozialwissenschaft und Sozialpolitik
Correspondenzblatt der Gewerkschaften Deutschlands—also titled *Korrespondenzblatt des Allgemeinen Deutschen Gewerkschaftsbundes*
Frankfurter Zeitung und Handelsblatt
Das Freie Wort: Sozialdemokratische Diskussionsorgan
Die Freiheit: Berliner Organ der USPD
Die Gesellschaft: Internationale Revue für Sozialismus und Politik
Jungsozialistische Blätter
Der Klassenkampf
Die Neue Zeit
Die Rote Fahne
Sozialdemokratische-Partei-Korrespondenz
Sozialistische Monatshefte
Sozialistische Politik und Wirtschaft (Levi Korrespondenz)
Vorwärts: Berliner Volksblatt, Zentralorgan der SPD

Section D:
Contemporary Books, Pamphlets, Articles, Memoirs

Adler, Marx. *Die Aufgabe der Jugend in unserer Zeit: Drei Reden an die Jugend*. Berlin: Jungsozialistische Schriftenreihe, 1927.
Aufhäuser, Siegfried. "Der politische Kampf um die Arbeitslosenversicherung und ihre sozialpolitische Bedeutung." *Die Gesellschaft* 7 (1930): 393–403.
Barth, Emil. *Aus der Werkstatt der deutschen Revolution*. Berlin: A. Hoffmann's Verlag, 1919.
Barth, Erwin. *Marxismus und Bolschewismus: Eine Auseinandersetzung*. Berlin: n.p., 1919.
Bernhard, Georg. *Wirtschaftsparlamente von den Revolutionsräten zum Reichswirtschaftsrat*. Vienna: Rikola, 1923.
Bernstein, Eduard. *Die deutsche Revolution: Ihr Ursprung, ihr Verlauf und ihr Werk*. Berlin: Gesellschaft & Erziehung, 1921.

————. *Evolutionary Socialism: A Criticism and Affirmation*. Translated by Edith Harvey. New York: Schocken, 1961.

————. *Was die Sozialdemokratie will: Die Ziele, die Grundsätze, und die Politik der Sozialdemokratie*. No information [1919?].

————. *Was ist Sozialismus? Vortag gehalten 28 Dezember 1918 im grossen Saal der Philharmonie, Berlin*. Berlin: Arbeitsgemeinschaft für staatsbürgerliche und wirtschaftliche Bildung, 1919.

Beyerle, R. *Die Bedeutung der neuen Reichsverfassung für Volk und Vaterland*. Berlin: Reichszentrale für Heimatdienst, 1919.

Bieligk, Fritz, et al. *Die Organisation im Klassenkampf: Die Probleme der politischen Organisation der Arbeiterklasse*. Die Roten Bücher der Marxistische Büchergemeinde, vol. 2. Berlin: Marxistische Verlagsgesellschaft, 1931.

Bischoff, E. *Die Entlarvung von der deutsch-bolschewistischen Verschwörung*. Berlin: Vorwärts, 1919.

Brahn, Max. *Politisches A-B-C*. Leipzig: Der Neue Geist [1919].

Brammer, Karl. *Fünf Tage Militärdiktatur*. Berlin: Verlag für Politik und Wirtschaft, 1920.

Brauer, Theodor. *Das Betriebsrätegesetz und die Gewerkschaften*. Jena: Fischer, 1920.

Braun, Adolf. *Die Sozialisierung: Volkswirtschaftliche und soziologische Bertrachtungen*. Nuremberg: Fränkische Verlagsanstalt, n.d.

Braun, Otto. *Deutscher Einheitsstaat oder Foderativsystem?* Berlin: Heymanns, 1927.

————. *Von Weimar zu Hitler*. New York: Europa, 1940.

Braunthal, Julius. *Kommunisten und Sozialdemokraten*. Vienna: Sozialistische Bücherei, 1920.

Brecht, Arnold. *Aus nächster Nähe: Lebenserinnenrungern 1884–1927*, vol. 1. Stuttgart: Deutsche Verlagsanstalt, 1966.

————. *Mit der Kraft des Geistes: Lebenserinnerungen 1927–1967*, vol. 2. Stuttgart: Deutsche Verlagsanstalt, 1969.

————. *The Political Education of Arnold Brecht*. Princeton: Princeton University Press, 1970.

————. *Prelude to Silence: The End of the German Republic*. New York: Oxford University Press, 1944.

————. "Reich und Länder: Tatbestand und nächste Schritte." *Die Gesellschaft* 5 (1928): 15–28.

Breitscheid, Rudolf. "Worum es ging und geht." *Die Gesellschaft* 7 (1930): 97–102.

Brüning, Heinrich. *Briefe 1946–1960*. Edited by Claire Nix with the Assistance of Reginald Phelps and George Pettee. Stuttgart: Deutsche Verlagsanstalt, 1974.

————. *Memoiren, 1918–1934*. Stuttgart: Deutsche Verlagsanstalt, 1970.

Buchwitz, Otto. *50 Jahre Funktionär der deutschen Arbeiterbewegung*. East Berlin: Dietz, 1973.

Calwer, Richard. *Die Währungspolitik des Kabinetts Stresemann: Kritik und Gegenvorschlag*. Berlin: Wirtschaftsstatistisches Bureau von Richard Calwer, 1923.

Caro, Kurt; and Oehme, Walther. *Schleichers Aufstieg: Ein Beitrag zur Geschichte der Gegenrevolution*. Berlin: Rowohlt, 1933.

Cohen (-Reuss), Max. *Der Aufbau Deutschlands und der Rätegedanke*. Revolutions-Streitfragen, vol. 2. Berlin: Generalsekretariat zum Studium des Bolschewismus, 1919.

Cunow, Heinrich. "Die Auflösungsprozess der U.S.P." *Die Neue Zeit* 39 (1921): 105–10.

D'Abernon, Viscount Edgar Vincent. *The Diary of an Ambassador: Versailles to Rapallo 1920–1922*. Garden City, N.Y.: Doubleday, 1929.

―――. *The Diary of an Ambassador: Rapallo to Dawes 1922–1924*. Garden City, N.Y.: Doubleday, 1930.

David, Eduard. *Verfassung und Verwaltung: Erläuterungen zum Görlitzer Programm*. Stuttgart: 1922.

Decker, Georg. "Faschistische Gefahr und Sozialdemokratie." *Die Gesellschaft* 8 (1931): 481–96.

―――. "Der Kampf um die Demokratie." *Die Gesellschaft* 6 (1929): 293–313.

―――. "Krise des deutschen Parteiensystems?" *Die Gesellschaft* 3 (1926): 1–16.

―――. "Nach den Preussenwahlen." *Die Gesellschaft* 9 (1932): 465–76.

―――. "Noch einmal: Kampf um die Demokratie." *Die Gesellschaft* 7 (1930): 193–200.

―――. "Tolerierung." *Die Gesellschaft* 7 (1930): 481–85.

―――. "Zur Soziologie der Reichstagswahlen." *Die Gesellschaft* 5 (1928): 1–12.

―――. "Zur Statistik der Reichstagswahl." *Die Gesellschaft* 2 (1925): 59–65.

Deutsch, Julius. *Antifaschismus*. Vienna: Wiener Volksbuchhandlung, 1926.

Diedrich, Franz. *Führer des Volks: Fritz Ebert*. Berlin: Schwetschke & Sohn, [1919].

Duderstadt, Henning. *Vom Reichsbanner zum Hakenkreuz: Wie es kommen musste, ein Bekenntnis*. 4th edition. Stuttgart: Union Deutsche Verlagsgesellschaft, 1933.

Düwell, Bernhard. *Einheit der Aktion und Parteidisziplin*. Sozialistische Zeitfragen. Berlin: Laubsche, 1931.

Ebert, Friedrich. *Schriften, Aufzeichnungen, Reden: Mit unveröffentlichen Erinnerungen aus dem Nachlass*. 2 vols. Dresden: Reissner, 1926.

Eckstein, Ernst. "Die Preussenkoalition." *Der Klassenkampf* 2 (1928): 335–39.

Enderle, August, et al. *Das rote Gewerkschaftsbuch*. Rote Bücher der Marxistischen Büchergemeinde, vol. 5. Berlin: Freie Verlagsgesellschaft [1932].

Engels, Friedrich. "Zur Kritik des sozialdemokratischen Programmentwurfs." In *Deutsche Parteiprogramme*. Edited by Wilhelm Mommsen. Munich: Olzog, 1964.

Erdmann, Karl. *Der Missbrauch der Revolution*. Berlin: Der Firn [1919].

Erdmann, Lothar. *Die Gewerkschaften im Ruhrkampfe*. Berlin: Verlagsgesellschaft des ADGB, 1924.

Erkelenz, Anton, ed. *Zehn Jahre Deutsche Republik 1918–1928: Ein Handbuch für republikanische Politik*. Berlin: Sieben-Stäbe, 1928.

Eulenburg, Franz. "Die sozialen Wirkungen der Währungsverhältnisse." *Jahrbücher für Nationalökonomie und Statistik* 122 (1924): 748–94.

Fabian, Lora. *Arbeiterschaft und Kolonialpolitik*. Jungsozialistische Schriftenreihe. Berlin: 1928.

Fabian, Walther. *Klassenkampf um Sachsen: Ein Stück Geschichte 1918–1930*. Löbau: Ostsachsen Druckerei, 1930.

Feder, Ernst. *Heute sprach ich mit . . . Tagebücher eines Publizisten 1926–1932*. Edited by Cécile Lowenthal Hensel and Arnold Paucker. Stuttgart: Deutsche Verlagsanstalt, 1971.

Fischer, Anton. *Die Revolutionskommandatur Berlin*. Berlin: n.p., 1922.

Fraenkel, Ernst. "Abschied von Weimar." *Die Gesellschaft* 9 (1932): 109–24.

―――. "1919–1929: Zum Verfassungstag." *Jungsozialistische Blätter* 8, no. 8 (1929): 226–31.

―――. "Um die Verfassung." *Die Gesellschaft* 9 (1932): 297–312.

————. "Zehn Jahre Betriebsrätegesetz." *Die Gesellschaft* 7 (1930): 117–29.

————. *Zur Soziologie der Klassenjustiz*. Jungsozialistische Schriftenreihe. Berlin: n.p., 1927.

Franke, Arno. *Nach Eden oder nach Golgatha? Eine ernste Frage an Deutschlands Arbeiterschaft*. Berlin: Der Firn [1919].

Friedensburg, Ferdinand. *Lebenserinnerungen*. Frankfurt am Main: Athenäum, 1969.

Geiger, Theodor. "Die Mittelschichten und die Sozialdemokratie." *Die Arbeit* 8 (1931): 619–35.

————. "Zur Kritik der Verbürgerlichung." *Die Arbeit* 8 (1931): 534–47.

Geyer, Curt. *Führer und Masse in der Demokratie*. Berlin: Dietz [1926].

————. *Der Radikalismus in der deutschen Arbeiterbewegung: Ein soziologischer Versuch*. Jena: Thüringer Verlagsanstalt, 1923.

————. *Die revolutionäre Illusion: Zur Geschichte des linken Flügels der USPD: Erinnerungen von Curt Geyer*. Edited by Wolfgang Benz and Hermann Grand. Schriftenreihe der Vierteljahrshefte für Zeitgeschichte, vol. 33. Stuttgart: Deutsche Verlagsanstalt, 1976.

Gieseke, Paul. *Die Rechtsverhältnisse der gemeinwirtschaftlichen Organisationen*. Jena: Fischer, 1922.

Göppert, Heinrich. "Sozialisierungsbestrebungen in Deutschland nach der Revolution." *Schmollers Jahrbuch für Gesetzgebung, Verwaltung, und Volkswirtschaft im Deutschen Reiche* 45 (1921): 313–47.

Greiling, W. *Marxismus und Sozialisierungstheorie: Eine Untersuchung des Ergebnisses der deutschen Sozialisierungs-Literatur*. Berlin: Vereinigung Internationaler Verlags-Anstalten, 1923.

Grotjahn, Alfred. *Erlebtes und Erstrebtes: Erinnerungen eines sozialistischen Arztes*. Berlin: Herbig, 1932.

Grzesinski, Albert. *Inside Germany*. New York: Dutton, 1939.

Guillebaud, Claude William. *The Works Council: German Experiment in Industrial Democracy*. Cambridge: Cambridge University Press, 1928.

Gurland, A. *Der proletarische Klassenkampf in der Gegenwart: Zur taktischen Orientierung der Sozialdemokratie in der Nachkriegsphase des Kapitalismus*. Leipzig: Leipziger Buchdruckerei, 1925.

————; and Laumann, K. *Spaltung oder Aktivität?* Sozialistische Zeitfragen Berlin: Laubsche, 1931.

Hamburger, Ernest. "Grzesinskis Leistung." *Die Gesellschaft* 7 (1930): 296–301.

————. "Parteienbewegung und Gesellschaftliche Umschichtung in Deutschland." *Die Gesellschaft* 2 (1925): 340–53.

Hanssen, Hans Peter, *Diary of a Dying Empire*. Indiana University Publications, Social Science Series, vol. 14. Bloomington: Indiana University Press, 1955.

Haubach, Theodor. "Die Richtlinien zur Wehrfrage." *Die Gesellschaft* 6 (1929): 97–112.

————. "Der Sozialismus und die Wehrfrage." *Die Gesellschaft* 3 (1926): 120–30.

————. "Wehrfrage und Sozialdemokratie." *Die Gesellschaft* 4 (1927): 493–501.

Heine, Wolfgang. *Wer ist schuld am Bürgerkrieg?* Berlin: Moeser, 1919.

Heller, Hermann. *Die politischen Ideenkreise der Gegenwart*. Breslau: Hirt, 1926.

————. *Sozialismus und Nation*. Berlin: Arbeiterjugend, 1925.

Hilferding, Rudolf. "Der Austritt aus der Regierung." *Die Gesellschaft* 7 (1930): 385–92.

_____. *Das Finanzkapital*. 2 vols. Frankfurt am Main: Europäische Verlagsanstalt, 1968.

_____. *Gesellschaftsmacht oder Privatmacht über die Wirtschaft: Referat gehalten am 4. AfA Gewerkschaftskongress*. Leipzig: Allgemeiner freier Angestelltenbund, 1931.

_____. "In der Gefahrenzone." *Die Gesellschaft* 7 (1930): 289–97.

_____. "In Krisennot." *Die Gesellschaft* 8 (1931): 1–8.

_____. *Nationalsozialismus und Marxismus*. Berlin: Volksfunk, 1932.

_____. "Politische Probleme—Zum Aufruf Wirths und zur Rede Silverbergs." *Die Gesellschaft* 3 (1926): 289–302.

_____. "Probleme der Zeit." *Die Gesellschaft* 1 (1924): 1–17.

_____. *Die Schicksalsstunde der deutschen Wirtschaftspolitik: Referat gehalten auf dem AfA Gewerkschaftskongress 15.–17. Juni 1925*. Berlin: Dietz, 1925.

_____. *Die Sozialisierung und die Machtverhältnisse der Klassen: Referat auf dem 1. Betriebsrätekongress gehalten am 5 Oktober 1920*. Berlin: Freiheit, 1920.

_____. "Theoretische Bemerkungen zur Agrarfrage." *Die Gesellschaft* 4 (1927): 421–32.

_____. "Unter der Drohung des Faschismus." *Die Gesellschaft* 9 (1932): 1–12.

Hirsch, Paul. *Der Weg der Sozialdemokratie zur Macht in Preussen*. Berlin: Stollberg, 1929.

_____. *Flucht vor Hitler: Erinnerungen an die Kapitulation der ersten deutschen Republik 1933*. Frankfurt am Main: Fischer, 1979.

Hoegner, Wilhelm. *Der politische Radikalismus in Deutschland 1919–1933*. Geschichte und Staat, vol. 118/119. Munich: Olzog, 1966.

_____. *Der schwierige Aussenseiter: Erinnerungen eines Abgeordneten, Emigranten und Ministerpräsidenten*. Munich: Isar, 1959.

Horton, Alfons. *Sozialisierung und Wiederaufbau: Praktische Vorschläge zur Sozialisierung und zur Wiederaufrichtung unseres Wirtschaftslebens*. Berlin: Neues Vaterland, 1920.

Hue, Otto. "Privatbergregale." *Die Neue Zeit* 37 (1919): 411–15.

_____. *Die Sozialisierung der Kohlenwirtschaft*. Berlin: Vorwärts, 1921.

Jäckel, Hermann. *Auf dem Wege zur konstitutionell-demokratischen Fabrik*. (no information).

Jansen, Robert. *Der Berliner Militärputsch und seine politischen Folgen*. Berlin: n.p., 1920.

Jenssen, Otto. *Erziehung zum politischen Denken*. Jungsozialistische Schriftenreihe. Berlin: n.p., 1931.

Kampffmeyer, Paul. *Der Geist des neuen sozialdemokratischen Programms*. Jena: Fischer, 1922.

_____. *Der Nationalsozialismus und seine Gönner*. Berlin: Dietz, 1924.

Kautsky, Karl. *Demokratie oder Diktatur*. Berlin: Cassirer, 1918.

_____. "Ein sozialdemokratischer Katechismus." *Die Neue Zeit* 12 (1893–94): 368.

_____. *Erinnerungen und Erörterungen*. Edited by Benedikt Kautsky. Quellen und Untersuchungen zur Geschichte der deutschen und österreichischen Arbeiterbewegung, vol. 3. The Hague: Mouton, 1960.

_____. *Gegen die Diktatur*. Berlin: Litfass [1918].

_____. *Nationalversammlung und Räteversammlung*. Berlin: Hermann [1918].

_____. *Der neue Staat: Demokratie oder Diktatur?* Berlin: Weisse Blätter [1919?].

————. *Richtlinien für ein sozialistisches Aktionsprogramm*. Berlin: Sittenwald, 1919.

————. *Sozialdemokratische Bemerkungen zur Übergangswirtschaft*. Leipzig: Leipziger Buchdruckerei, 1918.

————. *Texte zu den Programmen der deutschen Sozialdemokratie 1891–1925*. Cologne: Hegner, 1968.

————. *Volksherrschaft oder Gewaltherrschaft?* Berlin: Weisse Blätter, 1919.

————. *Was will die deutsche sozialistische Republik?* (no information).

————. *Das Weitertreiben der Revolution*. Berlin: Arbeitsgemeinschaft für staatsbürgerliche und wirtschaftliche Bildung [1919].

Keil, Wilhelm. *Erlebnisse eines Sozialdemokraten*. 2 vols. Stuttgart: Deutsche Verlagsanstalt, 1947.

————. *Wisst Ihr das? Was mit der demokratischen Republik erreicht wurde: Eine kurze vergleichende Übersicht*. Berlin: Dietz, 1932.

Kessler, Count Harry. *The Diaries of a Cosmopolitan 1918–1937*. Translated by Charles Kessler. Condensed edition. London: Weidenfeld & Nicolson, 1970.

————. *Tagebücher 1918–1937*. Frankfurt am Main: Im-Insel, 1961.

————. *Walther Rathenau: His Life and Work*. New York: Fertig, 1969.

Kirchheimer, Otto. "Legalität und Legitimität." *Die Gesellschaft* 9 (1932): 8–26.

————. *Politics, Law and Social Change: Selected Essays*. Edited by Frederic S. Burin and Kurt L. Shell. New York: Columbia University Press, 1969.

————. "Verfassungsreform und Sozialdemokratie." *Die Gesellschaft* 10 (1933): 20–35.

Klühs, Franz. *Die Spaltung der USPD*. Berlin: Vorwärts, 1921.

————. *Werden und Wachsen der sozialistischen Bewegung*. Berlin: Arbeiterjugend, 1929.

Knickerbocker, H. R. *The German Crisis*. New York: Farrer & Rinehart, 1932.

Korsch, Karl. *Schriften zur Sozialisierung*. Edited by Erich Gerlach. Frankfurt am Main: Europäische Verlagsanstalt, 1969.

Kuttner, Erich. *Otto Braun*. Leipzig: Kittler, 1932.

————. *Wie werden wir wieder reich?* Berlin: Verlag für Sozialwissenschaft, 1919.

Landsberg, Otto. *Die politische Krise der Gegenwart*. Berlin: Dietz, 1931.

Laumann, Kurt. "Zum Problem der Aktivierung der Partei: Randbemerkungen zu Schifrins 'Antikritik.' " *Die Gesellschaft* 8 (1931): 460–71.

Leber, Julius. *Ein Mann geht seinen Weg: Schriften, Reden und Briefen von Julius Leber*. Berlin: Mosaik, 1952.

————. "Zur Klärung des Wehrproblems." *Die Gesellschaft* 6 (1929): 125–30.

Ledebour, Georg. *Ledebour vor den Geschworenen: Seine Verteidigungsrede—Eine Anklage gegen die Regierung Ebert-Scheidemann 20.5.1919*. Berlin: Freiheit, 1919.

Lederer, Emil. "Die Gewerkschaftsbewegung 1918/19 und die Entfaltung der wirtschaftlichen Ideologien in der Arbeiterklasse." *Archiv für Sozialwissenschaft und Sozialpolitik* 47 (1920): 219–69.

————. *Planwirtschaft*. Tübingen: Mohr, 1932.

————. "Randglossen der neuesten Schriften Walther Rathenaus." *Archiv für Sozialwissenschaft und Sozialpolitik* 48 (1921): 286–303.

————. "Die Umschichtung des Proletariats." *Die neue Rundschau* 40 (1929): 145–61.

————, et al. *Das Kartellproblem: Beiträge zur Theorie und Praxis*. Munich: Duncker & Humblot, 1930.

Leichter, Otto. *Ende des demokratischen Sozialismus? Ein offenes Wort über die deutschen Lehren*. Vienna: Wiener Volksbuchhandlung, 1932.

Leipart, Theodor. *Carl Legien: Ein Gedenkbuch*. Berlin: ADGB, 1929.

Lenin, V. I. *Imperialism: The Highest Stage of Capitalism*. New York: International Publishers, 1939.

_____. *Left-wing Communism: An Infantile Disorder; a Popular Essay in Marxian Strategy and Tactics*. New York: International Publishers, 1940.

Lepinski, Franz. *Die jungsozialistische Bewegung: Ihre Geschichte und ihre Aufgaben*. Jungsozialistische Schriftenreihe. Berlin: n.p., 1927.

Levi, Paul. "Der Panzerkreuzer." *Sozialistische Politik und Wirtschaft* 6 (17 Aug. 1928).

_____. *Zwischen Spartacus und Sozialdemokratie: Schriften, Aufsätze, Reden und Briefe*. Frankfurt am Main: Europäische Verlagsanstalt, 1969.

Löbe, Paul. *Sozialismus, ja oder nein?* Berlin: Dietz, 1932.

_____. *Der Weg war lang: Lebenserinnerungen*. Berlin: Arani, 1949.

Luther, Hans. *Politiker ohne Partei: Erinnerungen*. Stuttgart: Deutsche Verlagsanstalt, 1960.

Luxemburg, Rosa. *Gesammelte Werke*, vol. 3. Berlin: Vereinigung Internationaler Verlags-Anstalten, 1925.

_____. *The Russian Revolution and Leninism or Marxism*. Edited by Bertram Wolfe. Ann Arbor: University of Michigan Press, 1961.

Marchionini, Karl. *Was trennt uns Unabhängige von den Rechtssozialisten?* Leipzig: Leipziger Buchdruckerei, 1919.

Marck, Siegfried. *Marxistische Staatsbejahung*. Breslau: Volkswacht, 1923.

_____. *Reformismus und Radikalismus in der deutschen Sozialdemokratie: Geschichtliches und Grundsätzliches*. Jungsozialistische Schriftenreihe. Berlin: n.p., 1927.

_____. "Sozialdemokratie." In Kurt Metzner, ed., *Die geistige Struktur der politischen Parteien Europas: Deutsches Reich*. Berlin: Pan [1931].

Maurenbrecher, Max. *Die Taktik der Parteien bei der Regierungsbildung Sommer 1920*. Dresden: Glaube & Deutschtum, 1920.

Maximilian, Prince of Baden. *Erinnerungen und Dokumente*. Edited by Golo Mann and Andreas Burckhardt. Stuttgart: E. Klett, 1968.

Menzel, Hans. *Carl Severing*. Berlin: Historisch-Politischer Verlag, 1932.

Michels, Robert. "Die deutsche Sozialdemokratie: Parteimitgliedschaft und soziale Zusammensetzung." *Archiv für Sozialwissenschaft und Sozialpolitik* 23 (1906): 471–556.

_____. *Political Parties: A Sociological Study of the Oligarchical Tendencies of Modern Democracy*. Translated by Eden and Cedar Paul. Glencoe, Ill.: Free Press, 1949.

Mierendorff, Carl. "Aufgeklärter Militarismus." *Die Gesellschaft* 6 (1929): 131–37.

_____. "Gesicht und Charakter der nationalsozialistischen Bewegung." *Die Gesellschaft* 7 (1930): 489–504.

_____. "Wieviele 'Bonzen' gibt es?" *Neue Blätter für den Sozialismus* 2 (1931): 142–43.

Mill, John Stuart. *Considerations on Representative Government*. New York: Holt, 1873.

Moellendorff, Wichard Georg von. *Konservativer Sozialismus*. Hamburg: Hanseatische Verlagsanstalt, 1932.

Müller, August. "Die Lehren der Staatsstreichepisode." *Sozialistische Monatshefte* 26 (1920): 217–25.

Müller, Richard. *Der Bürgerkrieg in Deutschland: Geburtswehen der Republik.* Berlin: Phöbus, 1925.

———. *Vom Kaiserreich zur Republik: Ein Beitrag zur Geschichte der revolutionären Arbeiterbewegung während des Weltkrieges.* West Berlin: Olle & Woltes, 1974.

———. *Was die Arbeiterräte wollen und sollen!* Berlin: Der Arbeiterrat [1919].

Müller-Franken, Hermann. *Die November-Revolution: Erinnerungen.* Berlin: Der Bücherkreis, 1931.

———. "Der Obmann als Geschichtsschreiber." *Die Gesellschaft* 2 (1925): 133–43.

———. "Vom deutschen Parlamentarismus." *Die Gesellschaft* 3 (1926): 289–305.

———. *Der Werdegang des sozialdemokratischen Programms.* Berlin: Vorwärts, n.d.

Naphtali, Fritz. *Abbau und Aufbau: Rückblick auf das Wirtschaftsjahr 1925.* Frankfurt am Main: Societäts-Druckerei, 1923.

———. "Debatten zur Wirtschaftsdemokratie." *Die Gesellschaft* 6 (1929): 210–19.

———. *Im Zeichen des Währungselends: Das Wirtschaftjahr 1922 und seine Lehren.* Frankfurt am Main: Societäts-Druckerei, 1923.

———. *Kapitalkontrolle.* Jena: Diedrichs, 1919.

———. *Konjunktur, Arbeiterklasse, und sozialistische Wirtschaftspolitik.* Berlin: Dietz, 1928.

———. "Die Kontrolle der Kartelle und Trusts." *Die Gesellschaft* 8 (1931): 43–53.

———. "Nachkriegskapitalismus." *Die Gesellschaft* 8 (1931): 533–40.

———. "Der organisierte Kapitalismus in der Wirtschaftskrise." *Die Gesellschaft* 8 (1931).

———. *Wirtschaftskrise und Arbeitslosigkeit, volkstümlich dargestellt.* Berlin: Dietz, 1930.

———, ed. *Wirtschaftsdemokratie, ihr Wesen, Weg und Ziel.* Frankfurt am Main: Europäische Verlagsanstalt, 1969. 3rd unrevised edition, originally 1928.

Neisser, Hans. "Sozialistische Analyse des Wahlergebnisses." *Die Arbeit* 7 (1930): 654–59.

Neumann, Sigmund. *Die Parteien der Weimarer Republik.* Stuttgart: Kohlhammer, 1970, originally 1932.

Neunerkommission für die Vorbereitung der Sozialisierung des Bergbaues im rheinisch-westfälischen Industriegebiet. *Die Sozialisierung des Bergbaues und der Generalstreik im rheinisch-westfälischen Industriegebiet.* N.p. [1919].

Nichts getan? Die Arbeit seit dem 9. November 1918. Berlin: Arbeitsgemeinschaft für staatsbürgerliche und wirtschaftliche Bildung [1919].

Noske, Gustav. *Aufstieg und Niedergang der deutschen Sozialdemokratie: Erlebtes aus Aufstieg und Niedergang einer Demokratie.* Zurich: Aero-Verlag, 1947.

———. *Von Kiel bis Kapp: Zur Geschichte der deutschen Revolution.* Berlin: Verlag für Politik und Wirtschaft, 1920.

Oehme, Walther. *Mein Ziel ist die Weltrevolution.* Berlin: Generalsekretariat zum Studium des Bolschewismus, 1919.

———. *Die Weimarer Nationalversammlung 1919: Erinnerungen.* Berlin: Rütten & Loenig, 1962.

Panzerkreuzer und Sozialdemokratie. Der Klassenkampf: Marxistische Blätter. Berlin: Laubsche, 1928.

Parvus [Alexander Helphand]. *Der Klassenkampf des Proletariats: Die Sozialdemokratie und der Parlamentarismus.* Berlin: Vorwärts, 1908.

Prager, Eugen. *Geschichte der U.S.P.D.: Entstehung und Entwicklung der Unabhängigen Sozialistischen Partei Deutschlands*. Berlin: Freiheit, 1921.

Pünder, Hermann. *Politik in der Reichskanzlei: Aufzeichnungen aus den Jahren 1929–1932*. Edited by Thilo Vogelsang. Schriftenreihe der Vierteljahrshefte für Zeitgeschichte. Stuttgart: Deutsche Verlagsanstalt, 1961.

———. *Von Preussen nach Europa: Lebenserinnerungen*. Stuttgart: Deutsche Verlagsanstalt, 1968.

Quarck, Max. *Sozialpolitik: Erläuterungen zum Görlitzer Programm*. Stuttgart, 1922.

Radbruch, Gustav. "Goldbilanz der Reichsverfassung." *Die Gesellschaft* 1 (1924): 57–69.

———. *Der innere Weg: Aufriss meines Lebens*. Stuttgart: Koehler, 1951.

Rathenau, Fritz. *Parlement und Räte*. Berlin: Stilke, 1919.

Rathenau, Walther. *Von kommenden Dingen*. Berlin: Fischer, 1918.

Reinhard, Ernst. *Abrüstung . . . zum neuen Krieg*. Jungsozialistische Schriftenreihe. Berlin: n.p., 1927.

Renner, Karl. *Karl Kautsky: Skizze zur Geschichte der geistigen und der politischen Entwicklung der deutschen Arbeiterklasse*. Berlin: Dietz, 1929.

———. "Der Streit um die Demokratie." *Die Gesellschaft* 4 (1927): 1–27.

Schacht, Hjalmar. *Das Ende der Reparationen*. Oldenburg: Stalling, 1931.

Schairer, Erich. *Rathenau-Brevier*. Deutsche Gemeinwirtschaft Schriftenreihe, vol. 5. Jena: Diedrichs, 1918.

Scheidemann, Philipp. *Köpfe in den Sand? Die wirklichen November Verbrecher*. Brunswick: Rieke, 1931?

———. *The Making of New Germany: The Memoirs of Philipp Scheidemann*. Translated by J. E. Mitchell, 2 vols. New York: Appelton, 1929.

Scheidemann, Philipp; and Müller-Franken, Hermann. *Deutschlands bürgerliche Regierung*. Berlin: Vorwärts, 1920.

Schiffer, Eugen. *Ein Leben für den Liberalismus*. Berlin: Herbig, 1951.

Schifrin, Alexander. "Gedankenschatz des Hakenkreuzes." *Die Gesellschaft* 8 (1931): 97–116.

———. "Kritik an der Organisation." *Die Gesellschaft* 8 (1931): 166–78.

———. "Parteiapparat und Parteidemokratie." *Die Gesellschaft* 7 (1930): 505–28.

———. "Der Streit um die Parteidemokratie: Erwiderung an Laumann." *Die Gesellschaft* 8 (1931): 472–77.

Schulz, Heinrich. *Sozialdemokratie und Schule*. Berlin: Vorwärts, 1920.

Seidel, Richard. "Aufstieg und Krise der Gewerkschaftsbewegung." *Die Gesellschaft* 1 (1924): 76–98.

———. *Die Gewerkschaften nach dem Kriege*. Berlin: Dietz, 1925.

———. "Gewerkschaften und Wirtschaft." *Die Gesellschaft* 2 (1925): 201–14.

———. *Die Gewerkschaftsbewegung und das Rätesystem*. Berlin: Der Arbeiter-Rat, 1919.

———. *The Trade Union Movement of Germany*. Amsterdam: International Federation of Trade Unions, 1928.

Sender, Toni. *Autobiography of a German Rebel*. New York: Vanguard, 1939.

———. *Grosse Koalition? Gegen ein Bündnis mit der Schwerindustrie*. Frankfurt am Main: Union, 1923.

———. "Kritik an den Richtlinien zur Wehrpolitik." *Die Gesellschaft* 6 (1929): 113–24.

Senger, Gerhard. *Die Politik der deutschen Zentrumspartei zur Frage Reich und*

Länder von 1918–1928. Hamburg: Lütcke & Wulff, 1932.
Severing, Carl. "Das Gebot der Stunde." *Sozialistische Monatshefte* 29 (1923): 1–3.
————. "Kiel: Ein Nachwort zum Parteitag." *Die Gesellschaft* 4 (1927): 1–5.
————. *Mein Lebensweg.* 2 vols. Cologne: Greven, 1950.
————. *1919–1920: Im Wetter- und Watterwinkel.* Bielefeld: Volkswacht, 1927.
————. "Randbemerkungen zu den Richtlinien." *Die Gesellschaft* 6 (1929): 197–205.
Siemsen, Anna. *Auf dem Wege zum Sozialismus: Kritik der sozialdemokratischen Programme von Erfurt bis Heidelberg.* Rote Bücher der Marxistischen Büchergemeinde, vol. 4. Berlin: Freie Verlagsgesellschaft, n.d.
————. *Parteidisziplin und sozialistische Überzeugung.* Sozialistische Zeitfragen. Berlin: Laubsche, 1931.
————. *Politische Kunst und Kunstpolitik.* Jungsozialistische Schriftenreihe. Berlin: n.p., 1927.
Singer. Kurt. *Staat und Wirtschaft seit dem Waffenstillstand.* Jena: Fischer, 1924.
Sommer, E. "Hilferdings Kritik: Parlamentarismus und Klassenkampf—Regierung und Opposition: Politischer 'Fehler' oder Lebensnotwendigkeit?" *Jungsozialistische Blätter* 9 (1930): 176–79.
Die Sowjetaktion gegen die Gewerkschaften. Berlin: ADGB, 1920.
SPD, Fraktion der Nationalversammlung. *Auszug aus dem Tätigkeitsbericht der sozialdemokratischen Fraktion der Nationalversammlung.* Dresden: Kaden, 1920.
————. *Bericht über die Tätigkeit der Nationalversammlung.* Dresden: Kaden, 1920.
————. *Bericht der sozialdemokratischen Fraktion der verfassunggebendenen Nationalversammlung des Deutschen Reiches Mai 1919–April 1920.* Berlin: Vorwärts, 1920.
SPD, Preussische Landesversammlungsfraktion. *Bericht über die parlamentarische Tätigkeit der Sozialdemokratischen Fraktion vom 13 März bis 18 Dezember.* Berlin: n.p., 1920.
————. *Die Arbeit der Sozialdemokratie im Reichstag von Mai bis August 1924.* Wie werbe ich für die Sozialdemokratie? Agitationsmaterial für die Funktionäre, vol. 2. Berlin: Vorwärts, n.d. [1924].
SPD, Reichstagsfraktion. *Bericht der Sozialdemokratischen Fraktion des Reichstages Juni bis Oktober 1920.* Brandenburg: Sidow, n.d.
————. *Bericht über die Tätigkeit der Sozialdemokratischen Reichstagsfraktion 1920–1921.* Berlin: Vorwärts, 1921.
SPD [VSPD] Reichstagsfraktion. *Materialien über die beiden Ermächtigungsgesetze.* Berlin: Vorwärts, 1924.
————. *Die Sozialdemokratie im Reichstage 1924: Bericht über die Tätigkeit der sozialdemokratischen Reichstagsfraktion von Mai bis August 1924.* Berlin: n.p., 1924.
————. *Die Sozialdemokratie im Reichstage 1925: Bericht über die Tätigkeit der sozialdemokratischen Reichstagsfraktion von Januar bis August 1925.* Berlin: Vorwärts, 1925.
————. *Das Steuerkompromiss.* Berlin: Dietz, 1922.
SPD, Vorstand. *Deutschland als freie Volksrepublik: Den aus dem Felde heimkehrenden Volksgenossen.* Berlin: Vorwärts, November 1918.
————. *Die vom Hakenkreuz: Hitler und Konsorten.* Berlin: Vorwärts, 1929.
————. *Diktatur!* Halle an der Saale: Hallische Druckerei, 1931.

_____. *Es lebe die Bolschewisierung! Die kommunistische Partei als Schutztruppe der Reaktion*. Berlin: Vorwärts, n.d.

_____. *Gegen die Parteispaltung*. Berlin: Vorwärts, 1931.

_____. *Das Gespenst der Arbeitslosigkeit und die Vorschläge der S.P.D. zu ihrer Überwindung*. Berlin: Heilbronn, 1931.

_____. *Handbuch für sozialdemokratische Wähler 1921*. Berlin: Vorwärts, 1921.

_____. *Handbuch für sozialdemokratische Wähler: Der Reichstag 1921 bis 1924*. Berlin: Vorwärts, 1924.

_____. *Das Heidelberger Programm: Grundsätze und Forderungen der Sozialdemokratie*. Berlin: Dietz, 1925.

_____. *Jahrbuch der deutschen Sozialdemokratie für das Jahr 1926*. Berlin: Dietz, 1927.

_____. *Jahrbuch der deutschen Sozialdemokratie für das Jahr 1927*. Berlin: Dietz, 1928.

_____. *Jahrbuch der deutschen Sozialdemokratie für das Jahr 1928*. Berlin: Dietz, 1929.

_____. *Jahrbuch der deutschen Sozialdemokratie für das Jahr 1929*. Berlin: Dietz, 1930.

_____. *Jahrbuch der deutschen Sozialdemokratie für das Jahr 1930*. Berlin: Dietz, 1931.

_____. *Jahrbuch der deutschen Sozialdemokratie für das Jahr 1931*. Berlin: Dietz, 1932.

_____. *Kampf dem Hakenkreuz: Rededisposition über die faschistische Gefahr. Mit einem Anhang: Referentenmaterial über die Rolle der KPD*. Berlin: n.p. [1930].

_____. *Der Kampf um die Arbeitslosenversicherung*. Berlin: Vorwärts, 1929.

_____. *Material für Redner: Haltung der bürgerlichen Parteien zum Frauenrecht*. Berlin: Vorwärts, 1919.

_____. *"Nur über meine Leiche!!"*. Berlin: Vorwärts, 1919.

_____. *Der preussische Landtag 1921–1924: Handbuch für sozialdemokratische Wähler*. Berlin: Vorwärts, 1924.

_____. *Das Programm der Sozialdemokratie: Vorschläge für seine Erneuerung*. Berlin: Vorwärts, 1920.

_____. *Regierungsbildung und Etatgestaltung im Reich: Materialen für Referenten und andere Funktionäre der SPD*. Berlin: Vorwärts, 1929.

_____. *Sozialdemokratisches Handbuch für die preussischen Landtagswahlen 1921*. Berlin: Vorwärts, 1921.

_____. *Was ist, was will der Sozialismus*. Berlin: Vorwärts, 1919.

_____. *Wir und die USP*. Berlin: Vorwärts [1920].

_____. *Worten und Taten der USP*. Berlin: Vorwärts, 1919.

Sozialismus ist Arbeit: An die deutschen Arbeiter: Ein Aufruf der Regierung. N.p. [1918].

SPD, Vorstand der Bezirksorganisation Gross-Berlin. *Generalstreik und sozialdemokratische Arbeit: Kritische Randbemerkungen*. Berlin: Vorwärts, 1919.

SPD, Vorstand des Bezirks Halle. *Die Wahrheit über den mitteldeutschen Generalstreik: Tatsächliche Feststellungen über seine wahren Ursachen und Ziele*. Halle: Schmidt & Eidel, 1919.

Spethmann, Hans. *Die Rote Armee an Ruhr und Rhein: Aus den Kapptagen 1920*. Berlin: Hobbing, 1930.

_____. *Zwölf Jahre Ruhrbergbau: Aus seiner Geschichte von Kriegsanfang bis zum*

Franzosenabmarsch 1914–1925. Vol. 1, *Aufstand und Ausstand bis zum zweiten Generalstreik April 1919*. Berlin: Hobbing, 1928.

Stampfer, Friedrich. *Das Görlitzer Programm erläutert*. Berlin: Vorwärts, 1922.

———. *Erfahrungen und Erkenntnisse: Aufzeichnungen aus meinem Leben*. Cologne: Verlag für Politik und Wirtschaft, 1957.

———. *Die ersten vierzehn Jahre der deutschen Republik*. Offenbach am Main: Bollwerk, 1947.

———. *Sie haben nicht kapituliert*. Berlin: Verlag für Gewerkschaftspolitik und Sozialwissenschaft, 1953.

———. *Verfassung, Arbeiterklasse und Sozialismus: Eine kritische Untersuchung der Reichsverfassung von 11 August 1919*. Berlin: Vorwärts, 1919.

Steffen, Hans. *Otto Braun*. Berlin: 1932.

Stein, Alexander. *Jungsozialisten und Arbeiterbewegung*. Berlin: Laubsche, 1928.

Stresemann, Gustav. *Vermächtnis: Der Nachlass in drei Bänden*. Edited by Henry Bernhard. Berlin: Ullstein, 1932–33.

Ströbel, Heinrich. *The German Revolution and After*. Translated by H. J. Stennig. London: Jarold [1920].

———. *Nicht Gewalt, sondern Organisation: Der Grundirrtum des Bolschewismus*. Berlin: Der Firn, 1920.

———. *Socialisation in Theory and Practice*. Translated by H. J. Stennig. London: P. S. King & Son, 1922.

Treviranus, Gottfried Reinhold. *Das Ende von Weimar: Heinrich Brüning und seine Zeit*. Düsseldorf: Econ-Verlag, 1968.

Troeltsch, Ernst. *Spektator-Briefe: Aufsätze über die deutsche Revolution und die Weltpolitik 1918–1922*. Edited by Hans Bewon. Tübingen: Mohr, 1924.

USPD, Zentralleitung. *Finanz- und Steuerkompromiss—Resultate der rechtssozialistischen Koalitions-Politik auf dem Gebiet des Finanz- und Steuerwesens*. Berlin: USPD, 1922.

———. *Handbuch für die Wähler der Unabhängigen sozialdemokratischen Partei, Reichstagswahl 1920*. 3 vols. Berlin: USPD, 1920.

———. *Koalition und Sozialpolitik*. Berlin: USPD, 1922.

———. *Die Wahrheit über die Berliner Strassenkämpfe*. N.p. [1919].

———. *Die Wahrheit über das Blutbad vor dem Reichstag 13 Januar 1920*. Berlin: n.p., 1920.

VSPD: Materialien zur demokratischen Politik. No. 70. Berlin: Litfass, 1924.

Wachenheim, Hedwig. *Vom Grossbürgertum zur Sozialdemokratie: Memoiren einer Reformistin*. Edited by Susanne Miller. Berlin: Colloquium, 1973.

———, ed. *Ludwig Frank: Aufsätze, Reden und Briefe*. Berlin: Verlag für Sozialwissenschaft, 1924.

Weber, Max. *Gesammelte politische Schriften*. Tübingen: Mohr, 1971.

———. "Politics as a Vocation." In *From Max Weber: Essays in Sociology*, edited by H. H. Gerth and C. Wright Mills. New York: Oxford, 1946.

Wilk, Kurt. "Krise des Parlamentarismus und sozialdemokratische Politik." *Die Gesellschaft* 8 (1931): 492–509.

Wissell, Robert. *Kritik und Aufbau: Ein Beitrag zur Wirtschaftspolitik der letzten zwei Jahre*. Berlin: Gesellschaft und Erziehung, 1921.

Wissell, Rudolf. "*Planlose Planwirtschaft*." Berlin: Der Firn, 1919.

———. "Zur Räte-Idee." *Die Neue Zeit* 37 (1919): 195–207.

Wissel[l], Rudolf; Hilferding, Rudolf; and Dissmann, Robert, eds. *Protokoll der*

Verhandlungen des ersten Reichskongresses der Betriebsräte Deutschlands,
   abgehalten vom 5.–7. Oktober 1920 zu Berlin. Berlin: Gewerkschaftliche Bet-
   riebszentrale des ADGB [1921].
Wolff, Theodor. *Through Two Decades*. Translated by E. W. Dickes. London:
   Heinermann, 1936.
Woytinsky, Wladimir. "Proletariat und Bauerntum." *Die Gesellschaft* 3 (1926):
   410–40.
_____. *Stormy Passage*. New York: Vanguard, 1961.
_____. "Zahl und Gliederung des Proletariats." *Die Gesellschaft* 2 (1925): 398–425.
Zehn Jahre deutsche Geschichte 1918–1928. Berlin: Stollberg, 1928.

Section E: Secondary Literature

Abendroth, Wolfgang. *Aufstieg und Krise der deutschen Sozialdemokratie: Das
   Problem der Zweckentfremdung einer politischen Partei durch die Anpas-
   sungstendenz von Institutionen an vorgegebene Machtverhältnisse*. 4th expanded
   edition. Cologne: Pahl-Rugenstein, 1978.
_____. *Die deutschen Gewerkschaften: Weg demokratischer Integration*. Kleine
   Schriften zur politischen Bildung, vols. 5–6. Heidelberg: Roth, 1953.
Adolph, Hans J. L. *Otto Wels und die Politik der deutschen Sozialdemokratie
   1894–1939: Eine politische Biographie*. Veröffentlichungen der Historischen
   Kommission zu Berlin beim Friedrich-Meinecke-Institut der Freien Universität
   Berlin, vol. 33. Berlin: de Gruyter, 1971.
Albertin, Lothar. *Liberalismus und Demokratie am Anfang der Weimarer Republik:
   Eine vergleichende Analyse der Deutschen Demokratischen Partei und der
   Deutschen Volkspartei*. Beiträge zur Geschichte des Parlamentarismus und der
   politischen Parteien, vol. 45. Düsseldorf: Droste, 1972.
_____. "Die Verantwortung der liberalen Parteien für das Scheitern der Grossen
   Koalition im Herbst 1921." *Historische Zeitschrift* 205 (1967): 566–627.
Anderson, Evelyn. *Hammer or Anvil: The Story of the German Working-Class
   Movement*. London: Gollancz, 1945.
Angress, Werner T. "Between Baden and Luxemburg—Jewish Socialists on the Eve
   of World War I." *Leo Baeck Institute Yearbook* 22 (1977): 3–34.
_____. *Stillborn Revolution: The Communist Bid for Power in Germany 1921–1923*.
   Princeton: Princeton University Press, 1963.
_____. "Weimar Coalition and Ruhr Insurrection March-April 1920: A Study of
   Government Policy." *Journal of Modern History* 29 (1957): 1–20.
Apelt, Willibelt. *Geschichte der Weimarer Verfassung*. 2nd edition. Munich: C. H.
   Beck'sche, 1964.
Arns, Günter. "Friedrich Ebert als Reichspräsident." *Historische Zeitschrift*, Supple-
   ment 1 (1971): 1–30.
_____. "Die Linke in der SPD-Reichstagsfraktion im Herbst 1923." *Viertel-
   jahrshefte für Zeitgeschichte* 22 (1974): 191–203.
Ascher, Abraham. "Russian Marxism and the German Revolution, 1917–1920."
   Archiv für Sozialgeschichte 6–7 (1966/67): 391–440.
Aviv, Aviva. "The SPD and the KPD at the End of the Weimar Republic." *IWK* 14
   (1978): 171–86.
Bach, Otto. *Rudolf Wissell: ein Leben für soziale Gerechtigkeit*. Berlin: Arani, 1949.

Bahne, Siegfried. *Die KPD und das Ende von Weimar: Das Scheitern einer Politik 1932–1935*. Frankfurt am Main: Campus, 1976.

Barclay, David E. "A Prussian Socialism: Wichard von Moellendorff and the Dilemmas of Economic Planning in Germany, 1918–1919." *Central European History* 11 (1978): 50–82.

―――. "Social Politics and Social Reform in Germany, 1890–1933: Rudolf Wissell and the Free Trade Union Movement." Ph.D. dissertation, Stanford University, 1975.

Bassler, Gerald. "The Communist Movement in the German Revolution of 1918–1919: A Problem of Historical Typology." *Central European History* 6 (1973): 233–77.

Bay, Jürgen. "Der Preussenkonflikt 1932/33: Ein Kapitel aus der Verfassungsgeschichte der Weimarer Republik." Ph.D. dissertation, Erlangen-Nürnberg, 1965.

Beck, Earl. *The Death of the Prussian Republic: A Study of Reich-Prussian Relations*. Tallahassee: Florida State University Press, 1959.

Becker, Josef. "Heinrich Brüning in den Krisenjahren der Weimarer Republik." *Geschichte in Wissenschaft und Unterricht: Zeitschrift der Geschichtslehrer Deutschlands* 17 (1966): 201–11.

Behrend, Hans-Karl. "Zur Personalpolitik des Preussischen Ministeriums des Innern: Die Besetzung der Landratsstellen in den östlichen Provinzen 1919–1933." *Jahrbuch für die Geschichte Mittel- und Ostdeutschland* 6 (1957): 173–214.

Beier, Gerhard. "Das Problem der Arbeiteraristokratie im 19. und 20. Jahrhundert." In *Herkunft und Mandat: Beiträge zur Führungsproblematik in der Arbeiterbewegung*. Schriftenreihe der Otto-Brenner-Stiftung, vol. 5. Frankfurt am Main: Europäische Verlagsanstalt, 1976.

Bennecke, Heinrich. *Wirtschaftliche Depression und politischer Radikalismus 1918–1933*. Munich: Olzog, 1970.

Beradt, Charlotte. *Paul Levi: Ein demokratischer Sozialist in der Weimarer Republik*. Frankfurt am Main: Europäische Verlagsanstalt, 1969.

Berlau, A. Joseph. *The German Social Democratic Party 1914–1921*. Columbia University Studies in History, Economics, and Public Law, vol. 55. New York: Columbia University Press, 1949.

Bermbach, Udo. *Vorformen parlamentarischer Kabinettsbildung in Deutschland: Der Interfraktionelle Ausschuss 1917/18 und die Parlamentarisierung der Reichsregierung*. Politische Forschungen, vol. 8. Cologne: Westdeutscher Verlag, 1967.

Besson, Waldemar. *Friedrich Ebert: Verdienst und Grenze*. Persönlichkeit und Geschichte, vol. 30. Göttingen: Musterschmidt, 1963.

―――. "Friedrich Ebert's Political Road from the Kaiserreich to the Republic." In *Friedrich Ebert 1871/1971*. Bonn-Bad Godesberg: Inter Nationes, 1971.

―――. *Württemberg und die deutsche Staatskrise 1928–1933*. Stuttgart: Deutsche Verlagsanstalt, 1959.

Bey-Heard, Franke. *Hauptstadt und Staatsumwälzung Berlin 1919: Problematik und Scheitern der Rätebewegung in der Berliner Kommunalverwaltung*. Schriftenreihe des Vereins für Kommunalwissenschaften e.V. Berlin, vol. 27. Stuttgart: Kohlhammer, 1969.

Biegert, Hans. "Gewerkschaftspolitik in der Phase des Kapp-Lüttwitz Putsches." In *Industrielles System und politische Entwicklung in der Weimarer Republik: Verhandlungen des Internationalen Symposiums in Bochum vom 12 bis 17 Juni*

1973, edited by Hans Mommsen, Dietmar Petzina, and Bernd Weisbrod. Düsseldorf: Droste, 1974.

Blackbourn, David G. "Class and Politics in Wilhelmine Germany: The Center Party and the Social Democrats in Württemberg." *Central European History* 9 (1976): 220–49.

Blänsdorf, Agnes. "Friedrich Ebert und die Internationale." *Archiv für Sozialgeschichte* 9 (1969): 321–428.

Blumenberg, Werner. *Kämpfer für die Freiheit*. Berlin: Dietz, 1959.

Bracher, Karl Dietrich. *Die Auflösung der Weimarer Republik: Eine Studie zum Problem des Machtverfalls in der Demokratie*. 2nd expanded edition. Stuttgart: Ring, 1955.

―――. "Der 20. Juli 1932." *Zeitschrift für Politik* 3 (1956): 243–51.

Braunthal, Gerard. "The German Free Trade Unions during the Rise of Nazism." *Journal of Central European Affairs* 15 (1956): 339–53.

―――. *Socialist Labor and Politics in Weimar Germany: The General Federation of German Trade Unions*. Hamden: Archon, 1978.

Braunthal, Julius. *History of the International*. Vol. 1, *1864–1914*. Translated by Henry Collins and Kenneth Mitchell. Vol. 2, *1914–1943*. Translated by John Clark. New York: Praeger, 1967.

Brehme, Gerhard. *Die sogenannte Sozialisierungsgesetzgebung der Weimarer Republik*. Berlin: Deutscher Zentralverlag, 1960.

Breitman, Richard. "Negative Integration and Parliamentary Politics: Literature on German Social Democracy 1890–1933." *Central European History* 13 (1980): 175–97.

―――. "On German Social Democracy and General Schleicher 1932–33." *Central European History* 9 (1976): 352–78.

Bresciani-Turroni, Constantino. *The Economics of Inflation: A Study of Currency Depreciation in Postwar Germany*. Translated by Millicent Sayers. London: Allen & Unwin, 1937.

Broué, Pierre. *Révolution en Allemagne 1917–1923*. Paris: Editions de Minuit, 1971.

Bry, Gerhard. *Wages in Germany 1871–1945*. National Bureau of Economic Research: General Series, vol. 68. Princeton: Princeton University Press, 1960.

Buse, D. K. "Ebert and the German Crisis, 1917–1920." *Central European History* 5 (1972): 234–55.

―――. "The Trustee, or Ebert as Reich President: An Approach to Political Leadership in the Early Weimar Republic." Paper presented to the Canadian Historical Association convention 1978.

Calkins, Kenneth R. "The Election of Hugo Haase to the Co-Chairmanship of the SPD and the Crisis of Pre-War German Social Democracy." *International Review of Social History* 12 (1968): 174–88.

Carsten, F. L. *The Reichswehr and Politics 1918–1933*. Berkeley: University of California Press, 1972.

―――. *Revolution in Europe 1918–1919*. Berkeley: University of California Press, 1972.

Caspar, Gustav Adolf. "Die Sozialdemokratische Partei und das deutsche Wehrproblem in den Jahren der Weimarer Republik." *Wehrwissenschaftliche Rundschau*, Supplement 11 (1959): 1–106.

Comfort, Richard A. *Revolutionary Hamburg: Labor Politics in the Early Weimar Republic*. Stanford: Stanford University Press, 1966.

Conze, Werner. "Brüning als Reichskanzler: Eine Zwischenbilanz." *Historische Zeitschrift* 214 (1972): 310–34.

———. "Die Krise des Parteienstaates in Deutschland 1929–1930." *Historische Zeitschrift* 178 (1954): 47–83.

———. "Die politischen Entscheidungen in Deutschland 1929–1933." In *Die Staats- und Wirtschaftskrise des Deutschen Reichs 1929/33*, edited by Werner Conze and H. Raupach. Stuttgart: Klett, 1967.

Czismik, Ulrich. *Gustav Noske: ein sozialdemokratischer Staatsmann*. Persönlichkeit und Geschichte, vol. 53. Göttingen: Musterschmidt, 1969.

Decker, Alexander. "Die Novemberrevolution und die Geschichtswissenschaft in der DDR." *IWK* 3 (1974): 269–99.

Diehl, James. *Paramilitary Politics in Weimar Germany*. Bloomington: Indiana University Press, 1977.

Domann, Peter. *Sozialdemokratie und Kaisertum unter Wilhelm II: Die Auseinandersetzung der Partei mit dem monarchischen System, seinen gesellschafts- und verfassungspolitischen Voraussetzungen*. Frankfurter Historische Abhandlungen, vol. 3. Wiesbaden: Steiner, 1974.

Dorpalen, Andreas. *Hindenburg and the Politics of the Weimar Republic*. Princeton: Princeton University Press, 1964.

Doss, Kurt. *Reichsminister Adolf Köster, 1883–1930: Ein Leben für die Weimarer Republik*. Düsseldorf: Droste, 1978.

Drechsler, Hanno. *Die Sozialistische Arbeiterpartei Deutschlands (SAPD): Ein Beitrag zur Geschichte der deutschen Arbeiterbewegung am Ende der Weimarer Republik*. Marburger Abhandlungen zur Politischen Wissenschaft, vol. 2. Meisenheim am Glan: Hain, 1965.

Ehni, Hans-Peter. *Bollwerk Preussen? Preussen-Regierung, Reich-Länder Problem und Sozialdemokratie 1928–1932*. Schriftenreihe des Forschungsinstituts der Friedrich-Ebert-Stiftung, vol. 111. Bonn-Bad Godesberg: Neue Gesellschaft, 1975.

———. "Zum Parteienverhältnis in Preussen 1918–1932: Ein Beitrag zu Funktion und Arbeitsweise der Weimarer Koalitionsparteien." *Archiv für Sozialgeschichte* 11 (1971): 241–88.

Eimers, Enno. *Das Verhältnis von Preussen und Reich in den ersten Jahren der Weimarer Republik. (1918–1923)*. Schriften zur Verfassungsgeschichte, vol. 2. Berlin: Duncker & Humblot, 1969.

Eisner, Freya. *Das Verhältnis der KPD zu den Gewerkschaften in der Weimarer Republik*. Schriftenreihe der Otto Brenner Stiftung, vol. 8. Cologne: Europäische Verlagsanstalt, 1977.

Eksteins, Modris. "The Frankfurter Zeitung: Mirror of Weimar Democracy." *Journal of Contemporary History* 6 (1971): 3–28.

———. *Theodor Heuss und die Weimarer Republik*. Stuttgarter Beiträge zur Geschichte und Politik, vol. 3. Stuttgart: Klett, 1969.

Elben, Wolfgang. *Das Problem der Kontinuität in der deutschen Revolution: Die Politik der Staatssekretäre und der militärischen Führung von November 1918 bis Februar 1919*. Beiträge zur Geschichte des Parlamentarismus und der politischen Parteien, vol. 31. Düsseldorf: Droste, 1965.

Eliasberg, George. "Der Ruhrkrieg 1920: Zum Problem von Organisation und Spontaneität in einem Massenaufstand und zur Dimension der Weimarer Krise." *Archiv für Sozialgeschichte* 10 (1970): 291–378.

Epstein, Klaus. *Matthias Erzberger and the Dilemma of German Democracy*. Princeton: Princeton University Press, 1959.

Erger, Johannes. *Der Kapp-Lüttwitz Putsch: Ein Beitrag zur deutschen Innenpolitik 1919/20*. Beiträge zur Geschichte des Parlamentarismus und der politischen Parteien, vol. 35. Düsseldorf: Droste, 1967.

Eschenberg, Theodor. *Die improvisierte Demokratie: Gesammelte Aufsätze zur Weimarer Republik*. Munich: Piper, 1963.

Euler, Heinrich. *Die Aussenpolitik der Weimarer Republik 1918/1923: Vom Waffenstillstand bis zum Ruhrkonflikt*. Aschaffenburg: Pattloch, 1957.

Eyck, Erich. *A History of the Weimar Republik*. 2 volumes. Translated by Harlan Hanson and Robert G. L. Waite. Volume 1, *From the Collapse of the Empire to Hindenburg's Election*. Volume 2, *From the Locarno Conference to Hitler's Seizure of Power*. Cambridge: Harvard University Press, 1967.

Fabian, Walter. "Arbeiterführer und Arbeiterbildungswesen im Freistaat Sachsen." In *Herkunft und Mandat: Beiträge zum Führungsproblem in der Arbeiterbewegung*. Schriftenreihe der Otto-Brenner-Stiftung, vol. 5. Cologne: Europäische Verlagsanstalt, 1976.

Favez, Jean-Claude. *Le Reich devant l'occupation franco-belge de la Ruhr en 1923*. Geneva: Droz, 1969.

Feldman, Gerald D. *Army, Industry, and Labor in Germany 1914–1918*. Princeton: Princeton University Press, 1966.

―――. "Big Business and the Kapp Putsch." *Central European History* 6 (1971): 99–130.

―――. "Economic and Social Problems of the German Demobilization 1918–1919." *Journal of Modern History* 47 (1975): 1–23.

―――. "German Business between War and Revolution: The Origins of the Stinnes-Legien Agreement." Comparative/International Series, Institute of International Studies, University of California, Berkeley, no. 369.

―――. *Iron and Steel in the German Inflation, 1916–1923*. Princeton: Princeton University Press, 1977.

―――. "The Origins of the Stinnes-Legien Agreement: A Documentation." *IWK* 19/20 (1973): 45–102.

―――; Kolb, Eberhard; and Rürup, Reinhard. "Die Massenbewegungen der Arbeiterschaft in Deutschland am Ende des Ersten Weltkrieges (1917–1920)." *Politische Vierteljahrsschrift* 13 (1972): 84–105.

Felix, David. *Walther Rathenau and the Weimar Republic: The Politics of Reparations*. Baltimore: Johns Hopkins University Press, 1971.

Fischer, Wolfram. *Deutsche Wirtschaftspolitik 1918–1945*. 3rd revised edition. Opladen: Leske, 1968.

Flechtheim, Ossip. *Die KPD in der Weimarer Republik*. Frankfurt am Main: Europäische Verlagsanstalt, 1969.

Flemming, Jens. "Parlamentarische Kontrolle in der Novemberrevolution: Zur Rolle und Politik des Zentralrats zwischen erstem und zweitem Rätekongress (Dezember 1918 bis April 1919)." *Archiv für Sozialgeschichte* 11 (1971): 69–140.

Fraenkel, Ernst. *Deutschland und die westlichen Demokratien*. 6th edition. Stuttgart: Kohlhammer, 1976.

Freyberg, Jutta von, et al. *Geschichte der deutschen Sozialdemokratie 1863–1975*. Kleine Bibliothek, vol. 58. Cologne: Pahl-Rugenstein, 1975.

Fricke, Dieter. *Die deutsche Arbeiterbewegung 1869 bis 1914: ein Handbuch über ihre Organisation und Tätigkeit im Klassenkampf*. Berlin: Dietz, 1976.

Fülberth, Georg; and Harrer, Jürgen. *Die deutsche Sozialdemokratie 1890–1933*. Darmstadt/Neuwied: Luchterhand, 1974.

Gablentz, Otto H. von der. "Zu unrecht vergessen: Wichard von Moellendorff." *Gewerkschaftliche Monatshefte* 5 (1954): 362–64.

Gates, Robert A. "The Economic Policies of the German Free Trade Unions and the German Social Democratic Party, 1930–1933." Ph.D. dissertation, University of Oregon, 1970.

———. "German Socialism and the Crisis of 1929–1933." *Central European History* 7 (1974): 332–59.

Gatzke, Hans. *Stresemann and the Rearmament of Germany*. Baltimore: Johns Hopkins University Press, 1954.

Gay, Peter. *The Dilemma of Democratic Socialism: Eduard Bernstein's Challenge to Marx*. New York: Collier, 1962.

Glees, Anthony. "Albert Grzesinski and the Politics of Prussia, 1926–1930." *English Historical Review* 89 (1974): 814–34.

Gordon, Harold J., Jr. *Hitler and the Beer Hall Putsch*. Princeton: Princeton University Press, 1972.

———. *The Reichswehr and the German Republic, 1919–1926*. Princeton: Princeton University Press, 1957.

———. "Die Reichswehr und Sachsen 1923." *Wehrwissenschaftliche Rundschau* 11 (1961): 677–92.

Gottschalch, Wilhelm. *Strukturveränderungen der Gesellschaft und politisches Handeln in der Lehre von Rudolf Hilferding*. Sozialwissenschaftliche Schriftenreihe der Wirtschafts- und Sozialwissenschaftlichen Fakultät der Freien Universität Berlin, vol. 3. Berlin: Duncker & Humblot, 1962.

Grebing, Helga. "Faschismus, Mittelschichten und Arbeiterklasse: Probleme der Faschismus-Interpretation in der sozialistischen Linken während der Weltwirtschaftskrise." *IWK* 12 (1976): 443–60.

———. "Konservative Republik oder soziale Demokratie." In *Vom Kaiserreich zur Weimarer Republik*, edited by Eberhard Kolb. Cologne: Kiepenheuer & Witsch, 1972.

Groh, Dieter. *Negative Integration und revolutionärer Attentismus: Die deutsche Sozialdemokratie am Vorabend des Ersten Weltkrieges*. Frankfurt am Main: Ullstein, 1973.

Grosch, Walther. "Der Reichswirtschaftsrat in seiner jetzigen und künftigen Ausgestaltung." Ph.D. dissertation, Hessische Ludwigs-Universität zu Giessen, 1931.

Grosser, Dieter. *Vom monarchischen Konstitutionalismus zur parlamentarischen Demokratie*. Studien zur Regierungslehre und Internationalen Politik, vol. 1. The Hague: Nijhoff, 1970.

Grund, Hennig. *"Preussenschlag" und Staatsgerichtshof im Jahre 1932*. Studien und Materialien zur Verfassungsgerichtsbarkeit, vol. 5. Baden-Baden: Nomos, 1976.

Hall, Alex. *Scandal, Sensation, and Social Democracy: The SPD Press and Wilhelmine Germany 1890–1914*. Cambridge: Cambridge University Press, 1977.

Hallgarten, George W. F. *Hitler, Reichswehr und Industrie: Zur Geschichte der Jahre 1918–1933*. Frankfurt am Main: Europäische Verlagsanstalt, 1955.

Hamburger, Ernest. "Betrachtungen über Heinrich Brünings Memoiren." *IWK* 15 (1972): 18–39.

Hamburger, Stefanie. "Die Krise der modernen Sozialpolitik in Deutschland." Ph.D. dissertation, Ruprecht Karl Universität zu Heidelberg, 1932.

Hartwich, H. H. *Arbeitsmarkt, Verbände und Staat 1918–1933: Die öffentliche Bindung unternehmischer Funktionen in der Weimarer Republik*. Veröffentlichungen der Historischen Kommission zu Berlin beim Friedrich-Meinecke-Institut der Freien Universität Berlin, vol. 23. Berlin: de Gruyter, 1967.

Haungs, Peter. *Reichspräsident und parlamentarische Kabinettsregierung: Eine Studie zum Regierungssystem der Weimarer Republik in den Jahren 1924 bis 1929*. Politische Forschungen, vol. 9. Cologne: Westdeutscher Verlag, 1968.

Hebel-Kunze, Bärbel. *SPD und Faschismus: Zur politischen und organisatorischen Entwicklung der SPD 1932–1935*. Frankfurt am Main: Röderberg, 1977.

Heer, Hannes. *Burgfrieden oder Klassenkampf: Zur Politik der sozialdemokratischen Gewerkschaften 1930–1933*. Neuwied: Luchterhand, 1971.

Heidegger, Hermann. *Die deutsche Sozialdemokratie und der nationale Staat 1870–1920: Unter besonderer Berücksichtigung der Kriegs- und Revolutionsjahre*. Göttinger Bausteine zur Geschichtswissenschaft, vol. 25. Göttingen: Musterschmidt, 1956.

Heine, Fritz. *Dr. Kurt Schumacher: Ein demokratischer Sozialist europäischer Prägung*. Göttingen: Musterschmidt, 1969.

Hellige, Hans-Dieter. "Die Sozialisierungsfrage in der deutschen Revolution 1918/19: Zu einigen neueren Darstellungen." *IWK* 11 (1975): 79–90.

Herkunft und Mandat: Beiträge zur Führungsproblematik in der Arbeiterbewegung. Schriftenreihe der Otto-Brenner-Stiftung, vol. 5. Cologne: Europäische Verlagsanstalt, 1976.

Hermens, F. A.; and Schieder, Theodor, eds. *Staat, Wirtschaft und Politik in der Weimarer Republik: Festschrift für Heinrich Brüning*. Berlin: Duncker & Humblot, 1967.

Hertzman, Lewis. *DNVP: Right-Wing Opposition in the Weimar Republic*. Lincoln: University of Nebraska Press, 1963.

Herwig, H. H. "The First German Congress of Workers' and Soldiers' Councils and the Problem of Military Reform." *Central European History* 1 (1968): 150–65.

Hirsch-Weber, Wolfgang. *Gewerkschaften in der Politik: Von dem Massenstreik zum Kampf um das Mitbestimmungsrecht*. Schriftenreihe des Instituts für Politische Wissenschaft, vol. 13. Cologne: Westdeutscher Verlag, 1959.

Hoffmann, Gabrielle. *Sozialdemokratie und Berufsbeamtentum: Zur Frage nach Wandel und Kontinuität im Verhältnis der Sozialdemokratie zum Berufsbeamtentum in der Weimarer Zeit*. Hamburg: Buske, 1970.

Honhart, Michael William. "The Incomplete Revolution: The Social Democrats' Failure to Transform the German Economy, 1918–1920." Ph.D. dissertation, Duke University, 1972.

Hüllbusch, Ursula. "Die deutschen Gewerkschaften in der Weltwirtschaftskrise." In *Die Staats- und Wirtschaftskrise des Deutschen Reichs 1929/33*, edited by Werner Conze. Stuttgart: Klett, 1967.

Hunt, James C. "The Bourgeois Middle in German Politics, 1871–1933: Recent Literature." *Central European History* 11 (1978): 83–106.

Hunt, Richard N. "Friedrich Ebert and the German Revolution of 1918." In *The Responsibility of Power: Historical Essays in Honor of Hajo Holborn*, edited by Leonard Krieger and Fritz Stern. Garden City, N.Y.: Doubleday, 1967.

―――. *German Social Democracy 1918–1933*. Chicago: Quadrangle, 1970.

Jacob, Herbert. *German Administration Since Bismarck: Central Authority versus Local Autonomy*. New Haven: Yale University Press, 1963.

Jansen, Reinhard. *Georg von Vollmar: Eine politische Biographie*. Beiträge zur Geschichte des Parlamentarismus und der politischen Parteien, vol. 13. Düsseldorf: Droste, 1958.

Jasper, Gotthard. *Der Schutz der Republik: Studien zur staatlichen Sicherung der Demokratie in der Weimarer Republik 1922–1930*. Tübinger Studien zur Geschichte und Politik, vol. 16. Tübingen: Mohr, 1963.

―――. "Zur innenpolitischen Lage in Deutschland im Herbst 1929." *Vierteljahrshefte für Zeitgeschichte* 8 (1960): 288–89.

Jones, Larry Eugene. "The Dying Middle: Weimar Germany and the Fragmentation of Bourgeois Politics." *Central European History* 5 (1972): 23–54.

Kaltefleiter, Werner. *Wirtschaft und Politik in Deutschland: Konjunktur als Bestimmungsfaktor des Parteiensystems*. Demokratie und Frieden, vol. 2. Cologne: Westdeutscher Verlag, 1968.

Kastning, Alfred. *Die deutsche Sozialdemokratie zwischen Koalition und Opposition 1919–1923*. Paderborn: Schöningh, 1970.

Kirchheimer, Otto. *Von der Weimarer Republik zum Faschismus: Die Auflösung der demokratischen Rechtsordnung*. Frankfurt am Main: Suhrkamp, 1976.

Kitchen, Martin. *The German Officer Corps, 1890–1914*. Oxford: Clarendon, 1968.

Klepper, Otto. "Das Ende der Republik." *Die Gegenwart* 2 (1947): 20–22.

Klink, Dieter. *Vom Antikapitalismus zur sozialistischen Marktwirtschaft: Die Entwicklung der Ordnungspolitischen Konzeption der SPD von Erfurt (1891) bis Bad Godesberg (1959)*. Veröffentlichungen der Akademie für Wirtschaft und Politik, Hamburg. Hanover: Dietz, 1965.

Klinkhammer, Reimund. "Die Aussenpolitik der Sozialdemokratischen Partei Deutschlands in der Zeit der Weimarer Republik." Ph.D. dissertation, Freiburg im Breisgau, 1955.

Kluge, Ulrich. "Essener Sozialisierungsbewegung und Volkswehrbewegung im Rheinisch-Westfälischen Industriegebiet 1918/1919." *IWK* 16 (1972): 55–65.

―――. "Der Generalsoldatenrat in Münster und das Problem der bewaffneten Macht im rheinisch-westfälischen Industriegebiet." In *Arbeiter- und Soldatenräte im rheinisch-westfälischen Industriegebiet*, edited by Reinhard Rürup. Wuppertal: Hammer, 1975.

―――. "Militärrevolte und Staatsumsturz: Ausbreitung und Konsolidierung der Räteorganisationen im rheinisch-westfälischen Industriegebiet." In ibid.

―――. *Soldatenräte und Revolution: Studien zur Militärpolitik in Deutschland 1918/19*. Göttingen: Vandenhoeck & Ruprecht, 1975.

Knapp, Thomas A. "The German Center Party and the Reichsbanner: A Case Study of the Political and Social Consensus in the Weimar Republic." *International Review of Social History* 14 (1969): 159–79.

―――. "The Red and the Black: Catholic Socialists in the Weimar Republic." *Catholic Historical Review* 61 (1975): 386–408.

Knüttler, Hans-Helmuth. *Die Juden und die deutsche Linke in der Weimarer Republik*. Düsseldorf: Droste, 1971.

Kocka, Jürgen. *Klassengesellschaft im Krieg: Deutsche Sozialgeschichte 1914–1918*. Kritische Studien zur Geschichtswissenschaft, vol. 8. Göttingen: Vandenhoeck & Ruprecht, 1973.

Koenen, Wilhelm. "Zur Frage der Möglichkeit einer Arbeiterregierung nach dem Kapp Putsch." *Beiträge zur Geschichte der deutschen Arbeiterbewegung* 4 (1962): 342–52.

Kohler, Erich D. "The Crisis in the Prussian Schutzpolizei 1930–1932." In *Police Forces in History*, edited by George Mosse. London: Sage, 1975.

————. "Otto Braun, Prussia, and Democracy, 1872–1955." Ph.D. dissertation, Stanford University, 1971.

Köhler, Henning. "Sozialpolitik von Brüning bis Schleicher." *Vierteljahrshefte für Zeitgeschichte* 21 (1973): 146–50.

Kolb, Eberhard. *Die Arbeiterräte in der deutschen Innenpolitik 1918/1919.* Beiträge zur Geschichte des Parlamentarismus und der politischen Parteien, vol. 23. Düsseldorf: Droste, 1962.

————, ed. *Vom Kaiserreich zur Weimarer Republik.* Neue Wissenschaftliche Bibliothek, vol. 49. Cologne: Kiepenheuer & Witsch, 1972.

Kollmann, Eric C. "Eine Diagnose der Weimarer Republik: Ernst Troeltschs politische Anschauungen." *Historische Zeitschrift* 182 (1956): 291–319.

Koszyk, Kurt. *Die Presse der deutschen Sozialdemokratie: Eine Bibliographie.* Schriftenreihe des Forschungsinstituts der Friedrich-Ebert-Stiftung; Historisch-politische Schriften. Hanover: Verlag für Literatur und Zeitgeschehen, 1966.

————. *Zwischen Kaiserreich und Diktatur: Die sozialdemokratische Presse von 1914 bis 1933.* Deutsche Presseforschung, vol. 1. Heidelberg: Quelle & Meyer, 1958.

Kotowski, Georg. *Friedrich Ebert: Eine politische Biographie.* Volume 1, *Der Aufstieg eines deutschen Arbeiterführers 1871 bis 1917.* Veröffentlichungen der Historischen Kommission zu Berlin, Sonderband 1. Wiesbaden: Colloquium, 1963.

Krause, Hartfrid. *Zur Geschichte der Unabhängigen Sozialdemokratischen Partei Deutschlands.* Frankfurt am Main: Europäische Verlagsanstalt, 1975.

Kritzer, Peter. *Die bayerische Sozialdemokratie und die bayerische Politik in den Jahren 1918 bis 1923.* Miscellanea Bavarica Monacensia, vol. 20. Munich: Stadtarchiv, 1969.

————. *Wilhelm Hoegner: Politische Biographie eines bayerischen Sozialdemokraten.* Munich: Süddeutscher Verlag, 1979.

Kuckuk, Peter, ed. *Revolution und Räterepublik in Bremen.* Frankfurt am Main: Suhrkamp, 1968.

Landauer, Carl. *European Socialism: A History of Ideas and Movements from the Industrial Revolution to Hitler's Seizure of Power.* 2 volumes. Berkeley: University of California Press, 1960.

Lange, Hermann. "Ideen und Praxis der sozialdemokratischen Aussenpolitik in der deutschen Republik (1918–1926)." Ph.D. dissertation, Erlangen, 1949.

Laubach, Ernst. *Die Politik der Kabinette Wirth 1921/22.* Lübeck: Matthiesen, 1968.

Laursen, Karsten; and Pedersen, Jørgen. *The German Inflation 1918–1923.* Amsterdam: North Holland, 1964.

Liang, Hsi-Huey. *The Berlin Police Force in the Weimar Republic.* Berkeley: University of California Press, 1970.

Lichtheim, George. *Marxism: An Historical and Critical Study.* New York: Praeger, 1966.

Lidtke, Vernon L. *The Outlawed Party: Social Democracy in Germany, 1878–1890.* Princeton: Princeton University Press, 1966.

Lösche, Peter. *Der Bolschewismus im Urteil der deutschen Sozialdemokratie 1903–1920*. Veröffentlichungen der Historischen Kommission zu Berlin, vol. 29. Berlin: Colloquium, 1967.

Lucas, Erhard. *Märzrevolution im Ruhrgebiet: Vom Generalstreik gegen den Militärputsch zum bewaffneten Arbeiteraufstand März-April 1920*. Frankfurt am Main: März, 1970.

————. "Ursachen und Verlauf der Bergarbeiterbewegung in Hamborn und im westlichen Ruhrgebiet: Zum Syndikalismus in der Novemberrevolution." *Duisburger Forschungen* 15 (1971): 1–119.

Luthardt, Wolfgang, ed. *Sozialdemokratische Arbeiterbewegung und Weimarer Republik: Materialien zur gesellschaftlichen Entwicklung, 1927–1933*. 2 volumes. Frankfurt am Main: Suhrkamp, 1978.

Maehl, William H. "The German Socialists and the Foreign Policy of the Reich from the London Conference to Rapallo." *Journal of Modern History* 19 (1947): 35–54.

Maier, Charles S. "Between Taylorism and Technology: European Ideologies and the Vision of Industrial Productivity in the 1920s." *Journal of Contemporary History* 5 (1970): 27–62.

————. *Recasting Bourgeois Europe: Stabilization in France, Germany, and Italy in the Decade after World War I*. Princeton: Princeton University Press, 1975.

Marcon, Helmut. *Arbeitsbeschaffungspolitik der Regierungen Papen und Schleicher: Grundsteinlegung für die Beschäftigungspolitik im Dritten Reich*. Moderne Geschichte und Politik, vol. 3. Frankfurt am Main: Herbert Lang, 1974.

Marks, Sally. "The Myth of Reparations." *Central European History* 11 (1978): 231–56.

Matthias, Erich. *Die deutsche Sozialdemokratie und der Osten 1914–1945: Eine Übersicht*. Arbeitsgemeinschaft für Osteuropaforschung. Tübingen: Osteuropa Handbuch, 1954.

————. "Hindenburg zwischen den Fronten: Zur Vorgeschichte der Reichspräsidentenwahlen von 1932." *Vierteljahrshefte für Zeitgeschichte* 8 (1960): 75–84.

————. "Die Sozialdemokratische Partei Deutschlands." In *Das Ende der Parteien 1933*, edited by Erich Matthias and Rudolf Morsey. Düsseldorf: Droste, 1960.

————; and Morsey, Rudolf. "Die deutsche Staatspartei." In ibid.

Maurer, Ilse. *Reichsfinanzen und grosse Koalition: Zur Geschichte des Reichskabinetts Müller 1928–1930*. Berne: Lang, 1973.

————; and Wengst, Udo, eds. *Staat und NSDAP 1930–1932: Quellen zur Ära Brüning*. Quellen zur Geschichte des Parlamentarismus und der politischen Parteien: Dritte Reihe; Die Weimarer Republik, vol. 3. Düsseldorf: Droste, 1977.

Mayer, Arno. *The Politics and Diplomacy of Peacemaking: Containment and Counterrevolution at Versailles 1918–1919*. New York: Random House, 1969.

Mayer, Paul. "Die Geschichte des sozialdemokratischen Parteiarchivs und das Schicksal des Marx-Engels-Nachlasses." *Archiv für Sozialgeschichte* 6–7 (1966/67): 5–198.

Meier-Welcker, Hans. *Seeckt*. Frankfurt am Main: Graefe, 1967.

Mendershausen, Horst. *The Two Postwar Recoveries of the German Economy*. Contributions to Economic Analysis. Amsterdam: North Holland, 1955.

Menzel, Walther. "Carl Severing und der 20. Juli 1932." *Die Gegenwart* 7 (1952): 734–35.

Merker, Paul Friedrich. *Sozialdemokratie und Gewerkschaften 1890–1920*. Berlin: Dietz, 1949.

Milatz, Alfred. *Wähler und Wahlen in der Weimarer Republik*. Schriftenreihe der Bundeszentrale für politische Bildung, vol. 66. 2nd edition. Bonn: Bundeszentrale für politische Bildung, 1968.

Miller, Susanne. *Die Bürde der Macht: Die deutsche Sozialdemokratie 1918–1920*. Beiträge zur Geschichte des Parlamentarismus und der politischen Parteien, vol. 63. Düsseldorf: Droste, 1978.

———. *Burgfrieden und Klassenkampf: Die deutsche Sozialdemokratie im Ersten Weltkrieg*. Beiträge zur Geschichte des Parlamentarismus und der politischen Parteien, vol. 53. Düsseldorf: Droste, 1974.

———. *Das Problem der Freiheit im Sozialismus: Freiheit, Staat und Revolution in der Programmatik der Sozialdemokratie von Lassalle bis zum Revisionismusstreit*. Frankfurt am Main: Europäische Verlagsanstalt, 1964.

———. "Zum dritten August." *Archiv für Sozialgeschichte* (1964): 515–23.

Mitchell, Allan. *Revolution in Bavaria: The Eisner Regime and the Soviet Republic*. Princeton: Princeton University Press, 1965.

Mitchell, Harvey; and Stearns, Peter. *Workers and Protest: The European Labor Movement, the Working Classes, and the Origins of Social Democracy 1890–1914*. Itasca, Ill.: Peacock, 1971.

Mittmann, Ursula. *Fraktion und Partei: Ein Vergleich von Zentrum und Sozialdemokratie im Kaiserreich*. Beiträge zur Geschichte des Parlamentarismus und der politischen Parteien, vol. 59. Düsseldorf: Droste, 1976.

Möller, Horst. "Parlamentarismus und Demokratisierung im Preussen der Weimarer Republik." In *Gesellschaft, Parlament und Regierung: Zur Geschichte des Parlamentarismus in Deutschland*, edited by Gerhard A. Ritter. Düsseldorf: Droste, 1974.

Mommsen, Hans. "Die Bergarbeiterbewegung an der Ruhr 1918–1933." In *Arbeiterbewegung an Rhein und Ruhr*, edited by Jürgen Reulecke. Hanover: Hammer, 1973.

———. "Die Sozialdemokratie in der Defensive: Der Immobilismus der SPD und der Aufstieg des Nationalsozialismus." In *Sozialdemokratie zwischen Klassenbewegung und Volkspartei*. Edited by Hans Mommsen. Frankfurt am Main: Athenäum Fischer, 1974.

———, ed. *Sozialdemokratie zwischen Klassenbewegung und Volkspartei*. Frankfurt am Main: Athenäum Fischer, 1974.

———; Petzina, Dietmar; and Weisbrod, Bernd, eds. *Industrielles System und politische Entwicklung in der Weimarer Republik. Verhandlungen des Internationalen Symposiums in Bochum vom 12 bis 17 Juni 1973*. Düsseldorf: Droste, 1974.

Mommsen, Wolfgang J. *Max Weber und die deutsche Politik, 1890–1920*. Tübingen: Mohr, 1959.

Moore, Barrington, Jr. *Injustice: The Social Basis of Obedience and Revolt*. White Plains: Sharpe, 1978.

Morgan, David. *The Socialist Left and the German Revolution: A History of the German Independent Social Democratic Party, 1917–1922*. Ithaca: Cornell University Press, 1975.

Morsey, Rudolf. *Die deutsche Zentrumspartei 1917–1923*. Beiträge zur Geschichte des Parlamentarismus und der politischen Parteien, vol. 32. Düsseldorf, Droste, 1966.

Müller, Klaus; and Opitz, Eckart, eds. *Militär und Militarismus in der Weimarer*

Republik: Beiträge eines internationalen Symposiums an der Hochschule der Bundeswehr. Düsseldorf: Droste, 1978.

Muncy, Lysbeth Walker. *The Junker in the Prussian Administration under Wilhelm II, 1888–1914.* Providence: Brown University Press, 1944.

Muth, Heinrich. "Die Entstehung der Bauern- und Landarbeiterräte im November 1918 und die Politik des Bundes der Landwirte." *Vierteljahrshefte für Zeitgeschichte* 21 (1973): 1–38.

Nettl, J. P. "The German Social Democratic Party 1890–1914 as a Political Model." *Past and Present* 30 (1965): 64–95.

————. *Rosa Luxemburg.* 2 vols. London: Oxford University Press, 1966.

Niewyk, Donald L. *Socialist, Anti-Semite and Jew: German Social Democracy Confronts the Problem of Anti-Semitism 1918–1933.* Baton Rouge: Louisiana State University Press, 1971.

"Die Novemberrevolution in der Sicht der Kommunistischen Geschichtswissenschaft: Thesen des Zentralkommittees des SED über die Novemberrevolution 1918 in Deutschland." In *Vom Kaiserreich zur Weimarer Republik*, edited by Eberhard Kolb. Neue Wissenschaftliche Bibliothek, vol. 49. Cologne: Kiepenheuer & Witsch, 1972.

Oberkommando des Heeres, Kriegsgeschichtliche Forschungsanstalt. *Die Wirren in der Reichshauptstadt und im nördlichen Deutschland 1918–1920.* Berlin: Mittler, 1940.

Oertzen, Peter von. *Betriebsräte in der Novemberrevolution: Eine politikwissenschaftliche Untersuchung über Ideengehalt und wirtschaftliche Arbeiterräte in der deutschen Revolution 1918/19.* Beiträge zur Geschichte des Parlamentarismus und der politischen Parteien, vol. 25. Düsseldorf: Droste, 1963.

————. "Die grossen Streiks der Ruhrbergarbeiterschaft im Frühjahr 1919." *Vierteljahrshefte für Zeitgeschichte* 6 (1958): 231–62.

Opitz, Eckart. "Exkurs: Sozialdemokratie und Militarismus in der Weimarer Republik." In *Militär und Militarismus in der Weimarer Republik*, edited by Klaus Jürgen Müller and Eckart Opitz. Düsseldorf: Droste, 1978.

Opitz, Reinhard. *Der deutsche Sozialliberalismus 1917–1933.* Cologne: Pahl-Rugenstein, 1973.

Orlow, Dietrich. *The History of the Nazi Party 1919–1945.* Vol. 1, *1919–1933.* Pittsburgh: University of Pittsburgh Press, 1969.

Osterroth, Franz. *Biographisches Lexicon des Sozialismus.* Vol. 1, *Verstorbene Persönlichkeiten.* Hanover: Dietz, 1960.

————; and Schuster, Dieter. *Chronik der deutschen Sozialdemokratie.* Hanover: Dietz, 1963.

Patemann, Reinhard. *Der Kampf um die preussische Wahlrechtsreform im Ersten Weltkrieg.* Beiträge zur Geschichte des Parlamentarismus und der politischen Parteien, vol. 26. Düsseldorf: Droste, 1964.

Petzina, Dietmar. "Elemente der Wirtschaftspolitik in der Spätphase der Weimarer Republik." *Vierteljahrshefte für Zeitgeschichte* 21 (1973): 127–33.

Pikart, Eberhard. "Preussische Beamtenpolitik, 1918–1933." *Vierteljahrshefte für Zeitgeschichte* 6 (1958): 119–37.

Pistorius, Peter. "Rudolf Breitscheid 1874–1944: Ein biographischer Beitrag zur deutschen Parteigeschichte." Ph.D. dissertation, Cologne, 1970.

Portner, Ernst. *Die Verfassungpolitik der Liberalen, 1919: Ein Beitrag zur Deutung der Weimarer Reichsverfassung.* Bonner historische Forschungen, vol. 39. Bonn: Röhrscheid, 1973.

Post, Gaines, Jr. *The Civil-Military Fabric of Weimar Foreign Policy*. Princeton: Princeton University Press, 1973.

Potthof, Heinrich. "Der Parlamentierungserlass vom 30. September 1918." *Vierteljahrshefte für Zeitgeschichte* 20 (1972): 319–32.

————. "Verfassungsväter ohne Verfassungsvolk? Zum problem von Integration und Desintegration nach der Novemberrevolution." In *Gesellschaft, Parlament und Regierung: Zur Geschichte des Parlamentarismus in Deutschland*, edited by Gerhard A. Ritter. Düsseldorf: Droste, 1974.

————. "Das Weimarer Verfassungswerk und die deutsche Linke." *Archiv für Sozialgeschichte* 12 (1972): 433–86.

Preller, Ludwig. *Sozialpolitik in der Weimarer Republik*. Stuttgart: Mittelbach, 1949.

Pryce, Donald B. "The Reich Government versus Saxony, 1923: The Decision to Intervene." *Central European History* 10 (1977): 112–47.

Quartaert, Jean H. "Feminist Tactics in German Social Democracy: A Dilemma." *IWK* 13 (1977): 48–65.

Ratz, Ursula. *Georg Ledebour 1850–1947: Weg und Wirken eines sozialistischen Politikers*. Veröffentlichungen der Historischen Kommission zu Berlin, vol. 31. Berlin: de Gruyter, 1969.

Raumer, Hans von. "Unternehmer und Gewerkschaften in der Weimarer Zeit." *Deutsche Rundschau* 80 (1954): 425–34.

Rengstorf, Ernst-Viktor. *Links-Opposition in der Weimarer SPD. Die "Klassenkampf-Gruppe" 1928–1931*. Texte zur Arbeiterbewegung. Hanover: SOAK, 1976.

Ribhegge, Wilhelm. *August Winnig: Eine historische Persönlichkeitsanalyse*. Schriftenreihe des Forschungsinstituts der Friedrich-Ebert-Stiftung, vol. 99. Bonn-Bad Godesberg: Neue Gesellschaft, 1973.

Ringer, Fritz, ed. *The German Inflation of 1923*. New York: Oxford University Press, 1969.

Ritter, Gerhard. "Kontinuität und Umformung des deutschen Parteiensystems 1918–1920." In *Vom Kaiserreich zur Weimarer Republik*, edited by Eberhard Kolb. Cologne: Kiepenheuer & Witsch, 1972.

————. "Die Niederlage des Militärs: Vom Scheitern der Offensivstrategie zur Waffenstillstandsforderung der OHL." In *Vom Kaiserreich zur Weimarer Republik*, edited by Eberhard Kolb. Cologne: Kiepenheuer & Witsch, 1972.

Ritter, Gerhard A., ed. *Arbeiterbewegung, Parteien und Parlamentarismus: Aufsätze zur deutschen Verfassungsgeschichte des 19. und 20. Jahrhunderts*. Kritische Studien zur Geschichtswissenschaft, vol. 23. Göttingen: Vandenhoeck & Ruprecht, 1977.

Rohe, Karl. *Das Reichsbanner Schwarz-Rot-Gold: Ein Beitrag zur Geschichte und Struktur der politischen Kampfverbände zur Zeit der Weimarer Republik*. Beiträge zur Geschichte des Parlamentarismus und der politischen Parteien, vol. 34. Düsseldorf: Droste, 1966.

Rosenberg, Arthur. *A History of the Weimar Republic*. Translated by F. Morrow and L. Sieveking. London: Methuen, 1936.

Roth, Guenther. *Social Democrats in Imperial Germany: A Study in Working-Class Isolation and National Integration*. Totowa, N.J.: Bedminster, 1963.

Runge, Wolfgang. *Politik und Beamtentum im Parteienstaat: Die Demokratisierung der politischen Beamten in Preussen zwischen 1918 und 1933*. Stuttgart: Klett, 1965.

Rürup, Reinhard. "Entstehung und Grundlagen der Weimarer Verfassung." In *Vom Kaiserreich zur Weimarer Republik*, edited by Eberhard Kolb. Cologne: Kiepenheuer & Witsch, 1972.

————. "Problems of the German Revolution, 1918–1919." *Journal of Contemporary History* 5 (1968): 109–36.

————, ed. *Arbeiter- und Soldatenräte im rheinisch-westfälischen Industriegebiet: Studien zur Geschichte der deutschen Revolution 1918–1919*. Wuppertal: Hammer, 1975.

Sauer, Wolfgang. "Das Bündnis Ebert-Groener: Eine Studie über Notwendigkeit und Grenzen der militärischen Macht." Ph.D. dissertation, Freie Universität Berlin, 1957.

————. "Das Scheitern der parlamentarischen Monarchie." In *Vom Kaiserreich zur Weimarer Republik*, edited by Eberhard Kolb. Cologne: Kiepenheuer & Witsch, 1972.

Saul, Klaus. *Staat, Industrie, Arbeiterbewegung im Kaiserreich: Zur Innen- und Aussenpolitik des Wilhelminischen Deutschland 1903–1914*. Studien zur modernen Geschichte, Universität Hamburg, vol. 16. Düsseldorf: Bertelsmann, 1974.

Schade, Franz. *Kurt Eisner und die bayerische Sozialdemokratie*. Schriftenreihe der Forschungsstelle der Friedrich-Ebert-Stiftung: Historisch-politische Schriften. Hanover: Verlag für Literatur und Zeitgeschehen, 1961.

Schieck, Hans. "Der Kampf um die deutsche Wirtschaftspolitik nach dem Novemberumsturz 1918." Ph.D. dissertation, Heidelberg, 1958.

Schiffers, Reinhard. *Elemente direkter Demokratie im Weimarer Regierungssystem*. Beiträge zur Geschichte des Parlamentarismus und der politischen Parteien, vol. 40. Düsseldorf: Droste, 1971.

Schmädeke, Jürgen. *Militärische Kommandogewalt und parlamentarische Demokratie: Zum Problem der Verantwortlichkeit des Reichswehrministers in der Weimarer Republik*. Historische Studien, vol. 398. Lübeck: Matthiesen, 1966.

Schneider, Michael. *Das Arbeitsbeschaffungsprogramm des ADGB: Zur gewerkschaftlichen Politik in der Endphase der Weimarer Republik*. Schriftenreihe des Forschungsinstituts der Friedrich-Ebert-Stiftung, vol. 120. Bonn-Bad Godesberg: Neue Gesellschaft, 1975.

Schorr, Helmut J. *Adam Stegerwald: Gewerkschafter und Politiker der ersten deutschen Republik; ein Beitrag zur Geschichte der christlich-sozialen Bewegung in Deutschland*. Recklinghausen: Kommunal-Verlag, 1966.

Schorske, Carl. *German Social Democracy 1905–1917: The Development of the Great Schism*. New York: Wiley, 1955.

Schröder, Wilhelm Heinz. "Die Sozialstruktur des sozialdemokratischen Reichstagskandidaten 1898–1912." In *Herkunft und Mandat: Beiträge zur Führungsproblematik in der Arbeiterbewegung*, Schriftenreihe der Otto-Brenner-Stiftung, vol. 5. Cologne: Europäische Verlagsanstalt, 1976.

Schuker, Stephen A. *The End of French Predominance in Europe: The Financial Crisis of 1924 and the Adoption of the Dawes Plan*. Chapel Hill: University of North Carolina Press, 1976.

Schulz, Gerhard. *Zwischen Demokratie und Diktatur: Verfassungspolitik und Reichsreform in der Weimarer Republik*. Volume 1, *Die Periode der Konsolidierung und der Revision des Bismarckschen Reichsaufbaus 1919–1930*. Berlin: de Gruyter, 1963.

Schulze, Hagen. "Ein Briefwechsel zwischen Otto Braun und Joseph Wirth im Exil." *Vierteljahrshefte für Zeitgeschichte* 26 (1978): 144–85.

———. *Freikorps und Republik 1918–1920*. Boppard am Rhein: Boldt, 1969.

———. *Otto Braun oder Preussens demokratische Sendung: Eine Biographie*. Frankfurt am Main: Propyläen-Ullstein, 1977.

Schustereit, Hartmut. *Linksliberalismus und Sozialdemokratie in der Weimarer Republik: Eine vergleichende Betrachtung der Politik der DDP und SPD 1919–1930*. Bochumer Historische Studien. Düsseldorf: Pädagogischer Verlag Schwann, 1975.

Schwarz, Gotthart. *Theodor Wolff und das "Berliner Tageblatt": Eine liberale Stimme in der deutschen Politik 1906–1933*. Tübingen: Mohr, 1968.

Schwerin von Krosigk, Lutz Graf. *Es geschah in Deutschland: Menschenbilder unseres Jahrhunderts*. Tübingen: Wunderlich, 1951.

Siemann, Joachim. "Der Sozialdemokratische Arbeiterführer in der Zeit der Weimarer Republik: Ein Beitrag zur Soziologie der Eliten in der modernen Parteigeschichte." Ph.D. dissertation, Georg-August Universität zu Göttingen, 1955.

Sigel, Robert. "Die Lensch-Cuno-Haenisch Gruppe: Ihr Einfluss auf die Ideologie der deutschen Sozialdemokratie im ersten Weltkrieg." *IWK* 11 (1975): 421–36.

Skrzypczak, Henryk. "From Carl Legien to Theodor Leipart: From Theodor Leipart to Robert Ley; Notes on some Strategic and Tactical Problems during the Weimar Republic." *IWK* 13 (1971): 26–47.

———. "Führungsprobleme der sozialistischen Arbeiterbewegung in der Endphase der Weimarer Republik." In *Herkunft und Mandat: Beiträge zur Führungsproblematik in der Arbeiterbewegung*. Cologne: Europäische Verlagsanstalt, 1976.

Sozialistische Einheitspartei Deutschlands, Institut für Marxismus-Leninismus. *Geschichte der deutschen Arbeiterbewegung in acht Bänden*. Volume 3, *Von 1917 bis 1923*. Berlin: Dietz, 1966.

———. *Illustrierte Geschichte der Novemberrevolution in Deutschland*. Berlin: Dietz, 1968.

Steenson, Gary P. *Karl Kautsky, 1854–1938: Marxism in the Classical Years*. Pittsburgh: University of Pittsburgh Press, 1978.

Stehling, Jutta. *Weimarer Koalition und SPD in Baden: Ein Beitrag zur Geschichte der Partei- und Kulturpolitik in der Weimarer Republik*. Frankfurt am Main: Haeg und Herchen, 1976.

Stein, Alexander. *Rudolf Hilferding und die deutsche Arbeiterbewegung*. Hamburg, 1946.

Steinberg, Hans-Josef. *Sozialismus und deutsche Sozialdemokratie: Zur Ideologie der Partei vor dem ersten Weltkrieg*. Schriftenreihe des Forschungsinstituts der Friedrich-Ebert-Stiftung: Historisch-politische Schriften. Hanover: Verlag für Literatur und Zeitgeschehen, 1967.

Stephan, Werner. *Aufstieg und Verfall des Linksliberalismus 1918–1933: Geschichte der Deutschen Demokratischen Partei*. Göttingen: Vandenhoeck & Ruprecht, 1973.

Stucken, Rudolf. *Deutsche Geld- und Kreditpolitik 1914–1963*. 3rd edition. Tübingen: Mohr, 1964.

Stürmer, Michael. *Koalition und Opposition in der Weimarer Republik 1924–1928*. Beiträge zur Geschichte des Parlamentarismus und der politischen Parteien, vol. 36. Düsseldorf: Droste, 1967.

————. "Der unvollendete Parteienstaat—Zur Vorgeschichte des Präsidialregimes am Ende der Weimarer Republik." *Vierteljahrshefte für Zeitgeschichte* 21 (1973): 119–26.

Timm, Helga. *Die deutsche Sozialpolitik und der Bruch der grossen Koalition im März 1930.* Beiträge zur Geschichte des Parlamentarismus und der politischen Parteien, vol. 1. Düsseldorf: Droste, 1952.

Trumpp, Thomas. "Franz von Papen: Der Preussisch-Deutsche Dualismus und die NSDAP in Preussen: Ein Beitrag zur Vorgeschichte des 20. Juli 1932." Ph.D. dissertation, Eberhard-Karls Universität zu Tübingen, 1963.

Turner, Henry Ashby, Jr. *Stresemann and the Politics of the Weimar Republic.* Princeton: Princeton University Press, 1963.

Varain, Heinz Josef. *Freie Gewerkschaften, Sozialdemokratie und Staat: Die Politik der Generalkommission unter der Führung Carl Legiens (1890–1920).* Beiträge zur Geschichte des Parlamentarismus und der politischen Parteien, vol. 9. Düsseldorf: Droste, 1956.

Vietzke, Siegfried; and Wohlgemuth, Heinz. *Deutschland und die deutsche Arbeiterbewegung in der Zeit der Weimarer Republik 1919–1933.* Berlin: Dietz, 1966.

Vogelsang, Thilo. *Reichswehr, Staat und NSDAP: Beiträge zur deutschen Geschichte 1930–1932.* Stuttgart: Deutsche Verlagsanstalt, 1962.

Vogt, Martin. "Die Stellung der Koalitionsparteien zur Finanzpolitik 1928–1930." In *Industrielles System und politische Entwicklung in der Weimarer Republik . . . ,* edited by Hans Mommsen, Dietmar Petzina, and Bernd Weisbrod. Düsseldorf: Droste, 1974.

Volkmann, E. O. *Revolution über Deutschland.* Oldenburg: Stalling, 1930.

Wacker, Wolfgang. *Der Bau des Panzerschiffes "A" und der Reichstag.* Tübinger Studien zur Geschichte und Politik, vol. 11. Tübingen: Mohr, 1959.

Waite, Robert G. L. *Vanguard of Nazism: The Free Corps Movement in Postwar Germany 1918–1923.* Cambridge: Harvard University Press, 1952.

Waldman, Eric. *The Spartacist Uprising of 1919 and the Crisis of the German Socialist Movement: A Study of the Relation of Political Theory and Party Practice.* Milwaukee: Marquette University Press, 1958.

Weber, Hermann. *Die Wandlung des deutschen Kommunismus: Die Stalinisierung der KPD in der Weimarer Republik.* Vol. 1. Frankfurt am Main: Europäische Verlagsanstalt, 1969.

Wehler, Hans-Ulrich. *Krisenherde des Kaiserreichs 1871–1918: Studien zur deutschen Sozial- und Verfassungsgeschichte.* Göttingen: Vandenhoeck und Ruprecht, 1970.

Weichmann, Herbert. "Kritische Bemerkungen Herbert Weichmanns zu den Briefen Brünings an Sollmann." *Vierteljahrshefte für Zeitgeschichte* 22 (1974): 458–60.

Wheeler, Robert F. *USPD und Internationale: Sozialistischer Internationalismus in der Zeit der Revolution.* Translated by Agnes Bländsdorf. Frankfurt am Main: Ullstein, 1975.

Wheeler-Bennett, John. *The Nemesis of Power: The German Army in Politics.* London: Macmillan, 1964.

Williamson, John G. *Karl Helfferich 1872–1924: Economist, Financier, Politician.* Princeton: Princeton University Press, 1971.

Winkler, Heinrich August. "Einleitende Bemerkungen zu Hilferdings Theorie des Organisierten Kapitalismus." In *Organisierter Kapitalismus: Voraussetzungen und Anfänge*, edited by Heinrich August Winkler. Kritische Studien zur Geschichtswissenschaft, vol. 9. Göttingen: Vandenhoeck & Ruprecht, 1974.

_____. *Mittelstand, Demokratie, und Nationalsozialismus: Die politische Entwicklung von Handwerk und Kleinhandel in der Weimarer Republik*. Cologne: Kiepenheuer & Witsch, 1972.

Witt, Friedrich-Wilhelm. *Die Hamburger Sozialdemokratie in der Weimarer Republik: unter besonderer Berücksichtigung der Jahre 1929/30–1933*. Schriftenreihe des Forschungsinstituts der Friedrich-Ebert-Stiftung, vol. 89. Hanover: Verlag für Literatur und Zeitgeschehen, 1971.

Witt, Peter-Christian. "Finanzpolitik und sozialer Wandel in Krieg und Inflation 1918–1924." In *Industrielles System und politische Entwicklung in der Weimarer Republik* . . . , edited by Hans Mommsen, Dietmar Petzina, and Bernd Weisbrod. Düsseldorf: Droste, 1974.

Wulf, Peter. "Die Auseinandersetzung um die Sozialisierung der Kohle in Deutschland 1920–1921." *Vierteljahrshefte für Zeitgeschichte* 25 (1977): 46–98.

_____. "Regierung, Parteien, Wirtschaftsverbände und die Sozialisierung des Kohlenbergbaues 1920–1921." In *Industrielles System und politische Entwicklung in der Weimarer Republik*, edited by Hans Mommsen, Dietmar Petzina, and Bernd Weisbrod. Düsseldorf: Droste, 1974.

Index